MINERVA SERIES OF STUDENTS' HANDBOOKS

NO. 6

General Editor

PROFESSOR BRIAN CHAPMAN

MA, D.PHIL (*Oxon*)

The Soviet Economy

The Minerva Series

The Soviet Economy

AN INTRODUCTION

BY

ALEC NOVE

James Bonar Professor of Economics
University of Glasgow

REVISED THIRD EDITION

London
GEORGE ALLEN & UNWIN LTD
RUSKIN HOUSE · MUSEUM STREET

FIRST PUBLISHED 1961
SECOND IMPRESSION 1962
REVISED SECOND EDITION 1965
SECOND IMPRESSION 1967
THIRD EDITION 1968
SECOND IMPRESSION 1970

© George Allen & Unwin Ltd., 1968

ISBN 0 04 330131 2

PRINTED IN GREAT BRITAIN
*in 10-pt Times Roman type
by C. Tinling and Co. Limited
Liverpool, London, Prescot*

PREFACE

The object of this book is to introduce the non-specialist with an interest in and some knowledge of economics to the study of the Soviet economy. The introductory nature of the volume must be stressed from the beginning. Many matters have had to be treated briefly, others have hardly been discussed at all. Thus there is practically no mention of natural resources, soil, climate, very little on the problems of transportation, or social services, or education. This is not to deny for a moment the importance of any of these things and readers interested in finding out more about them can be referred to the bibliography. Their omission is due to the fact that, within about 300 pages, I have attempted to cover at least in outline those features of the Soviet economy which particularly distinguish it from that of western countries. I have tried to do this by dividing the book into three parts. The first, Structure, is a fairly straightforward description of the institutional arrangements, going back into history in so far as it is necessary to explain how and why the present system developed. I start from the bottom, with the productive enterprise, and then go on to the planning and administrative organs, public finance and the structure of prices and wages. The second part, entitled Problems, seeks to identify those elements in the system which give rise to various difficulties, not in order to prove that the system does not work—obviously it does work—but in order to see which problems are of particular importance and how, in practice, means are devised and the structure modified to cope with them. The third part deals with Ideas and Concepts, and includes some attempt to explain and interpret the very interesting discussions which are engaging the attention of Soviet economists, notably on the theory of value and prices. This should not be beyond the understanding of the non-specialist, but whoever does not wish to immerse himself in controversies conducted in unfamiliar Marxist terminology can always skip that part of chapter 11, though this would be a pity. Finally, in the concluding chapter some (I hope) significant generalizations are attempted and a few very tentative morals drawn.

I am not at all sure that this is an ideal arrangement, for there are some regrettable overlaps between the chapters and the parts. But alternative schemes seemed to me even less promising.

Nothing is further from my intention than to pretend to 'solve' anything or to say the last word on any of the subjects discussed, the more so as detailed studies exist, listed in the bibliography, on most of the matters here all too briefly touched upon. The object is rather to encourage the interested reader to find out more for himself, and in particular, if he knows Russian, to look up the Soviet sources; to facilitate this task, I have been fairly lavish with footnote references to many Russian books and articles.

All or large parts of the manuscript were read at various stages of preparation by Ely Devons, Michael Kaser, Jacob Miller, Leonard Schapiro, Basil Yamey and Alfred Zauberman, and George Morton read the last two chapters. For their numerous and invaluable comments and criticisms I am very grateful. I must also express appreciation for the help given by other colleagues with whom I was able to discuss various points or ideas, to contributors to the seminar on 'Economic problems of the Soviet World' at the London School of Economics, and to the authors of the many books and articles on which I have drawn extensively, and references to which appear frequently in the pages that follow. I hope these numerous helpers will not take it amiss if I do not list them here. If, despite all this generous assistance, I have obstinately persisted in errors of fact or of opinion, the responsibility is entirely mine.

Finally, I would like to express appreciation for the help, patience and accuracy of Dubravko Matko, of the research division of the London School of Economics. Mrs Sarah Craig and Miss Mary Hutchinson performed miracles in translating my illegible scrawl into typescript. I do not know how they did it.

ALEC NOVE

PREFACE TO THIRD EDITION

So much has happened to the structure of the economy during the past few years, and so many new ideas and theories have been mooted, that a substantial revision has proved necessary. The majority of chapters have therefore been recast, rewritten, amended, although the general direction of recent change was foreshadowed by many articles and speeches, and duly found its reflection in earlier editions of this book.

The economy is still in a state of flux. The reform is still in a stage of experiment. There is no doubt whatever that many changes will be made, as a new balance is sought between plan and market, centralization and decentralization, traditional methods and mathematical-computer techniques. I hope that in this edition the issues will be adequately defined, so that the reader will not be taken by surprise when, as inevitably will happen, still more reform decrees are issued in Moscow.

I am grateful to Roger Clarke and Dubravko Matko, Glasgow University, for help in revision and to Mrs M. Chaney for typing and collation. I must also express thanks to Soviet colleagues for patiently discussing many questions put to them in the course of a visit to the USSR in 1967. Much of the rewriting was done during a period spent at the University of Pennsylvania, and I am indebted to Herbert S. Levine, for helpful comments and criticisms.

A. NOVE

Institute of Soviet and East European Studies
University of Glasgow

CONTENTS

ix

GLOSSARY

Russian words and abbreviations which appear in this book are always explained when first used, but it may still be useful to provide a glossary of some words which recur fairly frequently.

ASSR	Autonomous Soviet Socialist Republic (within a federal republic).
Gosstroi	State committee on construction.
Glavk	Department or division of a ministry.
Gosbank	State Bank.
Gossnab	State Committee on material supply.
Gosekonomkommissia	State economic commission (current planning body, 1955-57).
Gosekonomsovet	State economic-science council.
Gosplan	State planning committe (commission).
Khozraschyot	'Economic' (or business) accounting, profit-and-loss accounting.
Kolkhoz	Collective farm (sometimes refers to other kinds of collective economy).
Krai	Large province.
Mestnichestvo	'Regionalism', looking after own locality first.
MTS	Machine Tractor Station(s).
Nomenklatura	Appointments lists controlled by the Party.
Naryad	Allocation certificate, supply order.
Obkom	Oblast' committee of the Communist Party.
Oblast'	Province.
Obyedineniye	Industrial Association or Corporation
Raikom	Raion committee of the Communist Party.
Raion	District (sub-unit of oblast').
RSFSR	Russian Soviet Federative Socialist Republic, or Russia proper.
Sbyt	Disposals, deliveries organs.
Snab	Supply organs.
Snabsbyt	Supply-and-disposals organs.
Sovnarkhoz	Regional economic council.
Sovkhoz	State farm.
Stroibank	Investment Bank.
Tolkach	'Pusher', 'fixer', unofficial supply agent.
Torg	Trading department of a local authority.
Trudoden (plural: *trudodni*)	Workday units, labour units, on a collective farm.
VSNKh (*Vesenkha*)	Supreme council of national economy. (Used in the period 1960-62 also to designate the RSFSR *sovnarkhoz*.)
Zayavka	Application, e.g. for an allocation certificate.

NOTES:

On January 1, 1961, the Soviet Government revalued the internal rouble, ten old roubles equalling one new rouble. *Unless otherwise stated*, the statistics given in this book are in old roubles, when relating to pre-1961 figures, they are in new roubles since that date. This may seem confusing, but perhaps less so than, say, giving the annual wage in 1940 as 406·80 instead of 4,068 roubles.

Many references to books and periodicals appear in footnotes in abbreviated form. They can be properly identified in the bibliography. References to articles omit the title of the article, save where this is of especial interest, since they can be identified by details of author and publication, and one is saved from reprinting (usually) very long Russian titles.

A 'milliard' is a thousand million (an American billion).

Why and How

Why should we study the Soviet economy? There are a number of cogent reasons for economists and laymen alike to know more about it. Perhaps the most obvious reason is simply that the system developed in the Soviet Union is being applied, with some local variations, to a large part of the globe. Within the countries of the Soviet bloc, if Soviet statisticians are to be believed, there will shortly be produced half of the industrial output of the world. It seems desirable, therefore, to examine how the Soviet economic system works. As citizens, we should acquaint ourselves with its special features, with its strength and weaknesses, with the content and credibility of its statistical claims. As economists, we should surely be aware of the way in which so much of the world's economy is run.

Economists should also be interested in the fate of economic laws and economic theory in a philosophic and institutional setting quite different to the one to which they are accustomed. For example, what happens to resource allocation when there is no interest and no rent? Can market forces be replaced by administrative decision, or do they climb in through the window when driven out of the door? How far is centralized planning in practice consistent with any economic theory at all, Marxist or non-Marxist? What happens in their system to wage determination, consumer choice, and so on? An examination of the Soviet economic scene can help us to see our own economic concepts more clearly, to see how far they depend on western institutions or apply to all systems, albeit in altered or distorted forms.

Then, surely, economists, historians and interested laymen could usefully consider why the Soviet economic system is as it is, in response to what needs has the Soviet institutional structure taken its present shape, how far it is necessarily typical of a planned economy elsewhere, or indeed of the Soviet Union itself at a later date. How far has the system been a response to peculiarly Russian conditions, or to backwardness, or to the special problems of rapid industrialization? What lessons can usefully be drawn from Soviet experience

15

by under-developed countries seeking to industrialize? If Soviet growth has been unusually rapid, what special features of the economy facilitate such growth, and what distortions (viewed from the angle of optimum resource allocation) are explicable by the desire to achieve rapid growth as a primary objective of economic policy? These, and many other questions would seem to merit careful consideration. It is, of course, absurd to expect to find in this book a final 'answer' to them all. The author would be well satisfied if he were to provide some background, introduce some stimulating ideas into the minds of readers and persuade them to seek further information elsewhere.

Since it may seem rather obvious that these matters are important and ought to be studied, it may seem odd that so little has been done by professional economists, especially in Great Britain, to study them. Soviet economics has been the province, as a rule, of Soviet specialists, as if the ordinary economist needs to know nothing outside of the traditional theory and practice of Western Europe and America. Part of the explanation may lie in inertia and/or conservatism, but there are more weighty and more creditable reasons, which could usefully be examined here. One, of course, is the language barrier. Another is the belief that Soviet economics is politics, a belief which is by no means unfounded and which can be documented by citing declarations to this effect by Soviet politicians, and that, therefore, it is a matter for politicians rather than economists. It can be argued that while Soviet planners are indeed concerned with the allocation of scarce resources, they allocate resources to priority objectives determined from outside the economic system, a procedure somewhat analogous to the acts of a military supply organization. The Quartermaster-General to the Forces distributes scarce resources, but he is not an economist and his task is not one to which economic theory has much to contribute.[1] It may be further argued, with many examples, that the behaviour of various units composing the Soviet economy is regulated with great precision by the central administrative agencies; for instance, the ways in which maize or potatoes should be planted or cultivated, the number of shoes of children's sizes to be produced, the wage of fitters or clerks of a given qualification, and much else besides, are determined in Moscow for the remotest provinces. If such micro-economic detail is decided by officials, *a fortiori* this is even more typical of macro-economic matters. The drive to industrialize, launched by Stalin in

[1] Though programming techniques might enable him to choose optimum solutions to his problems.

1928, is often cited as a particularly striking example of purely political arbitrariness in the economic field. Finally, it is widely believed that the study of the Soviet economy is very seriously impeded by lack of information about its functioning and by lack of statistics. Let us examine the soundness of these objections.

We should, in my view, distinguish carefully between two kinds of political decision in the economic field, which both *look* 'arbitrary' but which in fact are fundamentally different in kind. In the one case, the politician issues an order which, affecting economic life, is essentially explicable by extra-economic considerations and is in no sense a response to economic necessity. For example, repeated measures to restrict the private activities of peasants are of this kind. However, a decree to expand the chemical industry, or to reform the wages system, though juridically and politically it looks just as arbitrary, may frequently turn out to be 'induced', an overdue response to necessity, or even, in the case of wages, a reflection of a *fait accompli*. In such cases, it may be useful to regard the government (or the central committee of the Communist party) as a species of super-board of directors, responding to economic forces which they only partially control, or to the economic-technical consequentials of policies which they themselves decided in their capacity as politicians. Even so 'macro' a decision as industrialization is not quite as arbitrary as it looks. There exist some political analysts who, while emphasizing the arbitrary, political nature of Stalin's decisions, also argue that, even without the revolution, Russia would have become a great industrial power. Indeed, Count Witte was urging the development of heavy industry thirty years before Stalin, for reasons in some respects similar to Stalin's. Of course, the methods used to impose rapid industrialization involved political choice between alternatives and coercion on a vast scale. But the general direction of the policy was not invented by the party leadership. At all stages of Soviet development, the central leadership has had to take into account not only technical but also economic criteria, since their efforts to achieve so much in so little time repeatedly presented choices between alternative uses of scarce means. It is true, as will be shown, that the role of purely *economic* criteria played at first a somewhat subordinate role, but this situation is rapidly changing. There is scope for economic analysis, even though in a number of important instances it will be seen that political considerations proved decisive.

The relevance of economics at the 'micro' level is also much greater than it looks. Centralization of decision is always more effec-

tive on paper than it can possibly be in reality. The proper understanding of the actual functioning of the economy (and not only of
the economy) is often impeded by the persistence of what might be
called the 'totalitarian myth'. The myth consists in the belief that
everyone does what he is told, and that everyone can be told exactly
what to do. In this picture, managers produce precisely the assortment of goods desired by the planners, peasants grow the crops prescribed in the decrees, workers receive the wage laid down in the
officially-published schedules, officials only issue instructions consistent with the desires of the top leadership, and the various inspecting and checking agencies ensure obedience up and down the hierarchy. This picture does, indeed, correspond to the version which
used to be found (paradoxically) both in official Soviet textbooks and
in the works of enthusiastic anti-communists. It does not, as will be
shown, correspond to reality. It is necessary to add that this is not to
deny the existence in the USSR of something which can be described as
'totalitarianism'. Perhaps the point is rather that the kind of totalitarianism sometimes imagined by western critics cannot exist at all,
anywhere.

The Soviet economist, Academician Strumilin, in criticizing his
own colleagues' traditional attitudes, put the point as follows. 'At
one time it was fashionable among us to deny the existence of any
objective economic laws in our society, in which, so it was said, the
plan was the basic "law", which meant the will of the lawgiver and
the *conscious* direction of the planned economy.' Emphasizing the
limitations imposed on the planners' will by objective necessity,
Strumilin contrasted the nature of juridical and economic laws. The
former are enforced by state organs. 'Economic laws also do not
lack an enforcement mechanism, even though this is not laid down
in any code . . . Economic sanctions operate independently, without
the help of any kind of coercive apparatus, as a result of the very
fact of a breach of (economic) law. To put it another way, economic
laws take their own revenge on those who break them.'[1] Therefore,
to take this thought a little further, planners ought to act in consciousness of economic principles, and, when they ignore them, the
chickens come home to roost, things go wrong. The fact that they
do so provides us with material for study as economists. It also
shows the limitations of 'totalitarian' power in this field, since the
things that go wrong often do so because of the behaviour of *homo
economicus sovieticus*, a close relation of the species found in the
west.

[1] *Vop. ekon.*, No. 7/1959, pp. 127 ,130.

There will be much more to say about economic laws in the Soviet context later on. In any case, whatever the situation was fifteen years ago, both the theory and practice of the Soviet economy today raise issues of direct relevance to our own economies.

The other commonly-held objection to the academic study of the Soviet economy concerns lack of reliable data. It must be admitted that difficulties exist, but they are certainly not insuperable. While in the last years of Stalin's life hardly any statistics were published, it is wrong to regard this situation as typical of the Soviet period. Up to the years 1936-38, there were vast quantities of statistics regularly available (with, it is true, some omissions), and since 1955 there has again been a much more liberal attitude to publication. Indeed, the flood of figures has been such as literally to overwhelm analysts who were used to the leisurely and selective trickle of the late-Stalin period. There still remain some conspicuous gaps. Thus systematic figures on wages have not been made available up to the time of writing. The figures on output, and especially indices, are of varying degrees of reliability and have to be used with care. Appendix A will be devoted to examining these questions of availability and reliability. However, the beliefs that Soviet statistics are confined to percentages of an unknown base-year, or that the figures are mere propagandist inventions, are now baseless legends.

It is not only figures which are needed, but also a picture of the organization and functioning of institutions. Here, too, there were grave difficulties in the late-Stalin era, because of the marked tendency to describe the desirable state of affairs rather than the one which existed. Thus most books on the collective farms, where the contrast between 'is' and 'ought' was perhaps most marked, were generally so misleading as to be downright useless. To this day, textbooks are apt to present an idealized version of whatever they may be describing. Fortunately, there is no need to rely on such textbooks (and it might be fair to add that the Soviet researcher into British economic organization is unlikely to find some of our textbooks very helpful either). Periodicals—party, economic, technical —supply the missing note of realism. They are concerned with the practical job of getting people to act 'correctly,' and so must perforce discuss real problems. Here again, the late-Stalin epoch was least productive of frank fact-facing. Many writers and editors were evidently scared of saying disagreeable things, and too often filled their pages with paeans of praise. There was some criticism, of course, but its authors played it safe, and made the criticisms particular rather than general: thus they would attack a local official or local abuse (if they were out of reach of that official's wrath), but without drawing any conclusions of national application. However, since his death there has been much more frankness. Major outbursts of criticism have, it is true, often followed a speech on the same subject by a party leader, but now it would be correct to say that a very large area of the Soviet economy is open to practical, business-like examination in the Soviet press by Soviet experts. There are certain solutions which they dare not put forward; but they can describe the stresses and strains of reality, and, outside the area of heresy, a range of practical suggestions to correct defects can be, and are, made. And in economics at least the area of heresy has shrunk, as we shall see.

This provides the western scholar with a great deal of evidence. But this evidence is seldom systematized, it is raw, it needs to be understood and assessed. The important must be disentangled from the accidental, 'self-criticisms' must be seen in their proper proportions. For the western literature, unfortunately, includes examples of mere assemblages of such self-criticisms, so arranged as to suggest extremely negative conclusions. Others, relying on the textbooks and shrugging off critical articles of Soviet periodicals merely as detailed and local aberrations, have produced unrealistic and over-favourable accounts. But the risk of error is not a reason for avoiding the study of a subject. On the contrary, this provides a challenge for a lively and inquiring mind. Evidence can be sifted with some confidence, if the analyst makes the realistic assumption that Soviet men (including planners, factory directors and workers) are human, and behave in a manner which, given the institutional forms, could reasonably be expected. This, and a general sense of the *vraisemblable*, should provide us with a sound basis for assessing the very wide range of critical material available to us from Soviet sources and building up from it a picture of the real system which should be near the truth Here are some not untypical examples of 'critical' material:

(a) Cracks have developed in a new apartment house in Kharkov, and in another in Baku.

(b) The director of a road transport undertaking, faced with a plan in ton-kilometres, refuses to carry loads for short distances.

(c) In order to fulfil his plan in terms of gross output, director A has produced the wrong assortment of textiles, to the annoyance of his customers.

(d) A new railway has wrongly been built across an area which was due to be flooded under a hydro-electric scheme.

Clearly, it would be wrong to deduce from (a) that most Soviet houses have cracks, though we may surmise from other reports that the quality of construction leaves much to be desired. Certainly we cannot judge the normal efficiency of planners from the error cited in example (d), though we may note that this is a failure of inter-departmental co-ordination which is not unknown in other sectors and indeed in other countries. However, (b) and (c) are in quite a different category, because, as will be shown in subsequent chapters, these particular 'deviations' were built in to the system itself; they are as much in the nature of the institutions concerned as, for example, the tendency of businessmen in the west to use every opportunity to avoid paying income tax. Indeed, it should be possible to deduce the general occurrence of (b) and (c) even if not a single published example could be quoted.

Thus there is ample printed material for study. To this must be added the fruits, actual and potential, of investigation on the spot. The USSR is no longer a closed country, and a number of students of Soviet affairs (notably from America) have paid visits to Russia and have discussed various problems with Soviet colleagues, often with fruitful results. But the limitations of the material should not be overlooked. Thus, to take an example at random, if workers at a building site in Kazakhstan go on strike or stage a riot, this would remain unreported in the Soviet press, and no one researching into Soviet labour relations (for instance) should forget that this is so when assessing the evidence available.

In this book, historical description will be kept to the minimum necessary for understanding the present Soviet system. However, some general remarks on the historical setting seem indispensable, even in this introduction. The Soviet Union has been the scene of an industrial and social, as well as of a political, revolution. Great changes have been compressed into a short space of time. They have been carried through under the leadership of the Communist party (or by leaders acting in its name), and they have transformed a backward, peasant country into a giant industrial power. This involved the tearing asunder of established ways of life, and indeed the systematic disregard of the pressure of existing economic forces. Soviet policymakers did not seek to adapt themselves to the demand pattern; the point was to change the demand pattern, the institutions, the structure of the economy. The economy was deliberately so organized as to facilitate this drastic and complex process, and this led to the neglect not only of non-priority sectors of economic life, but also of the finer adjustments required for 'optimal' resource allocation. For this reason, the student of the Soviet economy must bear in mind, in

making his assessments, the *purposes* of Soviet economic policy, and
the high priority given to rapid industrialization. Professor Oscar
Lange has described this stage of Soviet development as '*sui generis* a
war economy',[1] in the sense of all-out concentration of effort on a
major objective determined by political authority. No one would fail
to note, in analysing the effectiveness of the war economy of Great
Britain or Germany, that all kinds of desiderata had in practice to
be sacrificed to the concentration of resources for waging war (and
this without necessarily approving of the military objectives of the
governments concerned!). All that is required is that one should
bear in mind that Soviet institutions were created to serve certain
purposes, that many of the problems are intimately connected with—
and are often part of the cost of—the pursuit of rapid industrialization in a backward country, and that it is not always useful to criticize
the Soviet economic system as if its aim were to achieve the pure
static equilibrium of western textbooks.

It is important to insist on a sense of proportion in the study of
the Soviet economy because so many persons allow emotion to enter
into their assessment of anything Soviet. Economists are apt to compare Soviet reality not with western reality, but with an imaginary
model of the 'capitalist' economy. For instance, when (rightly) criticizing the illogicalities and confusions of Soviet agricultural prices
they implicitly overlook the illogicalities of agricultural prices in virtually every western country. Others seize with glee upon evidence
of the very real errors or waste in Soviet investment policy, with a
cavalier disregard not only for the inherent complexity of the problem but also for the errors or waste which can occur in their own
countries. Needless to say, Soviet economists are apt to do exactly
the same in reverse. This procedure might be called 'comparing
model with muddle'. It needs to be avoided. Of course, it is true that
the Soviet economic system contains within itself certain specific
weaknesses, certain kinds of waste which are not found (at least to
the same extent) even in the most imperfect world of western reality.
Part II of the present book will be largely devoted to analysing the
things which go wrong, or raise difficult problems which, within
their system, obstinately resist solution. This emphasis on difficulties is not without its dangers, since the reader may obtain a lop-
sided view of reality. If this were the whole story, a critic might
legitimately say, the Soviet economy would be far less effective
than it appears to be. Although an effort will be made in chapter 12
to assess in general terms the strength and weakness of the economy,

[1] *The Political Economy of Socialism* (Warsaw, 1957), p. 16.

such a criticism is not without point. It is, therefore, essential to stress that part II is entitled 'Problems', that it therefore emphasizes aspects of the economic system which involve various kinds of snags, just as a book or chapter entitled 'Problems of British education' would seize upon aspects of the British educational system which do not give entire satisfaction. The difficulties to be discussed are not by any means trivial. They are essential aspects of the system, and as such are causing concern to Soviet economists and planners. None the less, the very nature of this kind of analysis, under such a heading as 'Problems', does carry with it a certain unavoidable over-emphasis on things that go wrong. One does not write there about, say, the speed with which the Trans-Siberian railway has been electrified, or about the regular delivery of steel to this or that industry, but it should not be forgotten that many things are effectively and punctually accomplished all the same. Yet at the same time one should certainly not overlook the very considerable evidence of conspicuous misdirection of resources, of the sacrifices imposed or of the means adopted to impose them.

A last word about political bias. It is sometimes thought that it is impossible to write on the Soviet Union in an objective spirit. Some critics even believe that to attempt to do so is wrong, since it shows lack of proper militancy in the face of 'evil'. It is my firm belief that one can only usefully examine the Soviet economy if one is not trying thereby to find proof in support of preconceived notions, as by 'selective' research it is all too easy to 'prove' anything. In any case, the evaluation of economic activities can (indeed should) be politically neutral. A Soviet steelworks is a steelworks. If its products are used to shoot political opponents, its existence is doubtless deplorable, but no cause is advanced by pretending that its efficiency or its output are other than what they are. Opponents of the Soviet régime should remember that their opposition is not generally based on its alleged or real economic inefficiencies, but on its political-social system. It is pointless self-delusion to deny that it has to its credit, or is capable of, great achievements in the field of production and technique. There was a time when any Soviet writer who discussed the west without 'militant' epithets was denounced for 'objectivism'. Their understanding of the west has suffered, and to a great extent still suffers, in consequence. It is to be hoped that the reader will feel that the author is guilty of the sin of 'objectivism' which indeed it is his aim to commit.

It is certainly true and important that the Soviet economy is controlled at the top by persons who have the declared purpose of achieving a state of affairs which they describe as 'communism', that they wish to change society, and that they have an ideology which affects their choice among possible solutions to practical problems. It should be possible to note this, and also the dominance of the Communist party organization, as part of the basic facts. Whether what they do is morally justified is not a matter on which, in the present context, it is necessary to comment.

A note on political structure

The following is a brief sketch of the political framework.

The USSR is a federation of republics, which at present number fifteen. Sovereignty is nominally exercised by an elected body. Until 1937 this was the all-union Congress of Soviets, indirectly elected by lower territorial soviets. The congress elected an executive committee (known as VTSIK), which elected a praesidium. Since its first meeting in 1938 the sovereign 'parliament' is the Supreme Soviet, which consists of two houses, the Soviet of the Union and the Soviet of Nationalities, both elected directly by adult suffrage. In practice the deputies are nominated by the Communist party machine, and contested elections are unknown. The Supreme Soviet meets infrequently, often for no more than one week in the year, though its committees, including a finance committee, and an economic committee of the Council of Nationalities, now play a more active role. It elects a praesidium which exercises its legislative powers between sessions, subject to subsequent ratification. In principle at least, laws can only be adopted by the Supreme Soviet, and its praesidium can also issue decrees (*ukazy*) which are supposed to conform to existing laws, but in practice often change them. (Before 1938, laws and decrees emerged from a variety of bodies, including VTSIK or its praesidium, the government and even government committees such as the Council of Labour and Defence.)

The government was known before 1946 by the designation of the Council of People's Commissars, and since that date as the Council of Ministers. In this book, to avoid unnecessary brackets and qualifications, the terms Minister, Ministry, Council of Ministers, will generally be used, and *not* Commissar, People's Commissariat, etc. The Council of Ministers is elected by and is responsible to the Supreme Soviet (or its praesidium between sessions). It is empowered to issue binding orders (*postanovleniya*) within the constitution and the laws. In practice, it can issue *de facto* laws on any subject, since the Supreme Soviet has never used (and is most unlikely ever to use) its formal powers to challenge and revoke the actions of the government.

All the above relates to the all-union government, but the same structure was and is almost wholly duplicated in each of the fifteen federal republics. They have Supreme Soviets, praesidia, councils of ministers and so forth. Despite the apparently formidable powers with which they are endowed by the constitution, the republics are in fact subject to orders from the all-union government on any conceivable matter, though the amount of autonomy actually allowed them has fluctuated and has recently shown a tendency to decrease. The relationship between centre and republics in particular sectors of governmental activity varies, and has given rise to three different kinds of ministry: there are, first, the *all-union ministries*, which directly run from Moscow the activities of their subordinate units within the various republics. Secondly, there are *'union-republican'* *ministries*, which exist both at the centre and in the republics, in which case the republican ministry is simultaneously subordinate both to its elder brother in Moscow and to the Council of Ministers of the given republic. This is an example of 'dual subordination', which is very commonly encountered in Soviet administration: a local organ is simultaneously an integral part of the local authority and the representative in that area of the appropriate unit of the central government. Finally, there are purely *republican ministries*, which have no direct superior in Moscow, though naturally they have to conform where relevant to central policies and plans. The word 'ministry' does not cover all organizations of ministerial status either at the centre or in the republics: there are a number of state committees, commissions and other bodies, whose heads are members of the Council of Ministers. One such body, Gosplan, has been of key importance in the economy.

The republics are divided into provinces (*oblast'*, plural *oblasti*); there are also large provinces which are called *krai*[1], and finally certain national areas within some of the republics are given the dignity of Autonomous Soviet Socialist Republic (ASSR) and their top officials have the title of ministers; examples include Tartar, Chuvash, Komi and Bashkir ASSR. However, the power of these bodies *vis-à-vis* the authorities above or below them is hardly affected by the differences of designation.[2] In this book, therefore, when the word *oblast'* is used, it may be assumed that the same functions or powers apply to the ASSR and *krai*.

Local government in towns is run by elected town Soviets. The big towns have a status similar to the English county borough, in the sense of not being subject to the *oblast'* authorities but depending directly on the republican government.

At the very bottom of the scale are village soviets, with only minor powers. When the economic functions of local government are referred to, the village soviet can virtually be ignored.

Underlying all this elaborate governmental structure is the Communist Party of the Soviet Union, the 'directing nucleus' (as the Constitution itself emphasizes) of all state organs and social organizations. In a very real sense, the government at all levels exists to carry out the policies of the Party. Its own structure is as follows: party congresses are nominally supreme; they elect a central committee, which in turn elects other

---

[1] Some of these have autonomous sub-units, including even *oblasti*, but these refinements are hardly worth pursuing here.
[2] Except that the ASSR are represented as such in the upper house of the legislature, the Soviet of Nationalities.

committees, of which by far the most important is the politbureau (known in 1962-65 as the praesidium). The latter is in effect the supreme organ of government. At the party headquarters there are departments which duplicate the various governmental organs. There are also party committees corresponding to the various levels of government below the centre.

It is important to note that the party committees are wholly subordinate to the Moscow leadership, in the fifteen republics as well as at *oblast'* level and below. Thus, for example, the Ukrainian or Uzbek committees of the party have no greater rights *vis-à-vis* the all-union central committee than are possessed by, say, the Leningrad or Omsk *obkom*. Therefore the degree of independence of any federal or local body in the USSR must always be severely limited, in so far as it is at least partially controlled by a party committee on its own level, and the party itself is highly centralized.

The party's specifically economic functions will be dealt with in greater detail on page 107 below, along with other agencies of inspection and control.

PART I: STRUCTURE

CHAPTER I

Productive Enterprises

CATEGORIES OF ENTERPRISES

Before describing the governmental organs which plan and control the economy, it is desirable to start at the bottom and consider the organization and finance of enterprises and individuals actually engaged in the production of goods and services. These may be conveniently divided into the following categories:

(a) State enterprises.
(b) Non-agricultural co-operative enterprises.
(c) Collective-farms (*Kolkhozy*).
(d) The private sector, subdivided into

  (i) Agricultural holdings of collective farmers and state employees.
  (ii) Private craftsmen, individual peasants, professional services.

Before describing each of these forms, it is necessary to mention the types of economic activity, familiar in the west, which are not to be found in the USSR, or are illegal there. The laws and regulations have changed very little in these respects since the liquidation of NEP[1] at the end of the 'twenties.

It is illegal for any private citizen to employ anyone to produce a commodity for sale. For example, a private shoemaker, whose existence is legitimate under category (d)(ii) above, may not employ an assistant. It is legal to employ a domestic servant, who 'produces' nothing in the Soviet sense of the word, and no doubt many writers employ a typist privately, but in principle the 'exploitation of man

---

[1] NEP: New Economic Policy, which succeeded the so-called War Communism period in 1921, and under which a wide range of private economic activity was legalized.

by man' is repressed by law. It is also illegal for an individual to sell anything he has not himself produced (unless, of course, he is an employee or member of an organization which has the right to produce goods for sale). For instance, a peasant can sell a cabbage he has grown, any citizen can make coat-hangers in his spare time and sell them in the free market. But if a man buys on his own account a sack of cabbages from peasants and then resells them at a profit in a city where cabbages are dear, or if he buys a scarce commodity in a state store and resells it at a higher price, he is guilty of a criminal offence and, if caught, would probably serve a term of imprisonment. Of course, this does not mean that such activities do not exist. On the contrary, it may readily be observed that ticket touts outside a Soviet football stadium or the Bolshoi theatre are as active as their equivalents in London or New York, and there can hardly be a peasant in all Russia who has not committed the technical 'crime' of selling in the free market not only his own produce but that of some fellow-villager. However, none can doubt that the legal principles mentioned above deeply influence economic organization.

Since even within the sectors in which private or co-operative activities are nominally permitted, the state organs have and frequently use the right to refuse the necessary registration permits, it follows that a wide range of goods and services are either provided by state organs or are not provided at all. To take two small instances, it would not be open to an individual to open an agency to provide addresses for holiday accommodation, or a cafe, and if the appropriate state organs do not feel that it is necessary or desirable to provide them, then they cannot be brought into existence.

The relative importance of the various categories can be expressed in a number of different ways, according to the sector of the economy and the basis of the comparison. Thus, taking gross industrial production as a measure, the figures are as follows:

Gross industrial output by forms of ownership
(*Per cent of total*)

	1928	1937	1950	1958
State enterprises	69·4	91·8	92	94
Co-operative enterprises*	13·0	8·2	8	6
Private	17·6	—	—	—

Source: *N.Kh. 1958*, p. 127. For definition of industry, see p. 271, below. The 1965 figure, not given, is probably close to 99 per cent state.

*Includes some industrial production on collective farms.

Building is not included in the above table. The relative importance of the non-state sector there is much larger than in 'industry'. Collective farms erect various farm buildings and other constructions, while private persons built houses in substantial numbers throughout the Soviet period. Thus in 1965, out of a total new housing space of 79·2 million square metres (exclusive of peasant construction), 16·1 million were privately built; in addition, peasants and 'rural intelligentsia' put up about 371,000 dwellings.[1]

The following tables show the relative importance of the various sectors in agriculture, where the largest (though diminishing) private-enterprise activities in the Soviet economy are to be found. They show also the very substantial increase in the relative importance of state farms (sovkhozy):

	Per cent of total output					
	State farms*		Kolkhozy		Private**	
	1950	1965	1950	1965	1950	1965
Grain	11	37	82	61	7	2
Cotton	4	20	96	80	0	0
Sugar-beet	3	9	97	91	0	0
Potatoes	4	15	23	22	73	63
Vegetables	11	34	45	25	44	41
Meat	11	30	22	30	67	40
Milk	6	26	19	35	75	39
Eggs	2	20	9	13	89	67
Wool	12	39	87	41	21	20

* Including other state agriculture.

** Private plots of *kolkhoz* peasants and of state employees.

Source: N.Kh. 1965, p. 265 (Note: the share of the private sector in 1938, for instance, was much higher than in 1950.)

According to one source, in the RSFSR 17 per cent of gross agricultural output was private, in 1965 or 1966.[2]

---

[1] *N.Kh.* 1965, p. 610. Private house-building fell sharply after 1959, in town and country. The total of 'state' construction includes building co-operatives, partly financed by private persons. Private housing is due to expand spectacularly by 1970 (see *Vop. ekon.*, No. 8/1967, p. 8)

[2] M. Makeenko, *Vop. ekon.*, No. 10/1966, p. 57-67.

Sown area (millions of hectares)
(Soviet territory as of the given date)

	1928	1937	1956	1959	1965
Collective farms	1·4	116·0	152·1	130·2	105·0
State farms*	1·7	12·2	35·3	58·8	97·4
Private holdings, collective peasants	1·1 ⎫	⎫	5·65 ⎫	5·3 ⎫	
Private holdings, state employees	n.a. ⎬	6·24 ⎬	1·6 ⎬	1·9 ⎬	6·6
Private land, individual peasants	108·7	0·86	0·03	0·01	—

Source: *N.Kh. 1956*, p. 108. *N.Kh. 1958*, p. 312, 1937 figures—
N. Jasny: *The Socialised Agriculture of the USSR* (Stanford, 1949),
pp. 774, 788 and 790). *N.Kh. 1965*, p. 288.

*Includes other state enterprises (see p. 46).

A high proportion of livestock was, and is, privately owned;
though this proportion has been falling.

The relative figures for labour were given as follows for 1965:

	(millions, average over the year, agricultural work only)
State farms	8·0
Collective farms	17·6
MTS and RTS*	0·0
Private holdings (families of collective peasants and state employees)**	6·4
TOTAL	32·0

Source: *N. Khoz. 1965*, p. 435.

*Machine Tractor Stations and Repair Technical Stations.
**Private farm work done by those deemed to be regularly
engaged in collective farms and state enterprises is supposed to be
included, at least in part, in the other headings. This is controversial (see note by M. Feshbach, and reply by A. Nove, in
Soviet Studies, Jan. 1965).

State and 'co-operative' trade—the latter to all intents and purposes being a branch of state trade (see page 46, below)—was responsible for over 96 per cent of all retail trade in 1965 and 1966, the
remainder being accounted for by the free market. However, the free-
market data include only urban sales, intra-village trade being
omitted. The statistics also omit many unrecorded transactions between individuals.

Transport is run by state enterprises, with the significant exception of collective-farm haulage. There are a few privately owned horses, and some private cars run an illegal taxi service.

For other economic sectors, mostly services, no statistics are available for the relative importance of different types of enterprise.

THE STATE INDUSTRIAL ENTERPRISE

A state enterprise belongs to the state. From this apparently tautological statement of the obvious flow a number of consequences which are perhaps less obvious. In essence and in law, the enterprise is a convenient unit for the administration of state property. It is a juridical person, it can sue and be sued, but it *owns* none of its assets. The director and his senior colleagues—the chief engineer, who acts as his deputy, and the chief accountant—are appointed by state organs to manage the state's assets for purposes determined by the state. This is why there was no charge made for the use of the enterprise's capital, since it belongs to the state anyhow. This is also why the state is entitled to transfer the enterprise's profits to the state budget, save for that portion which the state's regulations or *ad hoc* decisions permit the enterprise to retain. That is why it is within the power of state organs to take away any of the enterprise's assets, if they think fit, without financial compensation, though this right is, for practical reasons, now being questioned and circumscribed.

The director is in sole charge, in the sense that he is responsible to those who appoint him and must be obeyed by his subordinates. However, this principle of 'one-man command' is subject in practice to a number of significant limitations. Not only are the director's hierarchical superiors liable to issue detailed orders on almost every conceivable subject, but he must also take into account a number of inspecting and checking agencies. The most important of these, which also exercises a controlling influence over other agencies, is the Communist party; this generally possesses an organized group within the enterprise, of which the director is usually a member but in which he holds no official position. There is also a trade union branch, to which certain questions (such as distribution of premia, overtime work, norm-setting, questions of labour discipline) must be referred. Since 1958, there is also an elected 'permanent production council', which, though without direct executive authority, is entitled to deliberate on many questions directly affecting planning and management. There are also outside agencies of inspection and control: the banks, financial inspectorates and some others; these will be examined in due course (see pages 105 and 127). The successful director requires to possess qualities of diplomacy, to obtain the support or avoid the opposition of these various controlling, checking and inspecting agencies. None the less, he is in command; he is to blame when things go wrong and is rewarded when they go right.

The role and function of management is in process of undergoing important, perhaps fundamental, changes. The primary task of the director was to fulfil, and if possible to overfulfil, the output plans, and to utilize the resources placed at his disposal with due regard to economy. The output plan specified the quantity of the product required in the given month, quarter or year, with some details of type, design, assortment, etc. The aggregate output plan of industrial enterprises was frequently expressed in physical measure (tons, square metres, etc.), or, where this could not be done, in terms of value (roubles of gross output). There were a number of other plan 'indicators': cost reductions, increase in labour productivity, wages, economy of scarce materials and sometimes other indicators appropriate to the given sector or the result of some campaign of the moment. Fulfilment of plans expressed in terms of these various indicators carried with it moral approbation and material benefits, in the form of substantial premia to the director and his senior staff, and so they could be conveniently designated '*success indicators*'. Over-fulfilment carried with it increased rewards, material and spiritual. Thus in the oil industry in 1956 the director received a bonus of 40 per cent of his salary for fulfilling the output plan, and 4 per cent for each 1 per cent overfulfilment. Those who overfilled received praise. Of course, not all of these plans were equally important, either from the standpoint of premia or in the weight given them by superior authority in assessing the success of the enterprise, and, since it often happened that directors were unable to fulfil all the various plans, they naturally chose the ones that seem to them the most important. This was generally the production plan in quantitative terms, reflecting the great emphasis on growth, though it was modified by insistence on cost reductions. The consequences of the 'success indicator' system will be discussed at length in chapter 6.

In September 1965, in a big speech to the central committee, Kosygin announced changes in the direction of greater management autonomy, part of the reforms which are now in process of being implemented.[1] At the end of 1967 roughly 7,000 enterprises had been

[1] See *Pravda*, September 28, 1965.

converted to the 'new system' and the process might largely be completed during 1968 ro 1969. Whereas in the past the enterprise directors were given a vast number of detailed instructions, with especial emphasis on gross output and cost reduction, these indicators were among those which henceforth would fall within the enterprise's own sphere of decision (we shall see that this is by no means yet the case). Gradually more autonomy will be granted in deciding the product mix and in purchasing at least some inputs. Enterprises will still receive from above the following indicators: sales (*realizatsiya*); 'the basic nomenclature of output'; the wages fund; total profits; profitability (i.e. the rate of profit as a percentage); contribution to and receipts from the budget; centralized investments and new productive capacity; 'the basic tasks in the introduction of new techniques'; and material supply indicators. To give one example of the change wrought by the reform: according to Kosygin's speech, there were until 1965 four plan indicators for labour: productivity, the number of workers, the average wage, and the wages fund. Now there would only be one: the wages fund. However, the management's freedom in labour questions will still be limited by staff establishment lists[1] and by the officially-laid-down wage scales. We will have much more to say about the enterprise's position under the reforms in chapter 6, where the whole background, scope and limits of the reform will be fully discussed.

Soviet enterprises, with very few exceptions, now operate as autonomous financial entities with their own profit and loss accounts, a status known by the Russian words *khozyaistvennyi raschyot* ('economic accounting'), usually abbreviated to *khozraschyot*. It was not always thus. In the period of 'war communism', that is, before 1921, most state enterprises had no funds of their own, wages and other expenses being met out of the state budget. In the years of NEP, before 1929, all except very large state enterprises were still 'not on *khozraschyot*', in the sense that their revenues were paid into, and their expenses were met out of, the accounts of trusts, which grouped together varying numbers of enterprises. It was only in 1929 that a decision was taken to place state enterprises on *khozraschyot*, and since this date there have been few exceptions to this rule. The basis of *khozraschyot* has been defined as follows: 'A method of planned operation of socialist enterprises . . . which requires the carrying out of state-determined tasks with the maximum economy of resources, the covering of money expenditures of enterprises by their own

---

[1] Thus he is not allowed to appoint anyone to a job not listed as applicable to his enterprise (see *Khozyaistvennaya reforma v deistvii*, M., 1967, p. 145.)

B

money revenues, the ensuring of profitability of enterprises'.[1] So far as the enterprise is concerned, prices of outputs are fixed, prices of inputs are fixed, and, as we shall see, the choice as to which inputs to use is severely limited by the system of allocation. Within these bounds, it is the director's job not only to fulfil the various plans already referred to, but also to cover his costs and to make a profit.

The whole question of the role of profit has become a key element in discussion of reform of the Soviet economic system. Some imagine that the profit motive is a fundamentally new element. This is quite wrong. For over thirty years before the reform there existed an *Enterprise fund* (known before 1955 as the Director's fund), which could be used partly for overplan investment (especially in housing) and partly for various welfare purposes. The rules governing this fund varied, with larger amounts provided for the favoured heavy than for light industry. To give just two examples: in the coal industry 6 per cent of the planned and 50 per cent of the overplan profit was paid into the fund; the figures for the textile industry were respectively 2 per cent and 30 per cent[2], all this subject to the total not exceeding 5 per cent of the wages bill and to the fulfilment of the output and other plan indicators. But in practice this fund made little difference, because, firstly, it was not used to pay bonuses to management; secondly, payments were in any case conditional upon the fulfilment of other elements of the plan; thirdly, the amounts were too small; thus in 1955 it amounted in all to $\frac{1}{2}$ per cent of the total wages bill, and many enterprises had not a kopek; fourthly, it was irrational to reward overplan profits disproportionately, since in this respect, as in so many others, it paid to persuade the authorities to accept a low plan. Finally with profits computed as a percentage of costs, this whole system led to glaring illogicalities. Thus, in mining, for instance, it was frequently the case that 80 per cent of costs consisted in wage payments, whereas in (say) the textile industry it was nearer 10 per cent. Under such circumstances, if the profit rate so defined was the same in the two industries, the enterprise fund was larger (in relation to workers employed, or the net product) in the textile than in the mining industry, despite the apparent discrimination in favour of mining referred to above.

For all these reasons, the decisions taken in 1965 to reform the system and to enhance the role of profit led logically to a decision to

[1] *Ekonomika promyshlennosti SSSR* (Moscow, 1956), p. 393. Sub-units of enterprises are sometimes said to be 'placed on *khozraschyot*', meaning that their profitability is separately calculated, though they have no financial independence.
[2] *Direktivy KPSS* (Vol. 4), pp. 457-9.

abandon the Enterprise fund and to substitute a new set of rules.[1]
There was set up under the reform three 'funds', into which the
enterprise is entitled to pay a proportion of its profits. These are:

(a) The material incentive fund
(b) The social-cultural and housing fund
(c) Fund for the expansion (development) of production, or investment fund

The first of these funds has become the principal source of payment
of managerial bonuses, and the size of these bonuses has now been
regulated by reference to the indicators to be cited below, instead of
in relation to gross output or cost reduction plans.

The amount paid into the *Material incentive* and *Social-cultural
funds* is determined by percentage 'norms', separately laid down for
each fund for economic ministries, sectors and groups of enterprises
(in some cases, it seems, also for particular enterprises). The norms
are then applied in a manner which seems, and surely is, quite
alarmingly complex. The actual amounts paid into these funds (the
investment fund is different, as will be seen) are given as percentages
of the wages fund of the given enterprise, in respect of three variables:

(a) The per cent increase in sales, compared with that planned for
the given year, over the previous year.
(b) The per cent increase in planned profits, compared with the
previous year.
(c) The rate of profitability (*Rentabel'nost'*) provided for in the
plan.

Of course, the planned sales, profits and profitability must be
realized (achieved) to 'qualify' for the present purpose. To discourage
bidding low, which is inherent in large rewards for plan overfulfilment, the payment into these various funds are roughly 30 per cent
lower in respect of sales, profits and profitability which exceed the
plan. Underfulfilment is penalized proportionately to the same extent.
In general, in the case of enterprises which 'for reasons outside their
control' have profits much higher than those of the sector, the 'norms'
are reduced, i.e. a smaller share of the profit goes to the above funds,
though it seems to be intended to eliminate these 'undeserved' profits
via rental payments in due course.

For the present, then, 'norms' vary. In practical terms, this means
that enterprise (or sector) X will be entitled to a different percentage
of wages and/or profits to the above funds than enterprise (or sector)

[1] The most accessible full text of the regulations is in *Ekon. gaz.*, No. 50,
1966, supplement.

Y. The reason would seem to be that of evening out the financial and incentive situation of enterprises which, under the existing price system, have widely differing profitabilities. The percentage link with the wages fund has the clear intention to relate incentive in some proportionate way to the size of the labour force: thus enterprise X may employ 5,000 persons and pay out 5 million roubles in wages, while enterprise Y may employ 500 and pay only 500,000 roubles, yet they could have identical financial results expressed as a percentage of the capital employed. In such circumstances, it is clearly intended that the two funds which benefit the employees should take a larger share of the profits in enterprise X than in enterprise Y. (It will be noted that this consideration led to a decision to allow for a higher rate of profitability in the light and food industries than in heavy industry, in the price reform of 1967, because the labour-capital ratio is generally a good deal higher in the former than in the latter).

It is also open to the planners to emphasize in particular industries the increase in profits instead of sales as a determinant of payments in these funds, or vice versa. This is the case in a cited example: 0·3 per cent of the wages fund for every 1 per cent planned increase in profits, and 0·6 per cent of the wages fund for every 1 per cent of planned profitability.

It is provided that the planners may draw up a list of key items which the given enterprise must produce to 'qualify' for its right to transfer profits to the above funds under these rules.

The Incentive fund may be used to pay premia to management, technicians and other workers and employees, subject to the various bonus regulations laid down by the planners, and also special bonuses and welfare payments. The social-cultural fund may be expended on holiday homes, canteens, kindergartens, sports facilities, medical arrangements, and so on, as well as the building and repair of houses.

The *Fund for the expansion of production* is used to finance investments and introduction of new techniques. It is formed from three sources: a part of the amortization (depreciation) fund, in the manner to be described below, the proceeds of sales of surplus equipment, and from profits by applying a formula which once again varies by sector and probably also by enterprise, and which lays down 'norms' (i.e. percentages) of the *planned value of basic capital*, the amount being dependent on increases in sales or profits *and* the achievement of the planned profitability rate (*rentabelnost'*). Again, overfulfilment of plans is discouraged by a 30 per cent reduction in the amount transferred to the fund in respect of overplan sales, or profit or profitability.

There is here too the prior duty of fulfilling 'the plan of production of key items'.

It is declared that the norms (i.e. percentages) used to calculate the sums payable into these funds should be stable, unaltered for a number (unspecified) of years, so that enterprise management can calculate on a firm basis. The decree also lays down that there should be a minimum below which allocations to these funds should not be allowed to fall: 40 per cent of the amount planned to go to these funds.

Planned by whom? This question raises a key issue in the whole reform. The rules about the rights and duties of the 'enterprise', its role in drawing up plans, are all to be found in the Enterprise statute (*Polozhenie o Predpriyatiyakh*), adopted just after the reform decisions, on October 4, 1965. It is admittedly the task of the enterprise to draft and propose financial as well as output plans. However, it will have been noted that both total profits and profit rate, as well as payments to the state budget, are included on the list of items for which plans are still laid down from above. Consequently the enterprise's proposals in these respects can be (and are) altered, and so not only the 'norms' but also the plans to which these normed percentages are applied are determined above the level of the enterprise. We shall see in subsequent chapters that this, and also the extraordinary complexity of the entire system of 'funds', are being criticized. It is highly probable that there will be many amendments to the rules.

For all the above purposes, profit is defined as being net of capital charges or other 'fixed' (rental) payments, and profits are expressed and calculated as a percentage of the enterprise's capital. These are significant innovations. Until the implementation of this reform there was no capital charge. (Rental payments are still exceptional, and would seem to be destined to be introduced only gradually). There were, of course, depreciation charges. It was felt that the absence of an explicit capital charge, plus the fact that much of the capital looked from the enterprise's standpoint like a free grant from the budget, encouraged overapplication for capital. It also distorted the financial results of enterprises, in that rewards for increased output and cost reduction were virtually unrelated to the amount of additional capital used to achieve them. Hence the adoption of this new principle.

Since selling prices are still, with few exceptions, fixed by the state authorities and not by enterprises, and since they remain based on 'average-cost-plus' (see chapter 4), it therefore follows that some enterprises still make planned losses, while others cannot pay the full capital charge. There are provisions made for payments into the incentive funds in relation to so-called 'theoretical profitability', this being cost reduction expressed as a percentage of the enterprise's capital.[1] The incentive scheme must then be modified, through the fixing of differential capital charges, or 'norms of profitability', or eventually perhaps differential rental charges so that the less favourably situated or less well-equipped enterprise is not unduly penalized for poor financial performance.

Capital and rental charges are paid out of profits instead of being included in costs. This is a gesture towards ideology, in that these payments are part of the 'surplus product' in Marxian terminology (see chapter 11). This makes little difference in practice, since, as we have seen, the profit which matters to the enterprise is net of the above payments.

Costs in state industry do not yet statistically reflect these new charges, as they are only just being introduced. The latest available data as at the time of writing are, so to speak, old style and are as follows:

	Per cent
Basic materials	63·8
Auxiliary materials	4·6
Fuel and energy	5·3
Amortization	5·0
Wages and social insurance contributions	18·0
Other	3·3

Source: N.Kh., 1965, p. 165.

Amortization (depreciation) allowances have been increased, especially following the revaluation of all capital assets carried out in 1959 and an upward amendment of norms in 1963. Thus its share in total costs has risen from 3·7 per cent in 1957 to 5·0 per cent in 1965. The amortization fund has, since 1938, been divided into two: for capital repairs and (nominally) for replacement. Until the recent reforms only the former part remained under the enterprise's control, and this could be spent only on capital repairs. While the original object of the division was to check a tendency to overspend on new investment and to neglect repairs, the effect in practice was not satisfactory. The enterprise management sometimes found itself spending more in repairing an old machine than the cost of a new one but was not allowed to use earmarked funds save for this purpose. This limitation has been abolished. The 'replacement' portion

[1] Ekon. gaz. No. 25/1967, p. 13; No. 22/1967, p. 9.

of the amortization fund used to be wholly transferred to the investment bank and used to finance investments decided upon at a higher
level, e.g. a ministry. Now a large part—usually around 40 per cent—
of this portion of the amortization fund remains at the enterprise's
disposal and is transferred to the 'Fund for the expansion of production'.[1]

The relationship between the budget and the enterprise is a complex one. The major part of the profits used to be transferred to the
state budget. Thus in 1961 66·2 per cent were so transferred, and
most of the retained profits could be used only for specified purposes
designated by the planning organs. On the other hand, budgetary
payments are made in respect of part of investment expenditure;
various subsidies were also paid (see chapter 3). Also it continues to
be the case that the planners can authorize the retention of profits
which would otherwise go to the budget to finance centralized
(planned) investments. The reforms now being implemented will alter
the 'traditional' pattern as follows:

(a) By dividing the payments to the budget between capital charges,
rental and the 'unused balance' (the latter being the designation used
to describe the planned payment into the budget of that part of the
profit whose retention for the various purposes described above is
not authorized. However, the rules do provide that enterprises can
retain a part of overplan profit, over and above the amounts which
can be paid into the various 'funds' and use them *inter alia* for the
repayment of bank credits before their due date).

(b) By increasing the total profit retained.

(c) By providing within the retained profit a wider range of purposes for which it can be used.

(d) By providing, as already noted, a greater role for profits both
in calculating the size of the incentives fund and making profits the
principal source for payment of bonuses (as distinct from normal
piece-rate pay and overtime, which continues to fall on the wages
fund).

(e) Subsidies and also direct budgetary financing of investment,
should be greatly reduced.

However, these propositions cannot yet be given any statistical
expression. It is simply too soon; the reform is still getting under way.

A Soviet economist has forecast that ultimately the allocation of
profits would be as follows:

[1] For details see Supplement to *Ekon. gaz.*, No. 50/1966, p. 13. A small part
of all the 'Funds' goes to the ministry (see chapter 2).

Per cent of total

Capital charge (to budget)	40·8
Incentive fund	12·3
Social-cultural fund	4·1
Fund of development of production	5·3
Finance of centralized investment, credit repayments, increase in working capital	15·9
'Free remainder' (to budget)	21·6

Source: A. Gusarov, *Ekon. gaz.*, No. 39/1967, pp. 14-15.

The enterprise's working capital (*oborotnye sredstva*, 'circulating resources') consists of two parts. The part which is required for normal operation 'belongs' to the enterprise, and increases in such working capital may be financed out of profits, if this is agreed by superior authority, or from the budget if profits are insufficient for the purpose. A new enterprise is endowed with its 'own' working capital from the budget when it begins its life. That part of working capital which is needed to cover seasonal or purely temporary needs —for example, the time-gap between production and payment, or, in retail trade, between buying and selling—is generally financed through short-term credits from the State Bank, at rates of interest of 2 per cent or less.

Investment finance will be separately considered (chapter 3). It is sufficient here simply to list the sources of finance available to expand the basic capital of an existing enterprise. These are: the state budget (until now the predominant source), retained profits, including the appropriate portion of the incentive fund, part of the amortization fund, so-called 'mobilization of internal resources' (for example unplanned economies, sale of surplus equipment, or the carry-over of stocks of building materials), and lastly bank credits. The latter are greatly to increase in importance under the reform now being implemented. The interest rate on such credits is 0·5 per cent for centralised, 2 per cent for decentralized investments.[1] Note that the fact that an enterprise *finances* investments out of its own resources, or on credit, by no means implies that the investment in question is unplanned or 'decentralized'. While investments out of the 'fund for the development of production' (as from the former Enterprise fund) are genuinely decentralized, it is clear that a large if not the major part of investments financed by credits will be part of the central plan for that particular enterprise.

[1] P. Bunich, *Vop. ekon.* No. 10/1967, p. 56.

Not only the bulk of the investment, but also most material inputs are subject to control. A large proportion of the materials and components required by enterprises may only be obtained against an allocation certificate (*naryad*), which commonly specifies not only the quantity but also the supplying enterprise, with whom the director must enter into a contract. Therefore, in most instances the enterprise is tied by the allocation system to particular suppliers or customers. It is true that contracts must be negotiated, containing detailed specifications, precise dates of delivery and so on. However, these contracts are based on the allocation decisions of the supply and/or disposal authorities. There is generally no right, in the case of allocated commodities, for enterprises to enter into free contractual relationships with one another. In particular, no long-term arrangements are possible between enterprises. For each year, or sometimes even a shorter period, enterprises must apply for a *naryad* for the required goods, and the supplying enterprise must await the issue of a *naryad* before the two enterprises negotiate the details of their contract, even though in practice they have been dealing with each other for many years and continue to do so. The contracts provided for in a *naryad* must be negotiated, and it is the task of the state arbitration tribunals not merely to settle disputes arising from alleged non-fulfilment of contracts, but also to compel the parties to agree to sign, in the event of disagreement over terms, using the intentions of the planners as the criterion for judgment. All this may now be altered. As we shall see, there is much talk of expanding free (i.e. unallocated), trade in material inputs, but administrative allocation remains the rule at the time of writing.

On the face of it, supply matters are decided very largely above enterprise level, save in the relatively few instances where the commodities are not subject to allocation. However, as so often in the USSR, things are not as strictly centralized as might appear to be the case. Thus the actual application for an allocation, initiated by the enterprise, has some influence upon the process of distributing the commodities in question, even though the planning organs amend or reduce the amounts, guided partly by material utilization 'norms' and partly by the suspicion (usually well founded) that enterprises tend to overstate their needs. Then the allocation certificates themselves are usually couched in general terms—so many tons of a given metal, for instance. But there are many varieties of this metal, and complicated negotiations are, therefore, set in train to obtain the desired variety. In this process, as well as in deciding what materials to indent for, the management is able to reflect its own initiatives in matters of design, technical changes, adjustment to demand. (For reasons which will be discussed in chapter 6 it may well fail to do so, but that is another question.) The system of materials supply will require separate consideration, in greater detail (see chapter 7, below). At this stage it is necessary to mention only that Soviet directors have had constant worries about their supplies, and that this has affected their behaviour in three principal ways. Firstly, they have often felt compelled to set up small-scale workshops to manufacture components, or castings, or tools, the delivery of which from outside could not be relied on. Secondly, there is a powerful inducement to hoarding. Thirdly, there have developed semi-legal materials procurement arrangements: lobbying for allocation certificates in Moscow, string-pulling through powerful friends or party officials, unofficial arrangements between enterprises ('I have a surplus of X, and will exchange it for Y', or, 'I will send you A if you promise not to let me down next month over B'), and even bribery. Specialists in such dealings as these are known in Russia as *tolkachi* ('pushers'). The personnel establishment of enterprises, which is determined by state authority, does not know such persons, who therefore nominally hold other positions. These semi-legal or illegal operations supplement and correct the official system, and it is often said that a Soviet director can hardly do his job without at least conniving at the breach of some law or regulation.[1] The wages bill, and the rules governing incentive bonuses to management and men, are also laid down from above (see chapter 4).

It is essential to look beyond formal degrees of centralization, to appreciate the fact that the Soviet system involves a complex interaction between planner-administrators and productive enterprises. Even where the former are in apparently full command—over production, investment, supplies, etc.—many of the proposals and much of the information upon which commands can be based comes up from below. Commands can be late, inconsistent, aggregated. Even in the worst period of centralization the directors had a good deal of room for manoeuvre. Indeed we shall see that many of the microeconomic problems, to which chapter 6 will be devoted arose out of the *de facto* autonomy of enterprise management.

As well as enterprises (*predpriyatiya*) in the sense described above, i.e. essentially factories or plants, there has been growing up in recent years some other categories of state economic unit. These are known

---

[1] For more on *tolkachi*, see chapter 7.

as *firma* and *obyedineniye* ('firm', or 'association' or 'corporation'). Each category in turn covers a multitude of variants, and no set pattern has yet emerged. However, their importance for the future justifies some attention being paid to them.

The *firma* is a grouping or amalgamation of enterprises, and covers several different kinds of organization. The *firma* was first invented in Lvov in 1962 when the then existing regional economic council (*sovnarkhoz*) found it expedient to join together a number of small footwear plants. The idea was given publicity and spread rapidly. There was and is no nationally-standardized structure, such as existed for the enterprise. Some *firmy* became in fact unified enterprises, with their sub-units (former enterprises) having no greater financial or legal autonomy than do workshops (*tsekhi*) of enterprises of the normal type. Others were federations of enterprises under a 'general director', with the enterprises retaining in varying degrees their separate existence. 144 *firmy* surveyed by a Soviet research team contained 849 enterprises, of which 282 were said to have 'retained their autonomy'. In 1964 a survey which its authors described as incomplete identified a total of 370 *firmy* employing 820,000 persons.[1] However, the restoration of ministries in 1965 led to an unknown number of disbandments of *firmy*, according to scattered reports, so their present importance is unclear.

The term *obyedineniye* is still sometimes used almost interchangeably with *firma*. A national gramophone firm was set up in 1964, with factories in Moscow, Leningrad, Tbilisi and Tashkent.[2] This proved to be a model for similar amalgamations, some regional and some national, which appear to be in process of developing into an important type of economic unit, broadly intermediate between the administrative ministry and its chief department (*glavk*) on the one hand and the ordinary enterprise on the other. It is to this that the term *obyedineniye* is often applied, though it is sometimes mixed up with *firma*,[3] sometimes with other administrative sub-divisions. It might be described as a species of Soviet corporation, with the constituent enterprises, under their directors, possessing some degree (as yet undefined) of financial and operational autonomy. There is taking place a drive to amalgamate thousands of small enterprises into these so-called *obyedineniya*, which increasingly resemble the

[1] M. Radomysilski and I. Shifrin, *Vop. ekon.*, No. 8, 1964, p. 15.
[2] *Ekon. gaz.*, August 8, 1964, p. 39.
[3] See *Pravda*, December 13, 1967 (R. Bobovikov *et. al.*) for one of many examples of the use of both terms interchangeably.

looser kind of *firma*. One likely development, already under way, is the granting to the *obyedineniye* the powers normally inherent in a ministerial chief department (*glavk*). This has been the case with the 'Sigma' *obyedineniye* in Lithuania.[1] This raises the important question of the boundary-line between the enterprise with its partially commercial (*Khozraschyot*) criteria and the planning-administrative organs, which will be further examined in chapter 2.

OTHER STATE ENTERPRISES

The above analysis has been concerned primarily with state industrial enterprises, but these general accounting and operating principles are common to state enterprises in general. However, certain peculiarities of non-industrial sectors call for brief comment.

Construction enterprises are of two types. The first, dominant in the 'thirties but now of less importance, is created *ad hoc* to do a given building job, by the organization for whom the job is being done. The nearest English equivalent would be the building of houses by 'direct labour', i.e. by a municipality directly. This species of building is known rather oddly as being done *khozyaistvennym sposobom*, literally 'by economic means'. The building unit undertaking the work possesses little or no working capital, since it only lives a temporary life. It has other financial peculiarities, into which it is unnecessary to go.

Most common is a building enterprise, carrying out work on contract (*podryadnym sposobom*). This is a true enterprise, with the degree of financial autonomy enjoyed by industrial enterprises in general, with working capital and other attributes of *khozraschyot*. They receive payment from their customers for building work. The customer could be another enterprise, or the building order may be placed by a ministry (or, in 1957-65, a *sovnarkhoz*).

In many localities, especially in large cities, there grew up a large number of construction enterprises, great and small, owing allegiance to many different organizations and ministries. To assure a necessary degree of co-ordination, a number of trusts were set up grouping together for operational purposes all the building enter-

[1] Described in *Ekon. gaz.* No. 23/1967, pp. 8-9. It makes electronic equipment.

prises located in certain large cities. Examples are Mosstroi (Moscow), Lenstroi (Leningrad), Kievstroi (Kiev).

Some construction enterprises make or procure some of their own materials, and to this extent contribute to industrial production in its Soviet definition. By contrast, many industrial enterprises carry out their own maintenance and repairs to buildings with their own labour, usually with a very primitive technology.

State farms (*sovkhozy*) for many years received very large subsidies. Thus in 1953 the subsidy of 4·6 milliard roubles amounted to 48·3 per cent of the cost of the produce which state farms delivered to the state.[1] However, from 1956 they have sometimes made a profit, and they are permitted to retain a large portion of this. State farms sell produce to state wholesalers, except that they sometimes sell also to collective-farms (for example, pedigree livestock, tested seeds) and also direct to the retail trade network (notably vegetables.) As state-owned enterprises, in which peasants become wage-earners, state farms are considered ideologically superior to collective-farms, and, as can be seen from the table on page 29 above, their numbers and relative importance have been growing.

An important development now in progress has been to place some *sovkhozy* experimentally on what has been called 'full *khozraschyot*'. In November 1967 there were 400 such *sovkhozy*. Their numbers are increasing. In practice this has meant paying them the same prices as those paid to *kolkhozy* (prices were usually lower), but out of the increased profits they (like *kolkhozy*) must pay for their own investments and purchases of machinery, instead of receiving them largely from the state. Greater initiative is provided in investment planning, greater autonomy in the field of labour and wages. These *sovkhozy* also have greater opportunity for selling direct to shops, processing plants, and in the free market those products which the state procurement organs do not purchase. The various 'funds' into which retained profits are directed are essentially similar to those which, under the reform, are being introduced in industry, except that there is also an insurance fund.[2] All this is said to be 'an experiment'. It will surely soon be the rule.

State agriculture includes not only *sovkhozy*, of which there were 11,681 in 1965, averaging 24,600 sown hectares and 663 employees,

---

[1] S. Nedelin, *Finansy SSSR*, No. 10/1957, p. 35.
[2] A useful summary of the new-type *sovkhozy* may be found in *Pravda*, November 20, 1967 (G. Lisichkin), and *Ekon. gaz.*, No. 23/1967, p. 32.

but also 'subordinate enterprises' (*podsobnye khozyaistva*), mainly small, run by industrial and other state enterprises, often to supply factory canteens. There were over 96,000 such enterprises, mainly small (averaging about 63 hectares of sown land).

Until their abolition in 1958, the Machine Tractor Stations (MTS) were a unique form of state enterprise, in that they were not based on 'economic accounting' but were wholly budget financed. They were closely linked with collective farms and will be discussed with them, below.

Trade and material supply organizations derive their revenues from authorized trading margins. The larger part of their activities are predetermined by plans handed down to them from above, but, like other state enterprises, they are expected to use their initiative in making applications to wholesaling and superior supply organizations, reflecting as far as possible the requirements of the purchasers, though this at times conflicts with the fulfilment of plans expressed in aggregate turnover. Trade and supply questions will repeatedly arise in subsequent analysis; at this stage it is sufficient to distinguish between organizational forms in retail trade, which might otherwise confuse the issue. Since the outlawing of private trade at the end of the 'twenties (except for the free or *kolkhoz* market), there have been two principal categories of retail outlets: state and 'consumer-co-operative'. The latter were confined to rural areas in 1935, and their urban network transferred to the state; consumer-co-operative activities in towns have been confined to the sale there of farm surpluses (in 1946-49, and again, on commission, after 1953) at and just below free-market prices. Their primary task has been to operate shops and stalls in villages. They are nominally co-operatives, in the sense that the bulk of rural householders (over 33 million of them) each hold one share and are entitled to 'dividends' which must not exceed 20 per cent of total profits. There are 16,000 co-operative associations, with 55 million members.[1] At their head is a central union of consumer-co-operatives, known as *Centrosoyuz*. But here the resemblance to a co-operative ceases. They act in practice as the rural branch of the state retail network. Trade plans are state-determined, managers are in fact state-appointed (though, at the lower levels, owing nominal allegiance to the consumer associations), employees are included in all statistics with state-employed persons. These 'co-operatives' run minor industrial enterprises,

[1] *Pravda*, January 20, 1968.

notably rural bakeries, and these are treated as state and not-co-operative in statistics of labour and of output. Finally, these 'co-operatives' have been used by the state to sell a wide range of producers' goods to collective-farms, and to act on the state's behalf as purchasers of farm produce.

State shops proper, in urban areas, are generally run by the trading departments of local soviets, commonly known by the abbreviation *torg*, and/or by republican or even all-union trading organizations; the repeated and complex changes in subordination of shops cannot be described here.[1] The normal state store is available to all the public, but there have at various times been 'closed' stores, reserved to particular groups of employees. These survive in the form of so-called 'workers' supply departments' (known by the initials ORS, *Otdel Rabochevo Snabzheniya*), which sell canteen meals and other goods to employees of particular factories. There are also military canteens. Their turnover is included in the statistics with state trade.

Transport enterprises raise few structural problems peculiar to the USSR. The railways are organized in a manner similar to that of West European countries. *Aeroflot* functions in a way very reminiscent of nationalized undertakings which run other countries' airlines. Perhaps the only point of difficulty is road transport, where one encounters the problem of the specialized haulage organizations *versus* the ownership of lorries by the user enterprise. In recent years, the policy has been in favour of developing lorry 'pools' to serve many different enterprises, especially in large cities. Trams, buses and taxis are operated by local authorities. Some transport services in rural areas are provided on hire by collective-farms, and here and there one encounters a lively but illegal ('pirate') taxi service. The charges levied by all state-enterprise providers of transport services are fixed by the state; there is a high degree of centralization of decision, applying even to the tram fares in all the towns of the Soviet Union.

Service undertakings of many kinds (baths, laundries, pawnshops, etc.) are organized by local authorities on a *khozraschyot* basis. State-owned *housing* either 'belongs' to the local soviet, or to other state enterprises or institutions (for example, factories, building organizations, even the Academy of Sciences, erect and administer housing space). Rents are centrally fixed at a low level, far too low to cover running costs and repairs, and substantial housing subsidies are the rule. Housing space is severely rationed, there being a very serious shortage.

[1] See E. Lomatovski and G. Gromova, *Upravlenie gosudarstvennoi vnutrennei torgovli SSSR* (Moscow, 1957). See also chapter 2, below.

Finally, there is one further special category of state enterprise: this is the *foreign trade corporation* (*Vneshtorgovoe obyedineniye*). The USSR has, since its earliest years, reserved all foreign trade dealings to state organs. After a period of experiment, there were set up trade corporations specializing in the export and/or import of particular commodities, under the general control of the Ministry of Foreign Trade. For example, *Exportles* sells timber, *Exportkhleb* sells grains and also (despite its name) purchases it. There are roughly two dozen such corporations, some specializing on imports, some on exports, but mostly on both. For any particular commodity, one corporation always has a monopoly position.[1] No detailed description of their functioning, or of their relations with Soviet commercial-diplomatic representations or foreign businessmen will be attempted here.[2] The corporations are autonomous enterprises, which, acting within the plan, buy abroad and sell to wholesalers and productive enterprises within the USSR, or place orders with Soviet enterprises and wholesalers for goods which they sell abroad. The corporations, in other words, act as intermediaries in all foreign trade matters. No ordinary Soviet enterprise has the right to import or export, save through one of these corporations.

CO-OPERATIVE ARTISANS

Through the 1920's and especially in the early 'thirties, the government sought to discourage the private artisan, by fiscal and other pressures, and to make them join producers' co-operatives, and these remained until 1960, a significant, though diminishing, sector of economic activity. These co-operatives undertook a wide range of production, such as making clothes, furniture, musical instruments and a variety of other consumers' goods. They also ran workshops for repairs, and sometimes also retail outlets for the sale of their own produce to the public. Unlike the collective farms (which, as will be seen, had no profit and loss account), the producers' co-operatives based their operations on the payment of what was in effect a wage to their members.

In 1960 the remaining producers' co-operatives, their assets and employees became, respectively, state enterprises, state property and state employees.

[1] Except that the all-union-consumer co-operative centre (*Centrosoyuz*) has made small-scale barter agreements covering commodities which also fall within the competence of other corporations.
[2] Readers are referred to A. Nove and D. Donnelly, *Trade with Communist Countries* (Hutchinson, 1960).

THE COLLECTIVE-FARM (KOLKHOZ)

The collective-farm is nominally a form of co-operative. The peasants of a given village or group of villages join together to cultivate land in common, under an elected management committee headed by an elected chairman. We shall see that reality is far removed from this definition, but it is legally valid and certain important organizational and financial peculiarities stem from the 'co-operative' nature of these *kolkhozy*.[1]

It is impossible to understand the nature and evolution of collective-farms without considering the political-social background, which has had a much deeper influence on structure than has been the case in industry. Thus the shape of the basic productive unit in industry, a factory, is largely predetermined by sheer technical necessities, and factories in Russia and in the West are in many respects similar. But there has been nothing like a collective-farm outside the Soviet bloc. For this reason, they have to be considered here in somewhat greater detail than other economic organizations.

After the revolution, the bulk of the land remained in the possession of private peasants. A small area was cultivated by state farms, and peasants were also encouraged to engage in joint productive activities of various kinds but the peasants remained obstinately attached to private farming. In 1927, all the various forms of state and co-operative farming covered a mere 2 per cent of the peasants. But in 1928 came the launching of the first five-year plan. To carry it through, Stalin's government needed assured supplies of food for the towns, and exportable surpluses to pay for machinery for industrialization. They needed labour to move from village to town. They needed finance for investment, and, in a market situation favourable to the peasant seller, they were anxious to obtain produce without having to pay the full market price. Experience in the period of war-communism suggested to them that no attempt to squeeze the peasants could succeed so long as land and produce was in peasant hands.[3] For this reason, and also on general ideological-political grounds (that the individual peasant is a 'petty-bourgeois' force

[1] *Kolkhoz* (plural *kolkhozy*) is the Russian abbreviation of the two words *kolletivnoye khozyaistvo*, literally 'collective economy'. The word *artel'*, a peculiarly Russian term designating a team of men working together in a self governing group, was and is also used to describe this general organizational form. The term *kolkhoz* is also used to describe a significant group of fishing co-operatives, whose members also cultivate some land.

[2] N. Jasny, *The Socialized Agriculture of the USSR* (Stanford University Press, 1949), p. 779, citing official data.

[3] For the background to all this, see the excellent survey by A. Erlich: *The Soviet Industrialization Debate* (Harvard, 1960).

hostile to socialism), it was decided to eliminate the individual peasant as quickly as possible as an economic force. This was achieved by coercion (notably by deportations on a mass scale of richer peasants and opponents of collectivization generally) and by fiscal and administrative pressures of many kinds. It is not possible here to go into the history of collectivization, and it seems hardly necessary to stress that by giving reasons for the policy pursued one is not for a moment arguing that the policy was reasonable. The point is that the structure of *kolkhozy* and the relationship between them, the peasants and authority cannot be understood unless one bears in mind the circumstances in which, and the purposes for which *kolkhozy* were created by a 'revolution from above'. After a period of experiment, in which the attempt to collectivize the bulk of private livestock ended in disaster (a large proportion of the animals were slaughtered by the peasants), a species of compromise was arrived at within the collective between interests of the farm and of its members, which became enshrined in the Collective-farm Statute of 1935, which lasted with only little change until 1958.

Under this statute, the collective-farm is a co-operative of peasants of the given village or group of villages, which occupies nationalized land[1] rent-free in perpetuity. Management is in the hands of a meeting of members; such meetings must be called to take important decisions affecting the work rules, membership and income distribution of the farm. The meeting elects a management committee and a chairman, the latter being the operational manager of the farm. He is assisted by a deputy or deputies, and also by an accountant. The peasants are organized for work purposes into 'brigades' each led by a 'brigadier'. A sub-unit of a brigade is known as a *zveno* ('link', or 'nucleus'). Until 1958, the power-driven machinery used by the farm remained in the possession of state Machine Tractor Stations (MTS), which were simultaneously service agencies carrying out work on contract, and supervisory agencies on behalf of the state. Each MTS had a political deputy-director (until 1953), or a party secretary based upon it (in 1953-57), for carrying out its political-control functions. The MTS were partly staffed by their own employees, and partly used collective-farm peasants on a seasonal basis. The collective-farm paid for MTS work almost wholly by deliveries in kind, based on a valuation of various operations, in terms either of a given quantity of produce or a stated share in the harvest. Exceptionally, payment was also made in money.

---

[1] All land was formally 'nationalized' in the USSR in November, 1917, but *de facto* ownership was the peasants' until collectivization.

Thus collective-farm production involved the joint effort of the farm and a state-owned machinery operator, the MTS.

The average size of collective farms varied, and varies, widely by area; in general, they are bigger in the prairies of the south and east than in the forest-and-bog country of the north and west. It has also varied over time. Thus in 1949 there were over 250,000 collective farms, averaging 80 households and 453 hectares (about 1,150 acres) sown area each. Amalgamation in the following years reduced numbers by 1957 to 76,500 averaging 245 households and 1,696 hectares of sown area, and numbers fell further to 53,436 by the end of 1959.[1] Partly because of conversions into state farms, but mainly through still further amalgamations, numbers of *kolkhozy* fell by the end of 1965 to 36,900, averaging 421 households, 2,843 hectares of sown area, 1,038 head of cattle, 667 pigs, 1,460 sheep. The number of MTS never exceeded 9,000, so that each served many collective-farms.

The influence of the state and party was exerted through the MTS, but was (and is) also to be felt throughout the collective-farm sphere of operations. The 'election' of the chairman was in reality in the hands of the party secretary of the *oblast'* or *raion*, and they could and did repeatedly reprimand or dismiss him. The output plan, sowing plan, livestock plan, even the dates of sowing and harvesting, were decided by state or party authority and 'handed down' (the Russian verb is *spuskat'*) to the farm to be acted upon. The basic duty of the collective-farm was to meet the state's compulsory delivery quota, and to hand over produce in payment for the services of the MTS. The quota was related until 1940 to the sown area under the given crop or to the number of animals owned; then the basis was changed to area of arable land. But, as Khrushchev stated,[2] this was in practice disregarded, because the local party and state authorities were themselves under pressure to meet delivery quotas imposed on their areas from above; in consequence, they often arbitrarily increased the delivery quotas of successful farms, in order to make up for the failures of the unsuccessful.

Subject to carrying out the requirements of higher authority concerning output and deliveries of produce, the collective-farm chairman and his colleagues have rather more control over their finances, operations and investments than do directors of state enterprises. This is due partly to the nature of agriculture, where local circumstances vary so very widely, and partly to the fact that the state's

[1] Full details may be seen in *N.Kh. 1958*, pp. 494-7, and *Sel. Khoz. 1960*, p. 51.
[2] *Pravda*, September 15, 1953. Brezhnev repeated it in March 1965, and promised that the practice *will* now cease!

primary interest has been to obtain deliveries of produce, and, despite a large number of decrees and orders of many kinds, the planning authorities have not in fact attempted any very tight control over what the farms do, once the required deliveries have been made. This may be seen from the financial and operational structure of collective-farms, to which we will now turn.

Cash revenues of collective-farms arise from a number of activities, not all of them agricultural. Thus, collective-farms have engaged in small-scale industry. This has taken the form of producing cartwheels, minor implements, bricks, or in some cases of processing vegetables (e.g. pickling, canning), as well as miscellaneous handicrafts. Income is also obtained from providing transport services (e.g. loaning out horses and carts, or lorries, to other enterprises). These non-agricultural activities have in some areas been a major source of revenue: thus in the Moscow *oblast'* in 1937, 63 per cent of all revenues were non-agricultural.[1] The authorities from time to time took measures to restrict these activities, because they were deemed to distract the peasants from their primary agricultural tasks.[2] The distraction was doubtless due in large part to the very unattractive prices paid for agricultural produce, of which more in a moment. In more recent years the agricultural sources of income have been dominant, and, as the table shows, total revenues have been rising:

(billions of old roubles)

	1940	1950	1957	1962
TOTAL REVENUES	20·7	34·2	95·2	152·4
of which:				
Sales of farm produce to state*	9·1	21·5	74·1	131·4
Sales of farm produce in market	7·3	9·1	13·6	12·3
Other revenues	4·3	3·6	7·5	8·7

Source: *N. Kh. 1958*, p. 498. *N. Kh. 1962*, p. 342.

*Including consumer co-operatives.

This large rise in gross revenues is *not* an indication of any similar increase in net revenues. Sales of produce rose sharply after the abolition of the MTS (because produce formerly handed over for their services was now sold for money), and also following the price reform of 1958. However, the *kolkhozy* had to bear a much heavier burden of capital and current expenditure, in connection with their newly-acquired machinery. As will be subsequently shown, the net effect on peasant incomes was not favourable.

[1] D. Abramov, *Vop. ekon.*, No. 6/1957, p. 80.
[2] See, for example, the decree of the Council of People's Commissars of October 23, 1938, and the resolution of the 19th party congress (October, 1952).

Sales to the state, until 1958 and for some products since 1965 also, were of two kinds. Firstly, there were *compulsory deliveries* of produce, at a low (sometimes purely nominal) price. Then, when this quota had been met, there were *over-quota purchases* by the state (*gosudarstvennye zakupki*) at higher prices. These over-quota sales were partly due to administrative pressure, in the many cases where the higher price was unattractive, and partly to *quid pro quo* inducements, in the form of state deliveries of scarce goods (or of goods at reduced prices) to those farms which made over-quota sales. In the case of industrial crops, this two-price arrangement bore a different designation, but was essentially similar. Thus a collective-farm selling cotton would undertake to sell its entire crop to the state, a given quantity being paid for at a low price, and additional quantities commanding a higher price. This arrangement was known as *kontraktatsia*. The level and principles of agricultural prices will be examined in greater detail on pages 153-158, below.

Mention must be made at this point of sales to consumer co-operatives, which act as *de facto* state agencies. In some years (e.g. 1946-49) they were empowered to purchase farm surpluses at free prices.[1] In others (1949-53, for example) they were limited to paying the prices applicable to over-quota sales. After 1953 they could buy from the farms for resale on free markets on a commission basis, at prices which were not fixed or limited by the state. These purchases by consumer-co-operatives are included in the revenues from sales to state agencies in the above table.

Then there is the *free or kolkhoz market* (*kolkhoznyi rynok*). Markets are maintained by the local authorities in all towns, and anyone may sell their produce there. While citizens may be observed selling non-agricultural commodities in these markets (such as home-made clothes-pegs, pictures and the like), the bulk of business is in foodstuffs. Collective-farms are among the principal sellers in these markets (though, as we will note, the peasants in their private capacity are more important). If there is a surplus of produce, after state needs have been met, then collective-farms can decide, if they wish, to sell them in the free market, at prices which have been generally much higher than any offered by the state. Farms located near big cities have often kept permanent stalls in the market precincts, and derive considerable incomes from these sales. There is scope here for enterprising chairmen; thus a prosperous farm near Alma Ata, visited by the author, sent vegetables and fruit to the free market of Novosibirsk, a distance of 1,000

[1] *40 let sovetskoi torgovli* (Moscow, 1957), p. 101.

miles. However, many farms have been unable to develop such trade owing to inadequate communications. The farms also obtain revenues from selling foodstuffs in villages, particularly to their own members, often at specially reduced prices.[1]

It must be emphasized that these free-market sales are within the discretion of the farm. For example, of a total output of 10,000 tons of potatoes, there may be 5,000 tons left after making deliveries to the state and providing seed potatoes for next year. This 5,000 tons can be used for fodder, for paying the peasants in kind (see below), or for free market sales, in proportions which are largely within the competence of the farm to decide. The only ruling on this subject is the frequently repeated injunction that the distribution in kind to the peasants should not be 'too large', in the sense of providing them with a surplus over their needs, which they might themselves take to the free market; but this in fact has often happened. A small amount must also be set aside for purposes of relief of aged and infirm members, since social insurance does not extend to collectivized peasants, though *kolkhozy* as well as the state contribute to an old age pension fund since 1965.

Thus the revenue of the collective-farm can be seen as consisting partly of the proceeds of sales (at different prices), and partly of produce used on the farm. Expenditures, similarly, are partly in money and partly also in kind.

There are no recent systematic statistics of the money expenditure of collective-farms. The following can be used as a basis for description.

Collective farm expenditures
(milliards of old roubles)

	1938	1952	1956
TOTAL	16·60	42·8	94·6
of which:			
Taxes and insurance	1·58*	6·9	10·9
(* including repayment of past credits)			
Capital fund contribution	2·32	7·4	16·7
Paid to peasants ('workdays')	8·70	12·4	42·2
Production expenses	3·25⎤		
Cultural fund	0·50⎬	16·1	24·7
Administration	0·25⎦		

Sources: A. Arina and T. Basyuk, cited in Jasny, *op. cit.*, p. 687.
           N.Kh. 1958, p. 498. *Pravda*, January 25, 1958. *Finansy SSSR*, No. 10/1957, p. 34.

[1] Proceeds of these sales are included in statistics of revenues from market transactions of collective farms, but statistics of free-market turnover is confined to urban areas, and so excludes these 'village' transactions.

The basis of taxes has been several times altered. Until 1958 they were differentiated between sources of revenue, (e.g. they were especially high on proceeds from free-market sales), and also included a tax based on a valuation of produce used within the farm and distributed to peasants, with certain exemptions. Until 1965, there was a flat-rate tax of 12½ per cent on all gross revenues, except those devoted to productive expenditures, and this rate of tax was also levied on the valuation, at state purchase prices, of produce distributed to peasants and used for such purposes as communal feeding (but that used for animal feeding was exempt). This way of assessing tax was very onerous. For example, the yield of tax in 1960 (12·1 milliard old, 1·2 new roubles) was of the order of 10 per cent of *gross* revenues, but may well have represented 35 per cent or more of the amount of cash paid to the peasants (the latter figure is unavailable for 1960). Therefore a change was made in 1965, and tax is levied only on the amount of revenue left over after the peasant members are paid a minimum sum. This was part of the change of principle affecting peasant remuneration, of which more will be said below.

Insurance is partly compulsory and partly voluntary. Collective-farms, unlike state enterprises, cannot expect to have their lost assets replaced at the expense of the budget, and are therefore bound to take out insurance against fire, natural disasters, etc.

The *capital fund* is officially entitled 'indivisible fund' (*nedelimyi fond*). Into it were paid the original contributions, in cash and in other assets, of the collectivized peasants. The total capital fund at any given moment covers the capital assets of the farm plus cash in the capital account. The annual contribution to the capital fund is laid down in regulations. It ranged for many years from 12½ to 20 per cent of gross cash revenues, but in 1958, after the absorption by the kolkhozy of the MTS, the proportion considerably increased, and was often near 30 per cent. The money is earmarked for expenditures on building materials, tools, lorries and other capital goods, and also the salaries of outside persons employed on capital work. Since 1956[1] the allocation to the capital fund can also be used to pay for the labour of collective-farm peasants engaged on such work. In assessing the burden of the capital fund contribution, it is again necessary to stress that the amount is based on *gross* revenues, and the impact is therefore greater than it looks. Investment by collective-farms may also be financed by *credits* from the banking system. Unlike state enterprises, collective-farms do not receive capital assets free.

[1] Decree of March 6, 1956, printed in *Direktivy KPSS* . . . , Vol. 4, pp. 603-5.

From 1966 there has been an important change in the status and significance of payments into the capital fund. Whereas up to this date it took priority over payment to labour, it has now ceased to do so, for reasons explained below. It therefore now varies widely according to the financial situation of the farm. It is now also the practice to allocate sums to an Amortization (depreciation) fund, whereas in earlier years no such separate fund existed; depreciation was not even calculated.

Production expenses largely speak for themselves; they include fuel, fertilizer, fodder, seeds and the like, and also payments to outsiders hired for operational purposes. It is important to note that most commodities bought by collective-farms were obtainable only at retail prices, which were generally higher than those charged to state enterprises for the same items.

The cultural fund is used for books, newspapers, the running of a clubhouse and similar objects. Up to 2 per cent of gross revenue may be devoted to it, under the model statute.

Administrative expenses include stamps, stationery, telephone, and also money salaries of administrative personnel. Total expenses under this head are limited to 2 per cent of revenue by the model statute, but this figure has often been exceeded.

Finally, there is *payment to peasants*. Until 1966 it was literally 'finally'.

When all the above expenditures had been met, the remainder was available for distribution to the peasants, along with produce set aside for the same purpose. This cash and produce was then paid to peasants in proportions determined by their contribution to the work of the farm. The proportions were measured in conventional work units (*trudodni*, literally 'workdays'). All work in farms was graded in these *trudodni*, piecework being widely used. This intricate system will be examined in detail later on (p. 138, below). At this stage it is sufficient to emphasize two aspects of this method of payment. Firstly, it involved no definite scale of payment. The amount available (in cash and kind), divided by the total number of *trudodni* earned, determined the earnings per unit of work. It is because the amount available could not be known in advance that the *trudodni* system was invented. Secondly, there was no fixed or minimum scale of payment.[1] The amount distributed was not a wage, it was a residual. It is true that it was within the competence of the farm to vary some items of

[1] Except that peasants employed for any period by the MTS were entitled to a minimum scale of payments while working for the MTS on collective-farm fields.

expenditure to some extent; for instance, it could decide to buy less fertilizer, or feed fewer potatoes to pigs, in order to make more money and potatoes available as payment for *trudodni*. However, this only partially modified the 'residual' essence of peasant rewards for their work. In most farms at least until 1958, the payments to peasants were irregular, often occurring only once or twice a year, as well as varying very widely from year to year and from farm to farm. It is also worth noting, as the above table makes abundantly clear, that the share of the peasants in gross revenues fell in post-war years, and was particularly low in 1952.

This system of payment had three consequences. Firstly, an un-certain and generally inadequate reward for collective work neces-sitated the introduction (formally in 1939) of a *compulsory minimum* number of collective workdays for each able-bodied person. The minimum varied by area, and has tended to increase. Since 1956 each collective-farm is empowered to impose whatever minimum is necessary to carry out the necessary work. Secondly, the normal principles of economic accounting (*khozraschyot*) could not be ap-plied to collective-farms, since, with payment of labour a residual, it was hardly possible to identify either the labour cost or the profit element (see chapter 6, below, for further discussion of this point). Thirdly, the peasants could not, in most of the USSR, obtain a live-lihood by working for a collective, and so it was necessary to permit the peasants to possess a *household plot of land* and some livestock, which constitutes the most important private-enterprise sector in the Soviet economy (see page 61, below).

However, from the standpoint of the authorities, the system should be judged by reference to the objects for which it was brought into existence. The compulsory delivery system ensured that the state took its share of the produce and thus supplied the growing towns. The fact that it took this share at well below the equilibrium price provided a vital source of revenue, since this produce could be re-sold at much higher prices to the population. The residual nature of payment of peasants meant that they shouldered not only much of the burden of industrialization, but also of the year-by-year varia-tions in the harvest. In a state-farm, the wages of the workers are a first charge on the revenue of the enterprise, and must be paid by the state if the enterprise makes a loss; in a collective-farm, the state had no responsibility to pay any given level of income, and any 'loss', which is in any case unidentifiable in the accounts of collective-farms, simply results in smaller distributions to members, i.e. is borne by the peasants. There will be much to say about the weaknesses of the system, but it must not be forgotten that these weaknesses are in part the consequence of organizing agriculture primarily with the object of obtaining at minimum cost the material and financial resources for industrialization. After Stalin's death in 1953, there were in fact a number of changes, designed to make the system work better. Thus prices paid by the state for farm produce were substantially increased, and some effort made to improve the planning and control system. In particular, the powers of the MTS were enhanced and there was a measure of decentralization. However, the basic pattern remained, until 1958.

In March, 1958, a law was adopted providing for the sale of machinery to the collective-farm and the abolition of the MTS over a short period of time. The reasons for this measure were essentially as follows. Firstly, the division of authority and responsibility (between the management of the farm and the machinery it used) caused unnecessary waste and much conflict. Not only were there 'two masters' in the fields, but their material interests were necessarily conflicting. The collective-farm was interested in maximizing the harvest and its net revenues in cash and kind. The MTS was rewarded by the authorities for carrying out its work plan (expressed in standard work units) and for earning produce in payment for its services; this encouraged it to carry out such work as was 'profitable' in respect of the above criteria, even if it was wasteful from all other points of view. The MTS were wholly budget financed, that is were not 'economic accounting' organizations. A decision to make them such was taken in 1953, but could not be implemented. The reason for this failure was, essentially, that the whole system of payments in kind, and indeed of MTS work, had no economic *rationale*. Thus, for instance, the payments in kind not only had no connection with the costs of the given MTS, but in a sense were inversely related to cost; they were higher in the south than in the north, though costs of operation were higher in the small fields of the north than in the southern plains.[1]

The higher level of payments in kind on the better lands of the south may be regarded as a disguised tax, or a species of land rent,

[1] This may be demonstrated in the following examples: in 1955 the MTS in the fertile Krasnodar region spent 301 roubles for every ton of grain received in payment in kind; by contrast, in Ryazan the MTS expenditures per ton of payments in kind were 1,149 roubles, and in Belorussia or the north they were higher still. Yet the scale of payment per conventional unit of tractor-work was 150 kilograms of grain in Krasnodar, but only 35 kilograms in Belorussia and 30 in Karelia. See S. Ilyin, *Gosudarstvennye zagotovki zerna* (Moscow, 1957), pp. 62 ff., and L. Kolychev, in *Voprosy sovetskikh finansov* (Moscow, 1956), p. 204.

but certainly it could have had no meaning as an economic measure of MTS activities. Thus no way was found to place each MTS on an economic basis. There was also no way of assessing the profitability of this or that machine or type of tractor, and no attempt was in fact made to do so. Machinery was centrally allocated to MTS, despite numerous complaints that it was often unsuitable to the requirements of the given area.[1] The inefficiencies of MTS operation had become a serious burden to the state, which had to cover their expenses out of the budget. Produce received as payments in kind, when measured against these expenses, appeared very dear. All these objections to the artificial separation of MTS and collective-farms were known for many years; for example, two economists, Sanina and Venzher, proposed to Stalin in 1951 that the machinery be transferred to the collective-farms.[2] The arguments of economic expediency were rejected; the MTS were still needed as state organs of control, and indeed in 1953 the powers of the MTS *vis-à-vis* the farms were actually increased. However, the anomalies of the relationship became abundantly obvious, while the mechanism of state and especially party control became strong enough to make it apparent that the MTS were unnecessary. There remained the ideological arguments that it was wrong to hand over state-owned assets to non-state ('co-operative') organizations, and that the payment-in-kind system was a higher, more 'socialist' form of exchange than straightforward buying and selling. But these ideological difficulties were overcome.[3]

The law of 1958 provided for the transfer to collective-farm employment of the staffs of the MTS, and for the purchase (usually on instalments) of the machinery by the collective-farms. It should be noted that the principle was maintained that non-state organizations must pay for their capital assets; state farms, like other state enterprises, received the bulk of their machinery free, but collective-farms must pay for theirs. The same law also provided for the setting up of a new species of state enterprise, the *Repair Technical Stations* (RTS), which were at first intended to sell machinery and spares to farms, and at the same time to carry out major repairs and to hire out specialized machinery (e.g. for carrying out drainage work) of

---

[1] For a typical instance, *Pravda*, February 25, 1957, printed complaints from north-west Russia, to the effect that machines supplied were ill-adapted to their type of soil. Similar complaints were common in 1960.
[2] The proposal was discussed by Stalin in 1952, See his *Ekonomicheskie problemy sotsializma v SSSR* (Moscow, 1952), pp. 88-94.
[3] The necessary adjustments to theory were carried out by K. Ostrovityanov, in *Pravda*, March 3, 1958.

types which collective-farms would not find it economical to purchase. The RTS were not supposed to possess the control function which formerly resided in the MTS, and to operate on *khozraschyot*. In 1960, a new agency, *Sel'khoztekhnika*, took over the function of selling machinery and other supplies to farms, both state and collective, and since 1961 it also carries out the repair functions originally assigned to the RTS, which have ceased to exist under that name.

The abolition of the MTS necessarily involved the state in buying from the farms the produce which was formerly handed over as payments in kind. Consequently, it was necessary to review prices. This was desirable also on general grounds, discussed in chapter 4, below. The wide 'spread' between the compulsory procurement (or basic *kontraktatsia*) price and the over-quota prices led to a number of undesirable consequences: successful or favourably situated farms were given a disproportionate bonus, since they had most to sell over the quota, while their less fortunate brethren were correspondingly depressed. In addition, the multiple-price system impeded economic calculation within farms. Consequently, in June, 1958, a decree[1] established new purchase prices for all farm products, differentiated by area. Farms henceforth would sell to the state at the one price applicable to the given product in their area.

In March 1965, however, the multiple-price system was restored, as part of the post-Khrushchev reforms, for a few key products. A quota of deliveries is to be determined for several years ahead, and any additional sales, (strictly voluntary, so we are assured) will be at higher prices. More of all this on pages 153-158.

In the same year, it was at last decided to tackle the problem of peasant pay. For nearly ten years the press had published criticisms of the *trudodni*, and many critics urged some guarantee for the peasants of a definite reward for their work, or at the very least a minimum share in the farm's gross income. Presumably the principal difficulty in implementing such proposals was financial: some money would have to be made available somehow to farms which had insufficient income. No doubt also the old habit of neglecting peasant needs also played some role. But with effect from July 1, 1966, it was decreed at long last that the peasant members of *kolkhozy* are entitled to the rate paid for the given work in *sovkhozy*, that this would be a priority charge on *kolkhoz* revenues (ahead of allocation to the capital fund), and that bank credits would be available to help farms which could not pay the peasants (hitherto *kolkhozy* were not

[1] Decree of Council of Ministers, *Pravda*, July 1, 1958.

allowed to borrow to pay their members). This fundamental change in the structure of collective farming has not gone through smoothly. Indeed there were press reports to the effect that some *kolkhoz* managements ignored the decree.[1] None the less, it is important in Soviet conditions to establish the principle, even if it takes time, effort and struggle to implement it. A new set of rules have been published: 45 per cent of the gross revenue of *kolkhozy* are to be set aside for basic guaranteed pay, a further 15 per cent for bonus payments (by results)[2] This, if fully implemented, would be a very big change indeed. Pay of peasants has risen very sharply since 1965.

A Congress of *kolkhozy* was to have met to adopt a new statute or rules, to replace those of 1935. It was promised repeatedly that it would meet, both by Khrushchev and, after his fall, by Brezhnev. It has still not been called (as at May 1968). A very likely reason may be seen in the fact that the changes noted above both in *sovkhozy* and *kolkhozy* have brought the two types closer together. A *sovkhoz* on 'full *khozraschyot*' has many features in common with a *kolkhoz* with a guaranteed wage. True, the one is a state, the other nominally a co-operative organization. But it may well be found sensible and convenient to merge the two varieties for all practical purposes into one 'socialist' agricultural enterprise. At the very least it may be surmised that the matter is under discussion. Hence no congress.

It should be noted that *kolkhozy* have been encouraged to form many thousands of *inter-kolkhoz enterprises*, in which neighbouring *kolkhozy* join together to make bricks, operate small generating stations and so on, sometimes employing outsiders as well as their own members. It seems likely that these organizations too may be affected by *kolkhoz-sovkhoz* link-ups in the future.

THE PRIVATE SECTOR

By far the most important private economic activity in the Soviet Union is in agriculture. Neglecting the individual peasant, who is not now significant, we must examine the two forms which this private agricultural sector takes: private plots of collectivized peasants, and private holdings of state employees.

The collective peasants' private plots are held by each household (*dvor*), as an entitlement under the 1935 model *kolkhoz* statute. Their size is normally $\frac{1}{4}$ hectare, sometimes higher where land is plentiful and/or of poor quality. There is also private livestock, with

---

[1] *Pravda*, December 28, 1966, for instance.
[2] *Ekon. gaz.*, No. 42/1967, pp. 33-6.

fixed maxima; usually the peasant household may possess one cow and one sow, with offspring, and some other animals also. The peasants benefit from *de facto* pasture rights in respect of their animals. In the first stages of collectivization (1930-32) an effort was made to collectivize all private livestock, with disastrous results. About half of the livestock was slaughtered. It was then decided to permit private ownership within collective farms of animals (other than horses and bulls, boars, etc., which could be used as a source of income from hire, though a very few horses remain in private hands).

Until 1958, peasants were subject to compulsory delivery quotas, at the low prices applicable to collective-farm deliveries. Before 1953, not only were the quotas exceedingly onerous, but the burden fell on the household regardless of whether or not they in fact produced the commodity in question. For instance, the milk deliveries had to be made even if there was no cow, and so the peasant was compelled to purchase milk, at whatever price it was necessary to pay, in order to deliver it to the state at a very low price. In 1953, the quotas were appreciably reduced. With effect from January 1, 1958, the compulsory delivery quotas on private plots of collective peasants and other private holdings (except for the few surviving individual peasants) were abolished altogether.

The reason for the burdening of private plots with delivery obligations was two-fold. In the first place, in many products the private sector predominated (see page 29, above), and, secondly, it was considered desirable to make the private sector relatively less profitable. This latter reasoning also operated in respect of the tax burdens on private plots. Whereas the receipts of the peasants from the collective-farm were and are untaxed, the private plot was assessed for a curious 'agricultural tax', which was based on the notional income delivered from private activity. The details of this tax were complex,[1] but in essence the basis of it was, until 1953, a valuation of area sown and livestock owned. For instance, a cow would be deemed to be 'worth' 2,400 old roubles, a hundredth-hectare under potatoes— fifty roubles, and so on. These valuations were added together to represent the 'income' of the peasant from his private holding. This was then subject to tax on a sliding scale, which, in 1952 ranged from 12 to 48 per cent. The valuations and the tax scale were such as eventually to cause a net fall in production in the private sector, and this must have been the object of the authorities. No doubt it was believed that, by making private activities less attractive, the

[1] For detailed description, see A. Nove, 'Rural Taxation in USSR', *Soviet Studies*, October, 1953, and *Was Stalin Really Necessary?*, pp. 174-85.

peasants could be persuaded to work for the collective-farms. However, since the latter paid so poorly at this period, the effect was to discourage all effort. Many households found themselves in a desperate situation: they were unable to live on what they received from the collective-farm, unable to pay the tax on their cow or pig, yet still liable to compulsory deliveries of milk and meat if they disposed of the cow or pig to avoid the tax.

In 1953, as part of the post-Stalin reforms, the 'agricultural tax' was much reduced, and its basis changed to land area actually held by the household, subject to regional variations.

The peasants can sell their surpluses in the free market. This they do on a large scale; for many years, they derived more income from this source than from any other. They also feed their families very largely from their private production, with the important exception of bread grains, which generally form the major part of payments in kind by the collective-farm. (In some areas specializing on industrial crops, as, for instance, in the cotton-fields of Uzbekistan, the bulk of collective-farm payment is in money, and the peasants buy bread or bread grains.)

The peasants generally take their own produce to market, thereby wasting a great deal of time on long journeys with a comparatively small quantity of goods. Millions of peasants waste millions of mandays in this extremely inefficient and primitive system of distribution. It is true that peasants can let the collective-farm arrange to take their produce to market for them, and there also exist sales on commission through the consumer-co-operatives. However, neither has so far replaced the peasant himself as a trader, to any decisive extent. This is due partly to lack of enterprise on the part (especially) of the consumer-co-operative organization, partly because of the peasants' inborn belief that they and no one else can strike a good bargain. The very great importance to peasants' welfare of this source of cash income causes them to exploit its possibilities very vigorously, often to the detriment of their work for the collective-farm. This has been a constant source of friction.

A decree in 1956 gave *kolkhozy* the right to diminish the private holdings of members who do not work when required for the *kolkhoz*.

After 1959, pressure to sell livestock to the collective-farm and to reduce private plots began gradually to be effective; private livestock numbers fell significantly. This process continued until Khrushchev's fall and took many forms: denial of fodder and pasture rights, a stricter definition of the permissible maxima of land and livestock, and so on. Coinciding as it did with a fall in collective income, it must have been exceedingly unpopular. Pressures were relaxed under Brezhnev.

State-employed persons' plots and allotments are to be found in all rural areas, and also in or near many towns. State-farm workers, railwaymen, even 'rural intelligentsia' (teachers, local officials, etc.) very commonly cultivate a small plot and possess some livestock, if only because the villages are so poorly supplied with shops. Many urban citizens, especially in smaller provincial towns, grow potatoes and vegetables and keep a small number of animals on allotments. These private holdings were also, until 1958, burdened with compulsory delivery quotas, and (with some exemptions) were and are subject to 'agricultural tax'. The government at first encouraged these private productive activities, since they relieved pressure on food supplies. They grew enormously during the war. However, in recent years the attitude has changed, in so far as these holdings distract the state worker, and even more his wife and family, from regular work. There were instances of private 'suburban' livestock being fed with bread, so as to fatten them to take advantage of the relatively higher price of meat. As a result, measures have been taken in 1958-59 to limit livestock ownership in urban areas, and state-farm employees have had to dispose of their cows.[1] These pressures too have been relaxed.

The relative importance of private activities in agricultural production has been particularly great in the livestock sector, and also in potatoes, vegetables and fruit. The reader is referred to the table on p. 29, above.

Soviet agriculture remains based on a species of compromise between state, collective and private sectors, so that a substantial portion of the labour force has private economic interests to pursue. The balance is changing appreciably, and it is official policy to continue the process of change. Brezhnev strongly criticized the negative and restrictive policy applied to private plots in Khrushchev's last years, and these restrictive measures were abandoned in 1965.[2] None the less, the share of private output in the land will probably resume its decline.

Little need be said about *non-agricultural private economic activities.*

[1] Khrushchev's speech, *Stenograficheski otchyot,* Central committee plenum, December, 1958 (Moscow, 1958), pp. 54-5. This was followed by a sharp increase in taxes on any livestock held over and above narrowly defined maxima. All these restrictions were lifted early in 1965.
[2] A most valuable analysis of private plots and a strong condemnation of this policy appeared in *Vop. ekon.* No. 4, 1965 (by G. Shmelev).

Artisans, seamstresses, shoe repairers and the like are permitted a precarious existence, subject to discriminatory rates of income tax (see chapter 3, below). There have been many reports of semi-legal gangs (*arteli*) of building labourers hiring themselves out in rural areas. There are also a wide range of other semi-legal or illegal economic activities: unlicensed taxis, 'speculation' of many kinds, and so on. Judging from things seen in Georgia, for instance, there must be a sizeable volume of unrecorded and quite unofficial economic transactions. Another source of private income is rent from letting rooms in privately-owned dwelling houses, which is legal unless the house-owner has acquired housing-space in excess of need in order to derive the major part of his income from rents, in which case action is taken against him.

CHAPTER 2

Administration, Planning, Policy Decision

INTRODUCTION: THE NATURE OF THE TASK

So far we have been considering the nature and organization of economically active enterprises. Now we pass to an examination of the ways by which the political, administrative and planning organs control and direct these enterprises, and thereby the economic life of the Soviet Union. There must be a flow of operational orders to enterprises, plans must be devised for various sectors and co-ordinated with those of other sectors. The orders given to enterprises about what to produce must be backed by the necessary material supplies, and the output plans must, of course, be related to the planned inputs. Every economic decision is interconnected with a great many other decisions, or involves a number of necessary consequential effects. Therefore, the situation appears to call for an all-knowing and all-seeing Planner, whose brain takes decisions in full awareness of all the relevant alternatives and of all the consequences of his acts. However, such a Planner cannot exist, outside the imagination of model-builders or of over-simplifying writers of textbooks. The tasks must be divided, and each possible arrangement of planning and operational powers involves its own set of advantages and disadvantages, solving some difficulties and creating others, a fact familiar to the management of large firms in the west. We should distinguish between several major aspects of organization. The first category lays stress on industrial *sector*; the process of planning and control is then based on the particular industry (e.g. textiles, metallurgy, coal), with general co-ordination between industries at government level. The second is often referred to as *functional*: powers are given to functional bodies, concerned on a national scale with supplies, labour, investment, wholesaling and so on, which give orders within the scope of their responsibility to subordinates in the industrial hierarchy. Finally, there is the *territorial* principle, which would devolve planning and operational powers to regional authorities. It must be emphasized from the beginning that none of these categories are ever present in pure form. Thus planning and control

66

which operate 'functionally' or territorially must involve separate consideration of the problems of each industry in some office in Moscow, headed by an official; the office may have the status of a branch of some larger organization, such as Gosplan, or possess the dignity of a 'ministry', but it is impossible to do away with it altogether. In any conceivable organizational arrangement, co-ordination between functions, industries and regions, between output plans and investment, between production and material supplies, and so forth, will present difficulties; these difficulties find their administrative expression in the creation of offices and departments to deal with them. None the less, the basis of organization chosen does make an appreciable difference to the chain of command, to the levels at which decision-making on various matters takes place, and to the weight given to certain species of problems within the planning machine; this should become apparent in the following pages.

v s n k h (Vesenkha)

Created as early as December, 1917, with the object of controlling economic life in what was still expected to be a largely privately-run economy, was the Supreme Council of National Economy, known by its Russian initial letters as vsnkh or Vesenkha. With the nationalization of the bulk of industry and trade, vsnkh became possessed of operational powers over the economy, subject to guidance by the government,[1] in which the chairman of vsnkh played a prominent role. In the NEP period, and especially in the years 1922-27, a large part of industry and trade was in private hands, and vsnkh was in charge of the state's economic activities, both in the field of industrial production and of wholesale trade. Its internal organization was repeatedly altered, and, as the recital of these changes would occupy much space without adding significantly to understanding, no attempt will be made here to list them. Essentially, vsnkh was sub-divided into two species of departments: functional and industrial-sector. The former dealt with such matters as finance, planning, economic policy, development and research, and the like. The latter, under a 1926 decree,[2] consisted of 'chief departments'

---

[1] That is, of the Council of People's Commissars, and of its powerful Council of Labour and Defence (*Sovet Truda i Oborony*, sto). Both were advised on long-term planning questions by Gosplan, founded in 1921, of which more below.
[2] Decree of Council of People's Commissars of August 24, 1926, and Order of vsnkh of September 4, 1926.

(*glavnye upravleniya*, or *glavki*) for separate industries, and in them must be seen the germs of the future economic ministries. The coverage and number of the *glavki* were several times altered, and for a time they became known as *obyedineniya* (associations), and then again as *glavki*, without changing their essence appreciably. The heads of all the various departments formed the actual council ǝf VSNKh, together with representatives of the union republics, in each of which there was a similar body, which was collectively subordinate to the all-union VSNKh. There were also regional economic councils, known by the abbreviation *sovnarkhozy*. In practice, enterprises of all-union significance (i.e. any large-scale industry) were administered by the appropriate *glavk* of the all-union VSNKh, subject only to occasional representations from republican or provincial councils on matters of local interest. However, minor industries, using local sources of materials and supplying local markets, operated under the direct control of the republican VSNKh and/or local *sovnarkhozy*.

Large-scale industry under VSNKh was organized for production, planning and accounting purposes into *Trusts*, which consisted of enterprises producing similar commodities, generally in some limited geographical area. In exceptional cases where enterprises were very large, they were directly subordinated to the appropriate *glavk* of VSNKh, without any intermediate Trust. Wholesaling was the responsibility of so-called 'syndicates' (*sindikaty*). In the middle twenties these trusts and syndicates had a wide measure of effective autonomy.

Co-ordination between the various functional and industrial-sector departments was supposed to be assured by including them all within one super-department, VSNKh. However, not for the first or last time, it was discovered that co-ordination is not necessarily achieved by placing the co-ordinees under one organizational umbrella. Departments A, B and C are not always easier to manage, or to keep in step with one another, if they are labelled A1, A2 and A3. In the end, especially after the launching of the first five-year plan (1928-29), the common problems of industrial sectors became so large and so urgent as to require a separate organization, with its own functional divisions, to cope with them. After some experimental changes in the VSNKh structure in the years 1929-30, VSNKh was finally abolished altogether by the decree of January 5, 1932. Trusts gradually ceased to be significant in most branches of industry, save where they provided a convenient geographical administrative grouping of several enterprises within the same productive complex.

THE RISE OF THE 'MINISTERIAL' SYSTEM

In 1932, three industrial People's Commissariats (Ministries) were created: heavy, light and timber industries.[1] Their numbers grew rapidly. By 1939 there were twenty of them. The all-time maximum was reached in 1946-48, when they (industrial and construction ministries alone) numbered thirty-two. After a drastic reduction immediately after Stalin's death to eleven, there was another expansion in 1954, and at the end of 1956 there were thirty-one industrial (including construction) ministries. Once again, there is no need to trace the very numerous changes in numbers, coverage and designation. It is sufficient to examine the essence of the system, which may be seen from a brief look at the features common to an industrial ministry.

A typical ministry is divided into a number of departments or chief departments (*glavki*), some of which are responsible for functional aspects (finance, supplies, investment, labour, etc.), some for sub-divisions of the given industrial sector (e.g. oilfields of a given area within the Petroleum Industry Ministry, or woollens within the Ministry of Textile Industry). Enterprises are, as a rule, subordinate to a *glavk* of 'their' Ministry.[2] They received their plans from the *glavk*, submitted their applications for materials and investment funds to the *glavk*. The ministry has its own supplies and disposals organizations. In some instances these powers are exercised through identically-named ministries (and *glavki*) of the union republics, i.e. through the so-called union-republican ministries (page 25, above), in others—the vast majority in the Stalin period—the republican authorities were totally by-passed, the line of subordination stretching straight from the enterprise to the *glavk* of the appropriate ministry in Moscow, regardless of the republic in which the enterprise was located. However, in the period 1955-56 there was a considerable move to strengthen the republican ministers' functions.

Many of the changes made when the numbers of ministries were increased or decreased consisted in promoting an existing *glavk* to the status of a ministry, or on the contrary 'demoting' it. Thus the Textile Ministry sometimes existed independently, and sometimes formed part of the Ministry of Light Industry, while in 1954-55 some

[1] In addition, much of the food industry came under the Commissariat of Supply.

[2] In some instances, notably in the coal and fisheries industries, there were and are intermediate organizations, e.g. a *kombinat* covering a coalfield and *Trusts* grouping together a number of adjacent coal mines, or a *kombinat* grouping the fisheries of Kamchatka.

glavki which, within existing ministries, were responsible for building operations were 'promoted' to ministerial rank (e.g. Ministry of Construction of Coal Industry Enterprises and several others). This last reform was due to a growing concern for the special problems of construction, and these 'building' ministries were supervised by a State Committee on Construction, which was (and is) headed by a deputy-premier.

The Minister, his senior deputies and his heads of chief departments (who commonly bear the title of Deputy-Ministers), together with a few other high officials, form the *collegium* of the Ministry, which meets regularly to transact business. Both the Minister and the Deputy-Ministers must be seen essentially as senior business executives or civil servants, not as politicians in the western sense; they are often promoted managers, with an engineering or technical background. They are technical executants, not policy-makers. When ministries became numerous, especially in the post-war period, it became customary to appoint senior party leaders as 'overlords', to supervise groups of ministries; these leaders held the rank of deputy-premier. Immediately after Stalin's death, no doubt because of the need to tighten control in the aftermath of that dictator's disappearance, party leaders became Ministers themselves, which explains the sudden reduction in numbers of ministries in 1953. They resumed their supervisory functions in 1954, and so the number of ministries returned to 'normal' levels.

Because of the activities of each ministry in ensuring or manufacturing supplies and components for 'its' enterprises, and also the habit of making consumers' goods out of by-products in many sectors of 'heavy' industry, the product coverage of ministries is often extremely heterogeneous.

Obviously, the existence of a large number of economic ministries, each controlling their own national network of productive enterprises and supply and disposal agencies, placed a heavy burden on the co-ordinating function. The *power* of co-ordinating plans and operational decisions resided in the government itself, and in its economic committee or economic cabinet, which was known until 1937 as the Council of Labour and Defence, and from 1937 to the war as the Economic Council (*Ekonomsovet*). After the war, it appears to have faded out. So unwieldy a body as the whole Council of Ministers was certainly unable to co-ordinate, and some evidence exists that an inner cabinet (or 'praesidium of the Council of Ministers'), composed of the premier and the deputy-premiers (the 'overlords'), took the necessary decisions. The body which carried out the work of co-ordinating, and drafted plans, was Gosplan; it had no powers to *order* any ministry to do anything, but its submissions appear to have been the basis of government decisions, the more so as it was intimately linked with the central committee of the party.

PLANNING AGENCIES BEFORE 1957

Before discussing the fate of the 'ministerial' system in 1957, it is necessary to refer to the development of the planning agencies, and notably of Gosplan. This body was founded in 1921 under the title of 'State general-planning commission' attached to the Council of Labour and Defence. Until the end of the 'twenties, it was essentially a body concerned with the elaboration of long-term plans, often of a somewhat abstract character. The practical planning, such as it was, fell to the planning department of VSNKh. When the first five-year plan was being drawn up in 1928, the Party's crash programme of industrialization was resisted by the moderate (and very able) economists of Gosplan. Several of these were former mensheviks, and their courage in sticking to their point of view led to their being removed.[1] Gosplan was reorganized, and, following the elimination of VSNKh, came to play an essential role of co-ordination within the government. Its head usually possessed the rank of deputy-premier. During the 1930's, Gosplan absorbed the Central Statistical Office.[2] Gosplan was responsible for drafting short-term and long-term plans, for allocation of materials and also for developing new techniques. In each instance, these functions were limited by the existence of the ministries. Thus the drafting of plans for enterprises in, for example, the Ministry of Ferrous Metallurgy was the job of the planning department of that ministry. Gosplan's job was to calculate the material needs inherent in the general development programme designed by the political leaders, that is, to draw up so-called 'material balances', which form the basis both of long-term investment planning and of general governmental directives to the ministries, and also to plan material supplies and deliveries.

[1] V. G. Groman was a leading defendant in a show trial of mensheviks in 1931. The world-famous economist Kondratieff vanished at the same time. Neither has been heard of again.
[2] This was known from 1931 by the clumsy abbreviation TsUNKhU, which stood for Central Department of Economic Accounting, the word 'statistics' being considered temporarily too bourgeois, since statistics suggests measuring random and uncontrolled events; the term Statistics was restored in 1941. See A. Ezhov, *Soviet Statistics* (in English) (Moscow, 1957), pp. 31-3.

In 1948-49, Gosplan, headed by the powerful Nikolai Voznesen-ski, ran into serious trouble. Its precise nature is by no means clear even today. Voznesenski was arrested and executed, for reasons which have never been disclosed. The name of Gosplan was changed from State Planning *Commission* to State Planning *Committee*, and it lost its material allocation department (*Gossnab*), its technical department (*Gostekhnika*) and the Central Statistical Office, each of which became separate committees of the Council of Ministers. Probably, this was intended to demote and weaken Gosplan. This state of affairs lasted until Stalin's death, when the *status quo ante 1948* was restored, temporarily, except that the Central Statistical Office remained a separate body attached to the Council of Ministers. Then, in 1955, came yet another major reorganization. It was alleged that Gosplan's preoccupation with current planning caused neglect of long-term considerations, and so it was split into, firstly, the *State Planning Commission* (still called Gosplan), which was concerned with long-term planning only, and the State Economic Commission (*Gosekonomkommissiya*), which was charged with current planning. *Gostekhnika* was also revived as a separate body, responsible for devising and introducing new techniques into the economy. This, then, was the position when the entire system went into the melting-pot at the end of 1956.

THE 'SOVNARKHOZ' REFORM

The reform of the system of industrial planning and administration was apparently touched off at the end of 1956 by the errors of the sixth five-year plan. This had been adopted by the twentieth party congress in February, 1956, but was found to be over-ambitious and unworkable, notably in its implications for investment in new industrial capacity. This caused a decision to be taken, at the central committee plenum of December, 1956, to revise the plan. Its principal author, Saburov, lost his job as the head of Gosplan. A general reshuffle of personnel and organization took place. *Gosekonomkommissiya* (i.e. the body in charge of current planning) was given powers over virtually all the economic ministries. Even the Ministry of Agriculture was at first put within its purview: the minister (like other senior economic ministers) became a deputy-chairman of *Gosekonomkommissiya*, under the chairman, Pervukhin. Thus while Gosplan retained separate long-term planning functions, all current economic matters were concentrated under the umbrella of *Gosekonomkommissiya*, which thus partially resurrected the situation of VSNKh.

But not for long. Khrushchev had other ideas, and in the spring of 1957 he piloted through a radical reform, which brought *Gosekonomkommissiya* to an end and abolished the majority of economic ministries altogether. The motivation was partly a political one; the reform was closely followed by the formation and defeat of the so-called 'anti-party group' (Molotov, Malenkov, Kaganovich, Bulganin, and to a lesser extent also Pervukhin and Saburov), who were against it. The political manoeuvrings were complex and it is no part of our purpose to analyse them here. Like many other important changes in economic and political affairs, this was partly a reflection of a genuine need for reform, and partly was devised (and opposed) by politicians to further their own ends. In any event, the Supreme Soviet formally adopted a law embodying the new structure in May, 1957, and it came into operation in July.

The economic arguments for a change were these.

Firstly, each industrial ministry showed strong tendencies towards becoming a self-contained economic empire. This was partly the consequence of the chronic uncertainties of supplies, which led to reluctance to rely on other ministries, and so to the setting up of one's own 'ministerial' supply bases, or ministerial factories to make necessary components. But another part of the explanation for ministerial autarky lay in the weakness of the co-ordinating authorities in the face of the growing complexity of the industrial structure. Gosplan, especially after Voznesenski's downfall, was too weak to keep the various ministries working together effectively. Ministerial autarky showed itself in many kinds of avoidable waste. Thus many small factories made components for nation-wide ministerial empires, and then transported them to all parts of the USSR. For instance, there could be a workshop in Sverdlovsk which supplied factories of the Ministry of Heavy Machine Buildings in Minsk and Kiev, while other ministries had identical workshops in Minsk and Kiev, supplying, *inter alia*, these ministries' factories in Sverdlovsk. This produced numerous instances of unnecessary cross-hauls on the already overloaded railways. In other words, both horizontal and vertical integration was stimulated or limited by ministerial boundary lines, rather than by economic forces. The maintenance of separate supply offices in all areas by every ministerial system caused much duplication and therefore waste.

Secondly, there was no effective authority responsible for regional planning. Despite some attempts to strengthen the role of republics after Stalin's death, all lines of command still led to Moscow, and no one in any area had authority to examine and act upon any assessment of the potentialities of the given area, from a viewpoint which transcended inter-industrial boundary lines.[1] All this particularly impeded the development of new areas, for instance, in Siberia. Factories next door to one another, but within different ministerial systems, had no means of collaborating, nor could any local body enable them to do so.

Thirdly, there was much avoidable waste in the utilization (or, rather, in failure to arrange for the utilization) of by-products. For instance, petrochemicals could be based on using the by-products of the oil industry, but there was no direct link between the Ministry of Chemicals and the Ministry of Oil Industry, and neither had any interest in taking any action in the matter.

Finally, the concentration of authority in Moscow over enterprises scattered over the country made for bureaucratic delays in settling the many everyday questions which unavoidably arise.

These weaknesses were part of the cost of basing planning and control on industrial sectors, and they had existed for many years, so the fact of their existence was not itself a sufficient explanation for the reform. But the burdens of planning and administration from the centre had grown with the growth of the economy itself, and this had led to a kind of elemental devolution of authority to the ministerial industrial systems, because of the inevitable difficulty of co-ordination. Just as a western firm which grows beyond a certain size eventually requires radical reorganization by reason of its size, so growth and complexity did present new and especially difficult problems, and the errors of the sixth five-year plan project showed that these problems were not being solved.

The new system was based on the territorial principle. All the USSR was divided into 105 (later 103) regional economic councils or *sovnarkhozy* (note resurrection of the old term), to which were directly subordinated the larger industrial and building enterprises, while local industry remained under local, mainly *oblast'* and city Soviets. The *sovnarkhozy* did not control agriculture, transport or retail trade, save where these activities were directly associated with industry (e.g. auxiliary farms, factory transport, canteens). The boundaries of the *sovnarkhozy* followed existing administrative borders in the main, though in some instances *oblasti* were grouped together. Therefore these boundaries did not, save by coincidence, represent economic regions.

[1] It is true that *oblast'* party and local-authority organs could do so, but they had no authority over any but the smallest enterprises in their area and probably lacked information also.

The members of each *sovnarkhoz* were to be appointed by the governments of the republics in which they were situated. In the case of the smaller republics (e.g. Georgia, Latvia, Armenia, Kirghizia), the republic was itself coextensive with a *sovnarkhoz*.

However, for reasons which will be further discussed below, the power and boundaries of *sovnarkhozy* were altered substantially in March, 1963, the number of *sovnarkhozy* was reduced to 47. The smaller republics remained co-extensive with *sovnarkhoz* boundaries with one conspicuous exception: the four Central Asian republics (Uzbekistan, Kirghizia, Tadzhikistan and Turkmenistan) were grouped together into a single Central Asian *sovnarkhoz*. At the same time, the sovnarkhozy gained control over local industry, which was taken away from *oblast'* and city soviets, and lost such control as they exercised over construction enterprises, which were transferred to a separate specialized hierarchy (see page 98, below). There was also an increase in the number of industrial state committees with some authority over production planning. In other respects, the powers of *sovnarkhozy* were, at least formally, unaltered.

The internal organization of a *sovnarkhoz* varied greatly from place to place, depending on the nature and extent of the industrial activity of the region. The powers and functions of the *sovnarkhoz* were laid down in a long decree of 138 paragraphs, issued by the Council of Ministers of the USSR on September 26, 1957.[1]

In its day-to-day operations, its essential task was to supervise the fulfilment of the plan decided by superior authority, though it has powers to decide the detailed composition of production where this was not prescribed by the plan. The *sovnarkhoz* had the duty to encourage new technique, and rational specialization within the region, in so far as this enables the plan to be fulfilled at lower cost and more expeditiously. It was guided in all matters by the orders it receives from its superiors, but had a range of choices as to how to carry them out. It could confirm or amend enterprises' investment projects of a value not exceeding 25 million (old) roubles, subject to general planned limits, it allocated some materials, and redistributed materials between enterprises,[2] authorized the overspending of the wages fund by enterprises. The *sovnarkhoz* also fulfilled an important function in the process of planning: together with 'its' enterprises, it drafted a regional plan and submitted it to the government.

---

[1] The most accessible source for this is *Direktivy KPSS* . . . , vol. 4, pp. 784-805.
[2] About 35 per cent of materials were either allocated or sub-allocated by *sovnarkozy*. M. Lyashko, *Finansy SSSR*, No. 10/1960, p. 49.

As originally designed, the formal situation was to be as follows. Enterprises were under 'their' *sovnarkhoz*, which, through its various industrial-sector departments, exercised the control over them formerly exercised by the *glavk* of the appropriate industrial ministry. The *sovnarkhoz* was subordinate to the republican government (in practice, the republican Gosplan was primarily involved), and this in turn took instructions from the all-Union government, within which a strengthened Gosplan played the vital co-ordinating and directing role. This, subject to the usual pervasive role of the Communist party, was the formal hierarchy. It never worked in this way in reality. The various divisions of Gosplan in Moscow, and others concerned with the planning and with the distribution of centrally allocated commodities, constantly bypassed the republican and the sovnarkhoz authorities and dealt directly with enterprises. Gradually the number of central co-ordinators grew, with the multiplication of state committees. In 1960, powers to ensure the implementation of plans were vested, in the three biggest republics (RSFSR, Ukraine, Kazakhstan) in *republican sovnarkhozy*.

INDUSTRIAL PLANNING AND ADMINISTRATION AFTER 1957: UNION LEVEL

The 1957 reforms eliminated all the specifically industrial ministries, with the exception of the Ministry of Medium Machine Building, which appears to be concerned with nuclear weapons, and the subsequently-abolished Ministry of Electric Power, which administered the interconnected electricity network. However, already in 1957 there were created six 'state committees of the council of ministers', five for branches of the defence industry, the sixth for the rapidly-expanding chemical industry. These committees were given the general function to advise on technique, design, research and planning, but were not placed in charge of enterprises, which remained formally under the *sovnarkhozy*. Their number increased rapidly in 1959-63. The effective economic 'boss' at all-union level was, beyond question, Gosplan. It absorbed the planning function of the ministries, and some of their staffs, and its production departments broadly corresponded to the ministries, though they had no enterprises subordinated directly to them. Gosplan also possessed at this period a large number of material allocation departments, these also absorbing many of the powers of the *snab* and *sbyt* departments of the defunct ministries (others passed to republics and *sovnarkhozy*). It had functional divisions concerned with finance, investment, prices and costs, foreign trade, long-term planning, current co-ordination of planning and material balances, labour and wages, and so on. Some of these functions it was to lose to other organs in the course of the next few years. As envisaged in the 1957 reform, and to a great extent also in reality, Gosplan's responsibilities were immense. It had to amend the plans submitted by republican planning organs, and make them coherent with one another, with the party and government's economic policies, with production possibilities, investment financing, estimated agricultural production, availability of labour and technicians. It had to watch plan fulfilment and amend production and supply plans as difficulties arose. All this lies at the very heart of the planning process. Yet Gosplan's *powers* were, formally speaking, small. Although there was some discussion of giving it executive authority, there was no mention of it in the legislation finally adopted in May, 1957. However, in practice its key role in planning, and especially its role in allocating materials, gave it great powers, the more so as it could normally count on the backing of the government and party for its decisions.

However, the decree of April 7, 1960, split Gosplan, by transferring the function of long-term planning, i.e. for periods of over five years, to a State Economic-science council (*Nauchno-ekonomicheski sovet*), which became known as *Gosekonomsovet*. Its tasks included the drawing up of long-term material balances, the working out of difficult questions (*problemnykh voprosov*) concerning the development of the economy of the USSR, the preparation of learned reports, forecasts and proposals on these questions. Confusingly enough, Gosplan was now left with current planning functions, whereas in 1955-56 it was given the job of long-term planning, while current tasks fell to *Gosekonomkommissiya*. The reason for the change, once again, was that long-term planning was being neglected under pressure of current work.

This arrangement was disrupted by the reform which was given publicity during the central committee plenum in November, 1962 and formally adopted in March, 1963. *Gosekonomsovet* vanished from the scene. Instead, following a precedent set in the large republics, the division of function was made on different principles: not between long and short term planning, but between planning and implementation of plans, the latter function including a substantial element of current planning, especially material allocation and the issuing of appropriate detailed production and delivery orders. Planning, with emphasis on long-term, fell to Gosplan, implementation to the *Sovnarkhoz* of the USSR. (One might suppose the the Soviet reformers were trying to make life difficult for students!) Needless to say, some of these changes left many officials and departments still doing the same as before, under another name: the upheavals caused by reorganizations are often less than they seem. Both Gosplan and the USSR *Sovnarkhoz* were made into union-republican organs, i.e. they were given *authority* over identically-named republican bodies, subject to the rules of dual subordination (see p. 25, above).

In March, 1963 (but not in the proposals published at the time of the central committee plenum in November, 1962) a new supreme central organ was announced: the Supreme Council of National Economy, new incarnation of VSNKh.[1] This body was to co-ordinate the co-ordinators in that Gosplan, the USSR *Sovnarkhoz*, *Gosstroi* (see p. 98, below), the State Committee for co-ordination of research, as well as a number of other state committees, were placed under its authority. It was, indeed, to have power to issue binding orders on matters within its competence to all organs and officials. Its head thus acquired authority as great as Pervukhin was supposed to possess in December, 1956. However, in practice its powers seemed rather limited. VSNKh's actual role hardly resembled that of a supreme controller. By contrast, Gosplan and the USSR *Sovnarkhoz* were constantly in the news.

SOVNARKHOZY AND 'REGIONALISM'

In assessing the importance and indeed the essence of 'regionalism'. it is necessary to study the nature of *sovnarkhoz* decision-making, Much of what they actually did consisted in the transmission of, or obedience to, instructions received from above, and in these respects they were cogs in the administrative machine. But the *sovnarkhozy*, as was indicated above (pp. 75-76), did have functions—drafting plans, organizing their fulfilment, supervising contracts and deliveries, and many other matters great and small—which were not covered by precise instructions and where they had to use their own initiative. What, then guided them when there were no orders from above to settle exactly what they should do?

Sovnarkhozy were interested in fulfilling plans for their areas—

---

[1] In 1960-62, this abbreviation VSNKh was used to designate the all-Russian (*Vserossiiski*) republican, i.e. RSFSR, *sovnarkhoz*, and care is therefore needed in reading documents and articles relating to this period, to avoid confusion.

gross output, cost reduction, adoption of new techniques, labour-productivity, and so on. Plans and resource allocation therefore tended to be geared to these purposes, or to the greater glory of the region (i.e. expansion, the attraction of investment resources from central funds). These aims may fit into the requirements of the economy as a whole, but this would be something of a coincidence. An average *sovnarkhoz* would possess within its boundaries roughly 1 per cent of the industrial productive potential of the USSR. The factories controlled by any *sovnarkhoz* drew their supplies from dozens, or even hundreds, of factories or mines located outside the given region, and supplied products to numerous factories or wholesalers similarly located. The major inter-regional deliveries were decided by Gosplan, at republican or all-union level, and these deliveries, once incorporated into the plan, had to be made by *sovnarkhozy* on pain of disciplinary measures or even prosecution before the courts. They had to be given priority over deliveries within the region. These disciplinary and legal measures dated from 1958,[1] and were sure signs that the economic mechanism was not working properly. Indeed, the press n 1957 was full of complaints about 'regionalism' (or 'localism'—*mestnichestvo*), showing itself in priority being given to the needs of the region instead of to outside customers. The following is a typical quotation:

'There are instances when officials bother only about enterprises subordinate to them, and do not think of the difficulties which their irregularities cause for enterprises in other regions. It is necessary to speak about this frankly, so that these defects do not grow worse ... *We have met clear instances of tendencies towards autarky.* The Dzerzkinski factory of the Dnepropetrovsk region supplies rolled wire to the Rezhitsa nail-making works. In July the Dzerzhinski factory underfulfilled its plan by 15 per cent but sent to Rezhitsa only 300 tons of rolled wire instead of 1,020 tons. When this outrageous fact was investigated, the managers of the Dzerzhinski factory declared that they had orders from the Dnepropetrovsk *sovnarkhoz* to give priority to enterprises in their own region and to supply them in full.' [Emphasis in the original.][2]

An assemblage of similar examples would fill many closely-printed pages. They show that 'regionalism' was a built-in deviation, which required to be repressed by invoking non-economic weapons. The weapons themselves were sometimes irrational. For, given that some

[1] Decree of praesidium of Supreme Soviet, April 25, 1958.
[2] *Pravda*, September 2, 1957.

material was unexpectedly short, it is no more logical to give priority to customers situated outside the given area, so that the entire burden of shortage falls on users within the region, than to do the opposite.[1] However, the 'regionalist' deviation was not cured by the 1958 decree, as the same complaints reappeared again and again.

There were many other instances. *Sovnarkhozy*, like enterprises, were guided by their success indicators, rather than the requirements of the customer. After 1957 a wide range of consumer goods was not subject to central allocation, and *sovnarkhozy* issued orders to curtail their production if local needs were met, since they could have no idea about the needs of outside users and had no incentive or interest to supply them. This explains the numerous complaints about *sovnarkhozy* which 'on various excuses stop production of much-needed cultural-domestic consumer durables'.[2] What mattered it to (say) the Tula *sovnarkhoz* that its hammers or tin-openers were in urgent demand in Orel and Voronezh? If any plan was more easily fulfilled by the use of the productive capacity for some other purpose, then it was used for some other purpose. In fact, it proved necessary to *forbid* the *sovnarkhozy* to cut production of consumer goods without special permission from superior authority, in the decree published on August 9, 1960.

In putting forward development plans, the *sovnarkhozy* were equally unable to take into account the impact of their plans on the economy as a whole. For example, while economists published articles seeking to prove that the lignite in the Tula area was high-cost and in-efficient, the chairman of the Tula *sovnarkhoz* attacked this view, and urged the adoption of a plan which envisaged a large increase in production of this lignite.[3] This was an aspect of the autarkic tendencies, or 'empire-building', familiar among the former ministries, but now transferred to a territorial rather than industrial-sector basis. The built-in tendency towards 'regionalism' necessitated the preservation or reinforcement of strict centralization. The right of *sovnarkhozy* to redistribute resources between different industrial sectors was in fact severely limited, in order to prevent any initiative which was inconsistent with centralized resource allocation. This led, for example, to complaints from the Karaganda *sovnarkhoz* that it was forbidden to shift funds from coal to building materials, and from

[1] This point was made in *Promyshlenno-ekonomicheskaya gazeta*, September 19, 1958.
[2] Decision of Central Committee of the Communist Party, *Pravda*, July 17, 1960, *Pravda*, September 6, 1958, and also many other sources.
[3] *Pravda*, August 17, 1957, V. Somov, *Vop. ekon.*, No. 12/1957, pp. 29-33; Z. Chukhanov, *Vop. ekon.*, No. 9/1958, pp. 42-4.

non-ferrous metals to coal, although this was needed to fulfil plans.[1] By a decision in 1959, *sovnarkhozy* were strictly forbidden to issue allocated materials to their enterprises without a *naryad* from above.[5]

This in turn led to complaints about 'excessive centralization' of the supply and disposals system, which in fact predetermined much of the enterprises' activities over the heads of 'their' *sovnarkhozy*. The representative of the Estonian *sovnarkhoz* complained that only 0·2 per cent of the production of his republic was allocated by republican organs; all the rest was under the control of Moscow.[3] In this respect recentralization continued steadily, especially after 1960. A number of all-union bodies had production and supply functions, and this gave rise to much administrative overlap and confusion in the localities. Thus in Rostov *sovnarkhoz* alone, apart from 27 *snabsbyt* offices organized under various departments of the *sovnarkhoz* itself, there were '13 supply offices subordinated to the *snabsbyt* of the VSNKh RSFSR (i.e. to the republican-level supply and disposals organs) and 32 supply-and-disposals offices and centres of various ministries and organizations of the USSR and RSFSR. Altogether there are in this region 72 *snabsbyt* offices and centres with an establishment of over 7,000 persons. Many of these organizations duplicate each other.'[4]

The consequence of a regional structure of this character must be, and was, a reconcentration of effective decision-making (above the level of minor details) at the centre. But, since the ministerial form of centralization was abolished in the reform of 1957, this means a recreation of central planning and administration on a new basis. This process led to the proliferation of central agencies which were referred to earlier.

But one generalized conclusion may be legitimately drawn from the experience of *sovnarkhozy*: it is that if production and sales are based not on directly economic criteria (e.g. profitability) but on plans and instructions, no *territorial* authority can be expected to make production decisions which are rational in terms of the needs of some larger area.

PLANNING OF PRODUCTION AND MATERIALS ALLOCATION

The first and most obvious problem of post-1957 central planning

[1] *Promyshlenno-ekonomicheskaya gazeta*, March 30, 1958.
[2] I. Baranov and F. Liberman, *Plan. khoz.* No. 9/1959, pp. 39-40. See also N. Podgorny (*Pravda*, January 12, 1961) concerning disposal of some of the products of local (i.e. non-*sovnarkhoz*) industry by the republics.
[3] *Ekon. gaz.* January 5, 1962, p. 12.
[4] N. Gal'perin, *Vop. ekon.*, No. 10/1960, p. 68.

was the multiplicity of interconnected and overlapping organs which dealt with a variety of overlapping and interconnected decisions. Under the ministerial system, each enterprise was *wholly* subordinated to 'its' ministry. Though it did draw some of its supplies from other ministerial systems under Gosplan's 'funded' material allocation schemes, its supply arrangements were in the care of its ministry, as also its production programme. While the system was not immune to error, it was administratively simple. The enterprise director had a clear boss, there were no doubts about the lines of subordination. But after 1957, most enterprises were nominally under the *sovnarkhoz*. But this body had been increasingly shorn of such resource allocation powers as it possessed. The effect was to subordinate each enterprise to as many 'controllers' as there were separately controlled products, both for output and for inputs. Of course, the single-product enterprise was in a happier position in this respect. However, let us take as an example an agricultural machinery factory in Tula. The director of the factory wrote the following:

'The multiplicity of planning organs, the absence of agreement among them, have become a brake upon the initiative of the director. The basic plan for farm machinery for the Tula combine factory (row harvesters) is decided by the USSR Gosplan; to this Gosplan RSFSR adds hemp and reed cutters; VSNKh, *Rosselkhoztekhnika* and *Soyuzavtoselmash* send us plans for motor vehicle spare parts and farm machinery components; and on top of this the *sovnarkhoz* gives us a variety of tasks for the manufacture of metal parts, units, sections and machines for the chemical, electrical, metallurgical and other industries of its economic region. The party *obkom* in its turn compels us to prepare, for the needs of the *oblast'*, battery holders, manure spreaders, silage combine-harvesters, spare parts for farm machinery and tractors, etc. As a result the factory is overburdened, but for some reason everyone considers that it is working at half-pressure and throughout the year gives us additional tasks.'[1]

THE RESURRECTION OF THE MINISTRIES

The confusions of the late-Khrushchev period were becoming obvious well before his fall. They could be fully documented from Soviet sources.[2] It was not surprising that after Khrushchev's fall the

---

[1] V. Pushkarev, *Ekon. gaz.*, February 15, 1962, p. 8.
[2] e.g. see A. Nove: 'The industrial planning system: reforms in prospect', *Soviet Studies*, July 1962. For a full account of the whys and wherefores of reform, see A. Kosygin, *Pravda*, September 28, 1965.

system was changed, though it took almost a year to decide just what to do. In the end, Kosygin's speech announced a return to the industrial-sector principle. Each industry or industrial group was once again placed under a ministry, and a surprisingly high proportion of these were all-union, not union-republican, ministries—see list at end of this chapter. This was not exactly a return to the *status quo,* in that the same speech announced the enhancement of the powers of enterprise directors, the intention to modify the powers of the ministries over their subordinates. But, at least in the initial stages, the ministries did acquire virtually all the powers of control over their enterprises which they possessed before 1957, with the single exception of supply-disposal functions, of which more in a moment. As we shall see, the hierarchical dominance of the ministries has created

The ministerial system restored

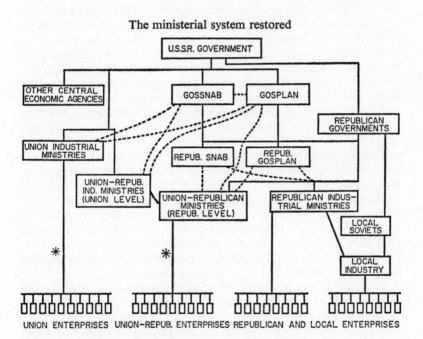

Notes * = *Obyedineniya* (see chapter 1), which in some instances constitute an intermediate stage between ministry and enterprise.
Gossnab = State-Commitee on Material-Technical supplies.
Snab = (Republican) supply organ.
List of union and union-republican ministries given at end of this chapter.

a problem which still awaits solution: how can rights to autonomy, even if established in an official set of regulations, be protected against the right of a superior to give orders to an inferior?

Ministries, then, exercise the overall power of drawing up, within their sphere, the major elements of the production, investment and technological development programmes.

The industrial state committees were scrapped. So was VSNKh, so was the USSR *sovnarkhoz*. The functions of planning were again concentrated in Gosplan. However, it was felt that the regional supply organs had justified themselves. The point was that the multiplicity of local supply agencies, providing often similar materials and components for enterprises owing allegiance to separate ministries, constituted one of the genuine defects of the former ministerial system. To obviate this, it was decided to preserve the *sovnarkhoz*-run regional supply depots which would provide supplies to enterprises regardless of ministerial subordination. These were placed under the State Committee on Material-Technical Supplies (*Gossnab*) which also took over at the centre the supply organizations which had been under the USSR *sovnarkhoz*, and the head of the latter, Dymshits, was placed in charge of *Gossnab*. The supply organs at regional level are being put 'on *khozraschyot*', and are therefore supposed to be influenced in their activities by profits, these in turn being a function of margins or handling charges to which the supply agencies are entitled.

Thus the planning of production and the planning of supplies are under separate bodies. Their functions inevitably overlap. Indeed, as we shall see, Gosplan retains the task of allocating key commodities, while a longer but less vital list is allocated by *Gossnab*. The tasks which, before 1957, used to be performed by the supply and disposals organs of economic ministries are now to be exercised by *Gossnab*, though it would seem that the ministries still retain some of their powers. So in practice a satisfactory organizational streamlining has not yet been achieved, as will be shown in chapter 7.

The State Committee on Construction (*Gosstroi*) has survived the reorganization of 1965. The State Committee on Scientific Research suffered no more than a change of name, to 'Science and Technology'. The abolition of VSNKh resulted in the placing of these and other committees directly under the Council of Ministers. A State Committee on Prices was set up, within Gosplan.

Mention must be made here of the *obyedineniye* (association), the species of semi-amalgamated group of enterprises described in chapter 1. Some of these have been accorded the powers of a ministerial *glavk*, and in this way we may be seeing the gradual emergence of commercially-orientated (*khozraschyotnye*) divisions of ministries, administering a multi-enterprise 'empire'. This could be the prototype of what might come to be called the Soviet corporation. It is not totally impossible that before long the ministries themselves will come to resemble nation-wide corporations. But more about this in chapter 9.

PLANNING AND ECONOMIC ADMINISTRATION: REPUBLICAN LEVEL

While theoretically the fifteen union republics have equal status, in economic and in other affairs, they are in fact of very unequal size and importance. The Russian republic (RSFSR) covers the major part of the USSR's territory and contains over half of its population. Obviously, organizational forms appropriate to it are unlikely to fit a small republic such as Estonia, with a population little over a million. In practice, for many years the RSFSR had no effective governmental and planning agencies, or any republican party organization, the all-union bodies being responsible for RSFSR business. However, in more recent years, and especially since 1957, the RSFSR's functions in planning have greatly increased in importance (as have those of other republics). Also since that date the republics, freer than before to take administrative decisions, have increasingly varied their organizational arrangements.

So far as republican planning organs are concerned, the situation is broadly as follows. Under the 1957 reform each republic's Gosplan acquired a key importance in planning and also in allocation of supplies, subject of course, to the authority of the centre and of 'its' republican government. In the case of twelve of the fifteen republics the *Sovnarkhoz* was coextensive with the boundary of the republic (though at first Uzbekistan was divided into several *sovnarkhozy*). In the three large republics—the RSFSR, Ukraine and Kazakhstan, however, Gosplan had the burdensome task both of planning *and* controlling the activities of the numerous *sovnarkhozy* into which the republics were divided. In 1960, it was decided to set up *republican sovnarkhozy*, with the task of implementing planning decisions, while leaving the Gosplans to plan. As we have already seen, this principle was later extended to the all-union level. In 1962, there was a change affecting the four Central Asian republics: they were combined into one *sovnarkhoz*, while Gosplans survived in each of the four.

In March, 1963 the *sovnarkhozy* at republican level, the Central Asian *sovnarkhoz*, and the republican Gosplans, were transformed into union-republican bodies, under the authority of the analogous all-union organs; this placed them under dual subordination, in that they also remain under their respective republican governments. It also meant that the practice was legalized by which all-union organs gave orders to republican planners without going through the 'proper' government channels. Indeed, as we shall see, the by-passing of republican organs, and dealing directly with regions or even enterprises, was and is extremely common.

There was superimposed upon the republican divisions, so un-were then seventeen of them: of which ten in the RSFSR, three in the Ukraine. The four Central Asian republics, the three Baltic states and the three Transcaucasians were grouped so that each was a big' region', as also was Kazakhstan. At first Belorussia and Moldavia stood aside from the big-region arrangement, presumably because geographical facts would have compelled them to be joined to a portion of a neighbouring republic. However, late in 1962 it was decided that Belorussia *was* a 'big region', bringing the number to 18.[1] When the number of *sovnarkhozy* was drastically reduced (November, 1962-March, 1963), it emerged that in several instances, the new *sovnarkhozy* became co-extensive with the 'big regions' (e.g. Central Asia, Belorussia, the Central black-earth, Volgo-Vyatka).

These big regions have no executive authority, though there are advisory planning commissions in sixteen of them (i.e. all except the two which are coextensive with republics). They are used as a basis for regional planning at the centre.

The 1965 reform of the planning mechanism altered the situation in the republics. The republican *sovnarkhozy* were all liquidated. The Republican Gosplan, the Supply organization[2] and a Ministry of Construction operate under dual subordination, i.e. are under effective control from the appropriate organs at the centre. Whereas under the *sovnarkhoz* system the lines of subordination were supposed to lead through the republican capitals, now there are numerous union ministries which control their enterprises directly. So the effect of the 1965 changes was to weaken republican powers. However, as we have seen, the republics were very frequently by-passed also before 1965. There was a chaos of all-union and republican supply organs,

---

[1] For a full list, see *Ekon. gaz.*, February 16, 1963 and October 19, 1963, or the Info. Supp. to *Soviet Studies*, January, 1964.

[2] Known not as *Gossnab*, in republics, but as *Glavsnab* (Chief supplies administration) 'attached to' (*pri*) the republican Council of Ministers.

which will now be run in a more tidy manner by the *Gossnab* system. Also there developed well before 1965 a number of industrial units controlled directly by various agencies outside the *sovnarkhoz* system, some all-union and others republican. The premier of Estonia complained that his republican *sovnarkhoz* did not control the republic's own Ministry of communal economy and the factories (making electrical motors, clothing, building materials) under the Ministry of Public Order.[1]

So in all these circumstances the changes in republican powers *may* have been intended for tidying up rather than diminution. However, it is worth observing that the logic of the present wave of reforms, which strengthens enterprises, ministries, and *obyedineniya*, is broadly inconsistent with territorial-administrative powers over the economy. Therefore republican powers have declined and complaints are being published to this effect.

The republics possess two kinds of economic ministries: those which correspond to union republic ministries, and which are therefore under dual subordination, and also purely republican ministries. The latter are responsible for a range of smaller-scale industries, and for local building. It has been reported that, at least in some republics, a Ministry of Local Industry has taken over workshops formerly operated by local soviets.[2] The number and designation of such ministries varies widely in different republics.

The republics are represented at the centre in two ways; firstly, their premiers are *ex-officio* members of the all-union Council of Ministers; secondly, a special Commission of the Soviet of Nationalities, the second chamber of the Supreme Soviet, examines the impact of proposed measures on the republics.

THE PLANNING PROCESS, AND MATERIAL SUPPLIES

The real importance of any territoral and administrative unit depends on the way in which the planning system operates in practice. The key to the entire system is in the material supplies organization, and this for two reasons: not only does the functioning of any enterprise in industry depend decisively on the provision of the necessary material inputs, but the basic planning procedures are themselves directly concerned with the 'material' consequences of economic policy decisions and react on these decisions. Let us take a

[1] V. Klauson, *Izvestiya*, August 25, 1964. (Is this prison labour?)
[2] For instance in the Ukraine: see *Ekon. gaz.*, No. 26/1967, p. 27.

simplified example. Let us suppose that the highest policy-makers in the land decide that the USSR should (let us say) become self-sufficient in steel and machine-tools and also develop oil as a major source of fuel. (In practice, these decisions too are not taken *in abstracto*, and bear some relationship to the expected utilization of steel, machine-tools and oil, but one must start somewhere.) These decisions call for certain inputs, which are calculated through technical co-efficients derived from past experience. Thus a given expansion in steel production requires X tons of iron ore, Y tons of coking coal, the construction of new smelting or rolling capacity, and so on. These call in turn for new mining machinery, constructional steel, cement, a new railway line to carry the iron ore, more locomotives (and still more steel, oil, etc., etc.) and all this has certain consequences which have other consequences. The process is repeated for each key element in the plan. Of course, amendments have constantly to be made, as when it is discovered that the requirements for a certain commodity cannot be met within the period in question, and/or if likely export earnings would be insufficient to enable imports to bridge the gap. Input and output calculations are necessarily connected and, in the process of planning, react on one another. Bottlenecks are discovered, and, if the sector is a priority one, become the subject-matter for an urgent investment programme and perhaps a 'campaign', with special inducements provided for those engaged in the enlargement of the bottleneck.

This is a continuous process, which must proceed on various time-scales. In the long term, the expansion of the economy must be expressed as far as possible in an integrated and consistent series of output targets, and the investment programme emerges as part of the process of ensuring that the capacity necessary for the achievement of future plans can be brought into operation when required; this in turn reacts upon these future plans themselves, since these must then include the investments in question. It is also necessary to take into account policy decisions—for instance, concerning the relative importance of consumers' goods, or agriculture, or housing. The central planners endeavour to combine all these data and projects and to calculate the material requirements, modifying the projects or the investment plan, or the foreign trade plan, in the light of discovered disproportions or inconsistencies. They must also take into account the submissions from below: from ministries, republics, regions, enterprises. It is important never to lose sight of the vital role of proposals, drafts, bids, appeals, from those who in the last resort will be the recipients of orders. In the process, the planners draw up a series of product 'balances', which are subject to modification in the light of representations from various economic and political agencies concerned. The process is never completed. The various bodies engaged in the process are constantly influencing each other in a multitude of ways, and one should not see things as happening merely by way of hierarchical and/or political subordination, although, of course, there is both a hierarchy and subordination. Major decisions are taken by the top Party organs, but many of them are 'induced', or based on advice of experts. Thus the Party decisions to triple the size of the chemical industry, taken in 1957, were doubtless based on submissions made to the Central Committee by planning experts charged with calculating input requirements. Plans prepared by those on the spot are influenced by knowledge of the priorities of the centre, which are in turn related to political decisions and to input requirements, bottlenecks, etc., which are partly reflected in these priorities.

This whole process is often labelled in Soviet literature as 'planning by material balances'. It involves a form of simplified 'input-output' procedure, carried out very largely in quantitative (physical) terms,[1] though there is some evidence of a rather rudimentary cost comparison in making choices between interchangeable alternatives. The considerable shortcomings of this system are referred to in detail in chapter 7, so are the modifications to this system, which are under discussion, and which, so it is hoped, will bring greater rationality into the process of choosing between alternatives.

The long-term (five-year, seven-year) plans which emerge from this highly complex process are not yet 'operational'. They do not directly order any enterprise to do anything. While they should in principle provide (for instance) enough iron ore to fulfil the steel plan, nothing is said about the supplies of ore to any one steelworks, or by any mining enterprise. Indeed, owing to the miscalculations unavoidable in planning far ahead, which frequently call for changes, it is clear that operational orders must relate to shorter periods and must take errors and delays fully into account. All kinds of things could go wrong with a long-term plan. Thus factories may not be finished in time, harvests may not come up to expectations, a big new discovery of minerals may be made, a new trade or aid agreement negotiated, or there may simply have been an under-or overestimate of material requirements, or of stocks, or labour proves unexpectedly scarce in a given area, or optimistic prognostications

---

[1] See W. Leontief, 'The Fall and Rise of Soviet Economics', *Foreign Affairs* January, 1960, for a critical but essentially true account.

concerning a rise in productivity are not fulfilled, or the Party itself may—as it often does—decree a policy change in the middle of a plan period. Stalin is often quoted as saying that, contrary to so-called western planning, Soviet plans are directives which have the force of law, but to take this to apply to long-term plans would be erroneous, except perhaps in the formal legal sense.[1]

Annual, quarterly, monthly plans, by contrast, are of direct operational importance. They are related to the long-term plan in the sense of being the practical expression of the same economic policy (as amended from time to time), and clearly the investment plans are of their nature a much more long-term affair, but, so far as any given industrial enterprise is concerned, its production and supply arrangements are geared only to short periods of time, and the rewards for success and penalties for failure are similarly concerned with a year, a quarter or a month, although, the enterprise itself should have a long-term plan and should relate to it its proposals concerning its plan for the coming year.

The annual plan is the basis of the supply arrangements and of the contracts which express them. It is obvious that production plans must be consistent with supply plans in total, and that in the end every enterprise's actual requirements in the next plan period must be matched by appropriate production, transport and delivery decisions. It is for this reason that, at a very early stage of the entire process, the enterprises submit applications for inputs. These go up through the ministerial system (in 1957-65 through *sovnarkhozy*) and are incorporated in the republican and all-union production and supply plan (we shall see that a range of supplies may now be obtained without prior application or allocation, but this is still exceptional). Gosplan is the body responsible for ensuring consistency, and the satisfaction of all-union needs (e.g. state reserves, defence, exports), and for ensuring the maintenance and development of rational links between sectors and areas, endeavouring to combat both 'localism' and ministerial empire-building. The immense complexity of the task of integrating output, supplies, deliveries and user-demand often led to delays in approving plans, and to complaints that enterprises did not know either their production plans or the materials to which they would be entitled until well into the year to which the plan was supposed to relate. Furthermore these plans are changed repeatedly,

---

[1] In fact, several five-year plans were not decreed until long after the beginning of the relevant five-year period. Thus the fifth five-year plan, which covered the period from January 1, 1951, was 'adopted' by the Party congress in October, 1952, the 1966-70 plan was still not in final form at the end of 1967.

despite frequent promises to ensure a stable plan.[1] Vigorous measures are being taken to avert this, by insisting that the plan submissions from the republics reach Moscow not later than August, and that the process of amendment and argument be completed and the annual plan drafted and approved already in October.

In practice, this has seldom been achieved. In theory the procedure for the drawing up of annual plans is as follows, according to a Soviet textbook. The details as published still related to the *sovnarkhozy*, and have been modified here to take their replacement by ministries into account. Ministries and republics are informed, in May-June, of the general pattern of requirements for the following year, and also any necessary 'limits' to the volume of materials likely to be allocated to them. This ensures that the plans to be submitted later from below are not wholly out of line with the national plan. This preliminary information is passed down to enterprises. Then, 'every enterprise, basing itself on its long-term output plan directives and the "limits" of which it is informed, elaborates its annual (production) plan, and prepares indents (*zayavki*) for the required means of production, including stocks, and submits these to the ministry. The (ministers) put together the indents received, relate them to the allocated "limits" and the production tasks laid down in long-term plans. .... The union republics elaborate consolidated indents on the wide list of products which the state plan contains, relating them to the draft output plans and construction plans and to the "limits" of product utilization. The consolidated indents and proposals for the output of principal products are sent to the Council of Ministers of the USSR on July 15-August 1.

'The central planning organs bring the requirements of economic sectors and union republics into conformity with the resources of the national economy, and, in the absence of such conformity, make proposals to increase production, decrease utilization, expand imports, etc.' After appropriate amendments are made to the republican and sector plans, a global plan of material supplies is submitted to the Council of Ministers by September 1. During September, 'the second stage of the supply plan is completed by the allocation of supply quotas to union republics, ministries and departments, which pass them down to enterprises.[2]

[1] See, among a great many examples, V. Selyunin, *Ekon. gaz.*, No. 17/1967 p. 35, and *Izvestiya*, May 25, 1967.
[2] M. Kolodnyi and A. Stepanov: *Planirovanie narodnovo khozyaistva SSSR* (Kiev, 1963), pp. 217-19. For a valuable account of the system see also H. Levine's contribution to *Comparisons between U.S. and Soviet Economies* (Washington, 1959).

Thus there takes place a process of sub-allocation by ministries and in union republics of supply quotas (*fondy*) for the principal items of industrial inputs. These should, at enterprise level, match the given enterprise's output plans. The planning organs and ministries try to achieve this by the use of material and fuel utilization norms. *Gossnab* then comes into the picture, firstly as 'systematically checking on timely passing down of supply plans to enterprises and construction sites', and, most important to arrange for contracts based on the supply plan, attach customers to suppliers, issue allocation certificates, and ensure implementation of the supply plan. (See also page 225).

There are thus three bodies at all-union level directly concerned with supply planning: *Gosplan, Gossnab* and the industrial ministries. There are also republican organs. In practice the task is divided. Gosplan in fact allocates only 2,000 commodity designations. No less than 18,000 are allocated at various levels by *Gossnab*;[1] though in some instances the allocation authorizations will still have been issued by Gosplan. One must distinguish clearly between allocation in the sense of issuing a certificate authorizing a planned purchase (*naryad*), and the process of negotiating a detailed supply agreement and/or drawing the actual material good from a store. The detailed agreement is supposed to be supervised by *Gossnab*, (for the 18,000 items it allocates it decides who supplies whom). But whoever decides on supplies, the actual goods, when not sent direct by the supplying enterprise, will frequently be obtained from a sub-division or store (*baza*) of *Gossnab*.

Gossnab has taken over, at the centre, the *snabsbyt* (supply-and-disposal) organs which had been within the USSR *sovnarkhoz*, and before that in Gosplan. There are altogether 19 such bodies at the centre, and they necessarily work closely with the industrial ministries. There are 3,200 supply-and-disposal organs scattered about the country, which form part of 56 territorial and republican supply organs, of which 42 in the RSFSR. According to the source, who is Dymshits himself, 10,000 commodity designations (presumably out of the total of 18,000) will be distributed by and/or through the local *snab* organs, thus saving much paper work at the centre.[2]

The above supply organs, which include the oil distribution organization (which has an identity of its own), provide about 60

[1] V. M. Kosachev, *Sistema organov upravleniya narodnym khozyaistvom SSSR*, izd. Mysl, Moscow, 1966, p. 42.
[2] V. Dymshits, *Pravda*, January 5, 1968.

per cent of supplies.[1] A recently-published account of supplies in Belorussia lists supply organs outside the *Gossnab* system. The largest of these, which together employ more persons than all the rest of the supply organs put together (in Belorussia) are: firstly, the supply department of the Ministry of Construction, and secondly the re-publican and local organs of *Sel'khoztekhnika*, which have the primary responsibility of supplying agriculture. It turns out that even the medium-sized town of Grodno possesses eleven supply offices, of which seven do not form part of the *Glavsnab* network.[2] Indeed, there has been a protest against the multiplication of ministerial supply organs: 'thirty all-union and union-republican ministries and departments have set up over 1,300 of their own supply offices, depots and stores, in which about 90,000 persons are employed. All this is wasteful duplication of the *Gossnab* organs.'[3]

It can be claimed that at least a partial tidying up has been accomplished. Yet the cost may be administratively quite heavy, as will be argued in chapter 7.

The totality of supply arrangements (between enterprises and to trading organs) must be more or less equal to the production plans. The output plans of enterprises for items specified in the central and republican plans are to a great extent predetermined by the in-structions they receive to produce and deliver produce to specified customers.

The centre, in making up its own 'balanced' plans, proceeds by estimating the needs of the economy of means of production and of consumers' goods in the coming year, or years (thus a two-year 'current' plan was drawn up during 1963 for the years 1964-65). In making up material balances, it proceeds, in the case of basic materials, by norms of utilization. The following example, used for teaching purposes by a Soviet textbook, illustrates the procedure in the case of a basic material, in this case a fuel: (*see table over-leaf.*)

In the case of consumers' goods, the planners proceed by estim-ating the balance of personal incomes and expenditures, and calculate likely patterns of and changes in consumers' demand. Availability of the relevant agricultural and industrial goods, less any necessary industrial utilization and exports, plus imports, are then balanced against estimated requirements. This serves as a basis for an outline

[1] V. Dymshits, *Ekon. gaz.*, No. 18/1967, pp. 7-8.
[2] A. A. Zakruzhnyi, *Organizatsiya i planirovanie material'no-tekhnicheskovo snabzheniya*, p. 32. Minsk, 1967.
[3] M. Viktorova, *Ekon. gaz.*, No. 49/1967, p. 38.

Use	Coal requirements Output in year		Coal Consumption Norm	Total Requirements (mill tons*)
	Unit	Plan		
Electricity generation	mlrd kwh	250·8	500 kgs per 1000 kwh	125·4
Steel	mill tons	60·2	180 kgs. per ton	10·8
Cement	mill tons	50·3	200 kgs. per ton	10·7
For running of steam locomotives	mlrd ton-kms.	820·0	180 kgs. per 10,000 ton-kms.	14·8

(and so on)

Source: Kolodnyi and Stepanov, op. cit. p. 87.

* Coal of standard calorific value.

of the central plan for the coming year. The longer-term plan is based partly on demand projection, and partly on estimated physiological needs for a desirable diet, and so on.

Bearing in mind, as one must, that all material supplies involve other enterprises in production and/or deliveries, and that the output of almost any commodity requires the supply of a number of different materials and components, let us now see how the plan provides for the material inputs required for its implementation.

Before 1957, the ministries were responsible for supplying 'their' enterprises, and each possessed a chief supply department (known as glavsnab). They were generally also responsible for disposing of the products of 'their' enterprises, and so they had a chief disposals department (glavsbyt). Each of these had local offices, as required. Almost all major materials and components were subject to central allocation and were divided into two categories: 'funded' (fondiruemaya) and 'planned' (planiruemaya) products. 'Funded' materials were the responsibility of the government, which meant in practice the snab department of Gosplan, which allocated to user ministries, who in turn allocated to enterprises via the appropriate glavk of the ministry. This meant that the producing ministry was told what sector of the economy they should supply, and in what quantities. 'Planned' materials, generally of lesser importance, were allocated by the disposals department of the producing ministries (i.e. by the glavsbyt). In addition there was a range of materials and components which were not centrally planned, but were either allocated by local authorites or based on contract between the parties concerned. Some of these were minor, others (like sand, gravel, clay) were of their nature a matter of local arrangement and were often procured by the user ministries.

After the 1957 reform, with the disappearance of nearly all the ministries, the distinction between 'funded' and 'planned' materials became obsolete, and it was formally abolished in 1958.[1] But it seems to have reappeared, in the form of a division between products allocated by Gosplan and *Gossnab*. There were a total of 19,000 commodity designations allocated centrally in 1962,[2] and the numbers were showing an upward tendency. It was seen that 20,000 were allocated in 1967.

Be it noted that the list of commodities for which material balances are calculated by Gosplan is nowhere near 20,000, it is nearer 2,000. These may not coincide with the items which Gosplan allocates. The point is that a commodity designation may be aggregated (e.g. tons of steel of all types, or all tractors) in a material balance, but require a greater degree of disaggregation in the plans of operational allocation.

The list of controlled commodities, and the procedures of control, vary from time to time. There is a good deal of talk about leaving enterprises free to buy what they wish, without any *naryad*, from stores maintained for the purpose. In fact the reform specifically provides for an expansion of what is called 'wholesale trade' in industrial inputs, in producers' goods in general. Such trade is growing. According to Dymshits, in January 1968 there were 246 such wholesale shops, which sold goods (presumably in the previous year) worth 392 million roubles, including 'equipment, electro-technical goods, chemicals, building materials' and so on. The shops draw their supplies from *Gossnab's* regional stores, and deliver the goods to the customers. They also sell surplus equipment for enterprises on commission. This is an important development, but up to the time of writing covers much less than 1 per cent of material supplies. However, it may grow rapidly. The same source refers to experimental sales of oil without limit or *naryad* to enterprises in the Voronezh province. It was found that consumption actually fell. The experiment is being extended.[3]

There has also been much talk of 'direct links' (*pryamye svyazi*) between enterprises, in the sense of contractual relationships freely negotiated between customers and suppliers. Of course, such negotiations take place even under the traditional supply system:

[1] For a useful account, see Y. Koldomasov, in *Plan. Khoz.*, No. 4/1959, pp. 54-65.
[2] *Ekon. gaz.*, November 10, 1962, p. 8.
[3] *Pravda*, January 5, 1968.

this calls for contracts to be concluded which provide for exact dates and specifications, based on the supply plan. The reformers had in mind, however, the *free* negotiation of contracts. This has so far happened only to a very limited degree, since production and planning continues to cover the bulk of industrial output. But efforts have been made, and publicised, to establish long-term planned links between enterprises, in other words to assign delivery and supply obligations for several years ahead, instead of having to be reconfirmed year by year.[1]

It is hardly possible, without actually working within the system, adequately to describe how the supply organization works in practice. It is known that some key projects or factories are in fact supplied by priority *naryady* issued at all-union level. In the case of construction, a decree of April 7, 1960, envisaged the drawing up of a list of projects of particular importance; these the all-union Gosplan is to supervise, ensuring deliveries of necessary building materials and of equipment for installation in new factories.[2] This practice has continued, through the so-called *Glavkomplekty*, which are responsible, within the planning and supply system, for supervising the placing of orders for, and deliveries of, machinery and equipment for important capital projects.

The process remains extremely complex, and the implementation of supply planning often involves improvisation and short cuts. Thus fully detailed allocations cannot in fact be integrated with production and with stocks throughout the economy, and non-priority sectors and minor users often have to make do with what remains when the big and important consumers have taken their share. Hence the frequent complaints of breakdown of supplies and also the scope for the 'pushers' (*tolkachi*). When, as often happens, it is recognized that total supplies of any commodity are plainly insufficient to meet requirements (this should emerge from a short-term analysis of 'material balances', of supply in relation to need), efforts will be made to increase supplies, which might well call for changes in the annual, or the five- or seven-year plan then current, or to the foreign-trade plan.

INVESTMENT AND CONSTRUCTION PLANNING

The general lines of the investment plans emerge from the interaction, within the planning organs, between 'material balances'

[1] V. Dymshits, *Ekon. gaz.*, No. 18/1967, pp. 7-8.
[2] See I. Maevski and A. Fomin, *Vop. Ekon.*, No. 10/1960, pp. 38-9.

analysis, requests from below and the guiding lines of Party policy. This is a highly complex task, which involves not only many divisions of Gosplan and *Gosstroi* at the centre, but also many other state committees and ministries directly and indirectly concerned in formulating investment plans, or plans which call for investments for their implementation. Each year's investment plan is submitted to the all-union government, with the largest projects specified by name. At many points investment decisions call forth production and supply decisions: building materials must be made available, machinery for new factories provided, new houses need furniture and water pipes, and so forth. These needs may themselves call forth other investment decisions, required to expand the production of such items. All this is part of the continuous process of planning, and constitutes an essential and continuous link between short and long-term planning, a link which has often been subject to severe strain, which is hardly surprising having regard to the difficulties of the task. Investments must be paid for, and so the Ministry of Finance is intimately concerned, since, as will be shown, most of these funds are provided by the state budget. Control by the financial organs, or 'limits' laid down in money terms, play an important role in restricting the opportunities of the various authorities and enterprises to indulge in investments additional to the central plan; these controls will be described in chapter 3.

Once the given investment decision has been taken, involving, let us say, the construction of a new cement factory, there remain two essential tasks of a planning-administrative nature: one is to choose which of a number of possible species of cement factory should actually be built, the other to organize the actual work of construction.

The task of comparing between alternative projects, estimating costs, preparing blue prints, submitting possible variants to higher authority for decisions if necessary, is the task of specialized 'project-making organizations' (*proektnye organizatsii*), which exist at all-union, republican and local levels, specializing in projects for particular types of construction. These organizations were at one time financed by a percentage addition to the value of the given project, but it was found that this encouraged them in extravagance, and from 1950 they have been largely budget-financed, at least so far as work on centrally-planned investments is concerned, though more recently many have been put on *khozraschyot*.[1] These organizations play an important role in the practical implementation of investment programmes, and, when we subsequently discuss the

[1] See A. Zverev, *Pravda*, December 23, 1958.

D

problems of choice between investment alternatives, it should be remembered it is in these offices that alternatives are weighed up, and technical recommendations are made. While the officials who work there (*proektnye rabotniki*) are not endowed with much formal power, their *de facto* position in the planning process is a key one.

Finally, there is the organization of building. As we have seen, before the 1957 reorganization there grew up a number of construction ministries, as well as construction *glavki* within industrial ministries. The building enterprises under their control worked not only within the sector suggested by their name; thus building organizations of the Ministry of Construction of the Coal Industry also worked on contract for others, and erected, for instance, hospitals for the Ministry of Health. None the less, there was a tendency towards an excessive number of building enterprises to be set up in any one place, owing allegiance to many different ministries, many quite small but each with its own office staff, lorries, supply organization; the state committee on construction (*Gosstroi*) had only the most general functions of supervision, though it did endeavour to lay down, not always successfully, standards of construction. In 1957, the separate construction ministries and *glavki* at all-union level had practically disappeared, except for ministries responsible for transport construction (railway building, etc.) and for building electric power stations.

Under the 1957 reform, building enterprises were placed under the *sovnarkhozy*, though a few specialized organizations (e.g. transport construction) remained separate. However, in March, 1963 they were all transferred from *sovnarkhozy* to a new 'construction' hierarchy, presided over at the centre by *Gosstroi*, which controlled several central (all-union) construction agencies. *Gosstroi* survived the 1965 reconstruction of the planning mechanism, but the other central agencies ('state production committees', as for instance for transport construction) disappeared, with the exception of the Ministry of Assembly and special construction work. It was therefore reasonable to suppose that it was decided to exercise operational control over building enterprises through the republican organs. However, second thoughts prevailed: as may be seen from the list at the end of this chapter, there are now four union-republican construction ministries. *Gosstrois* of republics (i.e. republican committees of construction) are charged with planning, norms and specifications for building and installation work, serviced by project-making and research organizations. They are subordinate to the all-union *Gosstrois*, and also to their republican governments, and more closely with their republican Gosplans. They do not control the building trusts and enterprises, however. The task of implementing the plans and issuing the appropriate instruction falls to the republican Ministries of Construction,[1] and in some republics also to other specialized construction ministries.

AGRICULTURAL PLANNING

There were and are a number of features peculiar to agricultural planning. There are several reasons for this. One is the division of agriculture between different forms of ownership. This led to the creation of two different ministries, of which one, the Ministry of Agriculture, dealt with *kolkhozy* and MTS, while the Ministry of State Farms controlled and planned the activities of *sovkhozy*.[2] Another reason has been the importance attached to the political aspects of agriculture, including the need to 'defend' *kolkhozy* against the private-enterprise activities of their own members. In the 'thirties, and again in the years following 1946, this led to the creation of a governmental Council on *Kolkhoz* Affairs (this faded out in the early 'fifties), and at all times to the very active role in all *kolkhoz* matters of the Communist party and its local committees. Still another relevant factor is the large proportion of agricultural output consumed on the farm, which led to the concentration of state organs less on total output than on the level of deliveries to the state. Though it is true that, until 1955, it was the practice of the Ministry of Agriculture and its local organs to specify in great detail the production plans of all *kolkhozy*, these were seldom fulfilled, and the planning organs were in fact more concerned with deliveries. In 1955, it was officially recognized that detailed planning of output was futile, and, so far as *kolkhozy* were concerned, only deliveries to the state were henceforth to be specified in the plans handed down to farms. However, there have been repeated instances since this date of the imposition by local agricultural officials and (especially) by local party secretaries of output targets on farms.[3] Procurements were, until 1956, the responsibility of a Ministry of Procurements, and then, until 1959, of the Ministry of Agriculture. The planning of deliveries was drastically overhauled in 1958, and

[1] For a valuable account of the division of tasks between *Gosstroi* and these ministries at republican level, see V. Pronina, in *Sov. Gos. i pravo*, No. 11/1963, p. 37.

[2] The Ministry of Sovkhozy was abolished in 1959, but such a ministry was re-formed in Kazakhstan to deal with 'virgin-lands' difficulties.

[3] See chapter 10.

was considerably decentralized. While a general procurement plan for major products was approved by the all-union government, in consultation with the republican governments, the latter (and also the local soviets) became largely responsible for supplying their own populations from resources within their own areas, with the centre responsible for acquiring produce for central reserves, export, and certain major deficit areas, as well as raw materials for industries which are centrally planned or which, like the cotton industry, draw supplies from other republics. As a result, centrally-planned state procurements tended to be confined to low-cost areas; thus many *oblasti* of central and northern Russia, and the Baltic states, were wholly or partly exempted from grain deliveries. The object was to encourage specialization on livestock, on the growing of fodder grain to feed them, but it did not work out that way. Figures cited by Khrushchev showed that grain harvest in the exempted areas declined, although consumption of grain (and therefore its 'import' from other areas) increased.[1] Consequently, procurement quotas again became the rule, since apparently local officialdom will not give due attention to products which are not on the list of state exactions.

At the same time, there was announced yet another reorganization of procurements. In 1959, 'the planning of production and procurements of agricultural products' became the responsibility of Gosplan instead of the Ministry of Agriculture. This entire task was transferred in 1961 to a new State procurement committee, whose local organs made contracts with *kolkhozy* and *sovkhozy*. Gosplan however, retained general responsibility for determining total needs. A further reorganization concerned the supply of tractors, machinery, fertilizer, and other producers' goods to farms. In 1959, Gosplan acquired from the Ministry of Agriculture the task of distributing most of these goods.[2] In January, 1961, however, a decision was taken to create a new all-union supply organization for agriculture, to act as intermediary between the farms and the agriculture machinery industry and other suppliers of inputs (e.g. the chemical and automobile industries). This central supply organ became known as *Soyuzsel'khoztekhnika*, with republican and regional administrations. The local offices of this organization took over the task of running maintenance and repair workshops. As suppliers and as service agencies, they cover both *kolkhozy* and *sovkhozy* in their areas.

[1] *Pravda*, January 21, 1961.
[2] Vlasov and Studenikin, op. cit., pp. 352-7, give details of the reforms up to 1959.

In 1962 these reforms were followed by yet another major overhaul of the agricultural planning system.

At the centre, the Ministry of Agriculture was reduced to dealing with research and technical advice. A State Committee for agriculture, was set up in March, 1962, headed by Ignatov who was then a party presidium member and vice-premier; members of the committee including the heads of *Sel'khoztekhnika*, of the state committee on procurements, of the Party's agricultural bureau, a representative of Gosplan and the Minister of Agriculture. However, it seems to have led a shadowy existence. Central policy and central guidance alike issued from the party, which, of course, has its own agricultural bureau. Below this level, there were supposed to be republican agricultural committees, with the first secretary of the republican party at their head. Each republic possessed a ministry of agricultural production and procurement, in charge of the planning of both these closely allied activities. At *oblast'* level, there was an agricultural administration subordinate to the republican ministry, and in practice under the guidance of the *obkom* secretary of the party. Finally, the former *raion* officials, both party and state, were 'amalgamated' in the Territorial Production Administrations (TPA). This was followed by an ill-advised division of the whole party into industrial and agricultural organs.

Khrushchev proposed still further administrative changes. He advocated the encouragement of product specialization by the creation of planning and control organs for each major product. The first of these, for poultry farming, was set up in 1964.

Khrushchev's arrangements and plans did not survive his fall. Neither the TPA nor the 'agricultural' party organs worked effectively, and systematic planning must have been impeded by the multiplicity of governmental organs (Gosplan, Procurements, *Sel'khoztekhnika*, the emasculated Ministry of Agriculture) with some partial responsibility for agriculture. The muddle would have been accentuated by the proposed specialized organs, and nothing more has been heard of this (surely unwise) scheme of administrative specialization.

In December 1964, the split between the industrial and the agricultural Party organs was healed, and the *raiony* were reconstituted under that name, though with areas larger than they were before the TPA came into existence.[1] This logically meant the dissolution of the TPA, but no legal enactment or decree on the subject seems to have been adopted. Instead, there are now *raion* agricultural administrations, no doubt dominated, as in past years, by the *raion* party

[1] In 1965 there are 2,434 *raikomy* in the USSR. There were 3,045 TPA in 1964.

secretary. They are now also the lowest rung in the hierarchy of governmental organs under the revived all-union Ministry of Agriculture, which was placed under a man whom Khrushchev dismissed, Matskevich, and which now has the basic responsibility for the planning of production, procurements, mechanization, organization of *kolkhozy* and *sovkhozy* and so on.[1] This represents a return in essentials to the organizational forms of before 1959. The new set-up has been implementing the policy adopted by the March 1965 plenum: higher prices, delivery quotas fixed firmly for six years, genuinely voluntary over-quota sales (at higher prices in some cases), increased investments, a higher priority for supplies to agriculture and particularly to the *kolkhozy* (which will, at last, be included in the allocation system for such badly needed items as building materials and other essential inputs). Matskevich, in the above-cited article, stated that the abolition of MTS (and the subsequent abandonment of the RTS; see p. 60 above) led to the sale or dispersal of many repair workshops. A new network of repair shops, based on *Sel'khoztekhnika*, has been created.

According to the spirit and letter of the decisions taken in 1965, both *kolkhozy* and *sovkhozy* do now have much more opportunity to draft their own production plans. However, many complaints were and are voiced concerning excessive detailed tutelage from above, not only in respect of procurements but also production and investment. *Sovkhozy* particularly suffered from control from above; party *raikomy*, the *oblast'* agricultural organs, sometimes specialized *sovkhoz* trusts (for instance a 'vegetable-dairying' trust in the Donetsk *oblast'*) were particularly prone to issue detailed orders and to require their permission for even the most minor investment decisions. Even kolkhozy had more autonomy, claimed the critics.[2] This kind of reasoning contributed to the decision to introduce gradually 'full *khozraschyot*' in *sovkhozy*, a trend to which reference was made in chapter 1.

We do not yet know how the new system will work. For example, despite the promise not to vary delivery quotas arbitrarily from year to year, officials may still be tempted to use pressures to compel deliveries from some areas to make up for deficiencies (e.g. due to drought) in other areas. Much depends on the degree of realism in the plans for both production and procurement. It is only right to suspend judgement for the present.

[1] See V. Matskevich, *Vop. Ekon.* No. 6/1965, pp. 1 ff. The ministry was given back its powers by a decree of March 1, 1965.
   [2] See for instance G. Lisichkin, *Novyi mir*, No. 2/1967, pp. 160-85 and also *Ekon. gaz.*, No. 6/1967, p. 32.

While industrial, transport and trade plans are often fulfilled and must always be taken seriously as evidence of serious intention, the same is not true of agricultural planning. Indeed, it is an exceptional occurrence, in Soviet economic history, for an agricultural plan to be fulfilled. This is due in part to the unavoidable dependence of agriculture upon a fickle climate, which makes all precise plans go awry, while tempting the authorities to set plans which assume good weather. In addition, under the special conditions of *kolkhoz* agriculture, ambitious plans (and, for many years, exaggerated harvest reporting) helped in the hard task of procuring produce from a reluctant peasantry. Another important reason for failures was the reluctance of the government, especially before 1953, to provide the necessary inputs and material incentives, reflecting the low priority of agriculture. There were also many instances of unwise policy decisions involving the misuse of resources; farming lends itself least of all to central direction, by reason of its infinite variety. The top leaders were industry-orientated, generally ignorant of farming, unsympathetic to peasants, and people with knowledge had insufficient political influence to correct this.

THE PLANNING OF TRADE

Until 1957, the Ministry of Internal Trade at all-union level controlled the distribution of major consumer commodities between republics, and key products within republics as well. It had taken over wholesaling responsibilities from industrial ministries. However, increases in the powers of republican ministries culminated, at the end of 1957, in the abolition of the all-union Ministry of Internal Trade. Its function in centralized distribution of key commodities passed to the all-union Gosplan, which, in 1960, was allocating between republics a short list of staple foods, textiles, footwear, also taking a special responsibility for supplying Moscow and Leningrad.[1] Gosplan's trade department was known as *Soyuzglavtorg*. In 1963, this was given a separate existence as the State Committee on Trade, because of the evident need for more systematic central control of distribution. After Khrushchev's demise this again became the Ministry of Trade. This ministry possesses all-union wholesaling divisions covering a wide range of goods. Following the general trend towards greater reliance on *khozraschyot* and commercial principles, there have also grown up a number of 'trading

[1] Also the armed forces. For a useful critical account of the system see Y. Sapel'nikov, in *Sovetskaya torgovlya*, No. 6/1960, p. 16 ff.

firms' (*torgovye firmy*) to carry out some of these wholesaling functions. In this respect as in others, the system is in a state of flux at the
time of writing. It is the task of the Ministry of Trade and its sub-
units to analyse *zayavki*, to serve as a link with production ministries
at all-union level, to ensure that all-union wholesaling organs function satisfactorily. It has also, in recent years, been encouraging all-
union *yarmarki* or fairs, at which retailers, wholesalers, and producers of a wide range of consumers' goods can meet together; this
serves, *inter alia*, as a means for republics to find purchasers for their
surpluses of such goods. Republics have their ministries of internal trade within which there are divisions responsible for allocating various commodities to the localities, and passing on requests
to the producers. There are also wholesaling departments within the
system of consumer co-operatives (i.e. of shops in rural areas, see
page 46, above). Some specialized shops are maintained by other
organizations; for example, medicines are sold in shops run by the
Ministry of Health, books—by the Ministry of Culture. Many goods
are procured and sold under local arrangements by the *oblast'* or
city authorities which organize retail trade and (in most cases)
actually control the shops in their areas: for instance, local industry, or *kolkhozy*, can and do sell direct to the retail chain. These
local trade authorities are representatives of the ministry, as well as
being part of the local soviet.

A wide range of consumers' goods must be allocated from central
or republican levels, since only thus can the necessary administrative link be assured between retail shops' requirements and the output and material supply plans of productive enterprises. Consequently, there are usually a large number of administrative stages
between the retail store and its ultimate supplier. As elsewhere in
the economy, planning involves reconciling the requests from below with the production and distribution plans at the higher levels.
Thus the requests of the shops of (say) Kharkov for wool cloth are
consolidated by the city soviets wholesale department (*torg*) and communicated to the republican Ministry of Trade. In this ministry
other requests (*zayavki*) from other Ukrainian localities are consolidated and eventually reach Gosplan in Moscow. This is clearly a
matter of inter-republican deliveries, as little cloth is produced in the
Ukraine. In due course, the Ukrainians learn the size of their allocations (*fondy*) for the coming year, and these are sub-allocated to,
among others, Kharkov. The actual task of distributing the cloth
belongs to *Glavtextil'torg*, the wholesaling division which exists at
both the all-union and republican (Ministry of Trade) level, and

has local offices. It is now for the Kharkov shops to turn the allocation into deliveries of the precise types of cloth they require; the *fondy* do not, as a rule, give detailed specifications. Once the allocations have been made, negotiations can be entered into with one of a number of bodies or institutions: the *glavk* of the all-union industrial ministry, an *obyedineniye* which sub-allocates orders received to 'its' enterprises, a republican ministry, or direct with the producing enterprise. There is infinite variety, which is understandable in view of the widely different quantities and types of goods involved. There is a gradual trend towards a new kind of direct relationship, between customer and producer (or wholesaler), untrammelled by prior administrative allocation, but this still covers only a small part of trade. Mostly one must obtain allocations (*fondy*), which may be specified in some detail, and to ensure a desired change in specifications it is often necessary to make application to the republican or even all-union level.

Finally, a contract for delivery is signed between the trading organization and the textile factory or wholesaler. Ultimately, the requests of the various trading organizations at all levels affect the behaviour of *Gosplan* and *sovnarkhozy*, but, as will be shown in chapter 6, the system remains clumsy and unresponsive.

INSPECTION AND CONTROL ORGANS

In the preceding pages, we have been concerned with various administrative and planning agencies which decide what should be done. It is also necessary to see that it is in fact done. For this purpose there are a number of agencies of inspection, checking and control. Some are essentially non-economic in character, though at times they can and do intervene actively in alleged malfeasances in the economic sphere: such are, for instance, the so-called secret police (known at various dates as Cheka, OGPU, NKVD, MVD, MGB, State Security Committee) and the *prokuror* (procurator, sometimes miscalled public prosecutor). Nothing needs to be said about them in the present context, despite their importance in Soviet life.[1] Separate mention must be made of the *Control committee* (or ministry). The name of this body varies. Its party analogy is the

[1] Large Soviet enterprises possessed, and probably still possess, a 'secret department' staffed by secret police, which organized a network of informers. However, they were more likely to be roused by a disrespectful remark about Stalin than by, say, the overspending of the wages fund. For a rare reference to these secret departments, see I. Evtikhiev and V. Vlasov, *Administrativnoe pravo SSSR* (Moscow, 1946).

Central Control Commission. In the period 1962-64, Khrushchev combined the two into a joint Party-State Control Committee. Now (1968) it is called the Committee of People's Control. The word 'control' should be read in its German-French-Russian sense of checking and inspection (e.g. the French *contrôle des billets*). The Committee is an all-union body, with subordinate committees in the republics. It has local teams of inspectors with the right of access to documents and accounts, and powers to interrogate. Its task is to seek out and report breaches of rules and instructions of all kinds, drawing in for the purpose anyone who is willing to help. Its functions are not confined to the economic sphere, but it is frequently engaged in checking on the carrying out of economic regulations, notably where it is in the self-interest of officials or managers to evade them. For instance, the Belorussian *sovnarkhoz* was alleged to have distributed premia, which should have been largely used to encourage those engaged on production, to its own officials, and this brought on it the wrath of the Control Committee.[1]

The Ministry of Finance, through its inspectors and regional offices, is another important 'cross-checking' agency. Thus it is the duty of its local officials to audit the accounts of enterprises, noting particularly any failures to earn the expected profits or, where applicable, to pay the planned amount of turnover tax. They must seek out causes, and report inefficiencies or breaches of rules. This Ministry is also responsible, through its Establishments Commission (*Shtatnaya kommissia*), for laying down the permitted establishment of managerial personnel and economic (as well as other) officials at all levels.[2]

The inspecting and checking role of the *State Bank vis-à-vis* enterprises arises from the fact that all the funds of the enterprises must be kept in the bank, and that it is the only source of short-term credits. The local branch of the bank has the duty of scrutinizing all payments and cheques to see that they conform to the plan and to the various regulations (e.g. relating to prices, wages, etc.). Under a decree of August, 1954, the bank assumes a more detailed tutelage over enterprises which find themselves in financial difficulties.[3] The State Bank is a centralized all-union institution, of whose control functions more will be said in chapter 3. Investment expenditure is

---

[1] *Pravda*, November 22, 1958.

[2] This has led to bitter complaints about the ministry's interference with staff establishments (see, for instance, G. Lopovok in *Ekon. gaz.*, June 12, 1960) These powers exist even after the recent reforms, as may be seen in the reference cited on p. 33 above.

[3] This includes provision for a species of socialist bankruptcy (see p. 128 below).

controlled closely by the specialized *investment banks*, which are under the Ministry of Finance (see chapter 3).

Arbitration tribunals settle the many conflicts between state enterprises, concerning the negotiation of contracts which they are compelled to conclude under the planned supply allocations, or the alleged failures to carry out the terms of contracts. Within an economic ministry, there is an internal arbitration tribunal to adjudge disputes between enterprises or other economic bodies within its own jurisdiction. For other cases the state provides a hierarchy of arbitration bodies, with, at the top, the State Arbitration Committee (*Gosarbitrazh*). Of course, none of these bodies have the right to arbitrate on disputes between a superior and an inferior in the same hierarchy, which are settled by the issue of appropriate instructions.

Other central and republican ministries and committees maintain local offices or send plenipotentiaries, inspectors and auditors. Some of these local offices also form part of organs of local government, under the system of 'dual subordination'. Thus the Kharkov city trading department is directly under not only the Kharkov city soviet but also the Ukrainian ministry of internal trade, and an *oblast'* soviet agricultural department is the representative in the *oblast'* of the Ministry of Agriculture. Naturally, the many bodies of this type can and do act as 'watchdogs' for the central or republican authorities.

Finally, and most important of all, is the *Communist Party*. It plays a vital role, at all levels, in the economic life of the USSR. At the top policy-making level, it is the party leadership which takes all basic decisions. 'No important decision is taken by the state organs of our country without previous instructions and advice from the Party.'[1] One often finds branches of the government (for instance, Gosplan) reporting to the Central Committee.[2] In republics and in other units of local government there is a parallel party committee which generally possesses more influence and power than the analogous government body (for example, the secretary of the party's *raion* committee—the *raikom*—is unquestionably the boss over the relatively insignificant chairman of the *raion* soviet executive committee—the *rai-ispolkom*). The party secretaries of the *oblasti* played a key role in the *sovnarkhoz*. In the republics and below, as at the centre, the party headquarters possesses economic departments. For instance, it seems probable that the real 'minister' of

[1] A. Denisov, *Sovetskoe gosudarstvennoe pravo* (Moscow, 1947), pp. 191-2.
[2] See, for instance, I. Kuzmin's speech to the Party congress, *Pravda*, February 5, 1959.

agriculture of the Ukraine is not the nominal holder of that post, but the party's agricultural secretary. Of course, the precise extent of party domination at any given level varies, and may in part depend on personalities, on the degree of support the various individuals can muster in Moscow and on the technical nature of the job. It must not be forgotten that senior government officials are also party members of some importance, and that there is some interchange in jobs between the governmental, economic and party hierarchies.

The party organs may be given powers of extremely strict control (in the English sense of the word 'control') of particular sectors of economic life. One example is a decision, taken in 1959, that all building projects 'are examined, in accordance with their importance, in *raikomy*, *gorkomy*, *obkomy*, *kraikomy* and central committees of the parties of the union republics, and only then can they be submitted for confirmation to the appropriate (governmental) organs'.[1] The greatest degree of party power over everyday economic life is, without doubt, in agriculture. As abundant evidence shows, *obkom* and *raikom* officials and plenipotentiaries are constantly interfering even in the routine activities of *kolkhozy*.

At the level of the enterprise, there is a party branch, with a secretary (who is a full-time official in the larger branches). This branch has no right to order the director to do anything, but it is in a strong position, since it can appeal to more senior party organizations in the event of any major clash. The party's task in enterprises is the twin one of mobilizing the employees to fulfil the plan and of checking on the director to ensure that he is acting 'correctly'. The party secretary in the factory, through the local party secretary, can also help to pull strings to secure necessary supplies or other requirements from the authorities. The party's tasks of supervision in enterprises were strongly re-emphasized in 1959, when the already-existing party groups were enjoined to keep a thorough and continuous watch on all aspects of the enterprises' activities and reorganized to do this more effectively.[2] The party exercises some of this power through the local trade union branch, which it firmly controls, and through mass bodies such as the 'production council' (page 31, above), *kolkhoz* meetings (page 50), the trade unions and so on.

Among the most important ways of exercising party leadership is in what is often called 'selection, training and distribution of

[1] I. Bocharov, *Plan. Khoz.*, No. 12/1960, p. 60.

[2] Party 'control' commissions were established in enterprises, with orders to report irregularities of any kind to the central committee and governmental organs (*Pravda*, July 13, 1959, and also August 3, 1959).

cadres'. This operates by means of the so-called *nomenklatura* system. *Nomenklatura* is two things: a list of appointments (e.g. in the state hierarchy, trade unions, enterprises, army, etc. etc.) for which given party committees are responsible, and a list of persons deemed to be qualified to hold such posts. The latter are often known as *nomenklaturnye rabotniki*, that is, as persons on this list, who can be appointed to jobs listed. For instance, it is known that *kolkhoz* chairmen are on the *nomenklatura* list of republican and *oblast'* party committees, and deputy-chairmen and 'brigadiers' on the *raikom* list.[1]

No significant economic appointment, whoever is nominally responsible for making it, can in fact be made without at the very least the approval of a party committee. In all important instances this involves the Central Committee cadres department, which controls the employment of party members above the lowest levels.[2] Knowledge that this is so inevitably affects the behaviour patterns of all state or economic officials. For example, a deputy-minister in Uzbekistan, nominally appointed by the republican government, is in fact appointed (or at least confirmed in his appointment) by the republican party organization, subject to the veto of (or on the suggestion of) the Central Committee cadres department. The high degree of centralization of the party is another essential political and economic fact; decentralization of authority to, for instance, the Ukraine or Uzbekistan must always be affected by the extent to which the party secretary in the republic is allowed some scope for decision. Of course, the converse is also true: the extent to which the party secretary in any republic or locality has power of decision partly depends on the number of matters which, in the governmental hierarchy, are to be settled within his territory. In any event, party control over policy and over its execution is an essential, if not always visible, fact of Soviet life, and affects not only basic planning decisions or the appointment and behaviour of a minister, but also the choices between alternatives which a factory director or a *kolkhoz* chairman may wish to make. This is why, although party organization as such is not a question to be dealt with here, it is necessary to emphasize that it affects all aspects of economic life. It is, so to speak, the board of directors of USSR Ltd and the institutional substitute for the motivating force of free competition, the driving force

[1] *Pravda*, March 6, 1954. For an interesting and well-documented discussion of *nomenklatura*, see M. Fainsod, *Smolensk under Soviet Rule* (Harvard University Press, 1958).
[2] For an example of how central committee officials in effect appoint the director of a major building project on the Volga, see F. Panfyorov's novel *Vo imya molodovo* (*Oktyabr*, No. 7/1960).

which tries (with some success) to overcome natural inertia. It is, of course, much else besides, but that is another story.

LIST OF MINISTRIES, etc.

The Industrial * Planning Structure after 1965

Gosplan (planning and co-ordination)
Gosstroi (as above, for construction)
State Committee for Material Supplies
State Committee for Science and Technique

All-union Ministries
Aviation industry
Automobile industry
Gas industry
Machinery for light, food and *bytovoi*** industry
Defence industry
General machinery
Instruments, automation equipment and control systems
Radio industry
Medium machinery
Machine tools and instruments
Construction, roadmaking and communal machinery
Shipbuilding
Tractors and agricultural machinery
Transport construction
Heavy—electrical and transport machinery
Chemical and oil machinery
Electronic industry
Electro-technical industry
Machine building

Union-republican Ministries
Light industry
Forestry, cellulose, paper and wood-processing industry
Assembly and special construction works
Meat and dairy industry
Oil industry
Oil refining and petrochemical industry
Food industry
Building materials industry
Fish industry
Coal industry
Chemical industry
Non-ferrous metallurgy
Ferrous metallurgy
Energy and electrification
Heavy construction
Industrial construction
Agricultural construction
Construction

*Omitting Transport, Trade and Agricultural Ministries, but including construction.

**'Domestic' consumer durables.

Source: *Ekon. gaz.*, No. 31/1966, pp. 3-5; also No. 45/1967, p. 27 and *Vedomosti verkhovnovo soveta SSSR*, No. 6, 1968, p. 54.

CHAPTER 3

Public Finance and Credit

THE STATE BUDGET

The role of the budget is (in all countries) to transfer resources, in accordance with government decision, from one part of the national economy to another. The USSR is no different in this respect. However, the relative importance of the budget is very great there, because of the direct responsibility of the state for the bulk of economic life. Thus in 1965 the Soviet national income (in its Soviet definition) amounted to 192·6 milliard roubles, while the revenues of the budgets of all public authorities totalled 102·3 milliard in the same year.[1]

However, Soviet finance has an essential feature which distinguishes it from the West: its intimate inter-relationship with the process of economic planning. Expenditures on investment and on other aspects of the economy are the financial reflection of decisions about economic growth and priorities. Revenues predominantly originate in the operation of the state sector of the economy, and, as we shall see, a large portion of expenditure also derives from the economic plan itself. Similarly, financial institutions operate with a copy of the plan before them. Their resources, and their allocation of moneys for credits and other purposes, are intimately related to the output and investment plan and are intended also to serve as a check on observance of regulations issued by higher authority in the course of organizing plan fulfilment. Thus financial plans and economic plans are elaborated simultaneously, and it has become the practice to submit the annual economic plan and the budget to the same session of the Supreme Soviet.

One feature of the state budget is that it includes the expenditure of all republics, and local authorities. Thus the expenditure of, say, the Omsk town soviet in repairing the drains will appear under the appropriate head in the budget voted by the all-union Supreme Soviet. This does not mean, of course, that the repair of the Omsk drains is specifically authorized by the Supreme Soviet. Republics

[1] *N. Khoz.* 1965, pp. 591 and 781.

111

and local authorities have their own budgets, and only the principal headings of expenditure require approval of the centre, though some detailed items are the consequences of plans decided at the centre, which also decides how much of the total revenue is made available to the republics (more of this in a moment).

The following table shows the principal items of *revenue* in some selected years:

Table 1. Revenue

	1940	1950	1958	1966
	(thousand million roubles)			
	(Old)	(Old)	(Old)	(New)
Turnover Tax	105·9	236·1	304·5	39·3
Deduction from profits	21·7	40·4	135·4	35·7
MTS revenues*	2·0	3·6	9·7	1·1
Co-operative tax, kolkhoz tax, non-commodity operations tax	3·2	5·5	16·6	0·2
State loans	11·4	31·0	10·6	—
of which:				
(Mass subscription loans)	(9·0)	(26·4)	(3·2)	—
(Savings bank loan purchases)	(0·2)	(3·1)	(6·5)	—
Direct taxes	9·4	35·8	51·9	8·4
Social insurance revenue	8·6	19·6	33·1	6·1
Other revenues	18·0	50·8	110·5	15·5
TOTAL	180·2	422·8	672·3	106·3
Of which from 'socialist economy'	160·1	354·0	604·0	97·0

Source: *N.Kh. 1958*, p. 899. *N.Kh. 1962*, p. 636. and *Strana Sovetov za 50 let*, (M. 1967) p. 40.

*Including other specialized agricultural organizations.

Turnover tax remains the largest item of revenue, though its relative importance has been falling in recent years. The nature of this tax is often misunderstood, and it plays an important role in the controversy about Soviet price policy (see chapters 4 and 8), therefore it must be examined in some detail.

'Turnover tax' (*nalog s oborota*) was first levied in 1931, when it replaced a variety of excise duties. It covers three kinds of tax, which are in significant respects distinct from one another. The first is an excise duty in all but name, levied at a fixed rate: the taxes on vodka, matches and salt are examples of this. The second may be described as 'tax by difference', and, beginning in 1939, has been commonly applied to industrial consumers' goods where there is very large assortment of product (for instance, textiles). Here the tax emerges as the difference between the retail price (less trade margin) and the wholesale price. In principle, the retail price is fixed in relation to supply and demand, and the wholesale price is based on average cost plus a small profit margin, and the tax emerges as equal to the gap between them.[1] The third species of turnover tax is in some respects similar to the second, but, so to speak, is a 'difference with a difference': it arises from the acquisition by the state of farm produce at low prices. Thus in 1936 the compulsory procurement price for wheat, plus handling costs, was fifteen roubles per ton. This wheat was sold to the state milling enterprises at 107 roubles per ton, the tax amounting to 92 roubles, or to over five-sixths of the wholesale price inclusive of tax.[2] The distinction between this and the tax on textiles is that, whereas the latter bears on the consumer of the textiles, the bulk of the tax on the grain clearly falls on the peasants who were compelled to deliver the grain so cheaply. It also implies that it is not very meaningful to calculate the percentage tax on bread grains and use the enormous percentage so obtained to prove that 'bread is heavily taxed in Russia', since the percentage would reflect the extent of under-payment of the peasants. If the grain were delivered free in the guise of a tax in kind, the tax percentage would become infinity! Revenue from this source has fallen rapidly in recent years, owing to upward amendment in state buying prices.

Turnover tax falls on consumers' goods or on materials predominantly intended for consumption, except that tax is levied on all uses of electricity, natural gas and oil. Actual rates are generally unpublished since the war.[3] Until 1949, there was a nominal tax of $\frac{1}{2}$ to 1 per cent on practically all products of heavy industry.

It is the Soviet habit, when reporting tax rates, to express the percentage in relation to the wholesale price inclusive of the tax. To

[1] This has consequences for the role of prices as 'transmitters' of demand (see page 152, below).
[2] The figures really were as given here! See S. Azarkh, *Oblozhenie khlebo-produktov* (Moscow, 1936), p. 20 ff. Example relates to the central-Russian zone, soft wheats; an additional tax was then levied on grain or flour sold retail.
[3] However, some rates are published. Thus electricity enterprises pay turnover tax on revenues, which, in 1956, varied from 0 in the Donets basin to 45-50 per cent in Armenia, with an all-union average of 15·8 per cent (Sh. Turetski, *Ocherki planovovo tseno-obrazovaniya v SSSR* (Moscow, 1959), p. 135).

illustrate this point, let us imagine cloth worth 100 roubles without tax and 150 with tax. In Great Britain we would call this a purchase tax of 50 per cent, but in the USSR the tax would be described as being 33⅓ per cent.

The actual method of collection of the tax varies: it is increasingly paid by the producing enterprise, sometimes by the wholesaling organization, which is now generally within the network of the Ministry of Trade, or, in the case of many farm products, by the procurement organization.[1] Sales of farm produce in the free market are exempt. Produce used for stockpiling, or for export, is also exempt.[2]

This tax causes some philosophical confusion. It has become customary for Soviet theoreticians to claim that this is not an indirect tax, but rather a 'profit of the socialist economy'. The state owns industry, and the difference between costs and the final selling price is the state's profit, so it is argued. The division of this surplus between the enterprise's profit and the budget's share is a mere matter of administrative convenience. The economics textbook avoids using the word 'tax', preferring to give the name 'the state's centralized net income' to all its revenues from the economy.[3] It is then claimed that, unlike capitalist countries, the USSR raises nearly all its state revenues without recourse to taxation! It is perhaps not so easy to explain how the vodka tax differs in principle from the whisky duty, or how the revenue arising from the procurement of farm products at low prices is part of the 'profits of the socialist economy', especially as many Soviet economists admit that this tax falls on peasants, either as a form of 'differential rent' or as 'the peasants' share in general state expenditure', or both.[4]

'Deduction from profits' (*otchislenie ot pribylei*) is the state's share in enterprise profits. This, until the reforms now being implemented, was a relatively simple item to describe: the state took all the profits other than that part which the enterprise was permitted to retain for a few specifically authorized purposes. Now, however, in respect of the enterprises transferred to the 'new system', it consists of several items, which have in common only that they are paid out of profit.

[1] In 1958, 60 per cent of turnover tax was paid by industrial enterprises, 40 per cent by wholesaling organizations of the Ministry of Trade (Turetski, op. cit., p. 56). There is a tendency towards direct payments by enterprises since that date.
[2] F. Uryupin, *Finansy SSSR*, No. 5/1957, p. 22.
[3] *Politicheskaya ekonomiya*, 3rd revised edition (Moscow, 1958), p. 596.
[4] See the interesting arguments on this whole matter by D. Allakhverdyan, *Vop. Ekon.*, No. 2/1954, pp. 50 ff., and M. Bor, *Vop. Ekon.*, No. 10/1954, pp. 79 ff.

There are the capital charge, rental and other 'fixed payments', and finally the so-called 'free remainder' of profits, i.e. the amounts left after payments into the various incentive and other funds described in chapter 1. It may be that before long these revenues will be separately identified; for the present they continue to be treated as coming under the single head 'deduction from profits'. It is an important feature of the price reform of 1967 that the profit margin was increased, and so the *relative* roles of profits and turnover tax as sources of budget revenue are continuing to change in 'favour' of the former. The table shows that the tendency is of long standing. There is a significant point which relates to this item and also to turnover tax: these revenues should not be regarded as 'net'. Enterprises often receive from the budget sums to cover some of their expenditures, even though the budget takes part of their profits. Turnover tax is sometimes paid by organizations which then have to receive a compensating subsidy; for example, for several years the food industry paid turnover tax and calculated profits on the assumption that all its milk and meat had been obtained at the low compulsory-procurement price, and the extra amounts which had to be paid out for over-quota purchases were covered by way of subsidy.[1] The object seems to have been to avoid having to recalculate industrial costs.

The same point arose also in considering the item 'MTS revenues', which has now disappeared with the MTS. These 'revenues' consisted principally of produce received in payment for their services, valued until 1958 at the low compulsory-procurement prices. The resultant sum appeared on the revenue side of the budget, and, when it was resold to processing enterprises or to consumers, the big difference was included in turnover tax revenue. Yet the consequence of so low a valuation was that MTS expenditures (until 1958) greatly exceeded income, though the 'loss' was 'book-keeping' rather than real.

Co-operative and *Collective-farm* taxes have been already dealt with (page 55, above). The *'tax on non-commodity operations'*, abolished in 1958, was levied on turnover of service enterprises, such as municipal laundries, baths and the like.

Revenues from *state loans* were of three kinds. The first, and for a long time the biggest, was the *mass-subscription loan*, which was to all intents and purposes a compulsory deduction from wages to buy premium bonds, the lottery-prize drawing representing at first 4 per cent, then 3 per cent and finally 2 per cent of the total sum

---

[1] In all probability this is how the bonus (over-quota) price for grain is now financed. It is also noteworthy that there are large subsidies in respect of livestock products, particularly since 1965.

subscribed.[1] In 1958, it was decided to abandon the practice, while simultaneously suspending lottery-prize drawings and repayments on already existing bonds. This is why the sum under this head shows so large a drop in 1958. The second kind of loan revenue arises from the fact that state *savings banks,* in which citizens are encouraged (by a 3 per cent rate of interest) to keep their savings, buy interest-bearing state bonds, their purchases in each year being roughly equal to the increase in deposits during that year. Finally, there are other bond sales, notably to individual citizens on a genuinely voluntary basis (these were not defaulted upon or suspended in 1958). All these loan revenues are included in the ordinary budget.

Direct taxes play a very limited role in the budget. They are of several kinds. There is, firstly, income tax,[2] levied on all revenues other than those of *kolkhoz* peasants. The rate of tax depends partly on the level of income and partly on its source. Thus in 1958 the rates were as follows:

Table 2. Tax rates (as at 1964)

Annual income (new roubles)	Workers and employees*	Writers and artists	(Per cent of income) Co-operative artisans	Lawyers doctors†	Individual artisans
200	Exempt	1·5	Exempt	3	4·6
400	Exempt	4·0	Exempt	6·65	9·8
600	Exempt	5·2	Exempt	10·1	14·2
1,200	8·2	8·2	9·02	18·5	24·5
2,400	10·6	10·6	11·66	27·6	35·7
3,600	11·4	11·4	12·54	34·9	43·6

Source: *Nalogi i sbory s naseleniya v SSSR* (ed. G. Maryakhin) (M, 1964), p. 22.

*On income from employment by state enterprises and organizations.

†In respect of private practice.

Workers and employees were in fact exempt if their total pay was less than 60 roubles per month. In September 1967 a decree was published[3] reducing income tax by 25 per cent on wages of 61-80 roubles per month, with effect from the beginning of 1968. *Kolkhoz* peasants

---

[1] The reductions were in 1953 (*Finansy i kredit SSSR*, Moscow, 1953, p. 210) and in 1955.

[2] Before the war income tax as such was quite small, there being also a local tax entitled 'cultural and housing levy' (*Kul'tzhilsbor*). This was merged with income tax in 1943.

[3] *Pravda*, September 27, 1967.

pay *'agricultural tax'* on their private holdings (see page 62, above), and nothing on their incomes from collective farms. Then there exists a *bachelor and small-families tax*, which was introduced during the war. Until 1958, it was paid by all single and married persons of child-bearing age at the rate of 6 per cent of income (a fixed sum in the case of *kolkhoz* peasants), and smaller rates were paid if there were less than three children. In 1958, however, all persons with children, and also unmarried women, were freed from tax, and persons with low incomes were exempted. This tax, and also income-tax, levied on 'workers and employees', was to have been gradually abolished in the period 1960-65, with some compensating diminution in upper-bracket wages and salaries. However, this process was interrupted in 1961, as a result of the increase in military spending in that year. The promise to abolish income tax was not renewed by Khrushchev's successors, but there was a further reduction in tax on on the low-paid workers in January 1968.

Social insurance revenues arise from the contribution paid by enterprises (see page 38, above).

There is also a large number of *miscellaneous taxes and other revenues*, of which the following is an incomplete list: net revenues of the state insurance trust (*Gosstrakh*), timber-cutting levy, stamp duty, automobile registration fees, repayment of credits granted to foreign countries,[1] passport fees, entertainments tax, customs duty, revenue from foreign trade (arising from the overvaluation of the rouble, until the 1961 reform), and also the carry-over from the previous year within the budgets of local authorities. There was also a 'buildings tax' and 'ground rent' levied on property occupied by state enterprises as well as other organizations. This was abolished, so far as the former were concerned, in 1959.

The bulk of these miscellaneous items, as of total revenues, arise from economic activities of enterprises and not from taxation of individuals, as can be seen from the last line of Table 1. In essence, all these revenues have as their source the gap between costs of production and the final selling price. It is sometimes argued by western propagandists that this is 'regressive taxation', contrasting it with the very much higher rates and steeper progression of taxes on personal incomes in western countries. To a considerable extent this argument is unsound. In so far as incomes from state employment

---

[1] This is mentioned by N. Kisman and I. Slavnyi, in the pamphlet, *Sovetskie finansy v pyatoi pyatiletke* (Moscow, 1956). Logically the credits themselves should be included somewhere under expenditure, but where?

are determined by the state, there is no reason why the fiscal system should be invoked to correct excessive inequalities, when the obvious way out would be to alter the relative incomes themselves. Indeed, there is no particularly compelling reason to charge tax at all on incomes derived from state sources, and this is doubtless why the decision was taken to 'abolish income tax', though nothing is being done to abolish the tax on incomes from private enterprise which, as can be seen from Table 2 above, are taxed at much higher rates.

Given the government's decisions about resource allocation, the budget must find means to cover state expenditures on non-consumption (e.g. investment, defence) or on social consumption (education, health and so on). Direct taxes are of minor importance. Voluntary savings can play only a minor role in the process. There remains the raising of revenue through the gap between costs and final selling prices of goods, and this, in various forms, is the largest source of income for the state budget. In western countries, such expenditures are financed by direct and indirect taxation, or out of the profits of private companies and individuals. In the USSR, the amount which requires financing is relatively larger than in the west, partly because of the higher proportion of the national income devoted to accumulation, and partly because social services play a bigger role relatively to distributed personal incomes. But in all countries these expenditures must be financed somehow. To put it at its simplest, men engaged in industries which do not make consumers' goods, or in the army, or teaching, or medicine, have to be paid and will demand consumers' goods with their money, and, unless heavy direct taxation sufficiently reduces personal cash income, the retail prices of consumers' goods must, therefore, exceed the wage cost of producing them by a considerable margin. This margin in the USSR consists principally of turnover tax plus profits. The magnitude of this margin reflects the proportion of total resources devoted other than to personal consumption. It is futile to 'blame' turnover tax for high prices in general, as if the state could simply lower the price level by reducing tax, though naturally the burden could be redistributed between commodities and sectors (e.g. by charging more on vodka and less on textiles).[1] The present price level of consumers' goods

---

[1] It is often alleged that turnover taxes are highest on 'necessities'. This view is partly based on the rather misleadingly high tax rates which were levied on the low procurement price of bread grains, and partly correctly reflects the fact that, to be effectively collected, the tax (or price mark-up) needs to be largely concentrated on goods with a low elasticity of demand; in any event, the range of luxuries has been comparatively small.

is not due to the fact that they bear most of the turnover tax; essentially the price level is determined by the relationship between personal disposable incomes and the goods and services available. Thus, if turnover tax were charged on all producers' goods, the cost structure would certainly be much altered, costs of production of consumers' goods would rise, turnover tax on consumers' goods would fall, but *of itself* such a rearrangement would not cause any fall in retail prices, whatever other advantages it may have. The way towards increased purchasing power of the consumer lies, of course, through increased supplies of consumers' goods. If these outrun the rise in money incomes, prices—and turnover tax rates per unit—naturally fall, as they did in the years following 1947. The reason for making these apparently self-evident assertions is that propagandists have often 'accused' turnover tax of causing high prices, when the problem is one of resource allocation, which can indeed be made the subject of legitimate criticism.

The main headings of budgetary *expenditure* are given in the table on the following page.

Allocations to the national economy represent non-returnable budgetary grants to enterprises and organizations, of which the largest portion is devoted to fixed investment, the financing of which will be examined separately. However, a large sum, rather over a third of the total, is spent on other things, and Soviet statistics are generally very vague about the actual amounts involved. Figures for two of these items only have been fairly regularly published: firstly, the costs of the MTS, which, it will be recalled, fell wholly on the

Table 3. Expenditures

	1940	1950	1958	1966
	(thousand million roubles)			
	(Old)	(Old)	(Old)	(New)
Allocations to the national economy	58·4	157·9	290·3	45·2
Social-cultural expenditures	40·9	116·7	214·2	40·8
Defence	56·8	82·8	93·6	13·4
Administration	6·8	13·9	12·0	1·4
Loan service	2·8	5·1	3·7	0·1
Other expenditure	8·6	38·8	28·9	4·7
TOTAL	174·3	413·2	642·7	105·6
Surplus	5·9	9·6	29·6	0·7

Source: as for revenues.

budget and greatly exceeded the revenue of the MTS valued at procurement prices (this item has now disappeared, with the abolition
of the MTS); and, secondly, the budget's share in increases of enterprises' 'own' working capital. Other items which come under this
head include subsidies; these are sometimes paid out openly as
such, under the name of *dotatsii*, and in some years these were
substantial;[1] but many other payments resemble subsidies in all but
name. These include so-called 'starting expenses' (*puskovye ras-
khody*), and also the quite substantial sums paid out to cover losses
on housing, which are due to the fact that rents are far from covering the running costs and repairs of houses owned by local soviets
and enterprises. In 1958-59, a payment seems to have been made
from the budget to compensate enterprises for losses due to the
changes in wages and hours, and this was not called a subsidy.
Here are also to be found the offsetting payments compensating for
overpayment of turnover tax, referred to under that head (page 115,
above). There are also subsidies of a special kind, paid to trade corporations by reason of the over-valuation of the rouble in terms of
foreign exchange, which caused a loss on export deals. These payments were substantial before 1961, owing to the overvaluation of
the rouble. But in recent years too one finds evidence that the major
part of the expenditures on 'trade' under this budgetary heading are
in fact devoted to foreign trade.[2] No doubt it is still necessary to
compensate for the fact that some internal wholesale prices are above
world prices, even though on average the new exchange rate seems a
reasonable one. Also financed out of these allocations are expenditures on stockpiling, and probably a number of other items on which
information is lacking. Thus it can be seen that these 'Allocations to
the national economy' are something of a ragbag, including as they
do investments, subsidies and certain types of operational expenditures. Statistics on these allocations by sector (e.g. agriculture,
transport, heavy industry and so on) are generally published annually,
though with gaps. A point to bear in mind in studying the published
material is that budget *estimates* include a contingency reserve, of

[1] In 1948, subsidies (*dotatsii*) reached 41·2 milliard roubles, of which 35·3
went to industry (A. Zverev, *Voprosy natsional'novo dokhoda i finansov SSSR*
(Moscow, 1958), p. 212). (A big price increase in 1949 eliminated most of these
subsidies.)
[2] Thus for example in 1965 the sum of 2,272 million roubles was devoted to
'Trade', according to the valuable statistical handbook on the budget (*Gosudarstvennyi Byudzhet SSSR, Stat. Sbornik*, Moscow 1966, p. 20) which presents
such systematic data as are published by sector. Yet the Minister of Finance
usually cites figures around 200 million for *Internal* trade (for instance in present-
ing the budget for 1967). The rest must be external.

which the bulk is used to finance unforeseen expenditures on the national economy.

The economic reforms now being implemented are bound to affect allocations to the national economy in a number of ways. Thus whereas in 1966 about 56 per cent of centrally-planned investment was financed by budgetary grants, the role of profits, amortization and bank credits will become much more important, as will be shown in greater detail later in this chapter. Therefore the biggest single component in this budgetary heading is due to decline. Subsidies should also fall, as a result of the industrial price increases of July 1967. However, the biggest single item of subsidy is undoubtedly paid in respect of meat and dairy produce. This is apparently to continue, owing to the government's reluctance to order an increase in retail prices of food.

Social-cultural expenditures include education, health, maternity assistance, social insurance and social security. The 'social insurance budget', which until 1938 was an independent entity, is now merged with the state budget, being used principally to cover expenditures on sick pay and pensions. Unlike the allocations to the national economy, the social-cultural budget is published in great detail. It has been growing rapidly. This is not the place for an examination of Soviet educational and welfare policies, and so no further comment is necessary, except to note that the education vote includes an item for '*Science*' (*nauka*, more properly translated Knowledge), under which it is thought that nuclear research is financed, as well as scientific and cultural activities of less dramatic kinds.

Defence is self-explanatory, but, since no information about the content of the defence vote is ever given, it is possible that some defence items appear elsewhere. Thus some military nuclear research may be financed under 'Science', and the stockpiling expenditures under 'Allocations to the national economy' could include stockpiling of weapons. Investment in arms factories quite logically belongs in 'Allocations to the national economy', and para-military security troops are financed out of the police vote (see below). However, investment in American or British arms factories is usually financed by private investment and not from the budget at all, while internal security troops in countries which possess them (France and Spain, for instance) also fall to the Ministry of the Interior budget. Nuclear research is separately financed in many countries. Thus there are no positive grounds for thinking that the coverage of the Soviet defence budget is very different from western practice, though the high degree of secrecy justifies a degree of caution or scepticism.

In particular, we do not know the prices at which weapons are acquired by the armed forces.

Loan service includes interest payments on bonds held by institutions (e.g. savings banks), and lottery prizes and repayments of bonds held by individuals.

The *Administration* vote covers, of course, local and republican governments, as well as the centre. It includes also the administration of justice, but not the police. By long tradition, the Ministry of Interior and the Security organization (OGPU, NKVD, MVD, KGB, etc.) come under a separate vote. No figures are available for recent years, but in 1948 it could be calculated that the interior and security services vote rose to the fantastic total of over 25 milliard (old) roubles, or about double all other administrative and judicial expenses.[1] The police vote is concealed among 'other expenditures'. Since Stalin's death the size of the police and expenditure upon it have fallen considerably, and this is reflected in the fact that in Table 3, above, the item 'other expenditures' was considerably smaller in 1958 than it was in 1950. No doubt some other kinds of expenditure are also financed under this miscellaneous group, but details are unavailable.

Before leaving budgetary statistics, it is desirable to mention a peculiarity which was of importance in 1953 and 1954. In these years, for reasons which have never been explained, both sides of the budget were inflated by the inclusion of 'expenditures on price reductions'. As far as can be ascertained, what happened was this: prices were reduced by aggregate equivalent of a given sum, which represented revenue foregone. This sum then appeared in the budget total, both in 'other revenue' and in 'other expenditure'. Therefore in these years these residuals were abnormally high. This had not happened before, and seems not to have happened since. These were the only two budgets presented during Malenkov's tenure of office as prime minister, though this could be coincidence. This was pure 'padding', in that the sums in question appear not to have ever been paid in and out of the budget, unlike the real in-and-out items which still exist and which do represent real payments.

---

[1] Zverev, in the stenographic report of the 1948 (budget) session of the Supreme Soviet, p. 323, gave total expenditure on administration, plus MVD and the MGB (Security Ministry) as 33·1 milliards for *union and republics only*, excluding local government. According to N. Rovinski, *Gosudarstvennyi Byudzet SSSR* (1949 edition), p. 47, local administrative expenses were 5·6 milliard roubles, and these would not include the highly centralized MVD/MGB. Total expenditures on administration and justice, excluding MVD/MGB, was given by Zverev as 13·5 milliards. 33·1 + 5·6 − 13·5 = 25·2. Q.E.D.

The detailed powers of republics and local authorities over their budgets has varied. For example, while in 1953 nearly four-fifths of the state budget was administered directly by the all-union authorities, reflecting the high degree of centralization of the Stalin period, in 1958 over half of total expenditure was within the separate budgets of the union republics (which include those of local authorities in their territories). To a great extent, however, the republics spend in accordance with central instructions. This applies particularly to allocations to the national economy, since allocations often pass through the republican budgets, even though the expenditure may be due wholly to the instructions of the central government. However, by a reform promulgated in 1959, republics retain certain revenues raised on their territories: all revenue from *kolkhoz* taxes, all agricultural tax, 50 per cent of income tax, the bulk of the budget's share in profits of enterprises, and some other items;[1] in addition they may or may not receive a portion of the turnover tax revenues, according to the union government's estimate of their needs. In general, as is only to be expected, republics or areas which are being developed (for instance, Kazakhstan) receive more from the centre than they pay in.

THE FINANCING OF INVESTMENT

Owing to its key importance in the planning process, and also the many sources from which it is financed, investment requires separate consideration.

The major part of investment in the state sector has been financed by non-returnable budgetary grants. However, a sizeable and increasing share is financed from enterprises' own resources, of which more in a moment. With minor exceptions, these sums are transferred to specialized investment banks (see page 129, below), which issue them when and if the expenditure is justified by the investment plan, or, in the case of extra-plan investment expenditures, falls within the regulations governing these. The central investment plan is submitted to the government of the USSR by Gosplan, and is a vital part of the general long-term planning process, for obvious reasons. The extent to which the process is centralized has varied considerably in Soviet history. From this standpoint, investments in the state sector can be divided into several categories. There is, first of all, the distinction between 'above-limit' and 'below-limit' (*sverkhlimitnye* and *nizhelimitnye*) investments. Investment projects of a value exceeding a

---

[1] *Pravda*, October 31, 1959. Before then they received much less as of right. However, the 1965 reform has increased the scope of all-union financing.

certain sum[1] must each be approved by the centre, while those below these value limits do not require approval separately, but form part of aggregate sums allocated for investment purposes to the given sector. There is also a somewhat different distinction between *centralized* and *decentralized* investments, the latter sometimes being confusingly designated *vnelimitnyi* ('beyond limit'). Centralized investments are those covered by the central investment plan, and include 'below-limit' investments if expenditure on these is provided for in the plan. The distinction must be made between centrally financed and centrally planned investments. Many of the latter are financed from enterprises' profits or even on credit, but are still part of the central investment plan, which provides for the use of these sources of finance. Decentralized investments are, of course, not planned. They are paid for out of the funds which exist at enterprise level for these purposes (see chapter 1, above), and also out of bank credits. For some reason, credits granted within the central investment plan are charged only $\frac{1}{2}$ per cent interest per annum, whereas credits for decentralized investments carry a 2 per cent interest rate.[2] The extent of decentralized investments was severely restricted during the last years of Stalin's life, and indeed the category as such was formally abolished in 1951.[3] Their importance increased rapidly after 1953. Khrushchev tried to cut back decentralized investment in 1961, but it grew again, particularly with the implementation of the reforms. Thus in 1967 centralized investments increased by 5 per cent, decentralized by 20 per cent.[4] Of course, these 'unplanned' investments are by no means uncontrolled. There are restrictions on the types of permitted investments; for example, a decree in 1958 forbade local investment in certain types of construction (offices, sports stadiums, etc.) without the special authorization of the republican government.[5] Then control over allocations of materials and equipment provides a further means of preventing diversion of resources into forms of investment not desired by the authorities. Indeed, as we shall see, there are many complaints that money available for decentralized investments cannot be spent, owing to shortage of capital goods, especially building materials.

In the 1957-65 period the republic and the *sovnarkhozy* had important functions in drafting and putting forward investment plans.

[1] This has varied between economic sectors and at different dates.
[2] P. Bunich, *Vop. Ekon.*, No. 10/1967, p. 56.
[3] D. Allakhverdyan, *Nekotorye voprosy teorii sovetskikh finansov* (Moscow, 1951), p. 168.
[4] *Pravda*, January 25, 1968.
[5] *Pravda*, October 5, 1958.

To some extent the effect of the restoration of the 'ministerial' system has brought about greater concentration of plan-drafting in Moscow. But it should be appreciated that proposals from below continue to be an important, indeed essential, part of the process of planning, in investment as in other matters. It is never only a matter of orders from above and obedience below. However, the basic responsibility remains central, and, in an economy of the Soviet type it is hard to see how it can be otherwise, though there have been many complaints that republics play a smaller role after than before 1965.

The financing of investment, as has already been pointed out, is due to be changed fundamentally by the reforms now being implemented, but the changes have yet to be fully operative. According to an article by a senior official of the Investment bank, 'the substitution of long-term credits for non-returnable grants will take place gradually, alongside the introduction of new planning and incentive methods in enterprises. This task should be completed in 1968. As a result, roughly 80 per cent of capital investments in industrial productive capital will be covered by enterprises' own resources (i.e. profits and depreciation) and long-term bank credits.'[1] Credits will be repaid partly out of the depreciation allowances, partly from profits.

It seems that outright budgetary grants will be confined, in respect of productive enterprises, to new investment projects which have a recoupment period, after completion, of over five years. The expansion of existing enterprises will not normally qualify for budgetary grants.[2] Naturally, a large proportion of the investments will continue to be centralized investments, in the sense described above. Of course, all these are forecasts, and the reform may in fact proceed slower, or even not proceed at all. But this is the way things are going at the time of writing. Evidently, these changes will place, and are intended to place, greater responsibility on the enterprise management. Much more of their own money will be involved, and credits will need repaying. There will therefore be greater reluctance to ask for investment authorizations or plans compared with the situation when these funds were, from the standpoint of the recipient, free gifts.

The cost of investment projects is carefully controlled. Based on prices of materials, machinery and labour, on centrally-approved norms (e.g. of depth of foundations or thickness of walls), and when

---

[1] P. Podshivalenko, in A. Rumyantsev (ed.): *Khozyaistvennaya reforma v deistvii* (M., 1967), pp. 55-6.
[2] P. Podshivalenko, *Plan. khoz.*, No. 10/1966, pp. 1-9.

possible on approved architectural patterns, costs estimates (*smety*) are approved, and form the basis of the issues of money by investment banks. The laying down of rules and designs for building is the task of the State Committee for Construction (*Gosstroi*), and, in detail, by 'project-making organizations'.[1]

Kolkhoz investments are financed out of the capital fund, and also from long and medium term credits (the rates of interest are as low as 1·75 per cent, under a decision made in 1957).[2] Individuals invest their own savings in private house-building, and may also borrow from the state bank for this purpose, though in the most recent years these credits have gone in the main to building co-operatives formed by groups of citizens, and private house-building has noticeably declined.

The following table shows the distribution of investment between different sectors of the economy:

(*Millions of new roubles, constant prices*)

TOTAL INVESTMENTS, *including kolkhozy and private persons*

		1960	1965
TOTAL		35,914	48,722
of which:	Industry	12,673	17,960
	Construction industry	1,021	1,324
	Agriculture	5,155	8,872
	Transport, posts	3,428	4,850
	Housing	8,209	8,152
	Communal, trade, health, culture, science	5,428	7,008
of the above total:			
	Kolkhozy	3,200	4,300
	Private (housing)	2,700	1,700

Source: *N.Kh.* 1965, pp. 528, 531-2.

The sharp drop in individual house-building was a feature of the period. The present (1966-1970) five-year plan provides for a spectacular increase in individual and co-operative house building as already noted in chapter 1.

There is a degree of statistical imperfection involved in adding together state and non-state investments. Thus *kolkhozy* (until very

[1] 'Project-making expenditure', i.e. quantity-surveying, designs, blue prints and other necessary investigations, were financed with investments until 1951. At this date it was decided to finance them separately, as a means of maintaining tighter control over projects. From January, 1959, they are again financed with investments. See page 50 above.

[2] K. Plotnikov (ed.), *Organizatsiya finansirovaniya i kreditovaniya kapital'nykh vlozhenii* (Moscow, 1954), p. 298.

recently) and individuals have paid much higher prices for building materials and other capital items than state enterprises.

The total is equal to something midway between gross and net fixed investment. It is more than net because it is financed partly out of the depreciation (amortization) fund. It is less than gross because a large portion of the depreciation fund—that earmarked for so-called 'capital repairs'—is not included in the figures. However, the concepts in question are by no means clearly defined anywhere, and differ widely as between western countries, so perfection should be neither sought nor expected.[1]

BANKING AND CREDIT

Banks were nationalized in one of the first acts of the Soviet government after the revolution, but it was not until the end of the Civil War that the State Bank (usually known by the abbreviation *Gosbank*) was founded, within the People's Commissariat of Finance. In the period of NEP, apart from the normal functions of a central bank, it also provided credits to the state and the private sectors of the economy, on both short and long terms. However, credits were also provided by enterprises to one another, until the credit reform of 1930-32. This did two things. Firstly, it gave Gosbank monopoly in granting short-term credits; secondly, it took away from Gosbank the tasks of financing investments, transferring this to specialized investment banks (see below), and basing investment financing of the state sector on non-returnable grants rather than credits. Its essential functions have remained broadly unaltered since, but its status was enhanced in 1954 by its separation from the Ministry of Finance and the promotion of the director to ministerial status.

Gosbank continues to carry out the functions of a central bank (issue of banknotes, keeping the gold reserve, making international payments),[2] as well as administering tax receipts and the paying out of the state's current expenditures. It also acts as an essential part of the economic control mechanism, carrying out so-called *kontrol' rublyom*—'control' by the rouble. All state enterprises must keep their accounts in Gosbank, must pay all but the smallest bills through Gosbank, which is thus able to check that cash resources are used only in accordance with the regulations, to pay wage rates

---

[1] For example, compare the treatment of repairs (e.g. to ships) in the capital accounts of Great Britain and Norway. Depreciation in the west is, in any event, more a fiscal than an economic category: it is what the tax inspector can be persuaded to accept.

[2] A specialized branch of Gosbank, *Vneshtorgbank*, deals with foreign trade payments.

and prices prescribed by the regulations, and in conformity with the plan. The Bank provides short-term credits, and this too provides an essential control mechanism. An eminent Soviet expert wrote: 'The Bank issues credits for the purposes and the amounts provided for by the plan. If the plan is overfulfilled, the enterprise can claim and the Bank must issue credits for the needs associated with plan overfulfilment; if the plan is underfilled, credits must be reduced. In this process, the Bank supervises not only the amount of the credit, but also its use for the particular purpose which the plan intends, not permitting unplanned redistribution of material and monetary resources in the socialist economy between and within enterprises'.[1] If enterprises are in financial difficulties and consequently do not keep bank credits at planned levels, or fail to repay them at due dates, a series of 'credit sanctions' may be applied; credits may be refused without the guarantee of a superior organ (e.g. the *glavk* of the ministry) and, in the last resort, the Bank can declare the enterprise insolvent, publish the fact in its journal and virtually take command over its assets (before such a desperate situation is reached, superior authority generally steps in to dismiss the management and reorganize the enterprise). On the contrary, if the enterprise is financially successful, it is given favourable treatment in obtaining credits.[2]

The role of credits is to facilitate the process of payment and to overcome the time-gap which must arise between payments and receipts. Gosbank credits provide about 40 per cent of all working capital in the economy.[3] However, the division between 'own' and borrowed working capital varies greatly in different sectors of the economy. Thus the role of credits is much greater in trade and in light industry than it is in heavy industry, apparently because the latter has been favoured with more lavish provision of own resources, another instance of the priority which it enjoys. Short-term credits to state enterprises carry an interest rate of 2 per cent, sometimes less, or 3 per cent if return of credits is overdue. (For the role of credits in enterprise finance, and the distinction between 'own' and borrowed working capital, see page 36, above.) Quarterly credit plans must be submitted by Gosbank to Gosplan and the government, since these must be carefully geared in with the general

---

[1] K. Plotnikov, *Finansy i kredit v SSSR* (Moscow, 1959), p. 167.
[2] For a valuable and detailed account of this and other aspects of the Bank's credit system, see I. Kirillov, *Finansy sotsialisticheskoy promyshlennosti* (Moscow, 1959), especially pp. 144-73.
[3] Excluding building and *kolkhozy*. M. Atlas, *Razvitie gosudarstvennovo banka SSSR* (Moscow, 1958), p. 349.

economic plans for which these bodies are responsible. The importance of Gosbank as an organ capable of enforcing centrally determined financial and credit policies increased after the 1957 reform
gave wider functions to republics and *sovnarkhozy*, for Gosbank is
essentially a centralized, all-union institution. Its monetary resources
come partly from deposits of enterprises partly from the transfer to
it of the bulk of budget surpluses, partly from budgetary grants.
The Bank also retains a portion of the profits which it makes.

Though, in principle, Gosbank is not concerned with investment,
it is found convenient to use it, rather than the investment banks,
for the provision of some short-term credits used to purchase equipment (small-scale so-called 'mechanization' credits, and for credits to
local, communal and producers' co-operative enterprises which are
used for investment purposes.

Individuals are encouraged (by a 3 per cent rate of interest) to use
the network of *savings banks* which are under the control of the
Ministry of Finance.

In 1932 there were created four investment banks: *Prombank*
(industrial bank), *Sel'khozbank* (agricultural bank), *Torgbank* (trade
and co-operatives), and *Tsekombank* (communal and housing bank,
which controlled numerous local 'communal' banks), under the Ministry of Finance. Their primary function was to administer investment funds, which reached them from two principal sources; from
the state budget and from enterprises (the latter transferred to the
investment banks the portion of the amortization fund and profits
earmarked for new investment). In the case of investments in the
state sector, the banks financed the necessary building or acquisition
of equipment. In addition, because of the special position of building enterprises as executants of the investment plan, the investment
banks provided credits for these enterprises. The importance of these
banks as a checking and controlling agency has already been emphasized. The appropriate banks also provided long-term credits to
kolkhozy and co-operatives, and for individual housing.

In 1959, however, the system was altered, and all these four banks
disappeared. In their place was created a construction bank (*Stroibank*), which took over the major functions of the defunct investment banks, shedding some minor ones to Gosbank.[1]

The reforms are affecting the role of the banks in a number of
important ways. Gosbank's control is being loosened, insofar as the
enterprises have greater flexibility in the use of their resources, as
shown in detail in chapter 1. Both Gosbank in respect of short-term

[1] For details, see leading article in *Finansy SSSR*, No. 6/1959.

E

and *Stroibank* for the increasingly significant investment credits, are now to use their economic judgement to a greater extent, instead of acting as a mixture of financial policeman and a 'conduit for budgetary investment funds', to borrow a phrase from a first-rate survey of this whole subject.[1]

Soviet currency, the rouble, is nominally on a gold standard. This has no practical significance, save that it determines official exchange rates. In theory Soviet currency should be, as is sometimes claimed, 'the most stable in the world'. Planning enables the authorities to limit effective demand to the quantities of goods and services available at established prices, by control over personal incomes and by controlling enterprises' claims on resources by physical allocation and various other forms of regulation. However, things have seldom been so simple, and there have been instances of acute inflation, sometimes open, sometimes concealed. Thus, in the hard years of the first five-year plan (1928-32) and in the period of the war, a sharp diminution of supplies of consumer goods stimulated an upward trend in money wages, which, as will be shown in detail, cannot be very effectively controlled even in more normal times. Despite efforts to keep down costs and to control wages funds, the banks in fact pay out rather more than planned, thereby increasing the volume of money in circulation. The credit reform of 1931, giving Gosbank a credit monopoly, had the effect of greatly stimulating inflation; credits granted by enterprises to each other were limited by their financial resources, but, in the context of the priority given to the achievement of rapid growth of output, Gosbank could and did issue whatever sums were deemed necessary, since financial soundness was repeatedly sacrificed to production achievements. If the level of money wages outruns gains in productivity, increases in prices of producers' goods are the only alternative to subsidies; if the level of money wages increases faster than the volume of goods and services available for sale to the citizens, a price increase is the only alternative to rationing. In the producers' goods field, it is true, rationing (i.e. administrative allocation) is the rule rather than the exception, and so inflationary pressures can show themselves by the severity of such rationing and by frequent breakdowns in material supplies—which happen often enough and are signs of overstrain. A disguised inflation in the consumers' goods sector is possible without any rationing, and indeed has shown itself by lengthening queues at various dates in Soviet history.

[1] G. Garvy: *Money, banking and credit in Eastern Europe*, Federal Reserve Bank of New York, 1966.

CHAPTER 4

Wages and Prices

PRINCIPLES OF WAGE DETERMINATION

In most areas of Soviet planning of economic life, as indeed in the west also, it is important to distinguish between formal principles and actuality. Nowhere is this more important than in the field of wages and salaries. The system appears to be far more centralized and far more tightly controlled than it really is. It would appear at first sight that wages can be systematically adjusted to conform to some set of desiderata, that the total level of disposable money incomes can deliberately be made to conform to the value of goods and services available, and that the government's authority over wage payments, in a totalitarian state in which independent trade unions do not exist, can readily eliminate anomalies and illogicalities. It will be seen that the truth is very different. However, it is first necessary to describe the formal structure.

The general level of wages, the 'spread' between grades and areas, and the rates payable in different industries have been the responsibility of the central government. Until its abolition in 1934, the People's Commissariat for Labour was responsible for these tasks. The All-Union Central Council of Trade Unions (AUCCTU) absorbed some (notably the social-insurance) of the functions of this commissariat; it also had, and still has, a central wages department. However, the AUCCTU is not part of the government, nor is it the task of trade unions to negotiate wage agreements, though they are directly involved in the definition of grading (of which more in a moment) and are also brought into discussions on incentive schemes; they doubtless also make representations about wage anomalies, but decisions on wage rates as such are clearly regarded as a governmental task. But until 1956 there was no body below the Council of Ministers which could decide these questions, or indeed even consider them systematically, in the absence of anything corresponding to a Ministry of Labour. Indeed, there was no *systematic* revision of Soviet wage-rates from 1931 to 1956. Obviously, wages were altered repeatedly between these dates; there were generally-decreed increases by given amounts, as for instance in 1937 and 1946, and many orders relating to particular groups or occupations, such as coal-miners, school-teachers, civil servants and the like. However, these piecemeal forms were, as a rule, due either to a necessary and indeed delayed adjustment to an inflationary situation, or represented yielding to the pressure of an economic ministry anxious to improve its chance of recruiting good workers. The government's response to these requests reflected its own judgment of priorities, as modified by its efforts to combat inflation. The ministries adopted different geographical zoning arrangements, and wages or bonus arrangements for similar work in different industries became inconsistent with one another, leading to numerous complaints. Under the circumstances, anomalies multiplied. It may seem extraordinary, in a planned economy, that 'there was no central organ which dealt with the question of labour and wages', so that 'in reality for years there was no unified wage system'.[1] But it was none the less a fact. In 1955, a State Committee on Labour and Wages came into existence, charged with the task of revising the wages structure from its foundations.

These anomalies were due in part to the fact that some wage-rates are, of their nature, far easier to control than others. Thus, at one extreme, pay of administrative, managerial and other specialized personnel (engineers, economists, accountants, or teachers, doctors, etc.) can be prescribed in detail in the regulations which lay down the establishments, promulgated by and enforced through the Ministry of Finance.[2] If it is laid down that the headmaster of a school or the chief engineer of a factory of a certain size are respectively entitled to a basic salary of 150 and 250 roubles a month, this bears the character of a clear instruction, hard to evade. But at the other extreme are the majority of factory workers, state-farmers, shop-assistants and so on, whose pay depends on individual or group piece-work, and therefore the amount they actually receive depends on the degree to which they fulfil the output norms. Here, too, the principles governing wage determination are clear. All workers are divided into grades, the government settles the wage of grade one (the lowest), each step upwards is calculated by co-efficients which are also laid down by the government,[3] and the qualifications required for each grade are published for each industry in a 'tariff-

---

[1] V. Maier: *Zarabotnaya plata v period perekhoda k kommunismu* (M., 1963), p. 138.

[2] The Establishments commission of this ministry (see p. 106, above).

[3] For example, in 1958 the typical scale of differentials, from bottom to top of the scale, was in the ratio of 1:2·8, in a progression of eight grades of skill (Rumyantsev, op. cit., p. 316). It is now much smaller.

qualification manual' (*tarifno-kvalifikatsionnyi spravochnik*) which also bears the signature of the secretary of the industrial trade unions concerned. The majority of workers are now included within a single consolidated manual, which covers trades and skills encountered in many industries, such as driver, fitter, electrician, carpenter. In this way, some consistency and standardization in grading was achieved. However, it does not necessarily follow that a person of a given grade is paid the same in different industries: for example, the grade 1 (lowest) rate, by reference to which other pay rates are calculated, was markedly lower in, say, the food industry as against the steel industry, though the difference has been much diminished by mini-mum-wage legislation, of which more will be said below. In theory the piece-worker should earn the rate laid down for his grade by just fulfilling the norm. Thus if the rate for a grade four piece-worker in the textile industry were fixed at 2 roubles, and if in a day's work the average worker should perform 100 operations, then the piece rate should be 2 kopecks. If by good work he overfulfilled the norm by, say, 10 per cent, then, under 'straight' piecework, he would be entitled to 2·20 roubles. However, in priority sectors of the economy there was often to be found a system known as 'progressive piece-work', which entitled the worker to double or even treble rates for output over the norm.[1] At regular intervals enterprises were supposed to revise the norms upwards, to offset and encourage increases in productivity. Timeworkers of the same degree of skill were to be paid less than pieceworkers. It was realized, however, that 'progressive' rates were wasteful; thus in the coal industry, there were cases where a 5 per cent overfulfilment of the output plan caused an increase of 53·8 per cent in wage and salary payments.[2] This, together with its inherent crudity and unfairness, led to a decision to abandon 'progressive piecework', and to substitute time rates (usually with group bonuses of some kind) in cases where any kind of individual piece-work system was unjustified.

The total wages bill for a given year is calculated centrally, Gos-plan and the Ministry of Finance being most directly involved, with, since 1955, the Committee of Labour and Wages. Under the minis-terial system, each ministry is informed of the size of its wages fund for the coming year, the magnitude being determined partly by what happened in the previous year and partly by the expected

---

[1] In the coal industry in 1956, double rates were paid when the worker ex-ceeded 80 per cent of his norm, treble rates for over 100 per cent, for coal face workers. See V. Nikol'ski, *Pooshchritel'nye sistemy oplaty truda* (Moscow, 1952).

[2] A. Zvorykin and D. Kirzhner, *Sotsialisticheski trud*, No. 2/1956, p. 70.

changes in the size and qualifications of its labour force. These, in turn, were related to the output and labour productivity plans for the given industry, in the light of general wages policy, which reflected the expected changes in availability of consumers' goods and services, and decisions on retail prices. The end-result was that a given economic ministry would know that its wages fund had been increased from, say, 20·5 to 21·5 milliard roubles.

They then subdivide the wages fund, until finally an enterprise which paid out a given sum in wages in the last year or quarter, is told that it may spend (say) 5½ per cent more in the coming year, or quarter. This plan is supposed to be in harmony with the expected numbers and qualifications of the employees, and their pay entitlements under existing rates. The State Bank has a copy of the relevant figures, and must not permit the paying out of wages in excess of these figures unless the enterprise overfulfils its plan. Such overfulfilment gives rise to legitimate additional expenditures on wages of piece-workers, and on bonuses, though some bonuses, especially for managerial technical staffs, are now financed not from the wages fund but frrom profits, as shown in chapter 1. The tightness of official control over wages has been relaxed under the reform, making it easier for enterprises to vary workers' take-home pay, but in principle they must apply the schedule of basic rates laid down by the government. The 'wages fund' limit has also been retained.

Thus there are two kinds of controls: over the rate for the job, and over the total amounts which can be paid out in wages and salaries. It would be wrong to assert that these controls are inoperative. At times they were more or less effective. Thus in the period 1947 to 1956, money wages rose by only 27 per cent,[1] which compares 'favourably' with the record of most western countries. Yet neither in aggregate nor in terms of wage relativities has practice conformed at all closely to theory; indeed, no general wage increase at all was decreed during the period 1947-56!

One difficulty has been the vagueness of the theory. Labour is not a 'commodity', it is paid in accordance with the quantity and quality of the work. But what is the objective measure of quantity and quality of labour? And, given that A is higher quality work compared to B, by how much should A be paid more? How is it to be related to the supply and demand position, bearing in mind that labour is more or less free to move and is only partially subject to direction? What if the rates laid down in the regulation fail to attract the necessary labour? The state's powers to 'allocate' labour are

[1] S. Figurnov, in *Sotsialisticheski trud*, No. 5/1959, p. 51.

now confined to the following circumstances. Firstly, graduates of any higher or technical institute must go to work where they are sent, for three to four years; there used also to be a call-up of youths to the so-called 'factory and workshop schools' (*Fabrichno-zavodskie Uchilishcha*, FZU), but these are based on voluntary recruitment since 1955. There is provision, too, for so-called 'organized recruiting' (*Orgnabor*) in villages for industrial and building labour, with preference given to important sectors short of labour, but this too is now a voluntary process. Last but far from least, Communist party members and (to a lesser extent) Komsomols—young-communists—may in effect be compelled to go wherever they are sent, on pain of expulsion. Since there are now twelve million members of the party, and many more million Komsomols, this represents an appreciable portion of the labour force, and, as so many of the Communists occupy leading positions, it means that a sizeable proportion of technical and managerial personnel are more or less liable to transfer if the cadres department of the party wishes it. None the less, the door is wide open for the operation of market forces in wage determination, since the major part of the labour force, and particularly of workers and clerical staffs, have the right and the real possibility of leaving their employment.

This was not always so. Decrees adopted in October, 1940, forbade all employees of state enterprises and institutions to leave their work without permission, save in a few narrowly-defined instances (e.g. qualifying for old-age pension, being the wife of a person sent to work in another town, etc.). Disobedience to this decree, as well as absenteeism or even lateness (by more than twenty minutes), were treated as criminal offences, punishable in the last resort by imprisonment, or by a mild form of forced labour ('at place of employment') and financial penalty. The unpopularity of these measures was such that judges and managers were threatened with punishment for failing to apply them. After the war, it was apparently found increasingly difficult to enforce these decrees, and they dropped from active use by 1953, before being finally repealed in 1956. At present, anyone may leave their work, with no penalty if they take another job within a month.[1]

The 'labour-market' in the USSR is highly imperfect, by reason

[1] Until 1960, those who changed jobs of their own volition lost their sick pay entitlements for six months and suffered other penalties under social insurance rules. This provision appears to have been repealed, presumably to encourage voluntary moves to the new factories in the east. Movement to cities is limited by the need for a passport and police registration, difficult to get in such places as Moscow, Leningrad and Kiev.

of the lack of adequate information, or of labour exchanges. One encounters a great deal of sporadic and unco-ordinated advertising of vacancies, e.g. on telegraph poles or public notice-boards, or even in local radio programmes, and information does percolate to many of those who think of changing their employment.

Where a factor of production is not—or is only partially—subject to administrative allocation, its price is bound to be influenced by market forces. Labour has the 'advantage' over inanimate factors of production of being able to move of its own volition, even in defiance of rules and regulations. There is therefore bound to be tension between the wages structure, as laid down by authority, and market forces. In some years the net result was a very large overspending of the wages fund, this being part-cause and part-consequence of uncontrollable inflation. This was particularly so in the chaotic period of the first five-year plan (1928-32), but even in the relatively stable second five-year plan years the wages fund was planned to increase by 55 per cent and in fact rose two-and-a-half-fold.[1] There was a large over-fulfilment of the wages plan also in the fourth plan period (1946-50). These deviations were due partly to unintended increases in average money wages and retail prices, partly to the fact that a much larger number of persons had to be given urban jobs than had been originally foreseen.[2]

In recent years the tendency to excess wage payments has been checked but not eliminated. Thus actual wage overpayments in industry, transport and trade were as follows, in percentage terms: 4·3 per cent in 1953, 3·1 per cent in 1956, 2·1 per cent in 1957.[3] This is by no means negligible, cumulatively, and probably accounts for the major part of the actual rise in average wages in these years.

For many years wage statistics were treated as state secrets. Only very recently has it been possible to compile a table of average wages from official sources:

(*Roubles per annum*)

1928	1940	1946	1955	1958	1964	1965
703†	3,960†	5,700†	8,580†	9,336†	1,081*	1,147*

† Old roubles.   * New roubles.

The figures include producers' co-operatives before 1961, and this pulls down the averages, as their members had been paid

[1] K. Plotnikov, *Byudzhet sovetskovo gosudarstva* (Moscow, 1948), p. 143.
[2] For instance, the fourth five-year plan envisaged 33½ million workers and employees in 1950. The actual numbers were 38·9 million.
[3] V. Popov, *Gosudarstvennyi bank SSSR*, 1917-57 (Moscow, 1957), p. 170. In 1967, as in many other years, wage payments exceeded plan (*Pravda* 25 Jan. 1968).

less than average. Thus the usual 1940 figure was 4,054.
Source: N.Kh. 1965, p. 567.

(Note: On page 126 of the second edition, using indirect and obscure data, I had calculated wage averages as follows: 1945—5,270; 1954—8,514; 1958—9,475; 1964—1,089 (new roubles). Not quite right, but by no means badly wrong.)

Needless to say, real wages presented a very different picture. Thus beyond doubt the purchasing power of money wages in 1937, 1940 and (particularly) 1947 was below 1928, though this needs to be calculated from indirect data, since no Soviet cost-of-living index is published with a 1928 base.[1]

The above are averages, and tell us nothing of differentials. Especially after Stalin's famous attack, in 1931, on 'petty-bourgeois egalitarianism', differentials were greatly increased, with the most skilled workers having roughly three-and-a-half times as much as the least skilled. The officially-sponsored Stakhanovite campaign, launched in 1935, caused very large rewards to be given to outstanding workers, increasing differentials still further. After the war, the wage adjustments of 1946 favoured the lowest-paid workers and this somewhat diminished differentials, although insistence on maximizing them continued to form part of official statements. As late as 1958, plans were based on differentials within the category 'worker' of 2·8:1. However, the seven-year plan adopted in 1959 envisaged a sharp rise in minimum wages and a reduction of differentials to 2:1. Of course, the gap between managerial personnel and unskilled workers has been very much greater than this, though this too is being reduced. Perhaps the biggest single step in this direction was taken on January 1, 1968, with the introduction of a minimum of 60 (new) roubles a month. The minimum introduced in 1956 was only 30-35 in new roubles. Yet the salaries of the higher-paid have not increased in these years.

It is important to note that the contradiction between formal regulations and market forces has led not only to unplanned money wage increases, but to other major departures from the regulations at enterprise level. Thus piecework norms are generally substantially overfulfilled, orders to revise the norms upwards have in various

---

[1] See a very careful survey by Janet Chapman, in *Review of Economics and Statistics*, May, 1954, which confirms similar calculations by N. Jasny, *The Soviet Economy during the Plan Era* (Standford University, 1951) and by S. N. Prokopowicz and others. An 'unofficial' Soviet index by A. Malafeyev, *Istoriya tsenoobrazovaniya, v SSSR* (M., 1964) shows real wages below 1928 levels not only in 1934 but also in 1937.

degrees been evaded, unskilled workers have been promoted to skilled grades, thereby upsetting the intended scale of differentials, the link between plan fulfilment and norm fulfilment barely exists in practice. These and other difficulties faced by planners in dealing with wages and labour will be discussed in greater detail in chapter 8.

PEASANT INCOMES

The reader was briefly introduced to the *trudoden*, or conventional workday unit. Since, unlike wages, this is an unfamiliar method of rewarding labour, it is necessary to examine it in a little more detail, though it is now vanishing.

The *trudoden* dates from 1931, and was supposed to relate the quantity and quality of work done to the amount available in each *kolkhoz* for distribution to the peasants, in cash and kind. Because this amount varied greatly, it was found impossible to value the work directly in terms of either cash or produce.

Differential payments for skill and effort were ensured by a system of grading prescribed by the central authorities. Average work of average quality was graded at 1 *trudoden* per day-norm. Unskilled occupations (e.g. night watchman, cleaner) were graded at 0·5 *trudodni*, the most skilled at 2·5 *trudodni*, for a day-norm,[1] with others in intermediate categories. Work on tractors carried out on *kolkhoz* fields, which was also remunerated in *trudodni*, was rated higher still, with 8 *trudodni* and more per day-norm for some tractormen and combine-harvester operators, for instance. Detailed norms were 'recommended' by the authorities in a number of decrees, but in practice they had to be left largely to local initiative, because conditions differed so widely. In principle, a person carrying out a task which was rated at 2 *trudodni* should be given a defined job to do which should take him a day to perform, and this job would then be valued at 2 *trudodni*. If he overfulfilled the task (for example, by weeding or cultivating more than the prescribed amount), the *trudodni* credited to him would rise proportionately. An important contrast with wage-earners lies in the fact that the job is rated, not the man. In industry, or in state agriculture, the man's grade of skill determines his wage scale, even if he is temporarily engaged on relatively unskilled work, whereas in *kolkhozy* it is the nature of the work which determines how many *trudodni* a particular individual earns. Another difference is that a wage-earner is entitled to be paid

[1] Up to 1948, the maximum 'spread' was from 0·5 to 2·0. See full details in H. Wronski, *Le troudoden* (Paris, 1956).

when his enterprise cannot provide him with work (e.g. in the event of a supply or power breakdown) whereas the *kolkhoz* peasant is only paid for the work he does. This is of importance because there are slack periods, especially in winter, in Soviet agriculture. As in industry, there has been a tendency to fix norms which can be over-fulfilled, or to overgrade work done, so that an average *trudoden* was earned in less than one actual day.[1]

The *trudodni* earned by particular individuals did not depend only on the number of graded day-norms of work they perform. There was also a very complex system of bonuses, related either to plan fulfil-ment (e.g. of the harvest plan in a field cultivated by a particular brigade or team), or to obtaining results above the average in that particular *kolkhoz* (e.g. if one team or brigade has a bigger harvest of a given crop than another). Additional *trudodni* were allocated to the successful, while up to 25 per cent of *trudodni* were deducted from those below plan or below average. To make matters even less simple, there arose in the post-war period the practice of earmark-ing a priority share in disposable income of the *kolkhoz* to those cul-tivating some particular crop. The system's many complications were and are frequently criticized, both because of this complexity and because of its unfairness; thus below-average harvests are often due to natural conditions, so it is unreasonable to penalize peasants who may have worked hard to save what they could. Criticism has also been made of the fact that the norms fixed in different *kolkhozy* have differed so widely that it is quite impossible to use the *trudoden* as a comparative measure of work performed.[2]

Trudodni were also allocated to the *kolkhoz* chairmen, who also receive a fixed sum in money, as do other officials (deputy-chairmen, accountants, etc.). Payments were varied by reference to the fulfilment of various plans (output, deliveries to the state, expansion of live-stock holdings, etc.).

At the end of the year, all the *trudodni* recorded by *kolkhoz* mem-bers (and officials, tractormen, etc.), were adjusted upwards or down-wards under the various bonus regulations, added together, and then

[1] According to E. Karnaukhova, in *Voprosy sotsialisticheskoi ekonomiki* (Moscow, 1956), p. 225, 1·4 *trudodni* were earned in each day's work, on average in the USSR in 1953-5, but there were substantial regional variations.
[2] K. Okhapkin, *Novoe v oplate truda kolkhoznikov* (Moscow, 1958), pp. 7-8, gives some startling examples, relating to *kolkhozy* in similar natural con-ditions. For valuable details of recent *trudodni* regulations, see G. Kuparadze, *Spravochnik ekonomista* (Tiflis, 1960), and also *Spravochnik predsedatelya kolkhoza* of various dates. Also A. Nove, 'Incentives for peasants and admini-strators', in *Soviet Agricultural and Peasant Affairs*, (ed. Laird), (Univ. of Kansas, 1964).

divided into the amount available for distribution, in money and in kind. The resultant sum determines the value of each *trudoden*. Thus this might be 1 rouble in cash, 1 kilogram of grain and 1 kilogram of potatoes (or some very different amounts, depending on the *kolkhoz* and the results of the given year). A peasant who had recorded 250 *trudodni* in the given year would then receive 250 roubles in cash, and 250 kilograms of grain and of potatoes. In most *kolkhozy* until recent years, distribution took place at the end of the year, so that, while they were working, the peasants had no idea of the value of the *trudodni* they were earning. However, since 1953 there was an increasing trend towards more or less regular 'advances' (payments on account) throughout the year, with a final adjustment when the year's accounts are made up. The difficulty has been that some farms are too poor, and in particular had no cash in hand until after the harvest.

The actual amounts paid out in *trudodni* have varied greatly not only between *kolkhozy* but also by geographical areas, due partly to the effects of price policy. Even after the reforms of 1953, these disparities continued. For example, in the three years 1954-56, if the USSR average is taken as 100, payments for a day's work to *kolkhoz* peasants were 148 in Kazakhstan, 143 in West Siberia, 138 in Uzbekistan, but only 60 in the 'central non-black-earth region', of which Moscow is the centre.[1] This must be borne in mind when assessing the significance of all-union averages which will be cited below, since in no other sector of the Soviet economy are there such enormous differences in payment for the same amount of work.

The cash element in *trudodni* pay may be see from the following table:

Old Roubles per trudoden		*Millions of trudodni recorded, USSR*	
1952	*1956*	*1952*	*1956*
1·40	3·80	8,847	11,103

Sources: M. Osad'ko: *Vop. ekon.*, No. 2/1959, p. 83.
N.Kh. 1956, p. 141.

The in-kind element has been more important than cash during most of the above period. As late as in 1956, distributions in kind were half of the total.[2]

It is noteworthy that the state had no *direct* means of determining the amounts which *kolkhozy* pay to peasants. Nor can it decide the amount which peasants earn by *sales in the free market*, which for

[1] A. Teryaeva, in *Vop. ekon.*, No. 1/1959, p. 110. See also examples cited on p. 190, below.
[2] T. Zaslavskaya, in *Vop. ekon.*, No. 2/1959, p. 113.

many years was by far their most important source of cash.[1] The organs of the state do, of course, estimate the likely levels of rural incomes, but they do not have direct power to determine what they should be.

Principally because of the financial burden of the purchase and running costs of the MTS machinery, *kolkhoz* peasants' incomes appear to have fallen in and after 1958. Statistics ceased to be published for the USSR as a whole, but the following figures cited by Soviet authors show the decline to have been considerable in many areas:

Value of cash and kind per working day in 1960, 1957 = 100

Ukraine	82
Belorussia	89
Uzbekistan	83
Georgia	86
Moldavia	71
Rostov oblast'	85

Sources: V. Khlebnikov, *Vop. ekon.*, No. 7/1962, p. 50 and E. Kapustin, *Ekon. gaz.*, April 9, 1962, p. 10.

This downward trend coincided with Khrushchev's policy of restricting the peasants' private livestock, and all this must have been resented by the peasants. Khrushchev's successors at once admitted the 'neglect of peasant material self-interest', and reversed the policy. After years of inconclusive discussion (the question had been publicly mooted at least in 1956), it was decided to eliminate the *trudoden* and to replace it by payments based on the rate for the job in *sovkhozy*, and, as set out in chapter 1, to give peasant pay a priority claim on the revenue of the farm. We still do not know if this quite fundamental reform is in full operation. Collective payments have risen sharply, the total in 1965 being 88% above the average for 1959-60, and it rose by a further 16% in 1966.[2]

Calculations of the total consumption of peasant families are in any case a hazardous undertaking. There is the income in cash and kind for collective work, plus occasional bonuses in kind (such as milk for milkmaids), together with the very important source of foodstuffs from the private plots and of cash from sales in the free market. In addition, many peasants work for part of the year for state enterprises, and many households contain one or more state-

---

[1] For example, in 1952 total cash distributions of *trudodni* amounted to 12·4 milliard roubles, while free market turnover in urban areas alone was worth 53·7 milliards, of which 35-40 must have consisted of peasant sales.

[2] I.Suslov, *Ekonomicheskie problemy razvitiya kolkhozov*, Moscow 1967, p. 64.

employed person whose income is pooled with the rest of the family's.

Hours of work on *kolkhozy* have for years been the subject of severe criticism, particularly of milkmaids, who work to a quite intolerable schedule, 3.45 a.m. to 9.45 p.m., (with breaks in between, but disruptive of normal life), and yet shift work is still the exception rather than the rule.[1]

TRADE UNIONS

Soviet trade unions are organized on an 'industrial' basis, covering all grades, including managers, in the given branch of the economy. The structure of the unions is nominally democratic, with elections of officials and the all-union central council (AUCCTU) elected at national conferences. However, the Communist Party is in full control at all levels, and indeed there was only one national conference to elect the AUCCTU between 1932 and 1954. This central body must be regarded as a quasi-governmental labour agency, which is charged with administering the social insurance fund, and with taking such action as will mobilize the workers in the struggle to fulfil output plans and other policies of the party and the government. At local level, trade union officials are supposed to reconcile these essentially official functions with the task of protecting workers from abuses on the part of the management. Collective agreements between the management and the union branch generally specify a number of measures concerned with welfare and amenities, as well as including undertakings on behalf of the workers to work harder and better, but they do not determine wage rates.[2] With the object of stimulating output, the unions endeavour to organize various forms of 'socialist competition' between workshops, groups and individuals. Subject to the over-riding general aim of increasing production and fulfilling the plan, union officials on the spot are concerned with planned piece-rates and thereby have a hand in deciding how much is in fact earned by the workers, even though they have no power to negotiate about basic rates. The local branch plays an important role in the settlement of disputes between individual workers and the management (e.g. over grading, demotion, bonus entitlements, allegedly illegal dismissals, etc.), participating on equal terms in the 'conflicts commissions' which, in enterprises, settle such disputes. If the trade union and the management fail to agree in the conflicts

[1] L. Shinkarev, *Ekon. gaz.*, No. 15/1967, p. 32.
[2] Collective agreements were revived in 1954, after a prolonged period of disuse.

commission, the matter is referred to the *trade union* for final decision.[1]

During the Stalin era, the task of mobilizing the workers was heavily emphasized at all levels, and the representational and protective tasks of trade unions took very much a second place. This was justified by arguments such as there being no need to protect the workers against the workers' state. The highly unpopular decrees of 1940, which forbade change of employment without permission and introduced severe penalties for lateness and absenteeism, were stated in the preamble to have been promulgated at the request of the AUCCTU. The trade union branch was directly concerned with the unpopular task of compelling everyone to subscribe to the virtually compulsory but nominally voluntary state bonds. Eventually, things reached a stage which proved intolerable to the government itself. There were too many instances of failure on the part of local trade unions to defend their members against local abuses, breaches of protective legislation were all too common, the so-called 'socialist competitions' organized by the unions frequently remained on paper; the unions, in other words, were failing to mobilize because, *inter alia*, they were not protecting the members and were not felt by their members to represent them. A sizeable crop of articles, expressing dissatisfaction with the trade unions, appeared in the years following Stalin's death, and these culminated in the decisions of the December, 1957, plenum of the central committee, which sought to stimulate the local unions to take their protective tasks more seriously, while re-emphasizing their role as 'mobilizers' of the workers and increasing their functions within enterprises, both directly and through the 'permanent production councils' in which they play a major role.

The argument that Soviet trade unions are not trade unions at all is often heard in discussions in the west. It is clear enough that they are not independent of state or Party, and that their purpose is to organize the workers for the carrying out of state and party policy. Against this, it is sometimes argued that, under Soviet conditions, it is unreasonable to expect conflicts between the managers and the labour force, because the managers are also employees of the state (and, indeed, members of the same union), and/or that the unions do in fact have powers to protect members against arbitrary acts or

[1] By decree of the praesidium of the Supreme Soviet, January 31, 1957. For details, see I. Dvornikov and V. Nikitinski, *Novyi poryadok rassmotreniya trudovykh sporov* (Moscow, 1957). If worker or management considers the decisions contrary to law, they can appeal to the courts.

neglect on the part of the management. Indeed, the powers are there and are impressive. The difficulty, however, is that the unions' task as a 'transmission belt' of party economic policies is often hard to reconcile with their 'protective' duties *vis-à-vis* their members, and, owing to the strong element of party control, in any conflict of loyalties the officials respond first and foremost to those above them, who in fact appoint them or arrange their 'elections', rather than to the membership. Thus if compulsory overtime or rest-day working is resorted to as a means of hastening plan fulfilment, it is in the highest degree unlikely that the union branch would fail to back the management, whatever the feelings of the members. In other words, in assessing the economic forces at work in the Soviet Union, it would be misleading to view the unions as any kind of independent pressure group, even though action is commonly taken by the local branch to ensure that, for example, an expectant mother receives the paid vacation to which the laws entitle her, or a grade IV carpenter is not unjustifiably demoted, though even here the union often neglects its duties.[1]

The trade unions administer the social insurance funds, and benefits to members are much higher than to non-members, which helps to explain why the vast majority of those eligible are members of their unions. *Kolkhoz* peasants have no trade unions and receive no social insurance benefits from state sources; the *kolkhozy* have to make their own arrangements to succour their members in distress. The one exception dates from 1965: old age pensions are paid to *kolkhoz* peasants, out of a fund to which both the state budget and the *kolkhoz* contributes. Social services as such are outside the scope of this book, but the reader will hardly need reminding of their great importance in peoples' lives and of the need to take them into account in any comparison of living standards.

THE PRICE SYSTEM: WHOLESALE PRICES

It is necessary to distinguish between the following principal categories of prices for industrial products:

(a) *Factory wholesale prices* (*optovaya tsena predpriyatiya*), being the transfer prices at which enterprises dispose of their products to wholesalers, exclusive of any turnover tax payable.

---

[1] Often the failures of the unions are corrected by the courts, especially in cases of unjustified dismissal in which the union branch supported the management. For two of many examples, see *Byulleten Verkhovnovo Suda SSSR*, No. 2/1960, pp. 1, 3. In one area, roughly half of all cases of appeal against dismissal were upheld by the courts (see *Sovetskaya Yustitsiya*, No. 5/1964).

(b) *Industry wholesale prices* (*optovaya tsena promyshlennosti*), these are prices at which goods are transferred to users outside the given industry, and include turnover tax when this is payable. This category is sometimes known as *otpusknaya tsena*, or 'release price'.

Agricultural prices, including those applicable to agricultural raw materials used in industry, and also some prices charged for industrial products to agricultural producers, have had a very different history and will require separate treatment.

Factory wholesale prices

Until 1957, decisions on prices were highly centralized. Virtually no price could be altered without the sanction of the all-union government; the industrial ministry, Gosplan and the Ministry of Finance were those principally concerned, together with the Ministry of Internal Trade if the commodity in question was a consumers' good. Prices for new products had also to receive the sanction of the centre, and, with many administrative organs involved, there was often excessive delay.

After the 1957 reforms, there was a tendency towards a somewhat lesser degree of centralization, culminating in a decision of the Council of Ministers on May 30, 1958. The new procedures are as follows. The Council of Ministers is responsible for general decisions on price policy. Actual prices for a list of key products ('the most important varieties of industrial production') are fixed or confirmed by the all-union Gosplan, acting as the executant of government price policy. Most other prices are decided by the republican governments, except that *oblast'* soviets confirm wholesale prices for small-scale local industry which is under their control. *Sovnarkhozy* had few powers in this field. They determined the prices at which 'their' enterprises delivered materials or semi-manufactures to one another, but only if 'for these products there are no prices which have been confirmed through the usual channels'. They also determined, within narrow limits, temporary prices of new products, these prices being based either on the existing price of analogous products, or on cost plus 5 per cent. Ministries have these powers since 1965. Enterprises and *obyedineniya* also have acquired some ill-defined powers to vary prices by agreement with the customer if some special variety of product, or an item of higher quality, is required. However, even temporary prices for 'major products' are the responsibility of the all-union Gosplan. The directors of enterprises still have only very limited freedom in deciding the selling price of their products, save for goods and services provided by the enterprise for its own internal needs, and also for components or instruments made to special order for which no prices exist, though this latter case is again subject to a limit of cost plus 5 per cent.[1] However, enterprises doubtless play some role in suggesting new or changed prices to the authorities above them.

General principles underlying price policy were considered by a 'committee of the praesidium of the council of ministers on prices', the existence of which has been mentioned in some Soviet publications.[2] This is now entitled the State Committee on Prices, and attached to Gosplan.

Neglecting the exceptions for the present, let us examine the principles on which the government has fixed or approved the prices at which enterprises dispose of their products. These are supposed to be based on the *average cost of production* of all enterprises producing the commodity in question, plus a profit margin. For decades this profit margin was defined in textbooks as being '3-5 per cent', the percentages being related to cost. In fact there was a steady increase in average profit rates, until in July 1967 a new set of prices allowed for a rate of profit out of which capital and other fixed charges could be paid. Profits are now, as already mentioned, computed in relation to capital. The net effect of the new policy was, of course, to push average wholesale prices up.

The other important reason for the price revision of 1967 was that no systematic price changes had been made since 1955, and as a result there grew up extremely wide variations in profitability, as well as many losses. Thus in 1965 iron ore prices covered only 75 per cent of costs, the coal industry made a loss of 16 per cent on costs and instrument-making a 60 per cent profit.[3] In the same year, the Ministry of Ferrous Metallurgy made a profit of 7 per cent but, one-third of its enterprises were expected (planned) to make a loss.[4] Because prices were too close to average costs, but above all owing to the tendency of planners to ignore costs and to require production of various items under unfavourable conditions, cost and profit variations were often extremely wide. Thus in the Sverdlovsk area alone the 'profitability' of ferrous metallurgy enterprises varied from + 15 per cent to −25 per cent, in ore mining from +27 per cent to −40 per cent, in building materials from +33 per cent to −55 per cent, and so on.[5] The 1967 price revision eliminated many anomalies.

[1] This account is taken from Rumyantsev, op. cit., pp. 367-70.
[2] A. Volin, *Kommunist*, No. 3/1959, p. 56, and also Turetski, op. cit., p. 157.
[3] Editorial in *Plan. khoz.*, No. 7/1967, p. 13.
[4] Turetski, *op. cit.*, p. 79.
[5] Turetski, *op. cit.*, p. 80.

Thus prices of coal rose by 78 per cent, of oil and iron ore by over 100 per cent, pig iron by 70 per cent, while some high-profit machinery had its prices cut. Thus instruments now cost about 12 per cent less. But electricity (except for agriculture and for domestic consumers) went up by 22 per cent, gas for industry by 51 per cent, non-ferrous metals by 22 per cent on average (though lead was reduced), fertiliser by 34 per cent, timber by 26-33 per cent, most building materials by amounts varying from 13 to 30 per cent, and so on. Surprisingly, the net effect of all this is said to be a rise of heavy industry (including machinery) by only 15 per cent, of all industrial prices by only 8 per cent.[2] The logic of this, and its consistency with other parts of the economic reform now in progress, will be further discussed in chapter 8.

Unfortunately it proved impossible to be wholly logical, even on the officially-approved basis. Thus the coal industry, despite the big increase in prices, will only have a profit rate (on capital) of 8 per cent and still not be able to pay the 'normal' charge of 6 per cent on its capital. Also political decisions were taken to hold retail prices steady, and not to allow any increase in prices of agricultural machinery. This limited the scope of the reform, which none the less did eliminate many anomalies and established new principles by accepting the capital charge (and rental payments) as part of the price structure.

In some instances, where there are very large disparities in natural conditions, a single selling price to users is combined with differential prices to producers. In the USSR, this system was applied for many years in the oil industry. These are known as 'accounting prices' (raschyotnye tseny). Under the 1967 price reform, however, oil prices have been drastically revised. One reason for the big increase (by nearly 130 per cent) is the inclusion of costs of geological surveying. Prices, furthermore, are now based on what is described as 'average-sized enterprises under worse-than-average conditions'. Only a very few exceptionally high-cost fields will still fail to cover costs. This is an approach to the marginal price concept. As far as can be determined, the oil users will continue to pay regardless of the source of the oil, and the better-situated, lower-cost oilfields will pay 'rent' to the budget, an amount estimated at 600 million roubles. Iron ore, too, will be subject to substantial rental payments. On the other hand, coal prices vary by basins, so that each basin makes a profit. Thus Donets coal is 17·49, Kuzbas coal 10·30 roubles per ton. Since Moscow basin coal is expensive, it is priced much higher (in terms of

[2] *Ekon. gaz.* No. 27/1967, p. 10; and *Plan. khoz.*, No. 7/1967, p. 15 ff.

calorific value) than Donets coal, even after allowing for transport costs to Moscow.[1]

After 1939, and especially in post-war years, most Soviet wholesale prices were fixed 'delivered to station of destination'. They, therefore, include an allowance for average cost of transport. Delivery prices are generally, but not always, differentiated by zones, and this differentiation does to some extent take transport costs into account; thus, for instance, the wholesale price of cloth or sulphuric acid delivered in north-east Siberia is higher than in the Ukraine. However, *any* supplier to north-east Siberia, be he located in central Siberia or in Leningrad, is entitled to charge only the one price laid down for the zone to which the goods are being delivered. This is logical under Soviet conditions, in that the recipient enterprise generally has its supplier designated in the supply plan, and its costs ought not to be adversely affected by the remoteness or otherwise of the supplier so designated. The supplying enterprise, or *sbyt* organization, in those cases in which it can influence the supply plan or the negotiation of contracts, is naturally interested in minimizing its transport costs, but the system does not adequately penalize the recipient enterprise for any initiatives which result in unnecessarily long hauls. There has been a shift towards 'price at station of despatch', which in the middle of 1967 applied to 60% of all tonnage transported, and included coal, ore, metals, most building materials, equipment, fertiliser. Prices 'delivered at station of destination' still apply to oil, timber, cement and some other products.[3]

The history of Soviet prices shows frequent departures from any coherent system or logic. In 1929-35 there was a sharp (and quite unplanned) increase in costs, but the government sought to maintain prices of basic materials and capital goods at unchanged levels, so that very large subsidies became necessary, with prices far below average costs. A sharp price rise in 1936 re-established a more logical relationship between costs and prices. Shortly before the war, both rose again. Then there was again an effort to keep prices of basic materials steady, in the face of a very large rise in costs due to the war and its aftermath. The result was that very large subsidies were again paid, and the price increase, when it came in 1949, was substantial. Thus a ton of Donets coal of type 'T' was 'worth' 34·43 roubles from 1939 to 1949, and was then increased at one bound to 91·83 roubles.[2] Since 1949, there have been several general price

[1] *Ekon. gaz.*, No. 25/1967, pp. 10-11; and No. 27/1967, p. 10, and *Plan. khoz.*, No. 7/1967, p. 15.

[2] Ibid., p. 123. Many other examples may be found in this and other Soviet sources. See also N. Jasny, *The Soviet Price System* (Stanford, 1950).

[3] B. Shafirkin, *Vop. ekon.*, No. 8/1967, p. 41.

reductions: in 1950, 1952 and 1955. But even when they were first in operation, the 1955 prices did not ensure anything like an equal profitability as between different industries, even different heavy industries: zinc ore was sold at an average loss of 19·5 per cent of costs, steel castings at a profit of 27 per cent.[1] Coal and timber was sold at a loss, and the loss increased as costs (principally labour costs) rose. Timber prices were raised, but coal prices remained unaltered until 1967, though, as we have seen, losses were very high. And the 1967 reform, though introducing new principles and a greater degree of logic, still regards cost-plus as a proper basis for pricing, relating the 'plus' to capital instead of costs, but still inconsistently: profits so defined are higher in light than heavy industries, lower-than-average in the coal industry, prices for farm equipment are 'frozen', retail prices are largely 'frozen' too.

It seems clear, therefore, that the practice of price determination is not easily reducible to any set of principles at all, and that this must affect the working of 'economic accounting' at enterprise level. To make things even less logical, there have been spasmodic efforts to relate prices of some interchangeable products to one another, and of some scarce products to their scarcity. An example of the latter is copper and some other non-ferrous metals,[2] while turnover tax on gas, electricity and oil is justified by the need to bring their prices into some undefined relationship with coal and with one another.

There have also been some instances of the use of what can only be called planners' shadow prices, different from those actually charged, which are designed to discourage the use of some particularly scarce material. Thus, in making investment choices planners were at one time using a 'co-efficient of scarcity' (*koeffitsient defitsitnosti*) for copper which increased its price ten to fifteen-fold.[3]

Before leaving the question of prices at enterprise level, it is necessary to mention the vexed problem of 'unchanged prices', used for comparisons over time. For many years—for some purposes until 1949—these were so-called 1926-27 prices, either those actually existing in that year or (for new products or models) nominal prices deemed to be those of 1926-27. Enterprises' plans were expressed in these 1926-27 prices, and, since the real prices were very different, a large disparity developed between planning prices and those in which the current financial accounts of the enterprise were conducted. The 1926-27 basis was finally abandoned in 1950, though

[1] A. Bachurin, *Finansy SSSR*, No. 1, 1960, p. 78.
[2] Referred to by V. Novozhilov in *Primeneniye matematiki v ekonomicheskikh issledovaniyakh* (Nemchinov, ed., Moscow, 1959), p. 43.
[3] A. Vaag and S. Zakharov: *Metody ekonomicheskoi otsenki v energetike* (Moscow, 1962), p. 9.

certain statistical consequences (growth indices, for instance) are still with us, as will be shown in the Appendix.

Building work has been valued on a different basis. The cost-schedules (*smety*) were expressed in 1936 prices, 1946 prices, then in 1950 prices, and, finally, in 1955 prices. Since actual costs reflected whatever were the current prices of the given year, there was generally some disparity between 'cost-schedule costs' (*smetnaya stoimost'*), in which investment statistics were frequently given, and actual cost. During the fifth five-year plan (1951-55), when prices were falling, actual costs were below the *smety*, and so the investment statistics of the period showed large 'economies', which somewhat illogically were included in the enterprise-financed portion of investment in the figures published at the time.

Wholesale prices of industry

These may be identical with factory wholesale prices, unless, firstly, there is a separate wholesaling organization through which sales to other enterprises are made, and which is entitled to add a wholesalers' margin to the factory wholesale price; and, secondly, because turnover tax may be payable. The latter is charged on a wide range of consumers' goods, and also on oil, gas and electricity.

In the case of many kinds of commodities which are used both by citizens and by state enterprises, one frequently finds partial or complete exemption from turnover tax for state enterprises, and therefore there emerge two wholesale prices of industry, which depend on the use to which the given consignment is to be put. Some examples are salt, many kinds of building materials, automobiles, oil products. *Kolkhozy* had to pay retail prices for many goods, inclusive of a sizeable element of tax. To take a particularly striking example, early in 1958 *sovkhozy* and other state enterprises paid 13,769 old roubles for a ZIL-150 lorry; a *kolkhoz* was charged 37,000 roubles.[1] The level of turnover tax on consumers' goods is inextricably mixed up with the retail price system; thus, in many cases in which turnover tax is calculated by 'difference' (page 113, above), the wholesale price of industry is equal to the state-fixed retail price less the retail margin, and is not actually listed anywhere as such.

THE PRICE SYSTEM: RETAIL PRICES

Except in periods of rationing (1929-34, 1941-47), retail prices are fixed so as to clear the market of available supplies save where

---

[1] Turetski, op. cit., p. 239. After 1958, *all* farms were charged the same price for lorries, tractors and fuel, intermediate between those previously existing.

there is some social reason for goods to be sold dear (e.g. vodka) or cheap (e.g. children's clothes). The total value of goods and services available should match the level of disposable personal incomes, and price increases or price cuts should follow if calculation shows them to be necessary. This general policy has not been consistently followed, the 'deviation' being usually in the direction of selling too cheaply, relatively to personal incomes (which tend to exceed plan), as may be seen from the prevalence of queues. Indeed, Stalin gave queues a certain *rationale* by suggesting that demand should exceed supply, so as to provide a spur for increasing production. There is a reluctance to make frequent changes in retail prices, and such changes are treated as a political matter, for the top leadership to decide. In the last years of Stalin's life and the period of Malenkov's premiership, it was considered politically expendient to announce price cuts every spring. In the period 1947-50 this had a logical basis; 1947 prices were extremely high, reflecting acute post-war shortages, and the big increase in goods available for sale certainly outpaced the rise in expendable incomes. However, in the next few years, i.e. the last two springs of Stalin's life and the only two springs of Malenkov's premiership, prices were reduced without adequate reason, with the result that shortages and queues developed. The surest indicator of unjustified cuts in food prices was a growing disparity between official and free-market prices, which can be illustrated by the following figures. Since in the base year (1950) market

	1950	1952	1953	1955
State food prices (1950 = 100) ..	100	87	78.5	74
Free market prices (1950 = 100)	100	100	93	107

Source: *Sovetskaya torgovlya* (Moscow, 1957), pp. 131 and 182.

prices were already above state prices, the disparity may well have been greater still.

The difference between the retail price, orientated at least in principle towards supply-and-demand equilibrium, and the costs of production and handling plus profit margin, is equal to turnover tax. This tax has been considered in chapter 3, where it was shown that in large measure the tax is a consequence rather than a cause of the retail price level. However, its impact on particular commodities does reflect state and price policy. Thus it was the practice for many years to levy a low tax on many kinds of consumer durables, even though they were very scarce. Motor cars, television sets, sewing machines, were systematically underpriced, despite long waiting lists and queues, while textiles and many kinds of foodstuffs bore substantial tax burdens.[1] Perhaps there is an element of irrational traditionalism in tax and price policy in the USSR; certainly no student of British purchase tax would be surprised.

Because differential rates of turnover tax in the USSR 'absorb' the differences between costs and retail prices, and because the retail margin is also a fixed magnitude, the producing and trading enterprises derive no benefit from providing more commodities with relatively very high scarcity prices; though these could act as a signal to the planning organs to direct investment resources into these branches, but so far this has not been the case, in practice or even in theory. Much more will be said of this in chapter 6.

Retail prices for key commodities are the responsibility of the central government and must be confirmed by Gosplan. Until 1957 detailed price lists on a very wide range of commodities, comprising nearly all retail trade, were issued centrally by the Ministry of Internal Trade. However, many commodities, amounting in aggregate to 45 per cent of total turnover, are now priced by republican governments, though complaints about excessive disparities have led to some effort to maintain coherence in policy in respect of this 45 per cent, the more so as in some instances the retail price indirectly determines the factory wholesale price (e.g. for furniture, on which no turnover tax is charged). Key commodities, including those with a large element of turnover tax in the price, remain in the province of the central government.

Prices vary by geographical zones, and were on average about 5 per cent higher in villages than in towns by reason of a 'rural addition' (*sel'skaya nadbavka*) which was justified by reason of the higher costs of rural distribution (for some commodities the difference was larger, for others it did not exist.)[2] In 1965, as part of the general policy of improving the relative position of the rural population, it was decided to eliminate the 'rural addition'.

Perhaps the biggest single 'irrationality' in retail pricing at present arises from the refusal to allow an increase in prices of meat and some dairy products, despite the fact that demand is rising and that the prices now paid to the producers make a large subsidy necessary. But

---

[1] Some other kinds of consumer durables, such as, in recent years, cameras and radios, pay little tax, but here the reason is simply that these goods are hard to sell even at present prices, and hire purchase was introduced in 1959 to keep stocks of these and some other goods moving. Retail prices of motor cars were greatly increased in 1959.

[2] Turetski, op. cit., p. 469. The average 'addition' was 7 per cent for those goods for which an addition is made.

this is only the most striking example of the impact of political considerations on retail prices.

THE PRICE SYSTEM: AGRICULTURAL PRICES

It is important to note that agricultural prices affect income distribution in ways in which other prices do not. For example, the trebling of the price of coal in 1949 did not change the income of anyone engaged in the production of coal, since wages and salaries were, when necessary, met out of a state subsidy. However, the incomes of collective farms and of peasants depended, and still depend, on the prices at which their produce is sold. Thus the question of agricultural prices is a matter affecting the distribution of income between town and country, and thus has been one of the very highest political importance, especially as it has a direct bearing on policy questions towards peasants as a class, and also on the problems of accumulation.

In the NEP period, after a very few years of genuinely free sales at free prices, the state intervened as early as 1924-25 in an effort to stabilize a grain price below the equilibrium level, though prices of many other farm products remained more or less free from control. This contributed to a grain collection crisis in 1927-28, when the government resorted to punitive measures against alleged grain hoarders, which was a foretaste of the even more drastic measures of the following years, which established collective farms.

Once these had been established, the state was able to insist on compulsory deliveries at prices approximating to those which it had fixed in the 'twenties, despite a very large increase in all other prices. Compulsory delivery prices for grain and almost all staple food products changed little until 1953.[1] Since the *kolkhozy* and peasants had to transport the produce to the state collecting point, and since in many cases the transport costs alone exceeded the 'price' paid, the element of sale was in reality absent: these were confiscatory prices, or a species of hardly-disguised tax in kind. Khrushchev gave an example to the central committee plenum of December, 1958: before 1953, potatoes delivered compulsorily by *kolkhozy* were 'paid' for at a price of 3 kopecks per kilo or less, which meant, allowing for transport costs, that the *kolkhozy* received less than nothing. An example concerning grain has been cited earlier (page 113), but here is another: in 1948, the wholesale price of 100 kilograms of rye

[1] See in particular an article by M. Moiseyev, *Vop. ekon.*, No. 7/1958, and also Malafeyev, op. cit.

was 335 roubles,[1] yet the *kolkhozy* received for compulsory deliveries a price of around 7 or 8 roubles, or a few per cent more than in 1928; however, a kilogram of rye bread cost 8 kopecks in 1928, 2·70 roubles in 1948.

By contrast, prices for certain industrial crops were much more favourable. Thus in 1935 raw cotton prices were increased three-and-a-half to four fold, and by 1952 they were ten times the level of 1928.[2]

For sales over and above the compulsory delivery quota (or, in the case of industrial crops, above the contracted amount), higher prices were paid. State policy with regard to these prices showed frequent variations, resulting in a bewildering multiplicity of prices. For example, sometimes these prices were maxima, sometimes they were definitive. Sometimes they were so little above the compulsory procurement prices as to provide no inducement to sell; this was true of grain, so that 'whereas between 1937 and 1945 [over quota] sales were insignificant, between 1947 and 1953 they did not in practice take place at all'.[3]

A full account of the entire system of agricultural prices and its many changes down to 1958 would fill a book. The actual prices were greatly increased in the period 1953-55, but the principles remained unaltered: that a quota of produce was to be delivered at relatively low prices, and amounts in addition to the quota were sold at higher, often very much higher, prices, subject to some regional variations. The following will illustrate the pattern; all the examples relate to the period 1956-58.

(old Roubles per centner = 100 kilograms)

	Quota price	Over quota price
Rye, central zone	30	85
Soft wheat, south-centre	28	92
Beef, all areas	150	380–410
Flax fibre (USSR average)	566	1,451

Source: Turetski, op. cit., pp. 229, 263, 265.

There were also still higher prices paid by consumer-co-operatives for sales on commission (page 53, above), and, finally, free-market prices.

To make things more complicated still, a confused and illogical series of measures provided for sales of some commodities to *kolkhozy* at advantageous prices, conditional upon their delivering

[1] A. Suchkov, *Dokhody gosudarstvennovo byudzheta SSSR* (Moscow, 1949). The figures relate to zone II, which includes central Russia.
[2] Malafeyev, op. cit., p. 267.
[3] Ibid., p. 226.

certain farm products to the state. For instance, bread grain, fodder, vegetable oil and sugar were made available, on a *quid pro quo* basis, to *kolkhozy* specializing on certain crops (e.g. on cotton, flax, vegetables), at well below retail prices. The object was to encourage specialization. In some instances, especially in years of acute short-age, *kolkhozy* which made over-quota deliveries were favoured by being given priority in acquiring a list of scarce commodities at the official price. Such transactions were known as *vstrechnaya pro-dazha*, or counterpart sales.

This whole system came under review in 1958. Its weaknesses were as follows.

Firstly, the existence of multiple prices confused all calculations. The success or failure of a farm in increasing its total production, or the rationality of its choice as to what to produce, depended de-cisively on the price basis chosen for the calculation (and what allow-ance could or should be made for the counterpart sales described above?).

Secondly, the prices were not rationally related to one another or to costs. The compulsory-procurement prices retained an element of taxation, while the over-quota prices were historic accidents which often encouraged the wrong disposal of resources. Thus, for in-stance, it was calculated that farms were reluctant to feed potatoes to pigs, because the relative prices of pork and potatoes made it far more profitable to sell the potatoes. Fodder was dear relatively to bread at retail prices, and it paid peasants to buy bread in the shops to feed their private livestock. A long list of anomalies could be, and was, drawn up.[1]

Thirdly, the principle of two or more prices, with a large gap be-tween them, produced economically absurd results. It meant that a farm with a poor crop and low productivity, for whatever reason, was paid less per unit of product than a high-yielding farm was paid. This can readily be illustrated using the prices cited above. Imagine two farms, A and B, both with a delivery quota of 1,000 tons of rye. A had a saleable surplus of 2,000 tons, B of only 1,200 tons. The total receipts would be:

Farm A: 1,000 tons @ 300+1,000 tons @ 850 = 1,150,000 roubles.
Farm B: 1,000 tons @ 300 + 200 tons @ 850 =   470,000 roubles.

The average price in farm A would therefore be 575 roubles per ton (57·50 roubles per centner), and in farm B it would be only 392

---

[1] Many examples were given in an article by M. Terentiev, in *Vop. ekon.*, No. 3/1958.

roubles (39·20 roubles per centner). Similar results could be obtained for all major varieties of farm produce, whether food or industrial crops. This provided disproportionate encouragement to the already successful farm, and depressed the unsuccessful. Undoubtedly these price arrangements contributed to the very wide disparity of income as between *kolkhozy*, especially if one bears in mind that surpluses could also be sold at still higher prices in the free market by those farms which had surpluses to sell. The situation was illogical not merely as between farms, but also on a national scale, since this multiple price system ensured that average prices for the USSR as a whole would be higher in a good harvest year than in a poor year, i.e. that prices would be lower in the event of scarcity. For example, although prices were unchanged, the *average* price at which the state bought grain from *kolkhozy* was about 3 per cent lower in 1957 than in 1956, although the harvest was almost 18 per cent lower (*Sel. Khoz.* 1960, pp. 27, 117), which was indeed topsy-turvy economics, explicable only by the long-ingrained habit of burdening *kolkhozy* and peasants with a semi-disguised tax through deliveries at low prices.

This habit, curiously, was allowed to affect the prices paid to state farms. Until 1940, they received only the low 'quota' prices paid to *kolkhozy* and peasants, and therefore received large subsidies. In 1940 there was an increase of 40 per cent, but this still left income far below costs, so subsidies continued. An upward price revision in 1954,[1] and again in 1956, greatly reduced subsidies. State farm delivery prices were varied by zones, but there was no multiple price system for them.[2]

In 1958, the multiple price system for *kolkhozy* and peasants was scrapped, and price relativities were reviewed. The state now bought at a single price for every product, with regional variations. For grain, this price was fixed a little below the former over quota price, but above the average actually paid in past years: the average for all grains was to be 74 old roubles per centner, against a national average 'compulsory' price of 25 and an over-quota price of 80-85 roubles. However, in any assessment of the impact of this new price, one must bear in mind the large amount of grain formerly handed over in payments in kind for the services of MTS, and now sold at this price following the absorption of the MTS by the *kolkhozy* (see page 59, above). Prices of meat were very sharply raised above even

[1] I. Novikov, in *Vop. ekon.*, No. 9/1954, pp. 31-4, gives full particulars. Until 1954, he says, the subsidy was the 'basic source of revenue' of state-farms.
[2] See V. Semyonov, *Finansy SSSR*, No. 1/1956, p. 35.

the over-quota prices of the past, while potatoes and some industrial crops were treated much less favourably. It was announced that the new prices would be long-term averages, and that they would be raised in poor harvest years and lowered when there is abundance.[1] However, already in December, 1959, at the central committee plenum, numerous powerful voices were raised in favour of cutting them. In fact, without publicity, prices were lowered. Thus instead of the promised 74 old roubles per centner, prices of grain in fact averaged 62 old roubles in the course of the next few years.[2] This contributed to the decline in peasant incomes, referred to earlier. The prices fixed in 1958 were below costs, in both *sovkhozy* and *kolkhozy*, in the case of meat and dairy produce, and this at a time when the farms were under heavy pressure to expand their livestock. In the spring of 1962 purchase prices for meat were substantially increased, and milk prices were raised. Further increases in prices of a number of products were announced in 1963-64, and another and larger price rise followed in 1965. The new prices were rather more logically interrelated, and the regional variations were rather closer to the estimated differences in costs (these differences are discussed in chapter 6, below). The new prices are associated with delivery quotas fixed for six years ahead, and, in the case of grain, there is a return to two-level prices: thus for over-quota sales will be at prices 50 per cent higher, though the arguments against multiple prices seem to be as valid in and after 1965 as they were in 1958.

The wholesale prices of agricultural materials supplied to industry have also had an odd history. Before 1953, the wholesale prices included a very large element of turnover tax, as has already been noted, and the farm price increases of 1953 and subsequent years did not, with minor exceptions, lead to any increase in retail prices, but were 'absorbed' in turnover tax reductions. The multiple price system greatly complicated the accounts of the procurement organizations, which found themselves paying a variety of prices for the same products, while selling to processing factories at one price, and also sometimes to retail stores at another price, and to some users (e.g. specialized *kolkhozy* under the above-mentioned counterpart arrangements) at yet another price. For purposes of assessing turnover tax payments, and for keeping the costs of user enterprises

---

[1] For details of the prices fixed in 1958, see *Pravda*, July 1, 1958.
[2] This figure is given by Khlebnikov, op. cit., p. 53; Malafeyev, op. cit., p. 294, gives 61 roubles for 1960. The reduction was confirmed by Matskevich, op. cit.

on an even keel, it became customary to assume that all produce had been procured at the 'quota' price, to pay turnover tax on this basis, and then to receive a compensatory payment from the budget in respect of higher prices actually paid. This is the item of budgetary expenditure mentioned on page 115, above. The result was to inflate turnover tax revenues, and also artificially to reduce the costs of the food-processing industry by providing 'subsidized' materials, though the subsidy at this period was not real. In 1955, there was some readjustment of wholesale prices which partially eliminated this purely accounting subsidy, with the result that costs in the food industry showed an upward jump.[1]

The 1958 price reform led to a complete overhaul of this price structure. In the case of a number of products turnover tax is no longer significant, because there is little or no difference between the price paid to the farms and the retail price, after allowance is made for handling costs. There is a considerable (but unfortunately unknown) element of tax within the prices of grain, flour and sugar. But already as from 1958 one had an odd paradox: while procurement prices of meat and dairy products were too low to cover costs of production on farms, the level of retail prices necessitated a subsidy. When procurement prices were increased in 1962, retail prices were raised in like proportion. But no increase in retail prices occurred when a further rise in procurement prices was decreed in 1965. In fact it is an open question whether, on balance, turnover tax revenue derived indirectly from agriculture is larger than the subsidies now paid. In any event, the contrast with Stalin's policy is striking.

Prices paid to *sovkhozy* have tended to be lower than to *kolkhozy*: thus in West Siberia *kolkhozy* are paid 95 roubles per ton of grain, *sovkhozy* only 64 roubles. The difference varies quite illogically as between various farm products.[2] The main rationale for a difference lies in the fact that *kolkhozy* have to finance their own investments, while the state supplies investment funds to state enterprises. Therefore, when it was decided in 1967 to transfer numerous *sovkhozy* onto full self-financing, including investment (see chapter 1), farms so transferred were paid the same as *kolkhozy*.

There will be further comments on the present situation in respect of agricultural prices in chapter 8.

[1] *Promyshlennost' SSSR* (Moscow 1957), p. 30.
[2] Figures given in *Ekon. gaz.*, no. 24/1967, p. 36.

Structure—Conclusion

Thus the structure of the Soviet economy consists at its base of quasi-autonomous enterprises, whose task it is to fulfil plans prescribed by the economic administration, supervised at all levels by the Communist party and by a number of inspecting agencies. Side by side with the hierarchy of administration and controllers, there exists a price and wage system, partly to provide the planners with guidance as to relative costs, and to the performance of their subordinates, and partly to encourage desirable initiative in the area of on-the-ground autonomy. Since the central authorities cannot in fact prescribe the behaviour pattern of all local officials and enterprises, even in the many instances in which they have the formal right to do so, the importance of the men on the spot and of their decisions should in no wise be overlooked. The formula 'democratic centralism', much favoured by Communist ideologists, is supposed to describe the proper balance between central control in essentials and local autonomy in execution, but the precise balance between the two is by no means easy to determine, especially because an essential element in the process—the Communist party machine— generally operates behind closed doors, and so many acts apparently taken by a republic or a ministry may in fact be the expression of a decision taken in Moscow at the central committee offices. But whoever actually decides, it may be surmised that a large proportion of the decisions are not the expressions of free choice, but are the consequences of policies, and often of a marginal character, especially so far as the enterprise is concerned, since almost always it will be doing the same as it did last year, only rather more so, and its material allocations will similarly change little. Central decisions play their biggest role in deciding basic investment programmes, for which the centre alone can provide the resources, but even these are partly shaped by the logical necessities of programmes adopted earlier. It is in adopting these programmes that the central authorities (i.e. the top party leadership plus the government) exercise to the greatest extent the freedom of choice which popular opinion supposes them to possess in all matters of economic planning. This is a point of some importance, since, as we shall see, it has led some Soviet economists to propose the application of mathematical techniques to work out the full consequences, in terms of investment and production, of the basic programmes and policies decided at the top.

The Soviet economy remains in essentials a 'command economy', because, despite all *de facto* operational autonomy, its functioning is based on instructions, and frequently the behaviour of men on the spot in their area of autonomy consists in manoeuvring to obtain the biggest advantage within the rules and instructions promulgated by the authorities. It is true that, in putting forward its own proposals to the authorities, the enterprise management is trying, so to speak, to draft the commands it would wish to receive. It is also true that the reform has enlarged the area within which management has the right to exercise choice. Yet in the last analysis instructions, when clearly and unequivocally expressed, still override considerations of micro-profitability. This is why a price system which would create an intolerable muddle if enterprises were free to react to the profit motive has not prevented the economy from functioning. It is to combat natural centrifugal tendencies that decisions on materials allocation, investment, credits, wage rates, depend in the last resort on the all-union authorities. Yet there must always be a search for a proper balance between centre and localities, between obedience to orders and initiative, between administrative decision and responses to economic incentives, just as there must be constant efforts to find an administrative and planning structure which gives the best results with minimum bureaucratic deformation. The primary policy object has been, and is, growth, and this permeates its structure and the leaders' attitudes to problems. Nor can we overlook the effect on policies of the régime's ideology. In the 'twenties, this was very much to the fore; the struggle against private enterprise and alleged *kulaks* took priority over economic assessment of costs or even of short-term growth. Nor is it possible to understand either *kolkhoz* organization or the history of agricultural prices without taking into account the party's attitudes to the peasants as such. However, these extra-economic influences on policy have become less marked, with the elimination of most of their causes. They remain significant in relation to *kolkhoz* agriculture, notably with regard to the surviving private sector, and to the minor pockets of private activity (craftsmen, etc.) in towns. Otherwise it could be said that the economic system is firmly established on the basis of state enterprises, and that it is seeking, on this basis, to overcome the many problems which complicate the achievement of a greater degree of efficiency. To consider these problems is the task of the next part of the present work.

PART II: PROBLEMS

CHAPTER 5

The Changing Nature of Problems

The economy which we are considering has developed rapidly over a comparatively short historical period, and one which has seen much violence and hardship. The structure and the problems which have arisen are intimately related to the process of change, and the development of the economy itself sets up new strains and throws up new problems. It is therefore most important to look at the questions discussed in the following chapters with some sense of historical perspective, not in order to argue that the solutions actually adopted were morally 'right', but to see why they were adopted, or why solutions apposite at one period are rejected or questioned at another.

The system of Soviet planning inherited by Stalin's successors was born as a direct consequence of the industrialization-collectivization drive, which began in 1928-29. Essential features of the system were: firstly, the use of extra-economic coercion to force social and economic relations into a new pattern; secondly, a high level of investment channelled into 'heavy industry', i.e. sectors which provided the sinews of future growth and also the basic defence potential; thirdly, the entire economy, as also other sectors of Soviet life, was under the strict control of a highly centralized Party machine, which, with the help of the police, could enforce the economic priorities decided upon by the authorities, despite the very substantial pent-up demand for a wide range of non-priority goods and services.

Of such a period of social and industrial revolution, Oscar Lange, in his lectures delivered in Belgrade in November, 1957, said the following:[1]

'Socialist industrialization and particularly very rapid industrializa-

[1] Op. cit., pp. 15-16.

tion, which was necessary in the first socialist countries, particularly in the Soviet Union, as a political requirement of national defence and of the solution of all kinds of political and social problems, due to backwardness, requires centralized disposal of resources. Thus the very process of transformation of the social system and in addition, in underdeveloped countries, the need of rapid industrialization, impose the necessity of high centralization of planning and management.

'The process of rapid industrialization requires such centralized disposal of resources for two reasons. First, it is necessary to concentrate all resources on certain objectives and avoid dissipation of resources on other objectives which would divert resources from the purpose of rapid industrialization. This is one of the reasons which leads to highly centralized planning and management and also to the allocation of resources by means of administrative establishment of priorities. The second reason why rapid industrialization demands centralized planning and management is the lack and weakness of industrial cadres. With the rapid growth of industry the cadres are new and inexperienced. Such old cadres which had some experience in management of industry and other economic activities are frequently politically alien to the socialist objectives. In consequence high centralization of managerial decisions becomes necessary.

'Thus the first period of planning and management in a socialist economy, at least according to our present experience, has always been characterized by administrative management and administrative allocation of resources on the basis of priorities centrally established. Economic incentives are in this period replaced by moral and political appeals to the workers, by appeals to their patriotism and socialist consciousness. This is, so to speak, a highly politicalized economy, both with regard to the means of planning and management and the incentives it utilizes.

'I think that, essentially, it can be described as a *sui generis* war economy.'

It was a 'war economy' because of the element of all-out concentration on politically-determined objectives, a situation full of campaigning and of emergency, of acute shortages and arbitrariness, which involved neglect of many economic desiderata. In such circumstances, just as in war economies in western countries, central decisions about resource allocation came to be decisive throughout the system. Theoretically, of course, it could all have been done through using traditional economic levers, just as the British econ-

omy in 1939-45 could (theoretically) have been geared to war purposes by proper manipulation of a free price mechanism, without
either rationing or allocation of materials. The government could
have competed for the steel it needed for munitions or warships
against the manufacturers of washing machines and private cars, and
let retail prices reflect the real scarcities of the moment. No government did this in wartime. All were driven to give some administrative expression to war priorities, and in consequence the price mechanism largely lost its traditional functions. The Soviet economy in
peacetime was engaged, in effect, in a politico-military operation.
Far from being willing to give expression to the socio-economic
forces in existence, it was seeking to alter or to repress these forces.
The sheer pace of advance and of change was such that a large part
of demand was itself a consequence of the process of change. Thus in
the early 'thirties the construction of some giant industrial complex
set up such acute and immediate difficulties that emergency programmes were constantly necessary: to overcome material bottlenecks, to train technicians, to build a new railway, to export enough
grain to pay for foreign machines, and so on. The planners were
constantly struggling with priority problems, which occupied most
of their time and demanded unremitting attention. 'Minor' requirements had to make do with what was left, and non-priority sectors
(agriculture, housing, textiles, drains, roads, and so on) seldom were
enabled to fulfil their plans, even though these plans were not nearly
as ambitious as those of the favoured heavy industry. 'Campaign
planning', central priorities centrally enforced, and particularly in
times of shortage of many necessities, meant the relegation of rational economic calculation to a comparatively minor place in the
thought-process of the leadership. The price mechanism was hardly
used for resource allocation at all, except to distribute to the citizens
in an orderly way whatever happened to be available for them.
As in Britain in wartime, all this by no means excludes some quite
considerable attention to need, but it is officialdom, not the citizen
through the price mechanism, which decides which needs can be
and should be satisfied. Differences between the choices made by
officials and the demand-preferences of the citizens are sometimes
ironed out in the USSR by rationing (e.g. of housing space), but most
often by varying the retail price so that the goods actually produced
are bought. This can be done by varying (or, where necessary, **abol-**
ishing) turnover tax rates, as we have seen.

Another feature of the situation in the USSR was the relative
abundance of labour. Of course, labour of particular skills or in

particular areas was often short. However, there was substantial underemployment in agriculture, and extra supplies of unskilled labour could generally be made available to fulfil planned tasks or to offset unplanned shortcomings in productivity or mechanization. As has been argued with some force by David Granick,[1] for purposes of decision-making it was largely possible to ignore labour cost. The point was, while enlarging the capital stock as fast as possible, to use existing equipment to the full. As might be expected, this was most easy to observe in *kolkhoz* agriculture, in which, since total remuneration of labour was independent of the amount of labour expended, the marginal cost of using extra labour appeared, from the standpoint of the management, to be *nil* (the more so as the additional labour would be at the expense of working on the private plot). Only thus can one explain the deployment of 70 peasants in two shifts (total: 140) on one grain-thresher, and this form of using machinery and peasants actually won a Stalin prize![2] Of course, in state enterprises the use of extra labour did make a difference to costs, but the priority given to growth and to plan fulfilment led, where necessary, to the overspending of the wages fund, and the controls designed to prevent this could be, and were, circumvented. The abundance of labour partially explains the institutional arrangements which permitted (or even encouraged) its wasteful use. It is also true that the existence of a large underemployed peasant population presents economists and politicians alike with problems which are not always to be judged by criteria of economic rationality which western economists regard as 'normal'.[3] In addition, if a deliberate programme of modernization is being carried through, there often occurs a long period of extremely uneven development, in which operations which are highly mechanized coexist with others (sometimes to be found within the same industry or in the same plant) in which the still relatively abundant unskilled labour force is working by antediluvian methods and in great numbers. In a sense, it would seem obvious that, with so much labour available—and at low wages—much of the mechanization is economically unprofitable. This may, however, be another way of saying that the industrialization drive itself would not have been launched if criteria of

[1] 'An organizational model of Soviet industrial planning', *Journal of Political Economy*, April, 1959.
[2] For a full description of how these peasants were used, see A. Nove and R. D. Laird, in *Soviet Studies*, April, 1953, pp. 434 ff.
[3] For some interesting ideas on this question in a non-Soviet context, see W. Arthur Lewis, 'Economic development with unlimited supplies of labour' *The Manchester School*, May, 1954.

'normal' economic rationality were used. In any case, the experience of many developing countries, from Tsarist Russia to modern Brazil, shows that the 'abundance' of unskilled labour can coexist with highly capital-intensive and labour-saving investment, by private entrepreneurs.[1] The Soviet authorities took as given the political decision that rapid industrialization is the overriding aim of public policy. Of course, it does not follow that they proceeded by the most rational route towards the aim they set themselves. There are (at least) two senses of the word 'rational' which should be carefully distinguished. The first relates to some kind of optimum behaviour designed to fulfil the requirements of the *existing* social-economic pattern. This would adapt economic policies to what the Germans (and the Russians) call *Konjunktur*, or the totality of market-determined trends. The second species of rationality takes the aims as determined from outside the economy, and then seeks the most efficient way to achieve these results. This may well require very different institutional arrangements. For example, Holland Hunter has argued that what he calls 'hortatory planning' (targets, strains, campaigns, etc.) may actually be the most rational way, in some circumstances, to achieve rapid 'development' results if certain costs can be disregarded.[2] There are in fact other aspects of this question, and we shall have much more to say on this theme in chapter 12.

But to return to the main line of argument. Revolutionary changes were in progress, imposed by a government disinclined to count the cost, in conditions of ample labour reserves in agriculture (and, we should add, also in forced labour camps). There were hardly any periods of normality in which the system could settle down. A few years after the 'crash programmes' of the first five-year plan, war preparations and the convulsions of the purges disrupted the advance.[3] Then came the war, then a period of recovery, then another arms programme, which takes one up to Stalin's death and even beyond. Therefore, given the nature of the régime, of the economic tasks with which it was endeavouring to cope, the disturbed history of the period, and also the hostility of the then existing ideology to any talk of economic rationality (see chapter 11, below), the net

[1] See A. Gerschenkron: *Economic backwardness in historical perspective*, (Oxford, 1962), and A. Nove: 'The Explosive Model', *Journal of Development Studies*, October 1966; also A. Nove: 'Irrationality and Waste', *Survey*, July 1967. Specifically on Russian experience in the 'thirties, see D. Granick: *American Economic Review*, May 1962, p. 150 ff.

[2] 'Optional tautness in development planning', in *Economic Development and Cultural Change*, July 1961.

[3] On the importance of these factors, see a valuable article l y A. Khavin, in *Istoriya SSSR*, No. 1/1959.

effect was to keep in being forms of economic organization designed to achieve rapid results in priority sectors by quantitative direction. As was also seen in the west during the period of wartime planning, such an approach renders impossible any systematic attempt to achieve rationality in its restricted sense, i.e. the most efficient use of resources to achieve politically-determined ends. This is because the institutional and price structures are geared to the primary task of mobilizing resources for the achievement of targets set in the process of quantitative 'priority' planning, and for this reason they become unsuitable instruments on which to base economic criteria in choosing between alternative means. We shall be concerned in the pages that follow with many examples of this.

However, this system tends to outgrow itself, to the very extent to which it succeeds in establishing a modern industrialized economy and emerges into a period of relative normality. There are a number of reasons for this, which are to some extent interconnected.

One is the ever-growing complexity of the economy. The innumerable interconnections between sectors and areas, the ever-widening consequences of any planning decision, are such as to overburden the authorities responsible. A comparatively unsophisticated system of 'material balances', with errors corrected by a series of campaigns to enlarge bottlenecks, becomes inadequate for the job.[1]

The second could be defined as 'the multiplication of priorities'. The centralized system of allocation can work only if priorities are few and well defined, and, conversely, if a large part of the economy can be treated as non-priority, its needs as 'expendable'. Only then can the planning authorities cope more or less effectively with their complex tasks; materials are then allocated to priority sectors, and the rest can take their chance. For many years consumers' goods industries, agriculture and housing were relatively neglected, and some quite important branches of heavy industry (for instance, chemicals) also remained underdeveloped, while big advances were made in branches considered to be of key importance. There are both economic-technical and social-political reasons why this can no longer be tolerated. Backward branches of the economy (e.g. chemicals, agriculture) became themselves bottlenecks, holding up the advance of the rest of the economy. The contrast between spectacular technological achievements and low living standards contributed to a political climate in which major improvements in food, housing,

---

[1] This point has been well made by, among others, W. Leontief, in 'The Fall and Rise of Soviet Economics', in *Foreign Affairs*, January, 1960. See also chapter 12, below.

retail trade, quality of textiles, and so on, were becoming increasingly a species of political necessity, and were seen to be such by Stalin's successors. This is not the place for a discussion of the political situation; we must simply note that the former 'cinderella' sectors now have enhanced priority, and that this makes the old style of planning correspondingly more difficult.

Thirdly, the period of labour abundance is drawing to a close. This, like all generalizations, is not altogether accurate. Thus the supply of skilled labour has much improved, there are pockets of little-used or misused labour, in small towns in the west, and there is still a large and inefficiently-utilized agricultural labour force. However, the release of more farm labour requires a marked change in organization, which is still geared to the period of abundance, and the natural increase in the working population is being adversely affected, in the period 1959-65, by the abnormal years 1942-48, when war and its aftermath had a drastic effect on birth and survival rates.[1] It is, in any case, easy to demonstrate that the change in the relative scarcities of labour and capital has added a new dimension to the problems of resource utilization as Soviet economists see them. For example, Academician Strumilin attributed the new interest of his colleagues in obsolescence, a concept whose very applicability to the USSR was denied before 1955, precisely to this factor. 'While the availability of labour permits it, one can utilize all equipment, old and new, and retain old equipment until it wears out . . . In the past, in the early stages of Soviet economic development, in conditions of abundance of labour, there was a tendency towards maximum quantitative increase in production; subsequently, as this abundance came to an end, the trend shifted towards maximum qualitative indicators in the use of labour, above all labour productivity. Hence the growing importance of obsolescence at present.'[2] This is an aspect of what the German economist Boettcher rightly calls 'intensification'.[3]

Fourthly, we must recall that Oscar Lange attributed part of the need for centralization of decision to the lack of capable and trustworthy personnel. Now, over forty years after the revolution, with a new and well-trained generation of managers at all levels, this argument gradually loses strength.

[1] According to the 1959 census, the numbers of 10 to 15-year-olds in January, 1959, was 17·1 million. In 1939, it was 28·4 million (*Pravda*, February 4, 1960).

[2] *Vop. Ekon.*, No. 8/1956, p. 46.

[3] *Die Sowjetische Wirtschaftpolitik am Scheidewege* (Tübingen, 1959), a most thought-provoking book.

Finally, in the USSR at least, we can note the virtual end of revolutionary change, of social upheavals, the carrying out of which so often led to the subordination of purely economic rationality to the achievement of social-political objectives. The one major area in which economically irrelevant arguments still deeply influence economic policy is in agriculture, in anything to do with the private sector and peasants as such. It is also important to note the importance of bureaucratic and party vested interest as factors highly relevant to the choice between possible chains of command and organizational forms. None the less, there are many signs of greater normality, of a more calm search for the best way and less slogan-mongering. Undeniably, political control or interference occur in all kinds of ways, but it remains true to say that the general atmosphere is much more business-like, much more congenial for discussions concerning rationality, optima, maximizing the return on investment, minimizing costs and other questions familar to economists the world over.

As a result of all this, Soviet economists and planners have been anxiously re-examining their theory and their practice, probing for weaknesses, suggesting remedies, and in doing so have provided the scholar with valuable evidence about the way things work. It is true that many, if not all, the criticisms which will be quoted here could have been, often were, made many years ago. The weaknesses now being discussed are not new. However, past criticisms were apt to be sporadic in character, and were particularly muted in the postwar period. They are now much louder and more systematic, partly because of the end of Stalin's terror, but perhaps principally because the defects and strains which are the subject of discussion appear to be less tolerable today, their correction more urgent. It does not mean that the weaknesses as such have become more glaring, or that the economy is about to fall to pieces. Indeed, time and experience have doubtless led to improvement in planning techniques, and the grosser errors of the early 'thirties are things of the past. Yet there is a widespread feeling that a qualitatively new situation now exists, to which the institutional structure devised in and for the Stalin epoch is increasingly unsuitable. It is hardly possible to read the many discussions of Soviet economists, especially after 1955, without coming to the conclusion that they know this very well.

In a sense, the analysis of problems which follows in the next chapters should be replaced by an all-inclusive picture of 'how it really works'. This, unfortunately, is an unattainable aim. No institutions in any country can be fully explained in terms of their formal structure, all are modified by a variety of conventions and informal links which play an essential role in their functioning. Similarly, the *de facto* exercise of authority is often quite different from the pattern suggested by the hierarchy of power as this appears in a law or a diagram. However, it is often extremely difficult to discover what the real pattern is, unless one has actually worked in the organization in question. As far as the Soviet Union is concerned, there is information on the formal structure, but accounts of what actually happens appear, if they appear at all, primarily in the context of problems, of frictions, of things that go wrong. In the course of examining these various frictions in the pages that follow, we will become acquainted with various aspects of the real life of the economy, as well as with those problems which cause perplexity to its economic administrators and planners. This will not, unfortunately, provide the fully balanced picture of reality which we ought to have, but such a picture is necessarily elusive, and will remain so until there is opportunity for a great deal of 'field work' on Soviet institutions. One should add that many economists and political scientists are very conscious of the fact that our information about how things 'really work' in western countries is often sadly defective.[1]

The plan for this part of the book is as follows. Firstly, we will consider, in chapter 6, entitled 'Micro-economic Problems', the frictions and difficulties that arise at the level of a productive enterprise, so to speak *within* the plan handed down by higher authority. Here will be discussed the consequences of the enterprises's efforts to fulfil the plans, the effect of these efforts and of the various inducements and controls on efficiency, innovation and so on, both in state enterprises and in *kolkhozy*. In view of the enlargement of the area of enterprise autonomy, including the right to draft and adopt certain plans, which is part of the present wave of reforms, the extent and consequence of these changes will have to be considered. Chapter 7 will then deal with planning process, including material allocation, material balances, investment choice, the behaviour of planning organs. In chapter 8 there will be covered questions concerned with prices of materials and of factors of production in general, including wage problems and agricultural rent. The division of the subject-matter in this way is no more than an analytic convenience, since the various micro- and macro-economic problems are intimately

---

[1] For instance, the Radcliffe committee spent years on enquiring into essential aspects of the British financial system, and many experts still dispute about whether their picture of the facts is correct.

F*

inter-connected. In fact one could argue that the inter-connections are in fact *the* problem, of which the chapters that follow provide the detailed illustrations. In a sense this is certainly true: the difficulties arise in large part out of the effort to 'translate' the authorities' macro-policy of rapid growth and priorities into effective action at working levels. The inter-connections are by no means one way. Clearly, the resource allocation and planning decisions which formally belong to the central government can be affected by the applications and requests from below, which are in turn influenced by the pressures of incentives and penalties to which directors and local officials are exposed. Thus prices influence both micro and macro behaviour, affect both the enterprise management and the central planners. The absence of agricultural rent affects the pay of peasants and the financial structure of *kolkhozy*, and these in turn react upon agricultural prices and planning, the marketing of food, and so on. All the various aspects constantly interact and affect one another. Yet they cannot be dealt with simultaneously, for obvious physical reasons. One can only urge the reader to keep the inter-connections constantly in mind.

CHAPTER 6

Micro-economic Problems

In the west, firms take decisions by reference to the profit-motive; in the USSR, all decisions must be based on and conform to the plan. This generalization, while not wholly accurate,[1] does underline an essential difference between the systems, despite the fact that considerations other than direct profit expectations do influence actions of managers in the west, and profits do affect to some extent the behaviour of managers in the USSR. The primary task of a Soviet manager, as we have already noted, is to fulfil the plan, or more strictly plans, since he is judged and rewarded under a number of plan indicators. We shall now consider the effect of this on Soviet managerial behaviour and on the output of goods and services, beginning with the influence of these 'success indicators' on the quantity and assortment of output.

This influence is related to the range of choice open to managers at enterprise level, and this in turn depends on two factors: the nature of the product and the degree of detail in which the plan is elaborated by higher authority. Thus, for example, an enterprise producing electricity, or a factory making large specialized machines (e.g. turbines), or arms factories producing to the precise specifications decided centrally by military experts, whatever their other differences, have in common the fact that the product mix depends hardly at all on decisions taken by enterprise managers. In most cases, however, the problem of the product mix is a real one: textiles, shoes, a wide range of metal goods and a long list of other commodities can be made in many shapes, sizes, styles, qualities, colours. It is generally impossible for the planning organs to specify the desired assortment in full detail, or, as we shall see, to enforce its specifications on the enterprise even if they made the attempt to subdivide the product mix. It is also important to note that the actual or potential production of any factory must always depend to some ex-

[1] It does not apply, for instance, to most nationalized industries in the west.

tent on the management on the spot, since the plan itself can hardly fail to be influenced by what the management declares itself able and willing to do in the next planning period.

The system is now in process of transition. In analysing its problems, we must never lose sight of the fact that many enterprises are still not 'reformed', and that, as will be shown, the reform is only partially operative even where it is said to apply. So this chapter can and should describe the problems of the 'traditional' planning system which may now be withering away, as well as the growing-pains of the new model which is taking its place.

It was the essence of the traditional system to specify plan indicators from above in some detail, and then to reward fulfilment and overfulfilment of these plans. If the fulfilment or overfulfilment of plans is to be rewarded, it is clearly necessary first to define what the plans are. To take three of the most common success indicators as examples: in each period there must be specified a quantity of output, a percentage reduction in costs, and a percentage increase in labour productivity. Managerial behaviour must naturally be influenced in the direction of endeavouring to fulfil the plans so defined, with results which may not be obvious at first sight.

Take the quantity of output first. The plan was generally based on the achievements of the previous period, to which was added a percentage increase. The quantity to be produced was usually intended to encourage effort, to induce the management to seek out 'reserves' of underused factors of production. In the process of plan determination, it pays the management of the enterprise to conceal its full potential and in other ways to manoeuvre to obtain an 'easy' plan; nor would it pay a wise manager to overfulfil it by too wide a margin, for, if he did so, he might be suspected of having concealed his potential, and plans for the subsequent period might be increased by an embarrassingly large percentage.[1] Of course, all this is known to the planning organs, and in the resultant manoeuvring the authorities try to utilize the various supervisory agencies, to check up on managerial behaviour. Plans may be deliberately 'tightened', on the not unreasonable assumption that the manager is not being quite honest about his production possibilities or his stocks of materials (as we shall see, it paid to hoard). These circumstances also help to explain the urge to 'overfulfil' output plans, which perfectionist

---

[1] These defects are discussed by G. Nikolaeva, in *Vovyi mir*, No. 7/1957, p. 74, comments on readers' letters in *Kommunist*, No. 1/1957, p. 49, and many others.

critics of planning often regard as proof of inefficiency, but which
springs in part from a knowledge that there are hidden reserves. On
the other hand, the 'supervisors' are often themselves interested in
being able to report plan fulfilment. Thus ministerial officials tolerated
understatements of production possibilities, while a *sovnarkhoz* was
said to have reduced a plan in mid-year so as not to have to report
that one of its major enterprises had failed to fulfil it.[1]

However, let us now assume that an output target for the next plan
period has been decided. One must now consider how the target
figure is expressed in quantitative terms. The ways in which this can
be done depend in part on the nature of the product: for example,
shoe output could be expressed in number of pairs or in roubles,
production of clothing or of furniture is too varied for the plans to
be expressed in anything but roubles, sheet metal plans could be in
tons or in square metres, cloth in square metres or linear metres or
roubles, and so on through a variety of other possibilities. The effect
of each of these is to encourage its own species of distortion. In the
context of an economic situation in which virtually all goods free of
major technical defects can be disposed of, the temptation always
exists to adapt the assortment of the product to the method of measuring the quantitative fulfilment of the plan. It will be noted that the
substitution, after 1965, of *sales* for gross output cannot solve the
problem, so long as there is a sellers' market.

Examples can be cited in very large numbers, drawing on material
published not only in the USSR but also Hungary, Poland and
Czechoslovakia, where a similar institutional structure involved
similar problems.[2] A plan expressed in tons encourages the production of heavy commodities; in any choice involving weight, the
'weightier' variant is bound to be favoured, since this facilitates the
fulfilment of the plan. Thus, for example, a metal works was reported
to have increased its output of roofing iron by 20 per cent over five
years in tons, but in terms of area the increase was only 10 per cent;
the plan, of course, was in tons.[3] Clearly, an output plan expressed
in terms of tons encourages the choice of a variant in which a given
weight is achieved with the least expenditure of those resources unrelated to weight. For instance, factories making prefabricated

[1] M. Sidorov, *Vop. ekon.*, No. 4/1957, p. 128, and *Pravda*, April 27, 1959.
[2] Particularly valuable in all matters pertaining to the present chapter is the
book by the Hungarian economist Janos Kornai, translated into English under
the title of *Overcentralization in Economic Administration* (Oxford, 1959). For
a discussion of Soviet experience, see A. Nove, 'Some Problems of "Success
Indicators" in Soviet Industry', in *Economica*, January, 1958, pp. 1 ff.
[3] V. Kontorovich, *Sotsialisticheskii trud*, No. 1/1957, p. 50.

cement blocks, prefer to make large blocks, which is the easiest means of fulfilling a plan in terms of tons, though, as it happens, the result is a shortage of small blocks necessary for completing portions of the buildings under construction.[1] Khrushchev himself gave a particularly absurd example: the chandelier plan was expressed in tons, so chandeliers were unnecessarily heavy.[2] The humorous journal *Krokodil* once pictured, in a cartoon, a factory which fulfilled its entire month's output programme for nails by the manufacture of one gigantic nail, hanging from an overhead crane the whole length of the workshop.

Output targets in roubles evade such difficulties as these, but at the cost of creating others. In most instances, the money measure was applied to gross value of output—*valovaya produktsiya*—which includes unfinished production, or, strictly speaking, the increase (if any) of unfinished or partly-processed goods over the previous plan period. This encouraged a number of distortions. In the first place, an advantage is derived from using dear materials. Obviously, to take a published example, an enterprise making tools, with a plan expressed in roubles of gross output, finds that it 'pays' (in terms of plan fulfilment) to use unnecessarily expensive quality steel, and for many years the production of inexpensive clothes was inhibited by the reluctance of manufacturers to utilize the cheaper cloths.[3] There is even involved in this method of measuring plan fulfilment a quite unintended discouragement of the production of spare parts. This is because, for example, a carburettor is 'worth' more in a completed motor-cycle or tractor, where it is combined with other goods and services many of which were bought from outside the enterprise, than if this same carburettor were produced and sold as a spare part.[4] Spare parts are notoriously short in the USSR, and it is noteworthy that a plan expressed in physical units also leads to neglect of spares. Thus *Pravda* (June 8, 1960) published a bitter attack on those who fail to provide spares for motor-cycles, in the course of which an imaginary person, deemed to be 'the director of an enterprise, head of a *sovnarkhoz* or official of a planning organ', undertakes to increase production of motor-cycles, and, when the question of spares is raised, answers as follows: 'I am not interested in your

[1] But if the cement blocks are calculated in roubles, they avoid making cheap cement blocks (*Pravda*, August 3, 1956).
[2] *Pravda*, July 2, 1959.
[3] See Kontorovich, op. cit., and N. Lyubimov and A. Petrov in *Plan. khoz.*, No. 1/1957, pp. 38-9.
[4] This point is made by N. Antonov, *Plan. khoz.*, No. 5/1957, p. 83, and V. Kontorovich, in *Plan. khoz.*, No. 3/1957.

calculations. All that matters is what is included in the statistical returns and counted in the plan, i.e. new complete machines. They interest me. As for piston rings, plugs and so on, these are just fiddling little things which don't appear in fulfilment indicators.' Spares, therefore, are unobtainable, for reasons connected with the success indicator system. At the same time, the failure of British car manufacturers to provide adequate spares and service in the first postwar boom years should remind us that these things are apt to suffer in a seller's market, even in a quite different institutional setting.

There is also a tendency to start work on production or on building which cannot be completed, which locks up resources unnecessarily, but counts in statistics of gross output (or of the volume of construction). It may appear simple to overcome some of these weaknesses, for instance by measuring plan fulfilment in terms of goods actually completed and sold, or to measure value-added only. However, it is clearly unfair not to include genuinely unfinished production in assessing the work of a factory over a given period of time. As for value-added, it has been found impracticable to use this indicator, since it would encourage *unnecessary* processing. In consequence, in a number of branches of the economy there was introduced a new indicator, *normativnaya stoimost' obrabotki* (NSO) or normed value of processing. This was the predetermined ('normed') cost of work done, which excluded materials bought in and also excluded profits, but oddly enough included the fuel used and a number of miscellaneous overheads.[1] However, this created many new problems. Thus there developed an illogical and varying relationship between *actual* processing costs and normed processing costs, and this caused irrational (but understandable) efforts to produce items for which the maximum normed value could be achieved at least actual cost, which distorted the product mix. Also the gross output indicator had to be retained alongside the NSO; for example the profits plan and the sales plan were related to gross values. In any case, the need to fix NSO values as well as wholesale prices in effect meant that the work of price-fixing had to be carried out twice, and many errors were inevitable. Therefore, despite much discussion and criticism, the 'gross output' measure remained predominant among monetary plan indicators. It is particularly common, unavoidably, in assessing the results of a group of enterprises, within a *glavk*, a ministry, a *sovnarkhoz* or a republic. The anxiety of these administra-

[1] For a detailed description of this indicator, see *Ekon. gaz.*, July 4, 1964, pp. 16-18. See also M. Nazarov *Ekon. gaz.*, November 11, 1964, p. 9. For a devastating attack on NSO, see I. Malyshev, *Vop. ekon.* No. 6/1965.

tive bodies to report plan fulfilment, arrived at by adding together the gross outputs of all the enterprises subordinate to them, results in constant pressure on managers to fulfil or overfulfil gross output plans, to the exclusion of many other relevant considerations, a state of affairs a Soviet economist has described as a veritable 'cult of the gross' (*kul't vala*).[1] We shall see that these considerations led to pressure to fulfil gross output plans even after the adoption of decrees which, supposedly, freed enterprises from the gross-output indicator.

Other measures of output plan fulfilment suffer from defects of their own. Cloth was 'measured' in linear metres for many years, with the result that it was made narrower than was desirable from other points of view.[2] Consequently from 1959 the basis was changed to square metres. But this is by no means always satisfactory, since other desiderata tend to be sacrificed to maximize square metres, at the expense, for instance, of quality or workmanship. Roofing metal which was too heavy when the plan was in tons becomes too thin when the plan is in square metres. If a plan for nails were expressed in quantity (e.g. thousands of nails) they would tend to be small, if in tons they would tend to be large. Highly original plan-measurement criteria were devised in some industries; for example, central-heating boilers were assessed for this purpose in terms of the area of heating surface (of the boiler); consequently, when a new model was devised which heated more efficiently with a smaller heating surface, no one would touch it, as it would worsen their success indicators'.[3] The Soviet economist Aboltin reported that the Stalingrad construction trust wasted metal because, for one of its projects, the plan was expressed in terms of metal used. In the course of an admirable survey of many of these distortions, the aircraft engineer O. Antonov cited the case of the management of a road transport enterprise which ordered useless journeys, often with empty lorries, at the end of a plan period in order to record the planned number of ton-kilometres. He rightly made the point that, in rewarding plan fulfilment in quantity for an intermediate good or service, the result may be one of inhibiting economy and stimulating waste: for, after all, ought one not to transport whatever needs transporting with a *minimum* expenditure of ton-kilometres?[4] Some restaurants avoid cheap dishes, as the plan is in terms of gross turnover. Other ex-

---

[1] D. Kondrashev, *Tsenoobrazovanie v promyshlennosti* (Moscow, 1956), p. 32.
[2] Kontorovich, op. cit., p. 50.
[3] *Pravda*, September 5, 1958.
[4] *Dlya vsekh i dlya sebya* (M., 1965).

amples, often even more grotesque, could easily fill several pages. One such recent example concerns fish. A great battle was reported, between the fisheries trust of the Far East, the Kamchatka fish *kombinat*, the State Fisheries Inspectorate, fisheries research institutes in Kamchatka and in Moscow, the RSFSR Gosplan, etc. The subject of the battle: is a certain fish a perch or a ruff? Why? Because if it is a perch it must be gutted, whereas no such rule applies to the ruff. 'To gut is not advantageous. It uses time and money, and, most important, the guts and head . . . are almost 15 per cent of the total weight of the fish. And, among other things, there is a gross output plan, which it is desirable to overfulfil (in tons, of course). It is particularly desirable for the managers of Far East fisheries trust. It is they who have discovered a gap in the fisheries standards, through which have penetrated countless ungutted ruff.'[1]

Repeatedly, it was stated that rewards for the fulfilment of output plans must be made conditional upon the fulfilment of the assortment plan, that it is inadmissable that the product mix be distorted in order to claim fulfilment in aggregate terms. These statements do not appear to have eliminated the trouble, which arose partly because of the very great emphasis given by the authorities to aggregate plan fulfilment, and partly because the product mix cannot be specified in all its detail in the plan.

Rewards for plan fulfilment require not only a clearly defined measure of results, but also a time-period to which the results must be related. Hence the great importance of the calendar, and the phenomenon of 'storming' (*shturmovshchina*), of a mad rush to fulfil the plan in the last few days of the month, quarter or year, followed by a slack and disorganized period in which production falls sharply until the next mad rush. Denunciations of *shturmovshchina* were, and are, extremely common, and the prevalence of the disease is a sign that it is, in a sense, built in to the structure of the economy. It is worth recalling that this particular form of distortion, as well as many of the other 'success indicator' problems referred to here, occurred also in British planning during the war.[2]

One weakness involved in 'calendar' planning is a certain short-sightedness; one has insufficient incentive to look to subsequent planning periods, the more so because, with a high turnover of directors, someone else might then be in charge. There is little or no in-

---

[1] *Krokodil*, June 10, 1960.
[2] See, in particular, E. Devons, *Planning in Practice* (Cambridge University Press, 1950).

centive for looking far ahead. This affects attitudes to resource conservation, as may be illustrated by a large number of articles pleading, apparently in vain, for preserving forests or the avoidance of pollution of rivers or lakes.

The effect of other 'success indicators' on the behaviour of managements may be partly to correct some of the deviations engendered by pursuit of quantitative plan fulfilment, but often they encourage similar distortions, or cause new ones. Thus an effort to fulfil a plan to increase labour productivity by 4 per cent would, clearly, discourage the taking on of large numbers of additional workers. On the other hand, the calculation of productivity necessarily requires comparing the labour force to total output, and this reinforces the tendency to try to simulate overfulfilment of the output plan in tons, roubles, or whatever the measure may be. Until 1958, the measurement of labour productivity involved only 'productive workers', i.e. excluded clerks, technical personnel and auxiliaries. The effect, not surprisingly, was that the management either neglected to mechanize the auxiliary work or endeavoured to classify as many of their employees as possible in non-productive categories. This particular deviation has been checked; from 1959, labour productivity statistics are based on the entire labour force.[1]

In 1959, after a period of experiment, a change was decreed in the 'success indicator' system, reflecting the realization that a system encouraging maximum quantitative results at any cost is no longer reasonable in present circumstances. Outside of a few particularly scarce commodities, the size of premia now no longer depended on the degree of fulfilment of the output plan, though fulfilment remains a precondition of receiving premia at all. The actual magnitude of the reward became primarily dependent on the fulfilment (and overfulfilment) of the cost reduction plan, subject also to fulfilling the plans for labour productivity, the introduction of new technique and the delivery plans.[2] Costs are commonly calculated as 'per rouble of commodity production', i.e. of output sold.

Admittedly, emphasis on this 'indicator' would discourage plan fulfilment involving a shift in the product mix towards using high-cost materials, but it would encourage lower-quality or lower-cost variants, which, in any multi-product enterprise, can be so selected as to make cost per unit appear to fall. The desire to achieve a 'statistical' cut in costs also influences the adoption or non-

[1] Rumyantsev, op. cit., p. 271.
[2] For two useful articles on these changes, see M. Mikhailov, *Plan. khoz.*, No. 12/1959, and V. Markov, *Plan. khoz.*, No. 6/1960, pp. 29 ff.

adoption of new models, according to whether or not they are considered to be 'comparable' for purposes of calculating costs. The influence of this on innovation and adaptation to consumer demand will be dealt with under these heads (pp. 181-186, below). Here again, there is a much better chance of ensuring that a downward change in costs is genuine if the given enterprise's product is homogeneous and unchanging, such as electric power, or coal of the only quality which the particular enterprise can mine. It is almost impossible to avoid simulation or distortion if the enterprise is able to vary the product mix.

There are a multitude of other 'success indicators', which cause distortions in varying degrees, or correct each other to varying extents. Incredible as it may seem, geological surveying units received plans in linear metres of drilling, 'and the planning departments want to know nothing else. If you have not fulfilled this plan indicator, you are classified as backward', even though the surveyors may have successfully discovered mineral reserves, so that the surveyors 'undertake work they know to be useless'.[1] There were many bonuses calculated in relation to economy of this or that material, or fuel. All were complex, all must of their nature stimulate forms of behaviour not intended by those who originally framed the rules.

Protests about the inefficiencies generated by this system mounted, and were widely used by reformers in the course of their efforts to change the system. In 1964 and in 1965 there were repeated instances quoted of enterprises producing 'not for the consumer but for the plan', to use Pravda's words (December 22, 1964). 'Gross output' was said to be 'the rock' against which all orders to conform to the requirements of the customers were in vain. New absurdities included the penalization of the Leningrad electricity network for reducing losses of current in transmission—since this led to the underfulfilment of the plan in value and in kilowatt-hours. The production of the wrong pottery at the wrong price continued to cause a pileup of unsaleable stocks, because the plan indicators rendered the necessary change in the production pattern virtually impossible, both for the enterprise and for their immediate superiors, and so on and so forth.[2]

It is essential to appreciate the cause of these and similar difficulties. They all spring from the fact that the activity of enterprises and

[1] *Pravda*, August 3, 1956.
[2] See *Ekon. gaz.* December 9, 1964 (V. Rodionov), January 6, 1965 (A. Malov), February 16, 1965 (V. Dykin), *Pravda*, October 18, 1964, December 22, 1964, etc., etc.

subordinate planning bodies is essentially based on *instructions*, and the incentives provided to the management are rewards for acting in accordance with instructions, with the plan.[1] The authorities are unable to issue unambiguous, all-inclusive instructions, and various aspects of the plan may be inconsistent with one another, as when overfulfilment of output plans may require some increase in costs, or when some other plan indicator or instruction (e.g. relating to saving fuel, or economizing in the use of some scarce material) contradicts the aim of increasing labour productivity, or involves the overspending of the wages fund. These ambiguities are further complicated by the inevitable imperfections and imprecision of the statistics which express the achievements of the enterprise by reference to the various indicators. There is thus an area of choice, of manoeuvre. The director, unless prevented by direct orders or *force majeure*, must be expected to act in such a way as to maximize his financial rewards and his standing with his superiors, and minimize the risk of loss of reputation, demotion, reprimand. Not only his own reputation, but that of his staff, of his superiors, of the enterprise itself, depends on plan fulfilment. The permitted wages fund is related to plan fulfilment. For these and many other reasons 'the director ... must, is bound, is compelled and certainly wishes to struggle to fulfil the plan and its quantitative and qualitative indicators'.[2] Obviously, his choices are complicated by his own assessment of the often uncertain prospects of risk and material and moral reward. He may shrink from exploiting too ruthlessly the possibilities of a situation, because this might well bring trouble. For instance, even if no details of sizes were specified in the plan, and it would be simplest from the angle of various 'indicators' to make all men's ready-made suits of one size only, no director of a clothing factory is likely to act accordingly. However, it is repeatedly a matter of complaint that plans for the production of children's sizes of both clothes and shoes are underfulfilled, because they are unpopular with directors as fitting badly into their 'success indicators'.

The instructions must leave much to be settled on the spot, or by negotiations between the parties directly concerned (e.g. the wholesaler and the factory), but the one thing which is not rewarded in any way is *use value*, or the satisfaction of demand. As Kornai well put it, 'if the article happens not to be faulty (i.e. is free of defects of workmanship) and is nevertheless not wanted by anybody, then this

[1] This thought is developed at some length, with impeccable logic, in the excellent book by Kornai, already cited.

[2] O. Antonov, *Znamya*, No. 2/1957, p. 151.

has no consequences. It does not affect the fact that it will be counted as part of the production value credited to the enterprise concerned'.[1] The system of instructions lacks an all-embracing criterion, which, at least in theory, is provided by profits in a market economy. Of course, the Soviet system did not produce vast quantities of useless rubbish. The system of plans and controls ensured that the bulk of what is produced served some purpose. However, the system of incentives which guided the director of the enterprise to choose between alternatives frequently worked in a misleading way, thereby causing some misdirection of resources.

This caused irrationalities both in the product mix and in the means chosen to fulfil plans. The word 'irrationalities', so often misleading, can be used here with confidence. It is not a question of conflicting criteria of rationality, such as might be suggested by the contrast between 'planners preferences' and 'consumers' preferences'. Obviously, planners seldom actually will the production of goods which the user prefers not to have, nor do they wish metal or road transport to be wasted. Such things are, in the main, *unwanted* consequences of the operation of the traditional system.[2]

Oddly enough, these unwanted consequences were often wanted not only at enterprise level, but also by intermediate administrative bodies: ministerial *glavki*, *sovnarkhozy*, and the rest. For, as a glance at any statistical report in the press can bear out, they were and still are judged by quantitative, aggregate plan fulfilment. It has been of little interest to them what the disaggregated product-mix was, so long as it added up to the prescribed total. This is why, far from checking or reproving their subordinates, the regional or ministerial organs often connived at or even instigated such malfeasances.

It is considerations such as these that led to the insistence on reform. But other matters were involved too.

INNOVATION, RISK-TAKING, INITIATIVE

The situation of the Soviet enterprise is somewhat paradoxical. On the one hand, great publicity is given in the USSR to inventors and inventions, and there are impressive statistics published from time to time about the number of new ideas put forward by employees. In

[1] Op. cit., p. 38. On all these questions, see also the valuable books by J. Berliner, *Factory and Manager in the USSR* (Harvard, 1957), and D. Granick, *Management of the Industrial Firm in the USSR* (Columbia University, 1954).

[2] See A. Nove: 'Planners preferences, priorities and reforms', *Economic Journal*, June, 1966.

addition, commercial secrecy does not exist, so that new methods or new models devised in one enterprise are available for the use of all enterprises, and effective new ideas are widely publicized on a nation-wide scale. But on the other hand the Soviet specialized press, and indeed also literature and drama, abound in criticisms of stick-in-the-mud directors who refuse to adopt new methods and continue to produce to obsolete designs. In some respects and in some industries, the Soviet economy shows striking progress in technique. In others, one sees a very different picture.

In the case of such 'naturally centralized' production processes as sputniks and jet aircraft, the 'micro' problems we are discussing scarcely arise. Development is essentially a matter of gifted designers and well-endowed research institutes, rather than of enterprise initiative. Nor does the presence or absence of such initiative make any decisive difference to the equipment or the product of large modern plant, erected in accordance with the latest technical know-how on the instructions of central project-making bodies. This applies, *inter alia*, to the wholesale adoption of the latest foreign techniques, and also to steelworks, hydro-electric power stations and the like; the problems here relate more to choices between investment variants, which are discussed in the next chapter. At the moment we are concerned with innovation on the scale of an enterprise, involving the rearrangement of a production line or a new design of a product.

The first snag is a consequence of the concentration on fulfilling the current output plan. Many new ideas involve a halt for retooling or for making other relevant changes, and it is hard to imagine doing this without adversely affecting the production figures of the current quarter. But it has been an essential fact of Soviet life that everyone is under pressure to report on the quarter's plan, and this includes the hierarchical superiors of the enterprise, who therefore show understandable impatience with any initiative which affects the current plan-fulfilment statistics.

The second difficulty relates to the financing of such investments as may be needed to change either the model produced or the methods by which it is produced. Retooling costs money. Until the last few years, there was virtually no source for financing such expenditure, without the specific authorization of the ministry concerned. In other words, the project had to be submitted up the hierarchy, which severely limited initiative. If the superior authorities supported the project, on the grounds that the output or costs would benefit by the proposed change, they were apt to amend the plans accordingly, so that there would be little or no gain to the initiators in the event of success, to balance possible loss of bonuses and reputation. There was, it is true, the cautious introduction, in 1958, of so-called 'mechanization credits', which could in some cases be granted by the State Bank, but the sums were small and the period of repayment absurdly short, usually 2 to 3 years.[1] Until the recent reforms, the total amount of the Enterprise fund available for productive investment was insignificant.

The third, and probably most important, snag concerns the impact of innovation on the 'success indicators' of the enterprise, and, linked with it, the failure to reward, or indeed even to recognize, risk-taking. Does the proposed innovation 'fit' into output and/or cost reduction indicators? Then it would be favourably considered. But what if it does not? One example has already been cited: that of the new central-heating boiler. There are other examples. Thus more durable kinds of electronic valves were not introduced, apparently because the existing ones satisfied the producing enterprise, whose 'success indicators' were in no way affected by whether the valves lasted three months or three years.[2] 'In order to provide effective checks on cost reduction,' wrote another critic, 'the greatest number of products are considered to be comparable,' even though the design may have been appreciably altered. Consequently, because the management seeks a cost-reduction bonus, 'the question of comparability is often in conflict with the improvement of the quality and range of the products of the enterprise, and sometimes acts as a direct obstacle in the path of introducing new and better products', because of the tendency to avoid 'those products which will be deemed "comparable" if the change in design involves increased costs per unit'.[3]

Innovation may, therefore, lead to difficulties. It is always simpler, in the circumstances, for managers to go on doing what they were doing before, unless some good reason (or order) to the contrary exists. Why take unrewarded risks? A Soviet literary periodical contained the following comment on this subject. 'The system of innovation is unfortunate. Innovation involves risk, and, as in all gambling, capital. If you risk, it is easy to lose. Isn't that so? But even if the director is given the capital, let him just risk and not win! ... No, it does not behove a director to take risks ... Suppose your direc-

---

[1] V. Markov: *Vop. ekon.*, No. 9/1959, pp. 41 ff., gives details.
[2] O. Antonov, op. cit., pp. 155-6. His article is significantly called, 'Why does the introduction of new techniques have to be fought for?'
[3] G. Vainshenker, *Vest. stat.*, No. 3/1957, pp. 20-1.

tor desires to bring into production a new (plastic) powder . . . , he would have to wait endlessly in ministerial reception rooms. There is a risk here. The risk is not that millions might be lost. He might take up these powders and, God forbid, the quarterly plan will be messed up, and the ministry will show up badly in the statistical report.'[1]

Finally, one must consider the effect on grass-roots innovation of the fact that virtually all prices are determined by superior authority. Since prices remain unaltered, wrote a Soviet critic, 'enterprises have no economic interest in the improvement of design'. It is true, he added, that in 1955 enterprises were allowed to charge extra sums to cover the costs of improvements to machinery, 'but this is seldom done in practice and is limited to certain kinds of equipment only.'[2] Another reason why new designs were unattractive is that a temporary price was fixed on the basis of cost plus 3-4 per cent, whereas, as several critics have pointed out, the average profit margin over costs in the machinery and engineering industries is often 15-20 per cent, in the case of possibly obsolete items already in mass production.[3] This did not encourage innovation.

A decree of the Central Committee and the council of ministers, published on July 2, 1960, somewhat improved the situation. Not only were premia received by directors and chief engineers made conditional upon the fulfilment of plans for the introduction of new technique, but some new incentives were provided for initiative at local level. Thus a new premium fund to encourage new technique will be formed by a levy on all industrial, building and transport enterprises, which will form part of production costs and which will vary from 1 per cent (for machinery) to 0·2 per cent (transport) of the wages fund. *Sovnarkhozy* were given more funds at their disposal to support new technical developments, including the production of prototypes and experimental work by enterprises. Prices of new machines will if necessary be kept below their initial costs by temporary subsidy from this fund.[4] A further decree on the same theme was published in September 26, 1964, also designed to encourage new techniques and new models.[5]

Obviously, these decrees do something to improve matters, if only by introducing and emphasizing new technique as a major success indicator. However, one can also envisage endless possibilities

[1] N. Lebedev, *Zvezda*, No. 5/1957, p. 155.
[2] V. Ganshtak, *Finansy SSSR*, No. 6/1957, p. 19.
[3] For instance see A. Basistov in *Vop. Ekon.*, No. 7/1964, p. 151.
[4] See text of decree in *Pravda*, July 2, 1960, and a good article by V. Markov, *Plan. Khoz.*, No. 6/1960.
[5] *Ekon. gaz.*, September 26, 1964, pp. 4-5.

of simulation, owing to the unavoidably imprecise definition of 'new technique', and also unnecessary innovation, 'for the record'. Many thousands of measures in this field are prescribed in central and republican plans; for example, in 1960, 'the plan for the introduction of new technique in the Ukraine envisages 2,900 measures', and, owing to fear of not being able to report fulfilment, 'already at the beginning of the year the *sovnarkhozy* of the Ukraine ask for 700 measures to be dropped from the plan'.[1]

The stimulation of innovation by administrative order becomes, in the circumstances, an important substitute for grass-roots incentives. Several bodies are charged with these duties.[2] At the top is the State Committee for Science and Technology. However, there are also republican organs, industrial ministries at various levels, Gosplan of the union and of the republics. When they existed, *sovnarkhozy* had such duties too. In those days, complaints were made that there were too many bodies concerned with innovation.[3] This is probably still the case under the ministerial system. The results, to repeat, appear to be patchy, with admirable achievement in some sectors and serious shortcomings in others. These contrasts may partly be attributed to the relative importance of initiative from below in the development of new models or techniques, but are also connected with the priorities imposed by planners. Thus, for example, all concerned may be aware of the advantages of some new sewing machine, but those in charge of the economy may be devoting attention and resources to matters which they consider to be of much greater importance. In these priority sectors, there has generally been much more active encouragement of new ideas, and much more money has been available to reward and develop them.

Here again we should not implicitly overlook the imperfections of the western system. Commercial secrecy, the buying up of inventions in order not to use them, trade-union resistance to new methods, sheer conservatism supported by a price ring and high import duties, these things may be found in various 'capitalist' countries. None the less, it remains true that the structure of the Soviet economy has done little effectively to encourage the search for the new at local level, and not a little to discourage it.

[1] K. Petukhov (chairman of Technical-scientific committee), *Pravda*, July 17, 1960.
[2] I. Spiridonov, the secretary of the Leningrad party committee, reported the existence of 'technical groups' (*tekhnicheskie kabinety*) attached to local party committees (*Pravda*, June 23, 1960).
[3] A. Kostousov, *Pravda*, August 28, 1959, Kostousov is the chairman of the State Committee on Automation and Machine-building.

The situation has been improved in these respects by the reform. As we have seen, more money is now available for decentralized investment, though a major snag repeatedly reported is that the equipment and building materials required to make a reality of this investment are unavailable. (We shall be referring again to this typical 'transition-disease'; if production plans are based on *zayavki*, i.e. on applications for planned supply, then obviously there will be trouble with *unplanned* supplies). The ministries have taken over from *sovnarkhozy* a fund which can be used in effect for subsidising technical improvements which would otherwise involve the enterprise in losses, or which would otherwise be too highly priced to be worth installing (more of this in chapter 8). The emphasis on profitability, the long-term nature of the profitability 'norms', the relative downgrading of 'gross output' as an indicator, should all help to overcome or mitigate the deficiencies mentioned above. Provided, that is, that the reforms are in fact fully implemented. More of this in a moment.

TRANSMISSION OF DEMAND TO PRODUCERS

Still on the micro-economic level, we must now consider the influence of demand on production decisions which can be taken at enterprise levels. We are not here considering the various ways in which a change in centrally-estimated requirements could lead to a corresponding change in the central plan. Obviously, if the top planning organs decided that the country needs more turret lathes, more soap and less vodka, the mechanism exists through which to issue the appropriate operational instructions and to make necessary investments. The problem here is one of adjustments within the general plan, rather than a change in the plan itself. We have repeatedly had occasion to note that detailed specifications and subdivision of assortment can only very partially be embodied in planning instructions.

Let us first examine the case of producers' goods, other than homogeneous products where questions of assortment do not arise. Suppose that a given enterprise desires to receive lathes, or yarn, or whatever it may be, of some particular type. How can its desire affect the producer enterprise?

It is certainly possible for orders to be placed for the required type. If it is defined as a separate variety of product in the commodity allocation lists, the user enterprise applies for an allocation certificate for the given variety. Alternatively, if it is not so defined, then, having obtained an allocation certificate for lathes or yarn, or whatever it may be, the customer approaches the producing enterprise or the wholesaling organization and requests that the required types be delivered. However, this request may be refused, and, unless backed by administrative instructions from superior authority, there is no particular reason why it should be granted, provided the customer can be compelled to accept the inferior substitute, which, in conditions of chronic shortage and a seller's market, he generally can be.

The reasons for this state of affairs are implicit in the preceding analysis of success indicators. The producing enterprise under the 'traditional' planning system, has no incentive to satisfy user requirements, and every incentive to fulfil output, cost-reduction and other plans which are irrelevant to the use-value of the product. If lathe A and lathe B are 'worth' the same from the standpoint of plan fulfilment, the fact that lathe A happens to be more efficient and more 'wanted' is a matter of indifference (economically) to the producing enterprise. If, for any of a large number of reasons, lathe B happens to be more convenient to manufacture, then, unless orders to the contrary are received from superior authority, lathe B will be produced.

A very good example of success indicators stimulating the production of a model undesirable from the user's standpoint was given by a Soviet engineer, and is worth quoting in full. He referred to several indicators peculiar to an aircraft factory, which serves as a reminder that ministries and *sovnarkhozy* frequently devised and devise large numbers of such indicators involving almost any conceivable aspect of the enterprise's activity.

'Suppose that the factory insists on a change in design which ensures an economy of 10,000 roubles a year but increases the weight of an empty aircraft "only" by 3 kilograms. What effect can this have?

'Suppose that the change consists in the elimination of a drilling operation after stamping, reducing the labour input by two hours. The labour input indicator is improved, and sure enough the annual plan of the factory prescribes a reduction in labour time. There is a reduction in machine-tool use—another indicator! There is less waste of metal—yet another indicator! A new "rationalizing" proposal has been adopted—that's an indicator too! There is additional annual economy as a result of adopting a new proposal—another indicator! And what an important one, too! The factory personnel has undertaken the obligation, under socialist competition, to economize 100,000 roubles over and above the (cost reduction) plan confirmed by the *glavk*. In a word, the factory is materially interested in the proposal.'

But, says the engineer, the effect of adding 3 kilograms to the weight of the aircraft is to reduce the carrying capacity of the aircraft by 2 kilograms, and, in the given example, assuming a freight rate of 2 roubles per ton-kilometre, the net effect could well be a loss to Aeroflot of 400,000 roubles, which hardly balances an economy of 10,000 roubles which the enterprise was so anxious to obtain.[1]

In the west, a product which is better from the user's point of view will, in general, command a better price, yield a higher profit, because the users can offer more if they think it worth their while. It is a weakness of the Soviet system that there is generally no means of doing this. Of course, there are efforts to impose minimum technical standards, but this can hardly cure this built-in defect. The system of allocation is itself a further impediment to flexible adjustment. Allocation certificates specify the supplying enterprise, and so the dissatisfied customers cannot threaten to buy elsewhere. In the many cases where specifications are closely defined by the central authorities, they cannot be changed at all at enterprise level, and the effort to secure permission to change them takes time and runs into bureaucratic delays involved in getting several departments to agree, a process known in Russian as *soglasovanie*. Where the proposed change can be made at enterprise level but requires delivery of some different material, nothing effective can be done until the allocation certificate is amended.

In a number of instances, failure to meet user demand is a direct consequence of 'allocation' decisions which neglect local requirements. One of many satirical articles in *Krokodil* (June 10, 1960) describes the repeated delivery of agricultural machines to *sovkhozy* in Kazakhstan which cannot be used there. 'The *Oktyabr'ski* sovkhoz of Pavlodar *oblast'* needs a flax thresher about as much as a fish needs an umbrella. Flax has never been sown in these regions and is not now sown there. Or why does the "Chekhov" grain *sovkhoz* receive all at once 136 tractor-operated reapers? Yet the *sovkhoz* was compelled not only to accept the reapers but also to pay 644,000 roubles for them. In vain it begged: "Take away these reapers, pass them on to someone who needs them." ' The very large number of similar complaints from other parts of the country suggest that the allocation of unsuitable machines to agriculture is a widespread phenomenon. No one in the allocation, wholesaling or, apparently,

[1] Antonov, op. cit., pp. 152-3.

manufacturing organizations has sufficient interest in the suitability of the machines for use in any given area, and numerous criticisms have yet to cure the weakness, though it is hoped that, following the creation of a new supply structure, the farms will exercise their rights as buyers and refuse unsuitable machinery.

Once again, the effect of these species of difficulty is very unequal in different sectors of the economy. The defects are most noticeable where there is a multiplicity of possible products, and a changing pattern of demand of a kind which no central planning agency can or should reflect in its detailed system of instructions. This is most clearly to be seen in the field of consumers' goods, to which we shall turn.

There is, first, the question of inducing manufacturers to meet the orders of the retail trade network. The latter can judge, by the length of queues, the views expressed by dissatisfied customers and the level of unsold stocks, that certain items should be ordered in greater quantity, and that others are unpopular with the public. But the retail shop, or local *torg* grouping the shops of the given town, has only very limited possibilities of action. It can place orders direct with local industry, but the large majority of supplies have to be obtained through wholesalers which operate at republican and all-union levels. As a Soviet critic put it, 'between the supplier and the user stands the disposals organization (*sbyt*), which, so to speak, depersonalizes the product'.[1] The wholesaling organs depend for their profits on fixed margins, their plans are expressed in gross turnover, they are remote from the customers and have no significant inducement to be responsive to their needs. They are not adequately penalized for holding unsaleable stocks, because stockholding is automatically covered by credits from the State Bank.[2] The wholesalers also operate, in the case of many major species of goods, within allocation quotas decided by the planners; thus Azerbaidjan or the Ukraine receives a given quantity of wool cloth or leather shoes, which are subdivided by the Ukrainian ministry of trade and Gosplan between *oblasti*, cities, etc., and the request of (say) the Odessa shops for more of a particular kind of shoes must be fitted into these various allocation quotas.[3]

[1] I. Kulyov, *Kommunist*, No. 9/1959, p. 27., also B. Zolotov et al., *Ekon. gaz.*, No. 19/1967, p. 40.
[2] Of course, the credits should not be automatic, but in practice are virtually so.
[3] According to R. Shniper (*Vop. ekon.*, No. 11/1960, p. 147), the Ministry of Trade of the RSFSR maintains an office through which local trading organs can dispose of the 'wrong' goods to other local trading organs, and acquire others.

However, let us now assume that, despite all possible obstacles, the order reaches the manufacturing enterprise. A plentiful literature shows that industry often fails to respond. It 'corrects' the trade orders, to take into account its materials allocation; it has hardly any choice in this, since if the right leather or a red dyestuff is not allocated to the producers, it cannot produce the required shoes or red cloth. Indeed, this problem of linking the ever-changing requirements of retail trade with the industry's material allocations is a peculiarly difficult one to solve. But, as one critic rightly put it, industry sometimes turned down requests from the trade network also because a 'change in the product mix would lead to an underfulfilment of the gross output plan'.[1] It is unnecessary to repeat here that efforts to achieve bonuses under various success indicators are often inconsistent with the satisfaction of the requirements of the consumer. A Soviet writer has commented as follows. '. . . The big rise in stocks in the trade network, together with the existence of unsatisfied demand for many commodities, is the result of discrepancies between the assortment and quality of goods produced and the pattern of people's demand. One reason lies . . . in the "aggregate" (*valovoi*) approach to the determination of commodities required to meet demand.'[2] Indeed, variants (usually less extreme!) of the stories about sending skis to Uzbekistan and textbooks on cotton-growing to north Siberia appear all too frequently in the press.

In fact the retail chain itself is very backward in studying consumer demand, as very numerous articles in the Soviet press make clear. Nor is this surprising. The trade margins are fixed, so there is no extra profit in providing a commodity in short supply. It is, or until recently has been, easy to sell anything. As in all countries under similar circumstances, employees in the retail chain develop a 'take it or leave it' mentality.

Retail prices are, with few exceptions, fixed by the central or republican governments, and at levels which should (and sometimes do) more or less equate demand with supply. This means that, in relation to costs of production, some retail prices are much higher than others. However, this does not encourage the production of commodities or models which sell at relatively high prices, because the bulk of the difference consists of turnover tax and does not benefit the producers. By way of illustration, let us take two commodities, A and B; costs are assumed to be 100 roubles in both cases. The following situation may frequently be encountered:

[1] R. Lokshin, *Vop. ekon.*, No. 5/1957, p. 132.
[2] R. Lokshin in *Zakon stoimosti (Kronrod)*, p. 458.

	A	B
Costs at factory	100	100
Profit margin	5	5
Factory wholesale price	105	105
Turnover tax	50	15
Wholesalers' margin	5	5
Retail margin	10	10
Retail price	170	135

Clearly, no one would find it worth while to switch to A rather than B on their own initiative. In the given example, they would be indifferent as between A and B, but in practice, such are the imperfections of pricing, it is not seldom found that the more desired goods work out to be less profitable. Thus this method of levying turnover tax eliminates a potential means of 'transmitting' the demand pattern to the manufacturers, because, as was shown above turnover tax is often deliberately calculated to cover the variable gap between the wholesale and retail price. Of course, it is arguable that the planning organs ought to use the size of this gap as a species of signal; if it is big, more should be produced of the particular good. However, there is little or no sign that they see it that way, though financial organs have been blamed for insisting on the production of items carrying high tax rates for which there was no demand.[1]

A further relevant factor has been the unresponsiveness of local authorities, who have many responsibilities in organizing trade, opening shops, restaurants, etc., to the needs of the citizens. This in turn was (and still is) due to the fact that elections are unreal, and that members of local soviets are primarily responsible to party and state officials above them. Only this can explain the remarkable degree of neglect so often encountered in Soviet cities, for example in opening enough shops. Efforts to put these defects right have been made,[2] and an extensive literature shows acute awareness of the problems of satisfying consumer needs in a more rational and more

---

[1] S. Partigul, *Ekon gaz.*, January 6, 1965.
[2] Notably in the decrees issued in 1959 on shops, and on restaurants and cafés, and in 1960 on wholesale and retail trade. See *Pravda*, February 28, 1959, and August 9, 1960, and A. Popov in *Sovetskaya torgovlya*, No. 8/1959, pp. 3 ff. There is currently a great and much needed drive to expand consumer services of all kinds.

flexible way. This is an inevitable consequence of greater abundance and wider assortment, compared with the acute 'goods famine' which prevailed for so many years. Unsold stocks of unsaleable goods are causing some worry to the authorities. The public is becoming more choosy, as supplies and living standards increase.

Progress is, however, also blocked by a clumsy system of planning consumers' goods production. A particularly notorious example—there are all too many of them—concerned electric irons and electric kettles. In 1955 they were in ample supply, so much so that it was decided to reduce production. But in the USSR nothing seems to be done by halves. The output figures developed as follows:

	1955	1958
	(thousands)	
Electric irons	5,290	2,130
Electric kettles	485	80

Source: N.Kh. 1958, p. 299.

Consequently, these goods disappeared from the shops, and *Pravda* denounced the acute shortages and published a decree increasing production again.[1] An example of another kind concerns lampshades. As all visitors to the USSR were able to observe, nearly all Soviet homes had old-fashioned, dark red or dark orange lampshades, with tassels. Why? Because, according to a *Pravda* article, no other kinds were made for retail sale; modern lampshades were made for hotels and public buildings, but, since no retail price had been settled for them, they could not be sold to the public and production was being cut down, as all hotels had been supplied.[2] Shortly afterwards, a decree of the Central committee of the party and the Council of Ministers of the USSR (*inter alia*) prohibited the production of old-fashioned dark red and dark orange lampshades.[3] It cannot be said that this is a good instance of flexibility in linking output, retail trade and consumer requirements.

One critic wrote: 'The most difficult is the linking of trade turnover and the plan of commodity deliveries,' and another, in the same journal, bitterly complained that the assortment of goods delivered by industry do not conform with the requirements and orders of the retailers, and that the arbitration organs systematically uphold the supplier's right to vary the nature of the goods supplied; 'for the

[1] *Pravda*, August 28, 1959, and October 16, 1959.
[2] *Pravda*, July 5, 1959.
[3] *Pravda*, October 16, 1959.

past ten years we have been unable to settle the assortment of goods with a single factory in good time.'[1]

The relative failure to adjust production and distribution to the requirements of the consumer has three aspects, or causes, which ought not to be confused in analysing defects or in endeavouring to see ways and means of overcoming them. The first, which has been much emphasized in the last few pages, is the unresponsiveness of the price system to demand, and, on the contrary, the responsiveness of directors to 'success indicators' and plans which cannot of their nature take consumer demand adequately into account. The second aspect concerns the habit of underpricing, the tendency towards tolerating queues rather than raising prices to the extent necessary to eliminate them, with the consequence of a chronic seller's market, with all that this implies in terms of quality of service and, indeed, responsiveness to demand.[2] The third is a question of priorities: during most of the Soviet period, scarce human skills and material resources have been systematically used in heavy industry rather than in consumers' goods industries or in trade; in these non-priority sectors, investments have been relatively low, the quality of managerial personnel relatively inferior. In the case of retail trade in particular, the effect of 'success indicators' is often extremely misleading. Thus labour productivity (in terms of turnover per shop assistant) is higher and distribution costs are doubtless far lower in the USSR than in Great Britain, but this is in large part due to such factors as the far smaller number of shops per thousand customers in the USSR, smaller stocks in relation to sales, much more intensive work of the shop assistants. Indeed, most British shop assistants spend a large part of the day waiting for customers, so in a sense they are 'inefficiently' used, though this is the inevitable consequence of a wider degree of consumer choice and the absence of queues.

But having said all this, it is important for the student of Soviet economics not to overlook a very essential point: whatever may be the inefficiency of the mechanism by which goods are distributed, whatever the inadequacies of the finer adjustments to the citizen's requirements, more goods tend to be produced, retail trade turnover increases by impressive percentages. In certain circumstances, even the appearance of a long queue may represent progress; there is no

[1] Y. Sapel'nikov, *Sovetskaya torgovlya*, No. 6/1960, p. 17, and M. Zykov, ibid., p. 25.
[2] Note the interaction of these two aspects: it is largely because of queues —i.e. of underpricing—that retailers, wholesalers and manufacturers can adopt a take-it-or-leave-it attitude, and concentrate on 'success indicators' without fear of not selling whatever is produced.

G

queue for goods which are not there. The Soviet system does, in normal years, ensure that there will be many more raincoats in three years' time than there are now, even though the styles, sizes, quality and range may all leave much to be desired. More cloth, clothin g shoes, television sets, handbags, and so on, are being produced. In so far as this is so, a steady increase in living standards does occur, and Soviet economists have some reason on their side when they accuse their western *confrères* of being so concerned with optimum distribution and the finer adjustments of output to demand that they overlook the quite essential point of the quantity of goods produced. A million raincoats, though they may not precisely correspond to what the citizen desires and may have to be queued for, are surely better than half that number produced and sold under the most perfect principles of the market and the capitalist price-mechanism.

This argument is certainly not to be ignored. Yet it contains a flaw which modifies its effectiveness considerably. Certainly, *ceteris paribus*, a million raincoats are twice as numerous as half a million raincoats (if one abstracts from the fact that other goods may be more urgently required). However, in terms of use-value, it is not always so. Two raincoats which do not fit are not worth twice as much as one which does. A given number of raincoats in fully assorted sizes and styles, which correspond to consumer requirements, are not 'equal' to the same number of raincoats which are available only in two styles and two sizes, in any but a purely numerical-statistical sense. All this is in the highest degree relevant when comparing Soviet output of consumers' goods with that of a 'capitalist' country. Standardization and a restricted range of choice are not necessarily a bad thing, but they have certain consequences in terms of aggregates of consumer satisfaction, which are none the less real for not being measurable. If a Soviet housewife wishes to buy a certain article and has to make do with another, her annoyance cannot be measured; only the thing she actually buys is statistically recorded. Yet in our conventional measurement of 'welfare', or in our aggregation of the value of goods, it is implicitly assumed that the consumer can choose from a wide range and that these goods are available at established prices. It is a scarcely deniable fact that the Soviet economy falls short in these respects of western standards. Plan-orientated production choices in the USSR are less effective instruments for adapting production to demand than are profit-orientated production choices under 'capitalism', sceptical as one may be about the reality of so-called consumers' sovereignty in the western world. This must have some unmeasured and probably unmeasurable bearing on the relative value of the consumer-goods produced under the two systems.[1] As will be shown subsequently, all this has a bearing also on growth rates.

The reforms now being implemented have as one of their principal objects the correction of these distortions. To some extent they must be disappearing. Thus *sovkhozy*, especially those who are being granted greater financial autonomy, are empowered to refuse equipment which they do not need. It is also intended that contracts between enterprises, albeit under the 'umbrella' of allocation decisions by Gosplan and *Gossnab* (and sometimes via freely-negotiated direct links), should more fully express the requirements of the customer-enterprises. The emphasis on profitability and *sales* as the principal success indicators undoubtedly detracts from the 'gross-output-for-output's-sake' approach. No sale, no bonus. In so far as the enterprise's own proposals affect the plan finally adopted— and to some extent this has been so even in Stalin's time—the new success indicators do orientate managerial thinking towards a study of demand, of the market. This applies also to consumers' goods. Trade organs have been urged to study demand, have been given greater flexibility. It has been recognized that one of the principal causes of the failings of retail trade has been the illogical and sometimes plainly absurd financial strait jacket within which they operated, and retail trade enterprises are being given some greater leeway, with fewer indicators imposed from above. However retail margins are often much too small, handling and storage facilities inadequate.[2] No doubt all this is historically explained by the prevalence of shortage, of 'goods famine', for a generation. Yet now that over-production is by no means uncommon, the new methods now being introduced should transform the situation, according to optimists.

But will they? Some of the causes of past troubles are still with us. Sales are perhaps a better indicator than gross output, but it is still a gross-value indicator. Material supplies are still, in the main,

---

[1] The following somewhat extreme example of 'output' for plan fulfilment instead of for profit might make the general point clearer to some readers. Suppose that a Soviet publisher of popular songs has a plan of 100 songs; a British pop song publisher has no plan, but seeks to maximize profits. The Soviet publisher, other things being equal, would tend to publish more songs (at least 100), because, until he fulfils his plan, he would choose to publish in all cases of doubt. Yet, even on the assumption that an increase in output of pop songs is a good thing (which God forbid!), what meaning would this 'superiority' have in any conceivable terms of worth, value or use? For a rigorous statement of similar arguments, see M. Polanyi, 'Towards a Theory of Conspicuous Production', *Soviet Survey*, October-December, 1960.

[2] See for instance *Sovetskaya torgovlya*, No. 10/1966, pp. 6 ff. and V. Mineev et al., *Vop. ekon.*, No. 4/1967, pp. 39 ff.

administratively allocated. The principal output targets in physical terms are still planned from above. Above all, prices are still inflexible, and profit margins are fixed (as in wholesale and retail trade), and are unrelated to fluctuations of demand, to scarcity or to abundance. The need for a new approach is well understood. But have there actually been any changes of principle yet? What has the reform accomplished?

THE REFORM AT MICRO LEVEL

Soviet economists rightly point out that a fundamental change in system cannot come overnight, that the process must be gradual, and that consequently it would be better to judge the scope of the reforms in 1970 or 1971 rather than today. This is a justified warning. In chapter 9 we will be examining the various models of reform (Liberman, the mathematicians and others). Here we shall examine the problems which have arisen in implementing the micro-economic reforms which have been described in chapter 1.

Firstly, a stream of complaints have appeared concerning the habit of ministries of issuing orders and 'passing down' compulsory plan indicators on matters which, according to the reform and the Enterprise Statute of 1965, are fully within the competence of the enterprise management. These include particularly the famous (or infamous) gross output indicator, but the list is long.[1] It includes, for instance, the detailed composition of the labour force, despite the clear provision to the contrary.[2] Supposedly, the enterprise itself should draft its own plans in respect of these indicators and they should merely be used for statistical-recording purposes. But it has frequently not been so in practice. The reasons are not far to seek: thus far, the ministries and their sub-divisions (glavki), like the sovnarkhozy before them, are judged by their own plan fulfilment record. They naturally exercise pressure accordingly. A second cause concerns the wages fund. This is still linked with the fulfilment of the gross output plan, and so any enterprise which cannot show the local branch of Gosbank that it has fulfilled (or overfulfilled) the output-value indicator is likely to be in financial difficulties.[3] Other plans, including labour plans, are 'given' to the ministry and,

[1] Evidence for this may be found in *Vestnik statistiki*, No. 6/1967, pp. 30-31 *Ekon. gaz.*, No. 17/1967, p. 35, and No. 22/1967, p. 10: *Vop. ekon.*, No. 11/1967, p. 78, and so on.
[2] See for instance full explanation of why this comes about by L. Levina, *Ekon. gaz.*, No. 6/1968, p. 30.
[3] *Ekon. gaz.*, No. 37/1967, pp. 13-15, and many other sources.

inevitably, passed down to its subordinates. These causes are recognized, and steps have been promised to alter the rules. Thus for example ministerial performance can now be measured in terms of profits, and the same trend may be seen in the experimental substitution of commercially-orientated *obyedineniya* for ministerial *glavki*, as described in chapter 1. In fact there exists, and is gradually being applied, a new set of rules (*polozheniye*) on industrial ministries and their *glavki*. A convenient example[1] happens to refer to the *glavk* responsible for the manufacture of combine-harvesters within the Tractor and Agricultural Machinery ministry. These rules would link the *glavk* much more closely to the financial results of its enterprises. Like them, it would have a fund for the development of production, a material incentives fund and a social-cultural fund, all these being a percentage of what its enterprises achieve (they must pay this small percentage to the *glavk*). The *glavk*'s own plan, as laid down by the ministry, is to include only *sales* (*realizatsiya*), plus the 'nomenclature of the most important products', goods for export and some quality indicators, total profits, profit rate, payments in and out of the budget, wages fund, centralized investments, new technique, and finally supply (i.e. delivery obligations laid down from above). Premia for *glavk* officials will depend above all on the magnitude of its enterprises' incentive funds, i.e. profits and sales. If—so it is laid down—a *glavk* official issues orders which lead to a reduction in the profits of an enterprise, he is to lose his premia and the enterprise is to be compensated.

Missing from the list of indicators is gross output, labour productivity, cost reduction and other 'traditional' plan goals. If these will indeed be the rules, if agrgegate ministerial plan fulfilment in respect of the above indicators is really now to be abandoned, then perhaps the situation is about to improve, and pressure from above to fulfil such indicators as these will be, is being, relaxed.

Unfortunately, such conclusions are premature, for several reasons. Firstly, even the new rules from which the above particulars are quoted provide for premia for 'overfulfilling the sales plan'. But sales (*realizatsiya*), it must be re-emphasized, is also a gross-value indicator. The difference between sales and gross output consists of unfinished production and production for stock. It is a money measure which includes the value of inputs. There can be conflicts between demand, or innovation, or profits, and the monetary measure of sales. We will return to these points in a moment. Then there is still no sign that the vital wages fund plan has been 'detached' from its

[1] N. Krasnikov, *Plan. khoz.*, No. 7/1967, pp. 29 ff.

connection with gross output. Also, as Soviet writers have pointed out, in any sector where there is a long production cycle it is hardly possible to measure plan fulfilment via sales.[1] Thirdly, just what exactly is meant by the 'nomenclature of the most important products'? It could be a long list specifying the product mix in physical terms in great detail. That this has happened in some instances is quite clear from complaints received. Thus from Magnitogorsk and Rostov came protests that the respective *glavk* planned in detail even production used only within the factory. A manager of a chemical plant protested that everything is planned 'down to the last kilogram'. Of course this need not be so, often is not so. But . . .[2] Under the rules, it is not at all clear where are the limits of central control over the product mix. Yet this is a key element in the reform. Fourthly, the ministerial and *glavk* grip over supply planning could nullify much of the reform. This control is a two-way process: control over supplies for enterprises (the ministries control the *fondy* of allocated commodities), and also supplies by enterprises to their customers as designated, supposedly, by *Gossnab*. The more detailed the material supplies plans and controls are, the more necessary it is to plan output and deliveries as well as inputs—since it is evident that if 1,000 tons of good A is to be delivered, according to plan, to enterprise X, it is necessary to ensure that it is produced. In other words, freedom of decision as to the product mix depends greatly on the conversion of the materials allocation system into free trade. This, however, is not yet far advanced, and this constitutes an important reason for the survival of detailed ministerial control. More will be said about the problems of supplies in the next chapter.

We have seen already that the enterprise's ability to utilize its unplanned resources (for investments in productive capital and in housing) was and is severely handicapped by shortage of goods, notably building materials and equipment. This shortage, in turn, arises precisely out of the unplanned nature of the demand, which meant that no one planned the supply. In come cases, building enterprises refuse to do the work, confining their efforts to planned (i.e. centrally-planned) construction.[3]

Various ways out of this situation have been discussed. One is to expand reserves to deal with this sort of unplanned demand. Thus the new rules for the *glavk*, referred to above, provide for reserves:

[1] Shipbuilding, for instance. V. Nikitin and I. Koslesova, in *Plan. khoz.*, No. 7/1967, discuss the 'sales' indicator very thoroughly.
[2] *Ekon. gaz.*, No. 22/1967, p. 10; No. 17/1967, p. 35 and No. 37/1967, pp. 13-15.
[3] *Ekon. gaz.*, No. 7/1967, pp. 6-7.

2 per cent of the wages fund, up to 3 per cent of material supplies, 10 per cent of the part of the depreciation fund intended for capital repairs, 5 per cent of the planned credits. All these percentages relate to the total of the amounts which enterprises within the *glavk* are to have.[1] They would provide some material and financial room for manoeuvre, though above enterprise level. The local organs of *Gossnab* are supposed to carry stocks. But one is once again up against the system of material allocation. One critic actually proposed the inclusion of decentralized investment work in the state plan![2] Of course this would make it centralized! Still another commentator noted that one of the principal obstacles to the development of direct contractual links (outside of the formal allocation system) was that delivery obligations omitted from the central plan are automatically regarded as of low priority and therefore would be omitted from the output plan.[3]

Many other snags have emerged. The whole incentive-fund system is clumsy, full of conditions, subject to much too much variation as between enterprises. It is extremely difficult to understand, and may well give rise to a whole series of ingenious and unforeseen bonus-maximizing manoeuvres. The element of unpredictability is further increased because 'confirmed' plans, (including profit plans) are altered many times by the ministries during the course of the year, just as they used to be.[4] The capital charge is varied between enterprises, so are the 'norms' by reference to which the various funds are calculated, which benefits the enterprise whose management succeeded in persuading the ministry to give them a low profits norm or a generous percentage of the wages fund or capital assets. What matters, in other words, is not so much actual profitability but the plan and the norms. But other illogicalities inevitably arise. The following are but a few of them:—

(*a*) There are still several indicators, which can be mutually contradictory. Total profits, the profit *rate* relative to capital, total gross values of sales, these objectives would frequently point in opposite directions. No hint is given as to what the manager is then to do. Needless to say, some other orders he receives, such as those relating to his product mix, can contradict all the above indicators. Nor is the situation improved by the fact that whereas the fulfilment of the sales plan is measured in enterprise wholesale prices (as fixed in July,

[1] M. Krasnikov, op. cit.
[2] *Ekon. gaz.*, No. 39/1967, p. 11.
[3] *Ekon. gaz.*, No. 37/1967, pp. 13-15.
[4] For instance *Ekon. gaz.*, No. 39/1967, p. 4.

1967), the profits are calculated in relation to actual revenues, i.e. the prices at which the goods are actually sold. The two can differ because of the existence of accounting prices, zonal prices (e.g. in respect of the food industry), different prices charged to different categories of customer (e.g. for electricity) and so on.[1]

(b) The actual formulae for the various enterprise funds bristle with anomalies, some of them comic. Thus the incentive fund is a percentage of the wages fund. Suppose that the extra profit arises out of an economy of staff which reduces the wages bill: it is possible that the net effect would be a smaller rather than a bigger incentive fund! The same is true of the effect of a reduction in capital on the calculation of the size of the investment fund. In the words of P. Bunich, 'the enterprise faces a dilemma: either increase profitability and profits by economising in capital funds, and thereby increase the norm (percentage) allocated to the Fund for the expansion of production, or lose by reducing the magnitude to which the norm (percentage) is applied'[2] So in the end it could be that the amount of the incentive is reduced by the very fact that, by economizing in wages or capital, one reduces the magnitude used for calculating the incentive, though the object of the exercise is precisely economizing labour and capital!

(c) There is criticism of the logic of depreciation allowances. A factory with old equipment, with therefore a low valuation of capital, has less to spend on repairs and renovations, when it needs more. A new factory, which needs to spend a great deal, has ample depreciation allowances and much more resources to finance decentralized investments.[3]

(d) There is lack of logic in investment decisions and finance in other respects too. Why should the rate of interest on investment credits be ½ per cent for centralized, 2 per cent for decentralized investments? Why the difference? Why so little, given that the usual capital charge is 6 per cent? (Capital charges are not payable during the period of repayment of credits in respect of credit-financed investment.) The capital charge is 6 per cent throughout the life of the asset, interest on credits is paid only on the outstanding part of the credit, so the disparity between the credit and the charge is greater than it looks and totally indefensible. All overdue credits are charged 8 per cent. Why? 'No one has yet told us why'[4] Nor is it

[1] Nikitin and Koslesova, op. cit.
[2] Vop. ekon., No. 10/1967, p. 48.
[3] Thus—Kudryavstev, Ekon. gaz., No. 4/1967, p. 12.
[4] Bunich, op. cit., p. 56.

clear why a part of profits is set aside in the financial plan for repayment of credits for centralized investments, yet no such provision is made for decentralized investments. Furthermore, as several critics have pointed out, differences in profitability norms as between enterprises naturally predispose them to adopt widely differing criteria for decentralized investment, for no reasons which make sense in terms of national-economic advantage. Thus 'enterprises with high profitability norms, say 15 per cent, will find unprofitable those investments which promise a final profit rate of 10 per cent. Any enterprises whose basic profitability norm is low, say, 3 per cent, would invest in anything which gives them a higher profit rate, such as 4 per cent or 5 per cent.'[1] But this is plainly nonsense. (More about investment criteria in chapter 7.)

(e) There is much criticism of the inflexible and often excessive transfer of the entire 'free remainder' of profits to the budget. Whatever the ultimate intention, at present this often means that the lion's share of profit goes to the budget, and the enterprise's interest in profit-making is greatly reduced.[2] Surely, too, enterprises could with advantage be allowed to accumulate reserves? These sums could be kept in the banks, which would pay interest, thus encouraging enterprises to wait until a good opportunity arises to spend the money.[3]

(f) As we have seen the material supply system is still very much what is was. It is said that the maintenance of the supply system in its present form is temporary, part of the transition to the 'wholesale trade' in inputs which many advocated and which was indeed mentioned in Kosygin's speech of September 1965, introducing the reform. However, experience suggests that, as the French say, *il n'y a que le provisoire qui dure*. Authoritative articles describing the system as it is, such as that by Ivanov[4], do not sound as if they are describing a fast-disappearing picture.

(g) Prices are, and must be, a vital element in any reform. Obviously, micro-economic decentralization of decision-making can only make sense if prices act to transmit economic signals. As will be made abundantly clear in chapter 8, the price system remains unresponsive. Indeed, there are some steps backwards in this respect. When, in 1963, two clothing firms (*Bol'shevichka* and *Mayak*) were the first to be put experimentally, onto 'the new system', they were given some limited but potentially very significant powers: to vary

---

[1] *Ibid.*, p. 47.
[2] Ibid., p. 47, and also *Ekon. gaz.*, No. 39/1967, p. 15, and many others.
[3] Bunich, op. cit., p. 49. Several Soviet economists, encountered in Moscow in 1967, advocated this procedure in the course of discussions.
[4] V. Ivanov, *Vop. ekon.*, No. 8/1967 (see next chapter for further references).

prices by agreement with their customers. This right was quickly withdrawn when these two firms were merged in the general reform, to avoid what was called 'the anarchy of the market',[1] to the irritation of their managements.

(h) The tendency to reorganize on the basis of *obyedineniya*, while in some respects both desirable and promising, has also the appearance of an ill-prepared campaign. There are still no set rules. There is great unclarity about the powers of headquarters. It is one thing to grant the powers of a *glavk* to some large inter-related industrial complex. It is another to take a group of medium-sized factories, scattered over a wide area, call one of them the chief over the others and hope for the best. The result in some cases is that the subordinate enterprises are treated as 'step-children' (*pasynki*) and are given the less profitable orders and the older equipment.[2] In any case, an intelligent commentator takes the view that the USSR badly needs large numbers of small autonomous enterprises. He points out the statistics of average numbers employed per enterprise, defined as financially separate units of production:—

	(*All industry exc. power stns.*)	*of which machinery and metal-working*
USSR	565	2,608
USA	48	74
W. Germany	83	139

The author argues strongly for the proposition that there is great advantage in modern industry to have large numbers of independent *small* firms, which in practice work closely with the industrial giants and supply them with all kinds of items. Thus General Motors has 26,000 supplying firms, many of them small, Renault obtains from sub-contractors 20,000 items for assembly. By contrast, the Soviet large enterprise often has to make its own components, in backyard foundries and workshops at high cost. The author claims that what is needed is 'small-scale industry composed of independent enterprises', and since this is inconsistent with state ownership, proposes the restoration of producers' co-operatives.[3] This is a lone voice at present, but clearly this sort of outlook, and the statistics cited above, do not suggest that further enlargement of the size of the management

[1] *Komsomolskaya Pravda*, June 23, 1967.
[2] *Sovetskaya Latvia*, September 2, 1967, also see A. Mozalevski, *Ekon. gaz.*, No. 5/1967, p. 11.
[3] Ya Kvasha, *Vop. ekon.*, No. 5/1967, pp. 26 ff.

unit is the right answer to some, at least, of the problems of Soviet industry.

(i) Finally, there are unsettled questions of labour and wages. Should enterprises be given the right and power to dismiss surplus labour, without having some responsibility for finding them another job? How far ought take-home wages vary according to the profitability of the enterprise? There is little evidence yet of clear thought on these subjects which, after all, relate closely to the effect and effectiveness of the reform.

The above pages may sound like an outright denial that the reform has accomplished anything. This would be going too far. It is essential to point out that the whole process is in its early stages; while the major part of the industrial structure was planned on 'traditional' lines, the logic of the system severely restricted any effective changes in those sectors which had 'gone over to the new system'. Things may be different by 1969. But even if they are not the new criteria for enterprise operation may make much more difference than might appear at first sight. Thus the greater interest in profits will inevitably affect what the enterprise management proposes. We have repeatedly noted the great importance of the application, the *zayavka*, in the process of planning. That is to say, the materials, output plan, investment projects proposed by the men on the spot have a big influence on what actually happens, even if ministerial or central-government authorization is required. Obviously, proposals from below must be affected by the new concern with profits, capital charges, and the rest. If ministries and *glavki* are concerned with these things too, and they are, this will affect resource allocation, which is also being more rationally discussed at higher levels of planning, as we shall see in the next chapter.

In any case, much in practice depends on the existence of a sellers' market. If demand exceeds supply at official prices, neither industry nor trade pay much attention to user demand. Under any reform or none, 'take it or leave it' will be the rule so long as the customers (be they citizens or other managers) are queuing for the goods. But when it is hard to find buyers, then even a poor system and incorrect pricing can operate. Thus several cases were reported in which the shift to *sales* instead of gross output caused a change in the product mix to a less profitable, but more saleable, pattern.[1] This is understandable, and would render 'wrong' pricing much less harmful than it would otherwise be. But one also encounters references to 'dependence of trading enterprises on their suppliers', to fear that

[1] See, for example, Ya. Pistrov, *Vestnik statistiki*, No. 9/1967.

complaints (about quality or wrong assortment) will be followed by victimization.[1] These, of course, are typical sellers' market phenomena.

Finally, on ministerial powers. Several Soviet analysts see that the problem is not one which can be solved by decrees. There are regulations for enterprises, and for ministries too as well as *glavki*. But no regulations can limit the power of a hierarchical superior over his subordinate. The latter must obey, though he can and often does protest. No arbitration tribunal can adjudicate between the boss and a more junior unit in the same hierarchy. It is hard to see, therefore, what can effectively be done to protect the enterprise from 'its' ministry. The solution being sought would seem to be that of giving the ministries basically the same material interests—in profits and sales—as the enterprises.

THE PARTY AND THE CORRECTION OF DISTORTIONS

It may be asked: what have the various controlling, inspecting and checking agencies been doing, to permit numerous deviations from the intentions of the party and government? In particular, we have had occasion to note the vital importance of party officials at republican and *oblast'* levels, their role as supervisors of *sovnarkhozy*, their very considerable influence over factory directors and others in the state's economic network.

There is a vast number of reports in the party press about this supervisory work. It is clear that in many instances the Party units do perform the task which they are meant to perform, notably in preventing disobedience to or direct evasion of plans and instructions, and also in stimulating the adoption of new methods, which might otherwise fall victim to inertia, organizing various forms of 'socialist competition', and much else besides. However, as must have become apparent in the present chapter, the essence of the present problem is not disobedience to orders, but manoeuvring designed to show (or sometimes simulate) the fact that orders have been obeyed, i.e. that the plans have been fulfilled. The Party officials are judged, in the economic sphere, by their ability to ensure the fulfilment of various plans within their area of jurisdiction. The secretary of the Party group within the enterprise often finds himself helpless *vis-à-vis* the director even if he wishes to act, because the director of a large enterprise is generally himself an influential Party member. But even the secretary of the Party's town committee (*gorkom*), or the *oblast'*

[1] *Komsomolskaya pravda*, September 9, 1967.

party secretary must inevitably be influenced by their own desire to report to headquarters that various key plans are fulfilled. For them, paraphrasing Dickens, '99·9 per cent—misery; 100·1 per cent—happiness'. It should surprise no one, therefore, to encounter numerous reports concerning the connivance of party officials at various distortions designed to facilitate plan fulfilment within the given plant or area.[1] There is hardly any need to list instances, since hardly a single one of the 'deviations' discussed in this chapter, or the next, would have occurred if the party supervisors had done their job. Criticism of this tendency among party officials has appeared at intervals in the party press, and there have been examples of party officials ordering local government officers to disobey orders received from the centre in the interests of plan fulfilment in the particular locality,[2] though, as already suggested, such direct disobedience is doubtless exceptional. No amount of appeals to doctrine and to discipline can eliminate it so long as the 'supervisors' are judged by the same criteria as the managers whom they supervise.

THE SPECIAL PROBLEMS OF AGRICULTURE

Soviet agriculture is peculiar in being divided between three very different forms of ownership: state, collective and private (see chapter 1, above), and the organizational and operational problems of each are in many respects different. One species of difficulty related to the existence of this division. If there are state farms and *kolkhozy* in the same area, there has been in effect no joint planning agency. *Kolkhozy* were controlled by the local party secretary, with the *raion* executive (and, until 1958, the MTS). State farms received their orders down their own state-farm line of subordination, and, though the *raion* party authorities had a formal right to interfere, this right was in fact hardly exercised. Lack of administrative co-ordination was accompanied by all kinds of wasteful duplication of supply agencies, complicated by the fact that *kolkhozy* were entitled to buy many kinds of producers' goods (e.g. building materials) at retail prices through the consumer-co-operatives, while state farms were supplied at much lower wholesale prices through the appropriate *sbyt* agencies.

Prices of the principal inputs (farm machinery, fuel, fertilizer,

---

[1] Thus a report appeared concerning directorial simulation of plan fulfilment in Leningrad, 'covered' by the party organization, trade union secretary and *sovnarkhoz* officials (*Pravda*, January 27 and 31, 1961). Superior party organs expelled and *dismissed* the director.
[2] See for example a leader in *Partiinaya Zhizn'*, No. 10/1958, pp. 4-7.

etc.) were equalized in 1958, and supplies were handled since 1961 by *Sel'khoztekhnika*, both for state farms and *kolkhozy*. (However, it still seems to be very difficult for *kolkhozy* to obtain building materials and tyres, to name two items which figure frequently in reports of shady dealings, and they have to pay high prices for these on occasion.) The two types of farms are both administered by the same production administration since 1962, and so the distinctions have become less with the years, so that we may be on the way to some single type of farm, a cross between *kolkhoz* and state farm.

Yet it is misleading to compare the selling prices of the two categories of farms, because they cover a different range of expenditures. A *kolkhoz* must, out of its revenues, pay for practically all its investments (or repay credits which it might receive for investment purposes), insure its buildings, animals and crops, issue produce and/ or money to its sick or aged members,[1] pay a sizeable tax on gross revenues, and has in recent years been encouraged to build schools and a variety of rural amenities. A state farm bears few of these burdens; a large part of its investment is budget-financed, any losses are covered by subsidy, its employees receive social-service benefits and qualify for old-age or disability pensions. Obviously, therefore, an equal selling price, *ceteris paribus*, would leave a *kolkhoz* far worse off than a state farm. All this greatly confuses one's assessment of the economic effectiveness of the two types of farm, both on a national and on a local scale.

It is no doubt for this reason, among others, that *sovkhozy* are being put onto 'full *khozraschyot*', being paid the same prices as *kolkhozy* and incurring almost the same costs (see chapter 1).

A state farm, whatever may be its other defects, has a system of cost accounting similar to that of other state enterprises, and there is no undue difficulty in determining what the costs are. It was quite otherwise on a collective farm. The essence of the problem was that of measuring labour cost, in a system in which the *trudodni* or other payments vary widely. Since the remuneration of peasants on a *kolkhoz* (unlike the wage-paying state farm) was a *residual*, with no fixed rate of pay and extremely wide variations from farm to farm and between area and area, it contained within itself such net profit or net loss as the farm has made, and so was of little use as a measure of costs as such (it will be recalled that the categories 'profit' and 'loss' do not appear in *kolkhoz* accounts, precisely because of the

---

[1] A budgetary contribution towards *kolkhoz* old age pensions was decreed in December, 1964. Of course, *Sovkhozy* pay social insurance contributions.

residual nature of peasants remuneration). Output statistics are still almost always 'gross', i.e. inclusive of goods and service bought from outside the *kolkhoz*. For many years, the very existence of 'cost' in *kolkhoz* production was denied by official economists. However, in more recent years both economists and planners have become acutely aware of the need for greater efficiency and for some effective action to reduce costs in general and labour inputs in particular. Therefore they must be measured. How?

Two schools of thought emerged. One argued that labour costs should be measured on the assumption that the peasants have received the pay rates applicable to state-farm labourers. Then, it is pointed out, one avoids some very confusing results. These could be illustrated by an example. Thus the total value of pay per working day in the *Strana sovetov kolkhoz* in North Kazakhstan was 21·70 roubles in 1956 (when it rained) and 3·70 roubles in 1957 (when it did not).[1] What sense is there in basing a calculation on the untenable proposition that labour cost, per unit of labour actually expended is almost six times greater in one year than another? What practical conclusions, other than misleading ones, could be drawn from such a measure of 'cost'? Efficient farms might falsely appear to be high-cost farms, just because they distribute so much more to 'their' peasants.[2] One can also see another advantage in the 'state-farm wage' method: that any actual expenditure of labour has a direct effect on cost calculation. Otherwise, by reason of the 'residual' nature of peasants' pay, one could envisage a situation in which a 30 per cent increase in labour inputs, which was totally unproductive, could lead to a 30 per cent decrease in the value of each *trudoden*, the total amount of peasant income remaining unchanged. In other words, in the *kolkhoz* the marginal cost of labour can appear to be *nil*—unless any additional work performed adds in some way to cost, as it would do if a notional value were assigned to it.

But this view was hotly disputed. It was pointed out that if state-farm wages are in fact not paid to *kolkhoz* peasants, it is quite unreal to measure costs on the assumption that they were paid. If, for instance, in a given area *kolkhoz* daily remuneration is 30 per cent below that of state-farms, then this must affect the real cost and cannot be assumed away. The distortion caused by large variations in pay was admitted, but, so it was argued, the greater efficiency of high-pay farms is such that costs per unit of produce will still generally

[1] G. Lisichkin, *Vop. ekon.*, No. 7/1960, p. 62.
[2] For this argument, see, for instance, M. Nesmi, *Finansy SSSR*, No. 11 1957, p. 92.

seem lower there.[1] The only basis for measurement, they claim, can be whatever is actually paid.

Still another method sought to evade valuation in money altogether, and tried to measure labour time. This foundered on the lack of reliable information. Assessment in uncorrected hours and minutes can mislead by ignoring quality and skill of work. Assessment in *trudodni* is useless for purposes of inter-farm comparison by reason of a wide divergency in work norms adopted.

This controversy has been partially resolved by the decision to pay *kolkhoz* peasants a minimum remuneration based on *sovkhoz* rates. Actual pay, in both types of farm, can differ from the official basic rates, by reason of bonuses and extras. Some *kolkhozy* distribute a good deal more than *sovkhoz* average pay, and will apparently continue to do so. But, by reducing the range of pay in different farms, the changes decreed in 1966 have greatly simplified the solution to the problem of identifying costs. The use of either *sovkhoz* pay rates or actual pay would give results which if not similar, would not differ to such an extent as to nullify the validity of cost calculations.

The impact of costs on *kolkhozy*, and their effects on remuneration, are intimately linked with prices, and also with the significance to be attached to land rent. These two questions are discussed in chapter 8. At this stage it is sufficient to make the point that the new price structure, while an improvement on the old, still failed to reflect cost differences, and the relative state purchase prices for different commodities in any particular area would only by accident be rationally related to local shortages or national requirements (except where, as in the case of fruit, prices are free). Therefore it is not in practice possible to base *kolkhoz* plans and programmes on price stimuli, the more so as most *kolkhozy* are also influenced by the free market price, which is generally much higher than either the official buying or retail prices. *Kolkhoz* chairmen do, of course, seek to manoeuvre to maximize farm revenues—net revenues in so far as they are able to identify them[2]—especially if they respond to the pressure of their members who desire higher incomes. Therefore, when delivery plans and administrative pressures permit,

---

[1] For several of the many statements of this side of the argument see I. Laptev and E. Karnaukhova in *Vop. ekon.*, No. 8/1957, pp. 80, 102, and N. Litvinov *et. al.* in *Sots. sel. khoz.*, No. 8/1956, pp. 35-42.

[2] The qualifying phrase is important. Often, thanks to the nature of *kolkhoz* accounts, it was impossible for chairmen or anyone else to discover whether a given activity was profitable in any sense. For example, see Litvinov. op. cit., pp. 35-42.

the chairmen adjust their behaviour to the available incentives in an effort to increase the value of distributed incomes, whether in *trudodni* or in terms of fixed pay plus bonuses; in either case the chairman as well as the members benefit.

Partly as a consequence of the continuing inadequacies of the price system, and partly because of long-ingrained habits, on-the-ground planning was constantly disrupted by administrative interference. *Kolkhoz* plans had to be geared not only into delivery plans imposed from above (this at least is in line with the rules adopted in 1955-58), but also with whatever current campaign the local party organization happened to be 'pushing'. All kinds of 'plenipotentiaries' (*upolnomochenye*) were despatched by party secretaries to run campaigns on the spot. An abundant critical literature has appeared in recent years concerning stupid forms of party intervention in *kolkhoz* planning and management, intervention motivated by the desire of party officials to report to their headquarters whatever the latter wishes to hear: that the sown area has been increased, even though fallow is desirable for soil conservation purposes; that a high percentage of harvesting was by the currently fashionable two-stage method, even though in the given instance it is unsuitable; that farms have been amalgamated to make bigger *kolkhozy*, even if local conditions are unfavourable for such large units; that milk output had to be increased, though there was no demand for more milk from this particular *kolkhoz*; that sowing had been ordered to be completed by some early date, though it is agronomically more sensible to delay it; that even seed grain had been delivered to the state, by order of the Party 'plenipotentiary', so as to claim that the plan is fulfilled; that more maize must be sown even if this disrupts the established crop rotation and makes no sense in that locality.[1] The encouragement given by the highest party authorities to regional 'competition' and to ambitious undertakings to double or treble production of, say, meat in some spectacularly short time, ensured the continuance of this highly 'political' agricultural planning. Khrushchev's campaigns included, in his last years, an effort greatly to reduce the area under grass and oats, substituting maize and sugar-beet. The harm

[1] A long bibliography can be assembled concerning these practices, which continue seriously to harm Soviet agriculture. The reader is particularly referred to V. Ovechkin: *Rayonnye budni* (Moscow, 1954), E. Dorosh's 'diary' in *Literaturnaya Moskva*, 2nd issue (Moscow, 1957) and, for more recent information, the speeches of Khrushchev and Polyanski to the central committee plenum (*Pravda*, January 12 and 21, 1961), and P. Prozorov, *Pravda*, January 6, 1961, A. Shevchenko in *Ekonomika sel'skovo khozyaistva*, No. 12/1960, especially p. 22, F. Abramov in *Neva*, No. 1/1963, V. Ivanov in *Novy Mir*, No. 3/1963, and many, many others.

done by these policies was given increased publicity after his fall, and promises were made that arbitrary political interference with farm management will cease. It may be thought that farming of all things is not suitable for such treatment.

All these deficiencies were vigorously criticised and attributed to 'subjectivism' and 'hare-brained scheming', in the course of the plenum of the central committee in March 1965, especially by Brezhnev, who once again showed that it is the party rather than the ministerial hierarchy which controls agricultural policy (Brezhnev spoke as party secretary, whereas the analagous speech on industry was made by Kosygin as prime minister). No longer are we to see these arbitrary political interventions, or so we are told. It is true that there has been no sign of Khrushchevian 'campaigning', and there is much greater emphasis on economic calculation. The Ministry of Agriculture, under the experienced Matskevich, is operating with reasonable efficiency and regularity. To this extent the deficiencies associated with central and party control were due to Khrushchev's personal predilection for interfering. But not all is either clear or satisfactory. The existing prices, especially after the 50 per cent bonus introduced in 1965 for grain, are more profitable for some crops than for others, and for nearly all crops than for livestock products (see next chapter for details). Pressure to deliver in accordance with plan continues, as it must do with such prices as these. Proposals have been made in print to the effect that the element of compulsion in procurements should be abandoned.[1] The critics also complain of the one-sided nature of the contractual obligation: *kolkhozy* must deliver, but the procurement organs do not have to accept. So far the element of compulsion has been retained for quota deliveries, i.e. for the obligations laid down under the new system introduced in 1965 and described in chapter 1. In fact the critics have been strongly counter-attacked, not only by Matskevich but by economist-defenders of the official line.[2] Indeed, there are signs that 'voluntary' sales over and above the quota can be semi-compulsory, judging by published criticisms of those who did not volunteer.[3] The language used there sounds all too familiar, though it must be admitted that the prices are much more advantageous than they used to be. Under recent rules, both *sovkhozy* (those on 'full *khozraschyot*' at least) and *kolkhozy* may sell direct

[1] A. Emelyanov, *Plan. khoz.* No. 1/1966, pp. 74 ff., M. Terentiev, *Vop. ekon.*, No. 4/1966, pp. 42 ff., and various works by V. Venzher.
[2] For such a statement, see M. Gritskov, *Vop. ekon.*, No. 8/1967, pp. 50 ff.
[3] Unsigned leading article in *Ekon. gaz.*, No. 29/1966, p. 3 ('The organization of overplan sales of grain surpluses . . . is a major state task').

to the retail trade network any perishables which the state procurement organs do not purchase in time.

Unequal profitability at *kolkhoz* level presents a problem of price-fixing policy, to be discussed in the next chapter.

Should prices vary with costs? Or should they, on the contrary, stimulate specialization in low-cost areas? Clearly, one cannot do both at once. This is linked, too, with compulsory procurement (or delivery) quotas: some otherwise orthodox commentators believe that high-cost areas should be exempt from delivery obligations, as these contradict the needs of specialization on products which, in the given area, are lower cost.[1]

The last but not the least among the difficulties engendered by the agricultural system concerns distribution. The problems here can readily be deduced from evidence given on the previous pages. Purchase prices are not logically interrelated and change little or not at all in response to shortage or abundance. This, of course, is not peculiar to the USSR, as any student of United States price support legislation must surely know. However, retail prices are similarly inflexible, fail to reflect scarcities and make grossly inadequate allowance for seasonal shortages. To make matters worse, the system of food distribution suffers from some inherent defects. This is partly a consequence of underinvestment; there is grave shortage of storage space, refrigeration, means of transport, good roads. But there is also lack of adequate incentives. With centrally-fixed prices often unattractive to the producers, with farm output plans often underfulfilled, and with the trading and procurement agencies having little material interest in showing enterprise, the situation is often extremely patchy. Matters are not helped by the delivery regulations to which *kolkhozy* are subject; for reasons of flexibility, the *kolkhozy* (and in some cases state-farms also) are entitled to substitute certain products for one another in meeting the delivery quotas imposed upon them, but in their choice they cannot be guided by actual requirements because these cannot be transmitted to them by any economic mechanism. One result is that deliveries of milk are generally made in the more readily transportable and less perishable form of butter, and liquid milk is notoriously short at many times of the year in most Soviet cities. Thus in 1958 no less than 65 per cent of all 'milk' delivered to the state in the USSR was in fact butter, over 80 per cent in some republics.[2]

Sales by farms direct to retail trade, while provided for in the rules,

[1] M. Gritskov, op. cit.
[2] R. Nazarov, in *Sovetskaya torgovlya*, No. 6/1960, p. 19.

run up against price-snags. In the case of meat, prices paid to farms are known to be higher than retail prices. This is sometimes true of potatoes too. The procurement price is 104·80 roubles per ton in Moscow *oblast*. Wholesalers sell to retailers at 87·50 roubles![1] Direct sales are therefore not made by the producers, except in the free market.

The consequence of erratic and unequal food supplies is a wide disparity in free market prices at different times of the year and in different towns. To some extent the uncontrolled free market can fill gaps, but the existence of the above-mentioned disparities shows that it cannot do so adequately. Peasants and (with some exceptions) *kolkhozy* are not generally in a position to supply remote markets, and communications are often a serious obstacle even to official food distribution, let alone to peasants with a sack of onions and no transport priority. The few who can make the journey glean a big profit from scarcity prices in ill-supplied areas. Thus peasants with two sackloads of citrus fruits find even an air journey from Transcaucasia to Moscow worth while. But there is no self-correcting mechanism, in the absence of a professional trader class and of adequate incentive for official trading initiatives. Indeed, the consumer-co-operative commission traders (p. 46, above) could theoretically market surpluses on the peasants' behalf, but they lack inducement to take much trouble to seek out supplies or to transport them over large distances, and they have made little difference to the situation.[2] With the gradual decline of the free market as a source of food, it is in any case essential to reorganize and strengthen the official food distribution machinery and its links with the farms.

There is also the perennial problem of the private plot, and its attractiveness as against collective work. Its importance for family consumption was highlighted as follows, for the RSFSR. It provided 90 per cent of the potatoes, 80 per cent of vegetables, almost 100 per cent of milk, meat and eggs.[3] Another analyst calculated that collective work absorbed 60 per cent of the family's time and provided only 37 per cent of income. In Lithuania the private plot absorbed the unusually high proportion of 40·8 per cent of the time, but provided 70·2 per cent of the income, whereas in the country as a whole the figures were respectively 30 per cent and 41·9 per cent. The author comes to the conclusion that an increase from 30 per cent

[1] V. Mineev, op. cit., pp. 39 ff.

[2] For criticism of the inadequacies of commission trading, see A. Gavrilov, *Sovetskaya Torgovlya*, No. 8/1957, pp. 13 ff., and also Khrushchev in *Pravda*, January 21, 1961.

[3] M. Makeeenko, *Vop. ekon.*, No. 10/1966, pp. 57 ff.

to 40·8 per cent in the share of private work could lead to a disproportionately high increase in income.[1] This conclusion seems unsound in detail, but does emphasise the fact that many peasants find that private work pays better than collective work. Perhaps the guaranteed minimum pay which now exists will change all that.

There remains the question: why, despite the many reforms of the post-Stalin period, do agriculture and food distribution retain so many elements of irrationality and clumsiness. Part of the explanation is historic: neither *kolkhozy* nor peasants were provided with incentives to produce what was required, and so arose the habit of ordering them about, which persists even when prices and incentives have been much improved. But, while this 'traditional' approach can wither away, another reason may prove more lasting: factors of production in agriculture are capable of producing many different things, can be combined in many different ways, and are subject to unplannable vagaries of weather. It is far more difficult to apply the techniques of central planning to agriculture than to—say—the coal or steel industries, or even textiles. Unplanned variations in output and availabilities are not reflected in prices, and the absence of adequate official inter-regional distribution arrangements (or of a private trading class) ensures spasmodic shortages and seasonal or local food queues. Lastly, as has been noted repeatedly, the social-political aspects of the peasant problem still affect policy, to an extent no longer true in other sectors of the economy.

THE SPECIAL CASE OF FOREIGN TRADE

As was noted above (p. 48), foreign trade is the monopoly of specialized corporations under the aegis of the Ministry of Foreign Trade. Import requirements and exportable surpluses are made known to these corporations by Gosplan and other internal economic agencies—though the corporations and the ministry, by their reports on trade opportunities, also affect the decision-making process.

The first problem that arises concerns calculating the profitability of trade, or calculation of comparative advantage. This is rendered very largely impracticable by the divorce between internal and world prices, as well as between the internal prices of the USSR and

[1] M. Sidorova, *Vop. ekon.* No. 5/1967, p. 51. In interpreting the above percentages, it must be noted that a considerable percentage of time was devoted to non-agricultural work.

those of other countries in the Soviet orbit. The unrealistic official exchange rate was not the primary cause of the difficulty, though it made things worse by introducing an additional confusion into the calculations. Though the rouble was in effect devalued in relation to the dollar in 1961, the essential problem remains. Soviet internal prices still bear a very varied relationship with world prices. A French delegation compared the prices of Soviet chemicals with those prevailing in France. Sulphuric acid, at a given exchange rate, is three and half times dearer in the USSR than in France, but caustic soda is one and a half times dearer in France than in the USSR; over thirty examples are cited in this report.[1] These examples are not in the least affected by such factors as turnover tax. They are explicable partly by wide differences in real costs in an economy sheltered for many years from world markets, partly by the consequences of the pricing irrationalities described at length in chapter 4. Then, in so far as Soviet prices do not reflect relative scarcities, they cannot be a useful guide to trade. For example, a 'cheap' commodity which, in terms of price comparisons, seems eminently exportable may actually be in short supply and need to be imported.

Calculation of comparative advantage therefore runs into most serious obstacles. But in practice these calculations were seldom made at all in the USSR. Trade decisions were very largely quantitative. It was decided that a certain amount is available for sale to this or that 'capitalist' country, or is earmarked under an agreement for China or Czechoslovakia; or the Soviet economy needs a quantity of rubber, copper, chemical machinery, and goods must be exported to pay for them. The quantities concerned are then disposed of, or bought, by the appropriate trade corporation. In deals with capitalist countries, their job is to strike the best bargain they can. In exchanges with Soviet-orbit countries, the general practice is to base payments on world prices. In either event, the trade corporation does not concern itself with the domestic price or domestic costs. It buys or sells as required, and the necessary financial adjustments are then made through the bank and the budget.

Soviet trade deals are very often bilateral in character. This bilateralism is not based on any ideological conviction, but stems from two factors: one is that quantitative exchange, a species of barter, lends itself far more easily to two-way arrangements; the other is that planning operates far more smoothly if both the prospective imports

[1] *Revue de l'Institut Français du Pétrole*, January, 1960, p. 246. The figures relate to November, 1959. See also very useful article on price relativities in *Economic Bulletin for Europe*, Vol. II, No. 1 (1959), pp. 39 ff.

and the prospective exports are integrated in the plan, and an element of untidiness is introduced when a trading partner earns a surplus which is transferred to some other country which then makes an unexpected demand for goods which the plan has earmarked for other purposes. Of course, none of these difficulties are insuperable, but the fact remains that, even within the bloc, the USSR has very largely stuck to bilateral trade deals, even though formal provisions for multilateral clearing have existed for some years. But the effect, as in all bilateralism, is to confine exchanges to the partner's surpluses, even where these may not be high on the importing country's scale of priorities. Thus, for example, the USSR imports tomatoes from Bulgaria, or dates from Iraq, largely because these happen to be commodities with which the countries concerned can pay for Soviet exports (or repay aid) to them.

It does not require much thought to see that such 'quantitative' trading at world prices unrelated to domestic costs is inconsistent with the application of the principles of comparative advantage. It is evident that the present system can permit sales or purchases to be made which are inherently unprofitable to the Soviet economy. The USSR's allies in Europe, who depend on trade much more than does the USSR itself, have been very conscious of these defects, and various attempts have been made to calculate when, whether, and how far particular trade dealings are worth while. Thus it was discovered that some Hungarian and Polish exports were sold at prices which barely covered the value of the imported raw materials used up in producing the goods concerned. Various ways have been discussed to ensure that choices are made on some objective basis. Thus one such method was as follows: the net earnings of foreign currency (i.e. export value less imports embodied in that commodity) were compared with the cost of production in zloty, and alternative variants were compared to find the most favourable zloty: foreign-currency ratios.[1]

This does not help appreciably in planning the production of exportable commodities, or, above all, in decisions concerning rational specialization within the Soviet bloc itself, of which there has been so much talk recently under COMECON[2] arrangements. Should Poland, or the USSR, or Czechoslovakia, specialize on some

[1] For more details on this subject, see *Economic Bulletin for Europe*, Vol. II, No. 1 (1959).
[2] Council for Mutual Economic Assistance (sometimes known as CMEA). All European members of the bloc and Mongolia, are full participants. China used to send an observer. North Korea, Yugoslavia and more recently Cuba do so. See M. C. Kaser: *Comecon* (2nd edition, London, 1967).

particular product, which could be produced in each of these countries at x zloty, y roubles and z crowns respectively? Indeed, imagin-
ing that only 'socialist' countries exist, at what prices would they
exchange various commodities? The fact that exchanges take place
at present at 'capitalist' market prices is a recognition that criteria
must be found outside the 'socialistic' system. Indeed, one eastern
official jokingly said—in private—that after the world revolution it
would be necessary to preserve one capitalist country: 'otherwise
how would we know at what prices to trade?'

This picture of crude barter and economic confusion should not
be pressed too far. The USSR still exports timber and imports cocoa.
The obvious kinds of international specialization, based on natural
conditions or traditional skills, do occur. The USSR does not try to
sell its high-price and inefficiently produced clothing in world markets. If it fails to buy cheap and good Italian clothes, it is not because the cheapness and quality are not known, but because of the
priorities of the plan. The USSR exports oil to Czechoslovakia because the USSR has oil and Czechoslovakia has not. East German
engineering products naturally exchange for Soviet raw materials
and fuels. Indeed, the obvious forms of trade are not really 'caused'
by market and price relations, but by underlying 'quantitative' realities. But this applies only to the obvious. In the very wide range of
goods where a calculation has to be made to determine relative
advantage, the Soviet planners are all but helpless, and serious and
unnecessary economic loss must result. However, before we in the
west adopt a superior attitude in these matters, it as is well to recall
that our practice has little in common with our own theories. The
discovery that goods can be produced 30 per cent cheaper in some
other country is far too often merely a prelude for the imposition of
a 35 per cent import duty, or, as in the case of farm products bought
by the United Kingdom, of some elaborate combination of quota
restrictions, import duties and subsidies to domestic producers. It
therefore behoves us to criticize the admittedly very crude Soviet
arrangements in the knowledge that we cannot compare them to
some pure comparative cost principle actually in operation in western
countries.

In another respect, however, Soviet practice is far inferior, and
this is a by-product of the monopolizing of trade by specialized corporations. These stand in the way of direct contact between Soviet
exporter and customer, the Soviet importer and his supplier, which
makes for clumsiness, delays, difficulties over precise specifications,
etc., on which it is hardly necessary to enlarge; these have caused

much criticism in Czechoslovakia and Hungary, among others,[1] and, one imagines, there must be a good deal of grumbling in the USSR also.

Why has this system survived in this very imperfect form? One suspects that much is to be explained by the development of this structure in a country—the USSR—which is largely self-sufficient and was anxious for most of its history to make itself so. Foreign currency was chronically scarce, and had to be strictly rationed by the centre on the basis of priorities centrally established. The USSR was, in its formative years, isolated politically, and it was a matter of faith that the forces of the world market were something to be guarded against. In any event, as the central plan was the foundation of economic activity, foreign trade had to be fitted into this plan. The planning process itself encourages an autarkic approach, since planners like to take decisions which can be enforced within their area of political-economic responsibility, and show an understandable disinclination to rely on the unforeseeable decisions of others, or on the unplannable vagaries of the world markets. On a less exalted plane of argument, one senses the vested interest of the Ministry of Foreign Trade and its corporations, concerned to channel all trade contacts through their own hands, even where, on general grounds, direct contact between firm and firm was desirable. In more recent years, the expanding levels of trade with countries of the Soviet bloc, and indeed with many other countries too, has placed heavier burdens on the system, so that major reforms of organization, of prices and some development in the still primitive theory of international trade can hardly be very long delayed. It is therefore not surprising to learn that a study of criteria of relative economic effectiveness of production in different countries has been launched by COMECON, which has set up a committee for that purpose. In the Soviet Union itself the level of the discussion has been raised by an excellent article by G. Shagalov,[2] which discusses the deficiencies of existing internal prices, and deals with the complex problem of assessing the effectiveness of export-orientated or import-saving ('anti-import') investments. There is now a recommended 'temporary methodology' for comparing the effectiveness of such investments in COMECON countries. But the argument continues, as does bilateralism and much dissatisfaction, especially in the

[1] For Hungary, see B. Balassa, *The Hungarian Experience of Economic Planning* (Yale University Press, 1959). The Hungarian government now permits a few large enterprises to engage in foreign trade deals directly, and is liberalizing further (see chapter 9).
[2] *Vop ekon.*, No. 6/1965, pp. 89-99.

smaller countries which rely so heavily on foreign trade. Voices are raised in some countries in favour of establishing a close relationship between internal and 'world' (i.e. capitalist) prices, but contrary views are also expressed. For instance a Soviet economist drew attention to this contradiction: prices of raw materials, minerals and grain have tended to fall relatively to prices of manufactures in the past ten years, which discourages investment in and production of these items for export, as and when calculations are made of their profitability. Yet in fact it is raw materials, many fuels and grain which are particularly urgently needed by many COMECON countries. Misleading price-relationships derived from world markets therefore impede rational specialization within COMECON, according to this critic, and lead to a tendency to barter bilaterally so as to balance two-way trade in sub-categories of goods known as 'hard' and 'soft', i.e. scarce and less scarce. This by-product of the wide gap between 'world' and internal prices leads the author into advocating a separate set of prices for a 'socialist' market,[1] but this is likely to be opposed. The level of the debate is rising all the time, but decisions are not taken.

The practice of trade with non-Soviet countries raises a host of other problems—for instance, discrimination, most-favoured-nation clauses, alleged dumping, the relationship between trade, aid and politics—which it is not the purpose of this book to pursue.[2] Nor is this the place to argue about the degree to which, so it is alleged, the actual prices at which trade within the Soviet orbit takes place favour the USSR, especially as the evidence is inconclusive.[3]

[1] O. Tarnovski, *Vop. ekon.* No. 10/1967, pp. 84-5.
[2] For some discussion of these problems, see A. Nove and D. Donnelly, op. cit., especially pp. 21-44, and especially F. Pryor (see next footnote).
[3] Interested readers are referred to H. Mendershausen, in the *Review of Economics and Statistics*, May, 1960, for a statement of the case for this proposition. However, the book by F. Pryor, *The Communist foreign trade system* (London, Allen and Unwin and Yale U.P.), and also articles by F. Holzman suggest that Mendershausen's case is weak.

CHAPTER 7

Planning and Investment

COMPLEXITIES

It is perhaps unnecessary again to stress the enormous and growing complexities of planning. Yet these underlie the problems we are considering here. The job must be divided between many offices, some concerned with the common problems of an industry, some with the common problems of an area, others with questions common to many industries and many areas. Production, supply, regional specialization, assessment of consumer demand, current planning, long-term planning, new technique, labour and wages, prices and public finance, all these interrelated and intermingled subjects are necessarily dealt with by different organizations. It is an illusion to suppose that the fact that all these organizations are part of the same 'state' machine makes it any easier for them to march in step. Certainly British experience of nationalized industries should teach us this. We are concerned here not with 'capitalist' characteristics, but with general rules of government and bureaucracy, and with the general tendency of human beings to seek personal gain, moral approbation or promotion, and to take responsibility for the sector or area with which they may be entrusted, rather than to concern themselves with a 'general good' which they can only obscurely apprehend.

An excellent illustration of these problems in their practical aspects can be based on the experience of regional organizations, the *sovnarkhozy*, under the 1957 reform, analysing why certain difficulties have arisen and where these 'fit' into the planning system as a whole. We have seen that the *sovnarkhozy* were set up as part of the effort to break up ministerial-industrial 'empires', which distorted the economy in the interest of ministerial particularism. It is important to note that the driving force behind this particularism was not selfishness or other defects of character of this or that official. The heads of some *glavk* in some industrial ministry set up their own supply arrangements and made their own components because of their anxiety to fulfil tight plan schedules. The reform of 1957 sought

219

to replace ministerial boundary lines with regional boundaries, though, as we have seen, the industrial sector divisions had to a great extent to be preserved or restored in practice.

AFTER THE SOVNARKHOZY

As was explained in chapter 2, the *sovnarkhozy* were replaced by ministries in 1965. In some respects this simplified the system, which was greatly confused by the proliferation of state committees, co-ordinating organs at the centre and the republics, plus the *sovnarkhozy*. At least there is now a clearer line of subordination. However, the difficulties are in large part due to the unavoidable necessity of dividing an extremely complex task, of planning production and supplies, between different offices at different levels. To see the problem more clearly let us return for a moment to the situation as it was under the *sovnarkhozy*.

The following is an example of post-Khrushchev criticism. It is by the Director and Chief Engineer of a knitting machine factory in Leningrad: 'The factory and the combine are under the Leningrad *sovnarkhoz*. But its work is planned by numerous organizations. The plan for the volume of output as well as profits and labour are passed down to us by the combine within the control figures decided by the Leningrad *sovnarkhoz*. The distribution of our production between branches of the economy is planned by Gosplan of the Russian Federation. The same body, through the Leningrad *sovnarkhoz*, after agreement with the republican *sovnarkhoz*, allocates investment funds to the combine. The product mix and technical design of mass produced machines are decided by the *sovnarkhoz* of the USSR. These indicators are then broken down in the republican *sovnarkhoz* on the basis of requests received from user enterprises by *Soyuzglavmash* attached to the USSR *sovnarkhoz*. The plan for spare parts is drawn up by *Rosglavsnabsbyttextildetal* within the republican *sovnarkhoz*. In a word the present planning system is excessively clumsy. The negative consequences of such methods are numerous. To agree a plan of output and all related technical economic indicators with all the above mentioned bodies is an extremely complex, lengthy and painful task . . . Take for instance the product design plan for 1965 . . . Four months went by in argument and endless reconciliations. But even the plan agreed at the centre cannot as a rule be used by us as a working document. After the plan is confirmed (in recent years this has been no earlier than November or December) *Soyuzglavmash* distributes our output between republican *sovnarkhozy*. Having received allocation instructions, we wait for the sub-allocations from the republics and then from the regional *sovnarkhozy*. Only when we can discover who our customers are, and the technical characteristics of the machinery they order are determined, can we prepare to produce machines ... So we still do not know what materials and components we will need (for 1965). But already last June (!) the factory had to indent for them! And indent we did! We invented something, based on experience of past years. Naturally we will get next year many materials and components which we will not need. Others, for which we did not ask, will be the subject of difficulty and much correspondence'.[1] The authors appear to see the solution, in the case of enterprises of all-union significance, in a more systematic centralization. Others have different views.

When the ministries were restored, the *glavk* of the ministry, in the above tale of woe, can be substituted for the Leningrad *sovnarkhoz* throughout, and *Gossnab* 'takes over' the USSR *sovnarkhoz*. The job is still divided, it is still necessary to indent (apply) for allocations months before plans are known. Delays in confirming plans, especially supply plans, remain all too common.

Of all these problems, the most intractable is the allocation of supplies. Literally millions of allocation certificates (*naryady*) are issued by different supply offices, in Moscow and in the republics. Each represents, in essence, a portion of the output plan of the enterprise which must deliver the allocated product. Yet not only are there many supply departments at different levels which raise difficulties of effective co-ordination (for example, where several products must be allocated to one factory or industry), but the supply departments are, since 1957, separated organizationally from the planning of production. In fact this is said to have been the one advantage of the 1957 reform, and so it has been retained after 1965, with consequences about to be examined in greater detail. Therefore there are numerous complaints about supply breakdowns, about plans for production which are inconsistent with plans for supplying the necessary materials and components. The interested student can readily convince himself of the serious nature of this problem by consulting any set of relevant specialized publications. For instance, one reads of a building site in Kuibyshev held up through failure to deliver machinery, which in turn is held up by failures to deliver components to the machinery manufacturers in Saratov, which failure is then traced up the line until it is discovered

[1] I. Solomonov, L. Fedorov, *Pravda*, December, 1, 1964.

that the Cherepovets steelworks had been expected to deliver steel from a workshop which had not yet been completed; or a Leningrad factory cannot complete textile machines because its plan has not been geared in to the output plan of a factory making one of the necessary components. The satirical *Krokodil* frequently publishes sarcastic comments. Thus a cartoon illustrated the statement of a Moscow party official to the effect that 'to receive ball-bearings from the first Moscow state ball-bearings factory, the neighbouring Likhachev automobile factory's requests for an allocation make a long journey, through fourteen republican and all-union *snabsbyty* and planning organs'.[1]

Uncertainties in supply cause *tolkachi* ('pushers') to flourish. The Dnepropetrovsk *sovnarkhoz* calculated that their metals and chemical factories were visited by 4,000 *tolkachi* in 1959, while 3,000 more descended on machinery factories and 1,000 besieged the *snab* and *sbyt* departments of the *sovnarkhoz* itself. Total: 8,000. All this is, of course, due to the failure of material supply arrangements to cover the production programme, or to fear of this.[2]

We do not know whether there are more or fewer *tolkachi* under the ministerial system.[3] We do know that, for instance, *Soyuzglavkhim* (chemicals disposal organ, *Gossnab*), responsible for tyre allocations, failed to name customers in 1967 for part of the factory's output, causing the management to make frantic appeals to *Glavshinprom* (its ministerial *glavk*) and the head of *Gossnab*, and this despite the fact that tyres are notoriously in short supply. There seems to have been a hold-up also at regional supply level. In the end, allocations were made only at the end of the quarter to which the allocations related, and then some of the 'customers' so designated did not need any tyres. The factory itself repeatedly found itself receiving materials which it did not need, and had to make appeals to the local organs of *Gossnab* and to its *glavk* to stop the flow.[4] Another good source, analysing the supply system, admits that many enterprises do not receive their authorization to purchase in time and have to place orders 'blindfold', in the hope that they will be forthcoming.[5] Of course, these could be seen as temporary consequences of change. But this interpretation is questionable.

Part of the difficulty arises from delays in confirming output and

[1] *Krokodil*, July 30, 1960.
[2] B. Zolotov, *Promyshlenno-ekonomicheskaya gazeta*, May 15, 1960. This article is an excellent analysis of the causes of this situation.
[3] *Tolkachi* in the supply process are discussed in *Izvestiya*, September 6, 1967.
[4] V. Shesternyuk et al, *Ekon. gaz.* No. 38/1967, p. 15.
[5] V. Ivanov, *Vop. ekon.* No. 8/1967, p. 115, and also many other sources.

delivery plans. For even if they are confirmed before the end of the previous year, this is only the signal for the detailed sub-allocations, decisions about which enterprise should supply whom, and negotiation of inter-enterprise delivery contracts, which can and do give rise to disputes. This can cause disarray.

Perhaps the best comment came from the economist Liberman. Writing, significantly, in the Party's leading fortnightly, he listed some outstanding examples of muddle over supplies. He pointed out that the system is both far too clumsy and too complex, making such muddles inevitable. So long as supplies are so organized, the complexities 'would overwhelm any apparatus of gosplans or supply-disposal organs (*snabsbyty*)'.[1]

Large numbers of *ad hoc* decisions are required to cope with disequilibria discovered after the plans have been approved, and this probably accounts for the continued practice of altering many enterprises' plans several times long after they were current; sometimes, wrote Liberman, this turns overfulfilment of the annual plan into underfulfilment at the last minute, which encourages the concealment of productive capacity and material reserves by directors.[2] As an example of how these alterations come about, a critic in the Party's fortnightly wrote that in 1958 the council of ministers of the RSFSR had to issue 140 statutory orders (*rasporyazheniya*) to secure additional supplies for Moscow region alone, because plans were not geared in with supplies. Possibly as a result, many received 'additional planned tasks' during 1958, but without the necessary materials being provided.[3] Worse, still, the organs of the Kazakh republican Gosplan were compelled to change their allocations of rolled steel 538 times, during the year 1959, because of various supply difficulties.[4]

Again, although the examples cited are pre-1965, the trouble continues. There are still repeated changes in plans, judging from many reports. This is due not to the fault of individual bureaucrats but precisely because the task, as Liberman put it nearly ten years ago, 'overwhelms' the apparatus. Unbalances, when discovered, must be put right. The plan must then be altered in the course of the year or even the quarter. New instructions must be issued to produce or to deliver. They then become 'internally inconsistent', because of incomplete amendment and because they are formulated by dif-

[1] *Kommunist*, No. 1/1959, p. 89.
[2] Ibid., p. 90.
[3] I. Kalinin, *Kommunist*, No. 18/1958, pp. 43-4.
[4] V. Saveliev and S. Ilyin, *Promyshlenno-ekonomicheskaya gazeta*, February 28, 1960.

ferent planning organs bit by bit.[1] It is abundantly clear, too, that the attempt to streamline supply planning and allocation has brought with it a series of new and predictable headaches. The task of planning supplies is divided between two totally separate bodies, Gosplan and *Gossnab*, and further involves, for various categories of materials, republican organs and regional supply agencies. But above all it also involves the economic ministries, and their *glavki*, as well as enterprises, since the ministries sub-allocate in their capacity of 'fundholders' (*fondoderzhateli*). Then the task of designating particular enterprises as supplying particular customers, and the supervision of the resultant contract negotiations and sub-specifications, is the job of *Gossnab*, or rather of its many sector and regional divisions and sub-units. In the *Gossnab* network are supposedly concentrated the *snabsbyt* (supply-and-disposals) functions which before 1957 were carried out by the industrial ministries. But ministries are in fact responsible both for sub-allocating *fondy* and for ensuring that 'their' enterprises do obtain their essential supplies and carry out planned deliveries. They would certainly be blamed for breakdowns. Indeed, the enterprise receives the finally-approved plan in respect of 'basic nomenclature of production', sales, profits, investment and the rest *from its ministry*.

It is therefore hardly surprising to learn that ministries in practice have held on to some of their *snabsbyt* functions. Even without reading about it in the press, one could foresee that ministries would have some local offices, that they would resist efforts of *Gossnab* to take them over. But one need not rely on imagination alone. Thus in Novosibirsk there were, in the second half of 1967, 37 *snabsbyty* under ministerial control, which, according to complaints from *Gossnab*, are duplicating the functions of its Novosibirsk regional system.[2] This is in fact a mass phenomenon, as we have seen already in chapter 2.

The enterprise's output and inputs must match. The chances of inconsistencies and confusions are still substantial, as is the likelihood of administrative overlap. The situation is tidier than in the last years of Khrushchev, but the basic problems have been rearranged rather than solved. It is true that there are now more officially-blessed and officially-planned long-term agreements between enterprises. It is true also that free sales of inputs through wholesale trade conducted by *Gossnab's* local organs is growing. The head of *Gossnab*, Dymshits, promised that it would continue to grow, as we have already seen

[1] See, for instance, *Ekon. gaz.*, No. 6/1967, p. 16.
[2] *Ekon gaz.*, No.30/1967, p. 20.

in chapter 2. But the logic of the system operates against partial freeing of production and supplies. The spirit of the past is well illustrated by an informative article by V. Ivanov. Here are some extracts:

'After the confirmation by the Council of Ministers of the USSR of the material supplies plan, the various ministries and departments distribute the allocated *fondy* between enterprises, construction sites and other subordinate organizations. This distribution takes place in accordance with indicators laid down in the national-economic plan for every enterprise and with detailed (*utochnennykh*) norms for the use of materials. . . .' He then criticises the slowness with which the *fondy* are distributed, and continues: 'Furthermore, the norms for the use of materials, confirmed by Gosplan jointly with the *fondy*-holders (i.e. ministries, A.N.), *as also the percentage average reductions in these norms for the planned year*, are sometimes also communicated late to enterprises' (my emphasis). . . . 'To create the conditions for successful implementation of the supplies plan, *Gossnab* must systematically ensure that the ministries (etc.) pass down to their enterprises the plan for supplies, material utilization norms, stock norms and differentiated tasks for reducing the use of materials, fuel, electricity. The *snabsbyt* organs . . ., on the basis of the confirmed supplies plan . . . sub-specify the distributed *fondy*, attach customer-enterprises to supplying-enterprises, issue alloca-tion-orders (*naryad-zakazy*) and so forth. This vital stage of the work . . . is vitally important, as it predetermines the successful implementation of the plan in respect of delivery dates, the quantity of the product, its assortment and its quality.'[1] The author does indeed advocate a greater use of direct inter-enterprise contracts, but obviously only as the basis of the supply plan.

Two points follow from the above. One, already mentioned in the last chapter, is that the kind of enterprise autonomy supposedly introduced by the reform is inconsistent with this kind of supply planning, and a *cri de coeur* on this very matter was printed recently in the house-organ of *Gossnab* itself, by a leading reformer.[2] Secondly, the appalling complexity, overlapping, delays, inconsistencies, in-herent in this kind of planning are evidently still with us, and will be with us for a long time yet on present showing. After all, supplies are just one problem. Other bodies, especially the industrial minis-tries, lay down or confirm production plans. Financial divisions of ministries, who no doubt receive a global profits plan from the Ministry of Finance, work out a disaggregated financial and profits

---

[1] Ivanov, op. cit., pp. 114-15.
[2] A. Birman, *Material'no-tekhnicheskoe snabzheniye*, No. 11/1967.

H

226   THE SOVIET ECONOMY

plan for 'their' enterprises. Wages, labour, investment, prices, the
plans for and deliveries to the retail trade network, the assessment
of relative costs in relation to particular production or supply
decisions, all belong either wholly or partly to different offices, or
ministries, or committees, or divisions of some large body (such as
Gosplan or *Gossnab*). Yet all of this has abstracted from the existence
of republican organs, which, for some of the less vital products,
have functions of planning and allocation too. Several years ago
there was vigorous criticism of confusion at republican level,
especially in respect of supply planning, and another republican
official said: 'To this day we have not eliminated inconsistencies
between the basic sectors of our plan: production, material supplies,
investment, the bringing into operation of new capacity.'[1]

Who co-ordinates the co-ordinators? The reform of 1957 replaced
centralized industrial structures with a system notionally territorial,
but in fact based on a multiplicity of central agencies, working
through territorial units, but unable to delegate any effective power
over resource allocation. These agencies could scarcely do anything
which does not impinge on other organizations. The task of keeping
them in harmony was of such a nature that new organizations were
set up to co-ordinate and to be co-ordinated. (Hence the new organs
set up in 1960-63, described in chapter 2, above.) The 1965 reform
altered the structure considerably. Has it altered it in such a way as
to resolve effectively the very severe problems which arise in treating,
for production and supply planning, a great industrial country as
if it were a great corporation, USSR Ltd.? Let us not forget that the
sovnarkhozy, for all their faults, did provide an institutional setting
for regional planning. The absence of such planning at any effective
local level, the weakness of the regional section of Gosplan at the
centre, are deplored by one Soviet critic, who fears its effect on the
development of Siberia.[2]

This whole section of the book is entitled 'problems', and therefore selects for analysis points of weakness or difficulty. Therefore
the above assemblage of criticism must not be misunderstood. The
economy works, most factories function most of the time. The punc-
tual arrival of materials is not news and would not be reported in
the press. As in all countries, most enterprises are doing this year
much what they did last year, and draw their supplies from what for
them has become the customary source. There exists an informal

[1] See V. Vasilyev, *Plan. Khoz.* No. 1/1965, and also *Pravda*, July 14, 1960.
[2] B. Orlov, *Ekon. gaz.* No. 29/1967, p. 11. This has been loudly re-echoed by
republican and regional planners.

network of personal links and contacts, which plays an essential role in overcoming a variety of obstacles. None the less, the problems discussed are real, not only because they have attracted and are attracting the critical attention of many Soviet planners, administrators and economists, but also because they are built in to the system. One has only to consider realistically each of the points discussed to see that it is not a question of human error or stupidity, correctable by appointing other officials or reorganizing the distribution of work between departments.

In the West some similar problems, though on a smaller scale, arise within a giant firm, and certainly our system does not insure against error and stupidity. Needless to say, delays in construction, unpunctual delivery of machines and other failures are no monopoly of the Soviet system. It is also only right to mention that many errors and scandals similar to those which are denounced or criticized in the Soviet press are unknown to the public in the West, because private firms' business is private. But the Western economy has the very substantial advantage that, in normal times, anything within reason (except large and highly specialized equipment) can usually be bought without any trouble. A workshop which indents on its company's headquarters for some needed tools or timber may sometimes curse headquarters for delay, but it is clear to all concerned that the tools or timber are available if needed. There is nothing approaching the confused maze of Soviet material supply organs. The Western system, it may be argued, is more haphazard and potentially more wasteful in deciding what to produce, in so far as each entrepreneur has less knowledge than have the Soviet central planners of the projects already on foot elsewhere in the economy and of the consequent need for the product in question. Far more effort must be spent on salesmanship, i.e. on disposals. If a *tolkach* is wasteful, so is a commercial traveller. The availability of stocks of materials, it could also be said, is often accompanied by a relative underemployment of productive resources, just as the troubles of Soviet material supply are a by-product of planning designed to use all resources to the full. But, be all this as it may, planning of the Soviet type does run into the difficulties described in these pages, and, at the risk of appearing to overemphasize the negative features of the economy, it is right to say so.

PLANNING BY 'BALANCES'

In chapter 2, above, a brief account was given of the planning based on material balances. This is a matter distinct from the actual job of current allocation of materials, though, of course, if done badly it would cause acute difficulties in the course of such allocations. The balances are needed primarily for development, for calculating the consequences of decisions on growth, and they are thus intimately connected with investment decisions. Whatever criticisms can and should be made of the system devised in the USSR, it is right to emphasize that they were pioneers in this very important field.

Until extremely recently, the 'balances' method was still somewhat crudely applied. For major raw materials and some other products widely used in industry, future requirements were calculated on the basis of technical coefficients, so as to enable the planners to foresee the material requirements inherent in their forward planning. But the inter-relationships were not adequately considered. No systematic working out of inter-sector relationships had in fact been undertaken. As has been pointed out by Soviet critics, while the methods used endeavoured to take direct material requirements into account, there was no adequate means of calculating indirect requirements. To use one example given by the Soviet source, the production of a ton of aluminium requires 18,950 kwh. of electricity; the various raw materials used in the production of aluminium also use electric energy, bringing the total to 20,042 kwh. But to this must be added the electricity used by other branches of industry supplying the aluminium industry, for instance, chemicals. When these are allowed for, the amount needed per ton of aluminium rises by a further 20 per cent, bringing the total to roughly 24,000 kwh.[1] It is surprising to learn that these calculations, confined experimentally to twenty-four products, were *begun* as late as 1959, using statistics for 1957[2] (of course, the plans for the chemical industry would include its own direct utilization of electricity, but this arises at a separate planning stage). The reasons for this shortcoming were in large part the same as those which inhibited a proper study of inter-sector relationships: statistical returns from enterprises and economic organs were incomplete, followed administrative rather than economic lines of demarcation, often grouped several products or several materials together. For instance, a factory making two different products does not, in its material utilization or allocation figures, distinguish which materials were used for which product.

---

[1] L. Berri, A. Efimov, *Plan. khoz.*, No. 5/1960, pp. 34-5. Presumably, though the authors do not say so, part of the extra utilization consists of investment requirements, direct and indirect, of the electricity industry itself.
[2] Ibid., p. 36.

Consequently, when in 1959 the research institute of Gosplan desired to create a true inter-sector input-output picture, information was lacking even in respect of direct material requirements, let alone the more complex indirect utilization data. Full data therefore required questionnaires, which were based on a sample survey covering 20 per cent of industrial enterprises. Progress in recent years has been rapid, and input-output tables have been devised, initially for 180 products, and some have been published in official statistical handbooks.

Of course, in Western countries we have been largely ignorant of inter-sector material relationships, but this had little practical significance for the functioning of the economy. In the USSR, however, when planning has been based on 'material balances', the slapdash nature of the calculations hitherto used does come as a surprise. How, one may ask, did the economy function at all? The answer seems to be in three parts: inspired improvisation often enabled rough calculations to be somewhere near correct; the many grievous errors were 'cushioned' by the existence of non-priority sectors which took the brunt of shortage; and, thirdly, some centrally-held stocks could be used in *ad hoc* rescue operations. Often enough there really was confusion, and the strains and stresses of material supply, already described, were presumably part of the everyday cost of doing things in this way. One wonders, too, whether the systematic failure to take *indirect* material requirements into account was not an important cause of the chronic shortage of many kinds of material.

With the help of mathematics and electronic computers, we may suppose that a more sophisticated version of material balances will be created within a short period. No doubt this will aid the process of planning, and make possible the avoidance of many errors. However, the limitations of the present programme must also be stressed. Obviously the list of products will only be a tiny proportion of the full range of commodities, models and types actually in production. Progress is being made, with Kantorovich (promoted Academician in 1964) put in charge of a mathematical-economics institute within the Siberian branch of the Academy of Sciences in Novosibirsk. A vast and impressive Mathematical-Economics Institute of the Academy of Sciences was set up in Moscow in 1963, under Academician Fedorenko, and is hard at work devising new techniques, methods, ideas, which will be referred to in chapter 9. Work is being done on inter-sector balances in both physical quantity and monetary terms. Thus twenty variants of inter-sector balances for the perspective plan (for 1970) were worked out with the help of computers. Efforts are being made to adapt the information flows and the organizational structure to the needs of computerization, but it is well understood that rapid implementation of the new ideas depends still on considerable advances in methodology, in computer design and in training of programmers and engineers.[1] Monetary balances are in fact being constructed for sixty-five sectors of industry, plus agriculture, building, transport, trade, supply and other branches which, in the Soviet definition, contribute to material production.[2] These will, naturally, be based on existing prices, and will reflect the irrationalities of these prices, and will fail to reflect relative scarcities in so far as prices do not do so. This severely limits the use of these balances as a criterion for planners. No wonder Nemchinov has called for 'a theory of planning prices', and the creation of a truly all-inclusive 'economic budget of Soviet society'.[3] Kantorovich, Novozhilov and others who are pressing for the adoption of programming techniques in Soviet planning are also greatly concerned with finding a suitable price-base for making possible rational choice between alternative plan variants. But much more about prices in chapter 8, below.

While the whole question of programming will be taken up again later on, it is necessary to dwell on one characteristic of planning by material balances, or indeed by the use of input-output techniques. It leads to a tendency towards a species of planners' conservatism. The reason is simple; these methods work best with fixed technical coefficients, (or they may be amended by arbitrary percentages, reflecting, for instance, hoped-for improved methods of economizing in the use of fuel or materials). The need for a different pattern of inputs does not emerge. One cannot see from an input-output table that there ought to be a shift from coal to natural gas, or from metals to plastics. In the context of rapid growth, it is simplest to plan on the basis of a general increase in production, on the already established pattern. There is therefore the much-criticized tendency to increase production of everything, this being the so-called 'ratchet' principle of planning: whatever you did in the previous plan period, do more of it in the next one. Change, usually ordered from above,

---

[1] See report of discussion of the whole subject in *Vop. ekon.* No. 7/1964, and also I. Bruk in *Literaturnaya gazeta*, August 27, 1964, and A. Efimov, *Plan. khoz.*, No. 5/1964, p. 15.

[2] See L. Berri and A. Efimov, op. cit., p. 28, and, on p. 30, a table giving the pattern of an 'inter-sector balance in monetary terms'.

[3] *Vop. ekon.*, No. 4/1959, pp. 26, 28.

then comes about only when it is abundantly obvious that the existing pattern is wrong, e.g. by comparison with a foreign country.[1]

INVESTMENT CRITERIA

This is a problem closely linked with that of planning by material balances, since the latter point the need to invest in this or that sector. Under the rough-and-ready system in operation so far, a decision to expand (for whatever reason) the aluminium industry was one of the factors determining investments in, and the location of, electricity generating stations, or of a railway line to take the bauxite to the aluminium plant. Let us first take the simplest aspect of the matter: the power station could be thermal or hydro; the railway line could be steam or electric. In each case, higher initial investments are more or less compensated by lower operating costs. Which variant should be chosen, and why? In this form, the question does not affect the rationality of the basic investment decisions as such, but only the means to achieve a given end.

The history of the discussions on investment criteria has been more thoroughly discussed by Western scholars than any other single aspect of Soviet economics,[2] and so the details of the debates can be passed over fairly briefly here. The need for a criterion for the planners is self-evident; if theory is unable to provide one, a rule-of-thumb approach has to be devised. But several institutional and theoretical obstacles had to be surmounted.

Firstly, there was virtually no capital charge, except amortization, the latter being generally too small to affect calculations significantly. This gave a spurious attractiveness to the capital-intensive variant. It was spurious because the loss to the economy in tying up resources in the capital project is not adequately reflected in the cost structure, nor is the factor Time. It was in fact Khrushchev who insisted on the importance of the time factor, in the context of choice between hydro-electric and thermal power stations, where this factor is particularly important.[3] His motive may have been a desire to achieve maximum results in his lifetime, but motives hardly matter; in any case, 'time-preference' is everywhere related, *inter*

---

[1] The whole question of the progress and frustrations in introducing mathematical and computing methods in the economy is dealt with at length in the book edited by John P. Hardt and the one written by Dr. A. Zauberman, of which particulars are given in the Appendix. Interested readers are referred to these works.

[2] Notably by A. Zauberman, G. Grossman, H. Hunter, M. Dobb, N. Kaplan, H. Chambre and J. M. Collette (see bibliography).

[3] In his speech at Kuibyshev, *Pravda*, August 11, 1958.

alia, to the fact that none of us live for ever. It remains true that capital charges—whether viewed as related to the time factor, relative scarcity of capital, or both—have been of quite minor significance in the USSR. This confused not only the central planners, but also the lower-level economic agencies and the enterprises for whom capital assets appeared to be a free gift from above, which naturally led them to apply for more than they could hope to get, and gave them no incentive to attempt, at that level, to decide rationally which and how much capital assets they require. Since some at least of the central decisions are influenced by applications from below, all this in no way helped in finding the best use for investment resources. One aspect of the time factor must also be mentioned: the large number of unfinished building projects are evidently due partly to overbidding for investment resources, resulting in breakdowns in supplies of building materials and partly to the lack of any penalty for delay. To put the matter crudely, if building operations are suspended for two years, the extra cost was limited to keeping a night-watchman plus perhaps deterioration of the half-completed building. As many critics have pointed out, the success indicators of construction enterprises in no way encouraged them either to economise or to finish the job: payments were made as work proceeded, no matter how slowly it proceeded. Bonuses depended on the 'volume of work', measured in roubles, not on completion (except, in recent years, in house-building). There is a very common tendency greatly to underestimate building costs, and as a consequence it happens that financial stringency so to speak builds non-completion into the investment plan: for example there were twenty-seven new projects for which only 11 per cent of their cost was provided for in the 1967 financial plan: at this rate, it will take nine years to complete them. Shortage of finance is a reflection of shortage of the material means of completing the project: cost underestimating, by as much as 32·5 per cent *on average*, means that more building materials, machinery and labour would be needed than had been planned. These facts, plus the lack of interest in completion and the desire to start a new project in the hope of getting more money with which to complete it, all contribute to a constant overstrain. There has been excess demand for investment goods, giving rise to the notorious *raspylenie sredstv*, the scattering of resources on too many building projects, with resultant freezing of capital assets and long delays in completion.[1]

[1] Good Soviet sources on all this include V. Krasovski, *Vop. ekon.* No. 4/1967, pp. 48 ff., *Finansy SSSR* No. 8/1967, pp. 3 ff., *Plan. khoz.* No. 4/1967, pp. 57 ff., and so on.

The introduction after 1965 of a capital charge is intended, no doubt, to discourage overapplication for investment resources from below, as is the shift from outright grants to credits. Yet one wonders what difference it will make, given that prices have been altered to 'make room' for the capital charges, and given also the very low rate of interest on credits. Perhaps of greater help will be the shift of more construction enterprises on to a system of payment-on-completion, with credits covering the period of actual building.

The second institutional-practical obstacle is the price system. Prices of materials, or of the end-products, often bear no rational relationship to one another, to their relative scarcity, or to their utility from the standpoint of the user. Consequently the relative profitability of this or that project could be quite misleading a guide to action, and some projects may be simply excluded by an absolute shortage of one or more products which are required to carry them out. All this is, perhaps, too obvious to require further comment.

If one also takes into account transport and labour shortages in some areas, and the complications of administrative and territorial demarcation lines, the practical difficulties in the way of finding objective criteria of judgment appear to be formidable. But to them must be added a theoretical-ideological obstacle: any objective criterion which would affect the *direction* of investment was resisted and resented, on two interlinked grounds. Firstly, many of the suggested criteria involved some measurement of a return on capital, which is a concept close to a rate of interest on capital, which was regarded as ideologically offensive. Secondly, the idea of adopting economic criteria for determining the direction of investment was itself suspect, save within the very narrowest range of choice. This view was strongly held by Stalin. He assumed that consumers' goods industries were obviously more profitable, that investment in these industries would provide a higher return than in most branches of heavy industry. The recognition of an objective economic criterion might suggest the shifting of resources into non-priority sectors. In any event, Stalin held the view that these matters are for planner-politicians, not economists.[1]

The principle that a given result (given by the plan) should be achieved with due economy of capital, by choosing the variant which 'pays for itself' most quickly, was accepted in principle without much argument at various conferences called to discuss the subject after Stalin's death. This is the so-called period of recoupment (*srok okupaemosti*). If project A requires more capital than

[1] Stalin, op. cit., pp. 22-4, 72. See also chapter 11.

project B but will save on current costs, or if the new project will reduce costs compared with existing practice, in such a way that the gain can wipe out the extra investment required over a given period of years, say, ten, then the given investment pays for itself in ten years. If, other things being equal, another variant pays for itself in eight years, then it should be preferred.

Various attempts were made to formulate this concept in forms which could be applied in all the relevant planning offices. The most recent is the *Tipovaya metodika ekonomicheskoi effektivnosti kapital'nykh vlozhenii i novoi tekhniki*, published by the Academy of Sciences in 1960. The formula for the recoupment (or 'pay-off') period may be given as

$$\frac{I_1 - I_2}{C_2 - C_1} = T$$

where I stands for the sums invested, C for the costs of production, in the two variants which are being compared, and T is Time, i.e. the period of recoupment.

The reciprocal of the above,

$$\frac{C_2 - C_1}{I_1 - I_2} = \frac{1}{T}$$

would represent the coefficient of efficiency of investment. In a choice of investment within any given sector, to the current cost of production involved in adopting this particular variant there should (so it is argued by the majority) be added a kind of imputed cost of capital, a *de facto* interest rate, representing the 'normative' rate of investment efficiency, a 'normative' recoupment period. Allowance must be made, in the recommended method of calculation, for complementary investment needs at least in the 'proximate' branches. The immobilization of capital assets during construction is also to be allowed for in this disguised interest rate. The recommendations do not insist on a single 'normative' rate for the economy as a whole, and in fact envisage the use of different rates in different sectors of industry and of the economy. However, the existence of a rate for the economy as a whole is recognized, it is referred to as a 'general' rate, and, at least by implication, it could be used in inter-branch and inter-sector calculations, where substitutable goods are involved. This is not clearly spelled out, which may be a sign of a compromise, since, as we shall see, this is a controversial question.[1]

[1] A very uneasy compromise, according to I. Malyshev, *Plan. Khoz.*, No. 1/1961, p. 48.

The existing rate of return in the given sector is to be used as a yardstick: the new project should not be less efficient, should not have a longer recoupment period, unless no possible alternative can be found. The use of sector 'norms of effectiveness' is implied by the use of different profitability norms as success indicators under the reform in different branches of industry. But in addition to these value indicators various other calculations are recommended, of a more general character: physical output per man, required inputs of materials and fuel, technical progress, and so on. While, bearing in mind the vagaries of Soviet costs and prices, resort to these non-monetary criteria is understandable, the effect may be to point to conflicting choices. The emphasis on other criteria—other, that is, than the return on capital—is greatest when new techniques are under discussion. Here there is much emphasis, as a rule, on comparison with foreign technologies, or on somewhat ill-defined increases in labour productivity. None the less the importance of the recoupment period (efficiency of investment) is now generally accepted. However, it is accompanied by vigorous argument on many unsettled questions.

The first of these has already been hinted at. It is increasingly realized that the search for criteria cannot in practice confine itself to any one branch, or closely inter-related branches, of the economy; it is not just a question of hydro *versus* thermal electricity, or two different projects for a steelworks. There are many permutations and combinations of energy, metals, chemicals, and so on, all inter-dependent. It is not enough, wrote Efimov and Krasovski, to 'compare variants of the same project'. What is needed is 'a more effective structure of capital investments which would correspond to the basic conception of the plan'.[1]

However, this immediately leads to a second difficulty. The actual 'periods of recoupment' in different sectors of the economy differ extremely widely; this was and is the consequence of basing investment decisions on plans for future production devised separately for separate products. The result has been that the recoupment period is in general much longer in heavy than in light industry; it is, according to Khachaturov, four to five years in light industry, ten years in transportation, sixteen to seventeen years in electric power.[2] Is this a sign of a misdirection of resources, or an inevitable consequence of Soviet-style 'priority' planning? On this there is still a sharp clash

---

[1] *Plan. khoz.*, No. 8/1959, pp. 66-7.
[2] *Vop. ekon.*, No. 9/1958, p. 121. Other examples were given by Vaag in *Zakon Stoimosti* (Kronrod), p. 424.

of views. Vaag argued that 'the normative recoupment period must be the same throughout the economy'; the deliberate introduction of the priority of heavy industry into the process of calculation must lead, in his view, to wasteful resource allocation.[1] Khachaturov disagreed.[2] Strumilin also argued that the priority of heavy industry must be firmly maintained.[3] Yet how can one make the inter-sector comparisons envisaged by Efimov and others of the more intelligent planners without a valid inter-sector criterion? (It should be noted that the revision of wholesale prices in 1967 only partially corrects these disparities, part of which arise because, at any given level of prices, projects in the priority group of industries are preferred, regardless of profitability). Vaag, of course, did not deny that some decisions must be made (and not only in Russia) for reasons other than estimated return on capital, but urged that planners must consider real costs, 'not those which we create in our imagination'.[4] The same thought was expressed by Zasyad'ko: 'Of course, the criterion of return on capital must not be obeyed blindly, it must be modified by political and strategic considerations, but always in the knowledge of the cost, the loss, arising from the decision.'[5] As the debate developed, virtually all the more serious economists increasingly came to agree that a single rate of return criterion, a standard capital charge, a single 'effectiveness norm' was desirable. This was vividly expressed by the talented young mathematical economist, N. Petrakov: 'The capital charge norm is of its nature a means of comparing the economic significance of different output. When compared with the actual effectiveness of capital, it will characterize the degree of relative advantage of the various spheres of application of means of production and labour resources . . . It is therefore proper . . . to compare the effectiveness of alternative investments in apparently quite different branches, such as electricity generation and the food industry.'[6] But, as the author well sees, the validity of his argument depends on prices which reflect supply and demand. In the absence of such prices, planners inevitably continue to derive investment decisions from material-balance considerations and confine their attention to alternative

---

[1] *Vop. ekon.*, No. 9/1958, p. 130.
[2] Ibid., p. 121, and also *Vop. ekon.*, No. 1/1961, pp. 72-5.
[3] Ibid., p. 123. But he simultaneously supported a single 'norm of effectiveness' (*Vop. ekon.*, No. 8/1959, p. 89).
[4] *Zakon Stoimosti* (Kronrod), p. 423.
[5] *Pravda*, February 3, 1959.
[6] *Nekotorye aspekty diskussii ob ekonomicheskikh metodakh khozyaistvovaniya* (M., 1966), pp. 43, 44.

means to a given end using different rate-of-return criteria in different sectors, and modifying even these in practice in the light of shortages of materials, which find no reflection in their prices.

A further point of both theoretical and practical significance arises. What precisely is the nature of the criterion we are discussing? In the discussions, Malyshev advanced the view that 'the economic content of the return on capital is profit', and consequently that 'profit norms should be the same throughout the economy'. He too pointed out the necessity of a rational price system if any calculations are to be soundly based.[1] But any criteria based on a price-system which fails to reflect *use*-value are liable to lead to confusing results. Thus, in the same discussion, the economist Shuster gave the following example. Suppose there are several possible machines which could be produced. Investment in their production would then be decided, according to the accepted criteria, by the return on capital (or profits) resulting from the adoption of this or that variant. By such criteria, machine A may be preferred to machine B. Yet the ultimate user of the machine, the enterprise which acquires it, is also investing, and from its point of view machine B may be much more productive and therefore preferable.[2]

One consequence of the reform in the field of the use and abuse of capital must be mentioned: the capital charge is levied both on fixed and working capital, and so should discourage enterprises from holding excess stocks and unused machinery, the more so as they would obtain some income from selling them. Previously the situation was much less satisfactory, judging from the comments of Z. Atlas: 'Enterprises have no incentive to reduce their capital funds.' In respect of unused equipment, 'enterprises by present rules do not even pay amortization'. The position in the case of working capital was even worse. 'The enterprise is (financially) indifferent whether it holds stocks to the value of one or of ten million roubles'.[3]

A capital charge (whether applied to basic capital only or to basic and working capital) has both a macro- and a micro-economic effect, and reminds one that the distinction between these categories is often blurred in practice. Thus central investment decisions are influenced in various ways by projects put forward from below, and these, as well as the utilization of capital assets on the spot, must inevitably be influenced by micro-economic stimuli; a capital charge

---

[1] *Vop. ekon.*, No. 9/1958, p. 135. Also see Z. Atlas, *Vop. ekon.*, No. 10/1960, p. 71.

[2] *Vop. ekon.*, No. 9/1958, p. 126.

[3] *Zakon Stoimosti* (Tsagolov), p. 279.

would affect enterprise behaviour by affecting their accounts. However, the inclusion of capital charges in costs—which is a form of interest rate—is also relevant to investment criteria calculations at the centre (see also chapter 8, below).

The entire debate has been taken on a higher level by becoming linked with a discussion of optimum planning and the utilization of mathematical techniques, which will be discussed separately, as its implications are so wide. Novozhilov argued, indeed, that the whole question of investment criteria is merely a special case of the general question of the proper valuation and utilization of scarce resources of all kinds throughout the economy.[1] Kantorovich, too, would treat this as an integral part of attaching values to scarce resources, as part of the application of linear programming methods to the Soviet economy. Indeed, Kantorovich favoured a capital charge ('efficiency norm'—*norma effektivnosti*—for investment) higher than Western interest rates, because of the enormous capital requirements of the Soviet expansion programme.[2] The eminent academician Kolmogorov also argued in favour of seeing the *norma effektivnosti* as a species of charge for time, basing it on the idea that, since in a progressing economy 'labour value will decline with time, the shifting of the expenditure of labour to an earlier period will permit . . . an increase in total production'. Having found a theoretically respectable foundation for Kantorovich's ideas, he continued as follows: 'We must not be upset by the formal analogy [of the *norma effektivnosti*] with the capitalist "interest on capital." '[3] The reform in some respects represents a clear advance in this field. Thus the capital charge is 'in', an important gain of principle, as is also the switch to computing profits as a percentage of capital. All this should lead to greater concern for the effectiveness of investments, greater care in the use of capital assets, less overapplication for capital grants. But the price system remains a very serious obstacle to rational calculation of alternatives, the actual capital charge varies in different branches. There are still large numbers of loss-making enterprises whose output is judged to be 'necessary' for the economy (no doubt it is, but this fact finds no reflection in prices). Profitability norms vary widely. The average capital charge (6 per cent) is nowhere near the rate which has been recommended by those who advocated its introduction. The rate charged for credits is, by any

[1] See his contribution to the symposium (edited by V. Nemchinov) *Primenenie matematiki v ekonomicheskikh issledovaniyakh* (Moscow, 1959), p. 129.
[2] *Ekonomicheskii raschyot nailuchshevo ispol'zovaniya resursov* (Moscow 1959), p. 220.
[3] *Vop. ekon.*, No. 8/1960, p. 114.

reasonable standard, illogical. One may be sure that many reformers are unhappy and are pressing for change.

The discussion continues. As will be shown in subsequent chapters, it is intimately linked with a more general reconsideration of both structure and theory. It is being increasingly realized that a greater attention to rational resource allocation is indispensable, and nowhere more so than in the field of capital investments. However, a balanced view of Soviet performance in investment planning requires at least some consideration for two relevant factors. One concerns the peculiar 'rationality' of moving out of a stage of underdevelopment, when general strategic considerations may logically take precedence over the 'micro-rationality' to which many Western economists pay almost exclusive attention. This point will be taken up again in chapter 12, and implies that it is at least possible that rapid development in the Soviet context (and perhaps also in some other developing countries) was necessarily inconsistent with the utilization of 'normal' investment criteria. Such an interpretation by no means excludes the view that the Soviet economy has moved into a more mature stage in which some of the 'traditional' criteria come into their own.

The second point to bear in mind is that Western practice too suffers from major weaknesses in this field. Of course, perfect competition should theoretically lead to an efficient disposal of resources, including investment resources. But, in the world as it is, this picture would be as unrealistic as would be a faultless all-foreseeing Gosplan. We must remember that major investment projects, involving the construction of a new factory, take several years to complete, and necessarily involve an element of guesswork as to demand and prices at a future date. Especially with chronic inflation and instability of relative prices, typical of the postwar years, few economists in the West would assert that would-be investors are able to exercise foresight under reasonable conditions. Nor does the role of interest rates, which also have fluctuated alarmingly from time to time, accord with rational economic principles of the textbooks. In these conditions, if misdirection of resources is to be avoided, investment decisions must in fact be often based on a forward estimate of demand in quantitative terms, the profits being assumed. This applies particularly to the many sectors affected by monopolies or quasi-monopolies. But it is certainly arguable that it is precisely in a planned economy that it is easier to foresee future demand, at least for basic industrial products. The central planners can forecast the requirements for, say, steel, sulphuric acid and hydraulic presses in 1965, because they have before them the plans for the output of industries using these commodities, and can take investment decisions accordingly. It is true that they may make mistakes, but the boards of directors of the relevant British undertakings are also capable of error, and in addition cannot have so much knowledge of future utilization, or of the development plans of competing enterprises. Investment decisions everywhere involve a mixture of calculation and 'hunch', are in part 'arbitrary' administrative decisions. It is surely arguable that the likelihood of error, and 'macro-error' at that, is somewhat greater in Western economies, even while they are noticeably superior in making adjustments to changing demand. Large investment errors become visible in the West when, as in periods of recession, capital assets are idle or underused, but major losses may also result from failure to take decisions, a failure which could be due precisely to the element of uncertainty. To take some British examples, insufficient investments in the steel and machine-tool industries may well be causing losses to the economy, which we would find it hard to measure, but which cannot be assumed not to exist unless one equates actual investment decisions with an imaginary optimum. As for the public sector in Western countries, perhaps the less said the better. One need only mention the sad history of the development plans of British railways, controversies on fuel policy, and the confused relationship between public and private investments. It would also be a very bold Western economist who could express satisfaction with the assessment of social costs involved in investment choices. Of course, many of these problems, including that of bringing social costs into the calculation, are unsettled in the USSR also. It is indeed not argued that Soviet practice, with its many errors and omissions, produces 'superior' results in the taking of investment decisions. The object of these final paragraphs is merely to emphasize that investment rationality, in any sense of the word, may in practice be just as elusive in London as in the planning offices of Moscow.

CHAPTER 8

The Pricing of Factors of Production

THE CONTRADICTORY OBJECTS OF PRICE POLICY

Prices in an economy of the Soviet type have several interconnected roles to play.

Firstly, as Grossman pointed out, 'pricing and accounting have the major purpose of exercising control over and evaluation of enterprise management'.[1] This was certainly Stalin's view, and Bachurin was reflecting it when he wrote, in 1954: 'prices of producers' goods ... serve primarily for "control by the rouble" over production and resource utilization, for developing and strengthening *khozraschyot*, the stimulation of reduction in costs.'[2] The doctrine at this period was loyal to Stalin's view that the 'law of value' does not apply to goods transferred between enterprises within the state sector (see chapter 11, below). If one assumes the capital stock, inputs and the output plan as given, which Stalin certainly would do in this context, prices then are important only in so far as they enable a superior to identify inefficiency and reward efficiency in carrying out the plan without undue waste. For such a purpose, the average costs incurred in producing the goods in question in all Soviet enterprises is an adequate basis. Obvious differences in equipment or other objective conditions can be allowed for in the cost plan for the particular enterprise, but a price related to average cost does provide the supervisory authorities with some basis for judgment. If costs are too high, it is a signal that something is awry, that work or management is on a low level.

However, since one finds that the assumption that the enterprise is told exactly what to produce is only partially correct, and that inputs are influenced in varying degrees by enterprises' own applications, therefore there is a second important role of prices: as a guide to enterprise decision at the micro level. If, other things being

---

[1] 'Industrial prices in the USSR', *American Economic Review*, May, 1959, p. 57. This article provides a thorough and stimulating discussion of these questions.

[2] *Vop. ekon.*, No. 3/1954, p. 35.

equal, price A is higher than price B, and the directors are able to choose, then they would emphasize A as producers, and B as purchasers of inputs. For these purposes, where, by definition, the central plan does not give precise instructions, prices would need to reflect relative scarcities and the requirements of the users.

Thirdly, prices guide the planners at all levels, and the authors of investment projects, in their choices as to how to devise means to further the economic policies of the government. Is it worth expanding plastics? Should aluminium be substituted for other metals? Is it worth building a pipeline to Chelyabinsk to replace locally-mined brown coal? Is it rational to supply forgings and castings to Chelyabinsk from Sverdlovsk? To what kind of textiles should new investments be devoted? Clearly, prices unrelated to costs could cause incorrect decisions to be made, while prices unrelated to scarcities would encourage planners to overindent for commodities in short supply.

Fourthly, there is the comparatively new question of devising prices adapted to mathematical techniques, notably linear programming, which bring up a number of matters of principle, of which much more will have to be said.

Fifthly, through prices the state obtains revenue, and in the case of agricultural produce the state also affects the distribution of income between town and country, and these considerations also affect action.

Finally, retail prices are used to distribute consumers' goods, to allow the citizen to choose which of the available goods he wishes to buy.

These various objectives can contradict one another in many different ways. Thus for 'control' purposes it is convenient to have stable prices. It would confuse the task of measuring success or failure if, half-way through the year, material A were suddenly increased in price by 15 per cent, especially if this material is administratively allocated to user enterprises, so that they cannot choose whether to use it or material B. Hence the general policy of keeping prices steady for long periods. However, this is plainly inconsistent with using prices as a 'micro' guide to scarcities or to demand. Similarly, from the 'control' standpoint the price of the output does not greatly matter; if it is below costs, a subsidy is paid, and here the matter ends. However, the planners could be confused if in their calculations they take coal to be 'worth' 150 roubles when its costs are 200 roubles.

The essence of the problem, as seen by Soviet planners, has been changing, with the growing necessity of devolving more functions to local bodies and with the interest shown in programming techniques. For these have at least one thing in common: prices become an essential element in 'feeding' back the relative scarcities and demand. To this task the Soviet price system is ill-adapted.

THE SEARCH FOR AN 'OBJECTIVE' BASIS FOR PRICES

Since 1955, Soviet economic literature has been full of debates on prices. Virtually all the participants agree that the existing system is far too illogical, as has indeed already been documented at some length in chapter 4. But they are much less clear about what is to replace it, and it is probable that this lack of clarity is connected with different ideas about the role which prices should play in the economy. Thus Turetski, while favouring the elimination of various anomalies, advocated for heavy industry 'a single price for all products of the same use value'.[1] Since the identical or interchangeable use-values—e.g. in the fuel industry—are associated with different costs, he is against relating prices to average costs or to 'values' based on cost. But at the same time he admits 'in certain cases . . . to the necessity of price differences in the interests of economizing certain scarce materials'.[2] For example, coking coal, being scarce, should be particularly dear for this reason. However, to him these are exceptions. The idea that all things are in some degree scarce seems hardly to have penetrated this professor's imagination. It looks as if he seeks a consistent and stable basis on which to judge enterprise performance, modified by a variety of considerations: acute scarcity, the need to encourage technical progress, social policies and so on. However, Turetski strongly opposed any mechanical linking of price with cost (or 'value'). To derive a consistent price theory from his ideas is a task beyond my powers. In the West, the absence of theory or criteria would make little difference, but in the USSR, with prices fixed by deliberate action, their absence cannot but have undesirable consequences.

But if there is to be a more adequate criterion for determining prices, what is this criterion to be? On this a vigorous debate has been raging. This is intimately linked with the more theoretical problem of the role of 'value' and the 'law of value' in the Soviet economy, which is discussed in chapter 11.

[1] Turetski, op. cit., p. 103.
[2] Ibid., p. 105. For a vigorous analysis of his ideas, see review of this book by M. Dobb, *Soviet Studies*, July, 1960, and Turetski's reply in ibid., April, 1961.

Essentially, the difficulty is this. Marxian theory was concerned with identifying the elements which determined value and price in a capitalist market economy, and accounting for such phenomena as exploitation and surplus value. Whether Marx was in fact successful in doing these things is a question we need not here pursue. The problem before Soviet economists in a search for an objective basis for prices is to find a means of using this theory in a situation in which a free market does not exist. A number of them responded to this challenge by asserting that prices of commodities should (as a rule) equal their 'values' in the Marxist sense. Various theories have been developed as to how values should be calculated, these being essentially concerned with deciding what should be added to prime cost (*sebestoimost'*). Most of this school believe that pricing in accordance with 'values' implies that all products should bear equally the burden of accumulation and unproductive state expenditures, which are financed primarily out of profits and turnover tax, though they put forward rival formulae about how this sum, the 'surplus product', should be shared out. Details of these ideas will be given in chapter 11.

These economists generally agree that some deviation from their recommended price bases should be permitted, in usually ill-defined exceptional circumstances. A favourite example is that vodka should be dear and children's shoes cheap. But, in principle, they argue, their respective formulae should determine prices.

These formulae presuppose that the basis for price-determination should be the same for all goods. The authors criticize the present system not only for its internal inconsistencies, but also for disproportionately burdening consumers' goods with more than their share of the 'surplus product', through turnover tax. At present, part of the 'surplus product' of the steel and coal industries, for instance, is 'realized' through the prices of various consumers' goods. This appears on the surface not to matter, since it is a mere revenue-raising convenience, and all payments are between state enterprises anyway. But, argue Malyshev, Kondrashev, Strumilin, Atlas and many other economists, this is an utterly false way of looking at things. This basis of pricing twists out of shape many essential cost comparisons, misleads planners in their assessment of the real magnitude of this or that portion of the national income. For instance, the veteran survivor of the 'twenties, Albert Vainshtein, claims that if the share of accumulation in the national income in 1964 were recomputed in prices which redistribute correctly the burden of turnover tax, this share would not be the official 27 per cent but 35 per cent.[1] Similarly, consumption is exaggerated in relation to accumulation, industry (to which the bulk of turnover tax is 'credited') in relation to agriculture, some regions in relation to others. Labour is paid in wages which must reflect the high consumers' goods prices, and which are therefore high compared with prices of machinery, the latter being exempted from turnover tax. Consequently even economically inadequate machinery looks profitable to use, since its cost appears low in relation to wages saved. If these critics' advice were taken, the effect would be an increase in prices of producers' goods, and of revenues derived by the state from heavy industry in the form of profits, turnover tax and/or a charge for the use of capital assets. There would be a reduction in such revenues from the consumer goods sector, but, if personal incomes are unchanged, this would be due not to a cut in retail prices but to an increase in costs caused by higher prices of materials and machines. Prices, they argue, would then reflect real social costs.

These proposals were vigorously opposed, notably by Turetski and by Maisenberg.[2] They do not deny that prices ought to have some relation to objective criteria, but regard much greater flexibility as necessary if prices are to be made to serve political objectives and other planning purposes. One of these is the encouragement of technical progress and growth, which, they maintain, demands low prices for the basic materials and machinery. Another is the usefulness of keeping enterprises up to the mark by cutting prices and not allowing 'comfortable' profit margins. Retail prices, they maintain, are different in principle, and there is no reason why wholesale prices of heavy industry should be brought into conceptual line with them.

It is a weakness of the 'law-of-value' price-reform proposals that prices are seen statically, as a reflection of costs, of average costs of production in the given branch, plus some amount determined by rival formulae. Though these proposals may appear more systematic, more worthy of economists, than the 'political' empiricism of Turetski and Maisenberg, the latter seem justified in accusing the authors of all these formulae of ignoring reality. They overlook the fact that Marx's theory of value, whatever its defects may be, was at least concerned with a competitive capitalist economy in which market forces operated and tended towards certain kinds of equilibrium. (The dynamics of any economy involve, of course, *departures* from these equilibrium positions.) In the USSR, as elsewhere,

---

[1] *Ekonomika i matematicheskie metody*, No. 1/1967, pp. 15-18.
[2] See Turetski's book, op. cit., and the thoughtful contribution by L. Maisenberg to the volume *Zakon Stoimosti* (Kronrod), pp. 405 ff.

if prices were to play the role of influencing decision making, whether by planners or at enterprise level, these static formulae become useless. *At best* they would make the price system neutral in decisions affected by relative scarcities and utility. Turetski and Maisenberg do see that prices should be influencing decision making. Their own weakness lies in their inability to suggest any systematic guide for price determination.

Such a systematic guide is advocated by Novozhilov and Kantorovich. Prices would be based, to use Kantorovich's phrase, on 'objectively determined valuations'. They would be efficiency prices, consequences of a programming exercise in optimization; given certain aims, the prices would be those which enable these aims to be most effectively attained. This approach involves the application to the USSR of the linear programming techniques in the development of which Kantorovich played a pioneering role.[1] There would be a species of market, if only within the computer. Relative scarcities and opportunity costs would then enter the picture, as would a rental charge for land and mineral workings. Clearly, this would mean a complete change in planning methods, as well as in prices. The arguments about prices and values cited in the present chapter would be swept away as irrelevant. The Novozhilov-Kantorovich approach has provoked strong opposition from the more orthodox economists. The arguments around these concepts, as well as the efforts of Nemchinov to bridge the gap,[2] take us far into the realm in which price policy and the theory of value dwell uneasily together, and detailed discussion of them must be postponed until chapter 11.

It is hardly necessary to stress the vital importance of the price problem, since, as we have seen, prices affect the behaviour of planners and enterprises, and 'wrong' pricing can lead to misallocation of resources and act as a barrier to possible forms of decentralization. Yet most serious theoretical and practical difficulties arise as one endeavours to devise a price system which can meet all the varied requirements which, in the Soviet setting, they are expected to meet. Neither a price system statically derived from prime-cost-plus-surplus-product, nor a series of 'objectively determined valuations' à la Kantorovich, provide a basis for the micro-economic

[1] See L. Kantorovich, op. cit,, which also contains a reprint of his pioneering work written as long ago as 1939, and ignored by official economics until very recently. Kantorovich also contributes to V. Nemchinov (ed.), *Primeneniye matematiki v ekonomicheskikh issledovaniyakh* (Moscow, 1959), but the main feature of this volume is the appearance of a long contribution by V. Novozhilov. An English translation, (Oliver & Boyd, 1965) has now appeared.

[2] *Vop. ekon.*, No. 12/1960, pp. 85-105.

role of the price mechanism. Therefore, with the emergence of arguments in favour of decentralization to enterprises on the basis of the profit motive, proposals were made to allow greater flexibility in prices, to allow for freer negotiation between customer and supplier. Liberman wrote rather vaguely of prices being 'both fixed and flexible'. Nemchinov more boldly argued for prices, save for a range of basic materials and fuels, being settled under quasi-market conditions, with enterprises putting forward competitive tenders.[1] In Czechoslovakia, the reforms being implemented specifically aim to free about a third of all prices from any control.

In the light of these considerations, the 1967 price reform, and the accompanying theoretical and practical explanations, can only be characterized as a blow to the reformers and contrary to the whole logic on which the reform was, or seemed at one time to be, based. Novozhilov, for instance, developed the idea that prices should inform the enterprise *what* should be produced, of what *quality*, and the 'socially-necessary limit (or margin, *predel*) of production costs.'[2] Petrakov claimed that supply-and-demand balancing prices are essential: if there is a disproportion, prices rise and profits rise, 'and thereby are created the conditions for the liquidation of the shortage and the restoration of proportionality.'[3] Now compare this with the view of Sitnin, the head of the Committee on Prices attached to Gosplan.

For him, the elimination of wide-ranging variations in profitability of different branches of industry, the elimination also of most subsidies, is a great step forward. He sees the need for certain minor changes: thus an increase in prices of tyres was intended to make possible the use of better materials, but he is concerned lest the enterprises use cheaper materials and then undeservedly cash in, or, somewhat less logically, if a cable enterprise shifts from plastic to lead covers and thereby saves money which in his view 'they are clearly not entitled to keep'. He is also worried about the prices of new machines, which are often fixed by the ministry concerned at too high a level. He is horrified by the misuse by some enterprises of their very limited freedom to negotiate prices for once-and-for-all special orders. He does see the need to change prices more frequently, to compel cuts in prices of the less modern machines for instance, though here he fears that too cheap an obsolete machine would

[1] V. Nemchinov, *Kommunist*, No. 5/1964. See also p. 296, below. See also A. Nove in *Economics of Planning* (Oslo), 1964.
[2] *Ekonomika i matematicheskie metody*, No. 3/1966, p. 328.
[3] Petrakov, op. cit., p. 48.

cause enterprises to buy it in preference to a dearer and more modern machine. (But might this not be rational in some circumstances!?) But the key arguments of his article are as follows:

(a) 'Socially-necessary costs', to which prices should conform, are seen by him in strictly cost-plus terms. Since costs are covered, 'the new prices can serve as a sufficient basis for all kinds of economic calculations' (regardless of relative scarcities, for instance).

(b) Prices of important goods must be fixed by the government.

(c) 'Market prices are, in our view, alien to our economy and contradict the task of strengthening centralized planning. In our view it is also totally incorrect to imagine that prices should balance supply and demand, should increase in the event of shortage of this or that product . . . The balance between demand and supply is achieved by proportional development of all (sic) parts of the economy, *and is the concern of the planning organs*.'[1] We shall have more to say in chapter 9 about the concept of market forces and their role under socialism. It is clear that officialdom is not at present prepared to allow prices to reflect market conditions. Sitnin is concerned about the enormously burdensome task of deciding millions of prices, but his idea is to devise a formula by which enterprises can 'determine' their own prices on a cost-plus basis related to 'normed costs'.[2]

So, in assessing the present (1968) structure of prices in relation to the reform, we must note the principles outlined by Sitnin, and also the importance which he attaches to the preservation of centralized planning and the role of the planning organs. But it is quite wrong to imagine that the prices which now exist are logical even in Sitnin's terms. For one thing, costs change and prices will soon be out of line with costs, let alone with demand, scarcities, etc. But in any event the prices are not cost-plus prices, or not consistently so. Coal prices do not permit the payment of the normal capital charge. Oil prices are semi-marginal, in the sense that almost all oilfields make a profit, and the better-off are subjected to rental payments. This has not been applied to coal. Loss-making enterprises have not been eliminated, but merely reduced in number: in ferrous metallurgy from 36 to 19, in non-ferrous metallurgy ('excluding Kazakhstan'!?) from 52 to 33, in the chemical industry from 56 to 30.[3] There are also unprofitable lines within generally profitable commodities: these have been reduced, in the cotton textile industry from 83 to 41.[4]

[1] *Ekon. gaz.*, No. 6/1968, pp. 10-11 (my emphasis).
[2] Ibid.　　　　　　　　　　　　[3] Sitnin, *Ekon. gaz.*, No. 25/1967, pp. 10 ff.
[4] L. Degtyar and V. Maslennikov, *Finansy SSSR*, No. 12/1966, pp. 7 ff.

There are also signs that the high profit margins in light industry based on cost have influenced price-fixing in ways difficult to reconcile with any principles, including Sitnin's. The point is that, under the old pricing principles of cost-plus-a-percentage-of-cost, the undercapitalized textile and clothing industries had a high profit in relation to capital (another reason was that costs included heavy expenditure on materials). The revised prices preserve this relationship to some extent, as the following figures show:

	Profit as % of costs	Profit as % of capital
Knitwear	17·9	44·4
Silk and rayon fabrics	12·6	26·9
Wool fabrics	8·0	33·7
Coal mining	11·5	9·6

Sources: Degtyar and Maslennikov, op. cit., and Sitnin, op. cit.

Coal is below average. But given an average of 15 per cent on capital, one can see a certain inconsistency. Then there are exceptions in respect of foodstuffs, and below average profits on agricultural machinery sales, supposedly because agricultural inputs must not be made dearer—except that a big increase in fertilizer prices has been authorized all the same.

But apart from considerations such as these, which are less important than the fact that prices still remain detached from supply and demand, two other matters require to be mentioned. One is the seldom-appreciated fact that, whether under the gross-output or sales indicator, it often does not pay enterprises to purchase cheap inputs. On the contrary, expensive inputs suit them, so long as the dearer variety is taken into account in the course of price-fixing. It is, of course, otherwise *after* the price of the output has been fixed, when it does pay the enterprise to switch, if it is able to do so, to a cheaper input, unless it fears that this will lead either to a price cut or to an increase in 'rental' payments or to a rise in its profitability 'norm'. Under the new draft rules for ministries and *glavki*, they will find that high prices and high costs 'pay', since in this way the value of sales and profits increase. Under the 'traditional' system, ministries were judged by output statistics and had less of an incentive to push up prices. They may now do their utmost in this direction. Efforts by Gosplan to check this tendency could well take the form of centralized inflexibility in this vast and complex question of price determination.

AGRICULTURAL PRICES AND LAND RENT

In discussing certain irrationalities in Soviet agriculture, notably the very large income differentials, the interlinked problems of prices and rent naturally arose. The problems are connected, because, in the absence of payments by *kolkhozy* of land rent as such, the price system is called upon to 'correct' differences in land fertility and location. Under the system as it existed before 1958 two other means existed for extracting a form of differential rent (under another name) from the better-situated farms: by varying the scale of payments in kind for the services of the MTS, and by varying the quota of compulsory deliveries at low prices. True, this was not done effectively, but these weapons were to hand for doing it. However, both the MTS and the multiple price system were abolished in 1958, and consequently the one important means available to the authorities to 'correct' for natural advantage is by varying the state purchase price between areas.

The 1958 'unified' prices suffered from grave defects. Not only did they provide very large variations in profitability (in so far as this could be ascertained) as between different crops and ensured heavy losses in the livestock sector, but they failed to allow sufficiently for the elimination of part of the disguised differential rent payments, referred to above. Cost variations were very great, as the following table shows:

GRAIN (1958)

Zones	Costs	Average purchase price	Price required to cover costs	Surplus or deficit
Caucasus	22·00	59·00	30·14	+28·86
Non-black earth centre	88·00	74·00	120·56	−45·44

Source: S. Nedelin. *Finansy SSSR*, No. 6/1960.

The total requirements of the USSR being what they are, state organs must rely on grain from these high-cost areas, and did indeed resume purchases in 1961. The farms of the non-black earth centre (i.e. such *oblasti* as Moscow, Tula, Kaluga, Vladimir) grow a great deal of grain, and the fact remains that zonal variations in prices are still quite inadequate. The inadequacy meant that the peasants, who absorbed the 'surplus' or 'deficit' in the above table, were much better off in one area than another. The magnitude of cost differences is partially explicable by natural conditions; mechanized extensive farming, to which *kolkhozy* have hitherto been most suited (or least unsuited) is most efficient in fertile steppelands (e.g. Krasnodar), and has been least successful in coping with the small fields and poorer soils of the centre, north and west, to which the available machinery is ill-adapted and where intensive methods (including much fertilizer) are needed to produce adequate yields. These areas also happen to have inherited a high labour density. Of course, costs per unit would in any case be lower in fertile Krasnodar, but the above factors increase the difference, especially in the absence of land rent.

The problem of rent has indeed come into the forefront of the discussion. In an interesting article, a Soviet economist showed conclusively that the pay of *kolkhoz* peasants depended decisively, and unfairly, on soil quality and location of the land. In order to put this right, he proposed a system of taxation (he could not call it rent, this would be ideologically incorrect) differentiated by land quality, which involves *valuing* land. This is obviously essential, he argued, since regional differentiation (e.g. as in price zoning) quite fails to take into account the wide differences in fertility and other advantages within quite small areas. He proposed the adoption of a system similar to that already in use in East Germany, where land is valued in accordance with the net income which might be derived from it by good husbandry, on a points system. If the existing *kolkhoz* tax system were related to these 'points', then the better-situated *kolkhozy* would pay much more tax, which would even out the unfairness of the present system. He appeared also to argue for the adoption of a similar valuation system for state-farm land, though without making it clear whether they should pay tax on the same basis.[1] As against this, Strumilin argued strongly against any use, even disguised, of the concept land rent. Logically its use should presuppose, in his view, prices which would cover costs on the worst (i.e. marginal) land, so far as *kolkhozy* are concerned, although prices in the state sectors, including the state-farm sector, are based and should (in his view) be based, on average cost. This, he asserts, would be nonsense. He therefore advocates a redistribution of net income within the *kolkhoz* system, on a regional, republican and even all-union basis.[2] The argument remains unsettled.

The whole problem of land rent was vigorously debated, and one such debate was published in full.[3] Tsagolov argued that, since pro-

[1] G. Lisichkin, *Vop. Ekon.*, No. 7/1960, pp. 61-8.
[2] A systematic statement of his case is in *Vop. ekon.*, No. 7/1960, pp. 81 ff.
[3] N. Tsagolov (ed.), *Zemel'naya renta v sotsialisticheskom sel'skom khozyaistve* (Moscow, 1959).

ducers on marginal land must live, prices must be fixed accordingly, and that a rental charge to offset natural advantages ('differential rent I') would be quite legitimate, although additional income due to investment, hard work and efficiency ('differential rent II') should belong to the farm. A complicated discussion ensued, with some protagonists even arguing that, while the 'value' of agricultural produce is based on marginal land, this does not exclude the payment by the state of a price related to *average* costs, to *kolkhozy* and *sovkhozy* alike. Another view is, of course, inherent in the Novozhilov-Kantorovich approach: land, like other scarce factors of production, would have to be given the valuation which reflected its relative scarcity in relation to the 'programme' regardless of who cultivates it, and a rental charge made accordingly.

The 1965 price revision improved matters in one respect: zonal differences in prices were increased considerably. Thus, to take the areas used above as an example, wheat in Krasnodar was increased in price by 13 per cent, while in the non-black-earth centre the increase exceeded 50 per cent. This is open to the objection, already raised, that 'rewarding' farms for producing high-cost output runs contrary to the logic of specialization. On the other hand, if state procurement organizations are instructed to minimize costs, they would tend not to buy at high prices if this can be avoided. Already delivery quotas are not assigned in respect of wool in the north and north-west, of potatoes in many southern areas, and the Soviet analyst urges 'greater boldness in reducing the areas of (planned) purchase' in the interests of specialization.[1]

There remains a wide and variable gap between costs and profitability. Taking costs in 1963-65 as 100, all-union average state purchase prices have altered as follows:

	As at 1960 (kolkhozy)	1967 Kolkhozy	Sovkhozy
Grain (excl. maize)	155	184	116
Potatoes	147	153	106
Sugar beet	164	140	107
Sunflower seed	—	589	407
Milk	86	98	87
Beef	65	109	87
Mutton and lamb	98	113	98
Pork	67	104	96
Eggs	65	83	108

Sources: (1960) V. Khlebnikov, *Vop. ekon.*, No. 7/1962, p. 53 and (1967) M. Gritskov, op. cit., p. 56.

[1] M. Gritskov, op. cit., p. 54.

The above figures underline the absurdity of Khrushchev's great meat and milk campaign, conducted at a time when all livestock products involved farms in heavy losses. It shows that the 1965 changes have not eliminated wide differences of profitability, though they have reduced them. In practice, the use of bonus prices (+ 50 per cent) for over-quota grain deliveries further distorts the pattern. Soviet critics have further charged that prices paid have encouraged quantity at the expense of quality.[1]

An explicit rent may yet be charged, as part of a reformed system of agricultural prices, applicable jointly to *kolkhozy* and *sovkhozy*, which is advocated by many economists. Even Strumilin, ninety-year-old representative of the oldest generation of Marxist economists, has denounced the treatment of land as a 'free gift of nature', not least because all agricultural land has a great deal of labour applied to it, and it is, in his view, plainly wrong to charge nothing at all for land taken out of agricultural use for industry, or urban construction, or for a hydro-electric reservoir.[2] But a revaluation of all the land of the USSR, even if started tomorrow, would take many years.

WAGES: A 'DE FACTO' LABOUR MARKET

On the face of it, wages, like prices of materials and equipment, are determined by the state. In practice, it is hardly so, despite the fact that wage schedules are indeed laid down centrally. The reason is essentially that labour is human and mobile, in a sense in which inanimate factors of production are not. This apparently obvious fact requires stressing because many students of the USSR are victims of what I have called the 'totalitarian myth' and suppose that all Soviet citizens obey all the rules all the time. If they did, then many serious problems of wage determination would not arise. Yet they do arise, and did so even when the law barred change of occupation without permission.

We have seen in chapter 4 that wage and salary scales are centrally determined, and cannot normally be varied by any enterprise or local authority. However, wage scales, in all countries, are not by any means the same thing as actual wage payments. This is as true in Birmingham as it is in Kharkov, and for the same reason: because workers are frequently on piece rates, or receive various

---

[1] Gritskov, op. cit., p. 56. See also devastating exposé of lowered quality of grain, in '*Russkaya pshenitsa*', Yu Chernichenko, *Novyi mir*, 11/1965, pp. 180-200.

[2] *Vop. ekon.*, No. 8/1967, pp. 60 ff. He strongly disagrees with some colleagues about *how* to value land.

bonuses, overtime and other extra payments. In the USSR, these payments are regulated centrally: thus overtime is normally paid at time-and-a-half; piece rates are either 'straight' (proportionate to output), or 'progressive' (extra payments per piece over the norm). But the essential point is that the majority of workers in the USSR are on piece-rate payments of some kind, and inevitably the determining factor becomes the fixing of the piece rates, rather than the basic wage as such. True, in a formal sense the basic wage should be equal to the number of 'pieces' normally produced in the given period multiplied by the rate per piece. But despite a long catalogue of decrees and orders demanding an upward revision of norms (time-and-motion study—'scientific' norm-fixing—was supposed to be applied), norms averaged well below the output of the average worker, and overfulfilment of norms grew steadily in the postwar years. Thus in 1950 the average industrial worker overfulfilled his norm by 39 per cent, by the end of 1956 by 55 per cent. In some industries the overfulfilment was much greater than this; thus at the end of 1956 it was 96 per cent in the electro-technical industry, 92 per cent in heavy machinery, 81 per cent in the automobile industry.[1] In others it was less, of course. Note that none of these figures imply that either the output or the labour productivity plans were overfulfilled, since these were and are based not on norms but on actual performance in the preceding year or years.

All this had several consequences. One, as has already been pointed out, was a tendency for money wages to rise faster than planned. Another was to muddle inter-industry wage relatives. Some gained much more than others, in a quite unplanned way. Within a given industry, the effect of efforts to prevent wage increases was often unjust and irrational. For example, orders to increase norms were sometimes applied uniformly to all workers, with the result that, while those who were working with improved equipment found that they would still comfortably overfulfil their new norms, those engaged in hard physical labour were unable to reach the new standards, which led to hardship in the building industry, where many operations were not mechanized.[2] In some enterprises, to avoid such unfairness, orders to increase norms were obeyed, but the increases were then cancelled by so-called 'corrective coefficients', which brought wages back to customary levels.[3]

---

[1] E. Kapustin, *Plan. khoz.*, No. 7/1957, pp. 29-30.
[2] For details of this, and of changes designed to remove the anomaly, see *Stroitel'naya gazeta*, September 21, 1955.
[3] See, for instance, N. Bulganin, *Pravda*, July 17, 1955.

However, the situation was by no means merely one of confusion. In part, what was happening could be explained by the forces of the market, which corrected obsolete and unsuitable wage scales. The market elements were present because good workers (often *any* workers) were scarce, because labour could drift away despite any legal restrictions, and because, though limited by restrictions on its total wages fund, the management has some room for manoeuvre. Let us now examine how things worked in practice.

Suppose an enterprise needed men in two occupations, rated respectively at 750 roubles and 500 roubles, and both were paid by piecework. Suppose further that the lower-paid job was difficult to fill. To attract workers into it, the management, unable to increase the basic rate, offered an 'easy' norm, easier, in terms of effort than other norms in that same enterprise. The real earnings of the 500-rouble worker could then be higher than those whose basic rates were 750 roubles; this example shows how the management, by juggling with norms, can make correctives to the official wage relativities by reference to its own labour-market situation.[1] To some extent, inter-industry and inter-area relativities were similarly affected by market pressures, operating gradually over long periods of time.

Another means of altering the rules while pretending to obey them is artificial upgrading. Unskilled or semi-skilled labour was extensively graded as skilled. This was particularly common among time-workers, who were unable to benefit from 'easy' piece-rates. Very few workers of any kind were to be found in the unskilled grades of Soviet industry. Still another method was to 'invent' bonuses, even, so it is alleged, for politeness and coming to work sober. The motives were by no means illegitimate: the regulations, if obeyed, would have involved impossibly low and irrational wage scales, and so, as Bulganin correctly explained, the rates were 'adapted' to ensure the payment of whatever was regarded as the proper wage.[2]

However, these substantial 'spontaneous' increases in money wages could not benefit those on fixed pay, doing work which could hardly qualify for real or simulated bonuses (though in some instances even they were given extras). Among them were white-collar office staffs, civil servants, teachers, railway staffs, cleaners and the

[1] The example given is not imaginary, but is based on actual figures obtained by the author in a factory in the Urals.
[2] Bulganin, op. cit., gave a useful account of many of these 'irregularities'. See also E. Manevich, *Vop. ekon.*, No. 1/1959, pp. 37-46, and I. Karpenko, *Ekon. gaz.*, January 13, 1965, pp. 12-13.

like. They were left far behind. There were also a multitude of other anomalies. These were tackled in instalments in the wage reforms of 1957-65, carried out under the aegis of the State Committee on Labour and Wages. The reform was simultaneously concerned with the reduction of hours of work, and with the implementation of a minimum wages law which raised the very low pay of auxiliary and unskilled labourers. New schedules were promulgated in various industries. Basic rates were raised substantially, and so were work norms; this was done in such a way as to correct excessive differentiation between occupations and skills, and brought earnings much closer to the (new) basic wages, and norms much closer to the amount of work actually done. Average wages were little affected, showing their usual tendency to rise slowly.

A jump in average wages is, however, the consequence of a substantial rise in the minimum wage, from 45 to 60 roubles, decreed just before the fiftieth anniversary of the revolution and operative as from January 1, 1968. There are also increases for some who earn more than this, in order to maintain some degree of differentials, plus longer paid holidays and reduced income tax for the less-well paid. A five-day week is being introduced. All this will benefit particularly those in low-priority industries and in the service sectors and also many railwaymen, and reduce the 'spread' between the low-paid and the high-paid. Another effect is a sharp increase in average wages. Even in 1967, before the implementation of the above measure, the total sum paid out in wages (the wages fund) rose by 7·4 per cent, against a planned increase of 5·6 per cent. Since the *kolkhoz* peasants also increased their incomes, it would seem to follow that, after the 1968 wage increases, shortages in the shops may become more serious, especially as the government rejects any general increase in prices.

It has been proposed, and rejected so far, that no wages fund limit be placed on enterprises. Since, however, they are somewhat freer to vary actual pay, within the limits set by the wages fund and fixed basic rates, there can now be greater flexibility. There is also room for manoeuvre in paying out bonuses, both out of the wages fund and the new incentive fund. But complaints have arisen over its use too exclusively for managerial and technical staffs.[1] No rules for its distribution yet exist.

Undoubtedly, these reforms have eliminated some of the confusion which crept into the Soviet wage system. However, the problem remains: how is one to enforce centrally-determined wage

[1] L. Pekarski et. al., *Vop. ekon.*, No. 11/1967, pp. 78-9.

scales, which cannot possibly reflect an ever-changing pattern of labour-market relations. It seems abundantly clear, from past experience, that even without free trade-union bargaining the market elements enter powerfully into the process of wage determination in practice. It remains the case that directors will manoeuvre to obtain the necessary labour, the extent of their deviations from rules depending on the circumstances of the case: how far the rules are realistic, how far labour in general, or of a particular category, is in short supply, and so on. In some instances, rules which favour some types of workers lead to difficulties: for instance, juveniles (under 18) are entitled to longer holidays, shorter hours, study leave; consequently managers prefer to avoid employing juveniles. In others, managers must overpay, on some pretext or other, to get labour at all. The same is now occurring in those *kolkhozy* which have gone over to fixed money payments. A job which is to be done by five peasants may be 'rated' at 500 roubles by the *kolkhoz* management, but the men may declare that they want 600 or 700 roubles instead; what then? Such cases actually exist.

Wages will therefore remain a sector of the economy in which planning is only very partially effective, either in terms of allocation (direction) or in terms of price (wages). Indeed, save in the unrealistic situation of all-round labour direction backed by military discipline, wages must be influenced by the labour market, though the authorities do exercise some influence on supply by training schemes, organized recruitment or migration, direction of students on completion of their courses, and so on. Either this will be in defiance of the formal regulations, or it will be found necessary to amend the regulations (usually *ex post factum*) to take the market realities into account. Thus in recent years the relatively unattractive wages and conditions in Siberia have led to a net migration *out* of an area which was planned to expand particularly rapidly, and this has led to strong pressure (surely irresistible) to alter the relative wage levels and improve amenities.[1] Of course market influence applies more to some categories of labour than to others. In the USSR, as also in many Western countries, it is relatively easier to control salaries of white-collar staffs, and consequently their relative position tends to decline in comparison with industrial workers. It is an interesting and worth-while exercise to compare the social consequences of this

[1] E. Manevich, *Vop. ekon.*, No. 6/1964, p. 109 ff. Detailed sociological and statistical studies underline the continuing conflict between official wage scales and Siberian realities: see particularly D. Valentei: *Teoriya i politika narodonaseleniya* (M., 1967), and V. Perevedentsev: *Migratsiya naseleniya i trudovye problemy Sibiri* (Novosibirsk, 1966).

I

in East and West. In both, the office staffs have lost ground, and, in both, the status of the foreman has been adversely affected by the fact that he often earns less than do skilled men working under him.[1] The many similarities of development of wages structures, in countries with such different systems of wage determination, suggest common influences.

Quite recently, a new problem, familiar in the West, has emerged in the USSR: that of unemployment, virtually unknown in the towns since 1930. It is never discussed under that name, since unemployment as such does not exist in Soviet statistics. It arises in several ways. One is an aspect of the location of new industries; these are seldom built in or near many cities in European Russia, but young people reach working age in these cities and have inadequate avenues of employment there. This raises the problem of so-called *trudoustroistvo*, or placing at work, rendered difficult by the virtual absence of labour exchanges (or of course of any private-enterprise employment agencies) and by the fact that employment in new projects in the east is often blocked by shortage of housing and also sometimes hindered by unwillingness to go. A second category is explicable by overproduction of some commodity, in an area where alternative occupations are few.[2] Another, familiar in some Western countries, is the difficulty of finding work for women in districts where heavy industry employs largely men; this arises increasingly because women are being freed from unsuitable work, e.g. in coal mining, for instance in the Kuzbas. Finally, there are the consequences of automation, referred to several times as a social problem of surplus labour in the given area.[3] These difficulties have been discussed particularly frankly by the labour economist E. Manevich. He pointed out that, apart from shortage of employment for women in the East, there are many cases even of men, in smaller towns in the West, North Caucasus and Central Asia, who have no alternative but to engage in 'domestic and individual auxiliary' activities. Many factories are compelled to keep surplus labour because, in the absence of any labour exchanges, they bear the responsibility of finding alternative work for them.[4] The same complaint was made by a 'reformer': suppose the pursuit of greater efficiency leads to a

[1] On this type of anomaly, see N. Maslova, *Vop. ekon.*, No. 12/1960, p. 51, and figures cited by L. Pekarski et al., *Vop. ekon.*, No. 11/1967, p. 79.

[2] Oil is mentioned in this context by Panfyorov, in his semi-fictional tale, *Vo imya molodovo* (*Oktyabr*, No. 7/1960).

[3] See Panfyorov, op. cit., and also A. Khavin, *Novyi mir.*, July, 1960.

[4] *Vop. ekon.*, No. 6/1965, pp. 26-7. On unemployment in small towns, see also *Trud*, February 15, 1967.

reduction in the labour force, how is the enterprise to find jobs for the workers rendered redundant?[1] In recent years the lack of effective control over labour has been a source of worry to planners. Thus labour drifts out of Siberia, with many recruits staying less than a year before returning westwards. This unplanned and unwanted movement out of labour deficit areas in fact proceeds mainly in the direction of areas where labour is already plentiful, but where living conditions are more agreeable: the North Caucasus, Central Asia, the Ukraine, Moldavia and Transcaucasia. In perhaps the best book yet published on the subject, it is shown that, for instance, Russians go to Central Asia and work in towns, while Central Asian villagers, despite overpopulation, tend to stay in the villages.[2] Far from this being due to a deliberate policy of Russification, as imagined by 'anti-colonialists', this is a quite unintended development, deplored by the planners. There just happens to be more fruit and sunshine in Dushanbe or Frunze than in Krasnoyarsk. (In Tashkent earthquakes act as a disincentive).

The same author makes the interesting point that restriction on movement out of villages and into the biggest cities, through the passport system, sometimes has the effect opposite to what is intended. Thus people avoid living in villages in case they cannot move to towns in the future, and avoid leaving Moscow and Leningrad in case they will never be able to return. This last point was made also by a scientist, to explain why over half of all the doctors of science live in these two cities.[3] There have been criticisms elsewhere too of the lack of one body clearly responsible for what the Russians call *trudoustroistvo*, job placement, and the elimination of confusion, irresponsibility and administrative overlaps between many bodies, from the Ministries of Public Order and Education to the Komsomol and the trade unions, who have some functions in the matter.[4] It seems clear that some new organization will shortly be set up. Job placement offices do already exist in at least some cities, and in some republics, but appear to be essentially information centres. These are needed, but so is a national body with some powers and resources, particularly if the reform is to encourage the shedding of surplus labour in some areas Indeed the impact of the reform on labour is the object of special study: the greater leeway given to management in determining the levels of take-home pay, the greater role of bonuses

[1] N. Arutynov, *Ekon. gaz.*, No. 4/1967, p. 13.
[2] Perevedentsev, op. cit.
[3] S. Lisichkin in *Novyi mir*, No. 8/1967.
[4] See K. Urzhinski, *Sovetskoe gosudarstvo i pravo*, No. 12/1967, pp. 133 ff.

based on profits, as well as the need to encourage the transfer of redundant workers, all raise new problems and pose new challenges, not least to the trade unions.

There are other unsettled issues. What should be the scale of managerial bonuses? Should the workers have a major share in profits, or rely, as they still do, principally on the wages fund for their piece-rate and other bonuses? If so, would this constitute unfairness between workers in different enterprises, and lead to cumulative depression in the less successful enterprises? The best workers would leave. In what form should managerial risk-taking be encouraged and rewarded? Circumstances are inevitably placing such questions as these high on the agenda. It is hardly necessary to add that, as in most countries where there is a numerous peasantry, seasonal unemployment has long been a problem in agriculture. Indeed, with *kolkhozy* there was (to some extent still is) a considerable labour surplus, which helps to explain the wasteful methods of labour utilization typical of *kolkhozy*. One way in which seasonal slack is being taken up is by the development of inter-*kolkhoz* industrial activities, referred to in chapter 1.

Needless to say, the West has no claim to having any magic formula for the solution of the problems of labour relations and wage relativities. But neither has the existence of wide central powers over wages in the USSR eliminated the difficulties inherent in trying to deal with millions of human beings at their work.

CHAPTER 9

Trends Towards Reform

REFORM IS IN THE AIR

This book is in imminent danger of being out of date, in its description of structure, by reason of constant efforts to overcome problems by reforms and amendments of existing arrangements. Some of these changes are being actively discussed, others have been tried out in smaller countries of the Soviet bloc. In any case, it is of evident interest to see how far, within the basic pattern of Soviet-style economies, various reforms can overcome the difficulties which we have been analysing in earlier chapters. While there can be no sound basis for prophesying the course of future reforms, at least it should be possible to indicate likely trends; the observant student should have been able to identify some major causes of such reforms. When they come, their precise shape will doubtless be affected, as were the *sovnarkhoz* reforms of 1957, by political factors and personal ambition. But it would be misleading to regard these factors as determinants, just as it would be misleading to ignore them altogether. No doubt when, in 1932, VSNKh was abolished, it could have been viewed as a blow against the then head of VSNKh, Ordzhonikidze. Indeed, perhaps it was. However, on a long-term view we would hardly regard this as the fundamental explanation, and would be right to emphasize the less personal elements in the chain of causation.

WHAT IS TO BE DONE?

In the USSR, a variety of proposals have been put forward. Some are of quite moderate character, requiring little change of system. Thus it is generally agreed that price illogicalities should be eliminated as far as possible. Some economists have urged amendments in the success indicator system, to establish targets for several years ahead, to reduce the number of detailed indicators, to devise a composite indicator of efficiency. Numerous examples of proposals on these lines have appeared since 1956. To take an early instance, Liberman urged that each enterprise should have a 'long-term economic perspective' on which it could rely, for five to seven years ahead, in terms of which its efficiency should be measured; such objective criteria of efficiency should be, in his view, output relatively to basic and working capital, labour productivity and profitability.[1] Only in this way would enterprises be able to consider long-term development, be guarded against ever-changing plan indicators and the distortions which arise from striving to fulfil them.

Many economists have urged that an increasing role be granted to commercial relations and the profit motive. Gatovski repeatedly made this point, speaking of an increasing role of 'price, costs, profits, etc.', at the expense of 'purely administrative methods of control from above'.[2] He argued that 'mechanical allocation of output' should, through 'the development and perfection of trading methods' be based increasingly on 'commercial agreements directly negotiated between enterprises'. This will ensure 'the influence of the demands of the purchasers on the production programmes of the suppliers'.[3] Many others have argued on similar lines. In particular, they have concentrated their attention on the clumsy and bureaucratic system of material allocation. Nemchinov has argued for 'the gradual conversion of material allocations into state trade', with enterprises buying their supplies as required from wholesalers.[4]

Pravda declared: 'The plans of enterprises engaged in production of consumers' goods will be confirmed on the basis of orders by trading organizations and contracts made with them. Trading organs are forbidden to accept goods if the assortment, quality, pattern, do not conform to the orders placed . . .'[5] If plans were in fact based on contracts, it would mean that factories would not be tempted to produce goods which trading organs do not require, merely in order to 'fit' into plan fulfilment indicators, as is the case frequently at present. If selling became more difficult, if prices were such as to eliminate queues and therefore also the chronic seller's-market situation, no doubt the requirements of the consumers would have a greater influence on what is produced. All concerned are urged 'systematically to study consumer demand and changes in market trends (*konyunktura rynka*)'.[6]

The logic of all this demanded that a growing importance be

[1] *Kommunist*, No. 1/1959, pp. 90-1.
[2] Ibid., p. 71.
[3] *Voprosy stroitel'stva kommunizma v SSSR* (Moscow, 1959), p. 146.
[4] *Vop. ekon.*, No. 12/1960, p. 99.
[5] *Pravda*, October 23, 1960.
[6] Leader in *Sovetskaya Torgovlya*, No. 9/1960, p. 6.

attached to profits, or, as many Soviet economists put it, a greater role for 'value' categories and *khozraschyot*. However, there remain major disagreements about a proper basis for prices, both practical (see chapter 8) and theoretical (chapter 11), and it remains problematical whether the solution chosen will be a satisfactory guide for enterprise decisions. Yet this is a key aspect of any reform.

It is in this context that new proposals emerged into the full light of publicity in 1962. In the West they have often been associated only with the name of Liberman, and are thought to have been first put forward by him in an article in *Pravda* on September 7, 1962. Yet, as we have already seen, many of the ideas involved in the proposals have been discussed in the specialist press for years, and Liberman himself had been developing these thoughts on the subject in print beginning already in 1955.[1]

The arguments he advanced in an article published in 1959[2] were actually more far-reaching than those of 1962, as he then advocated openly the dismantlement of the materials allocation system, while at the later date he thought it best to keep silent on this point. He left it to Nemchinov to put the case for 'free trade' in producers' goods.[3] The essence of the Liberman plan was as follows. The basic criteria of success of enterprise operations were to be profits expressed as a percentage of the enterprises' capital. The management was to devise their own plans based upon orders negotiated with customers. Once approved or amended by the planning authorities, the output and delivery plan would be obligatory on the enterprise. (Liberman left rather vague what the relative functions of enterprise and planners would be in determining just what should be produced, and in the subsequent discussion he was variously interpreted by his critics.) Once this plan is approved, the enterprise's financial and labour plans would be left wholly to the management to decide, though they were to conform to the official wage scales. It would no longer be the job of the planning authorities to decide wages fund, profits plan, costs plan and productivity plan for the enterprise. Liberman was very conscious of the harm done by the tendency, built-in to the traditional system, for management to conceal their production possibilities in order to obtain an easy plan. To encourage management to bid high, he proposed that the bonus rules be such that full bonuses should only be payable in respect of *planned* profits and output.

[1] See *Vop. ekon.*, No. 6/1955, p. 34.
[2] *Kommunist* No. 1/1959, pp. 88-97.
[3] *Pravda*, September 21, 1962.

Anything over-the-plan would be rewarded at half-rate. Under the Liberman rules, the amount of retained profits and of bonuses would depend on the relationship between the profit percentage and the value of the enterprise's capital, though in a later article he conceded that it might also be related to the wages fund.[1] He envisaged differential profit norms in different sectors and perhaps for different enterprises, to offset the 'unearned' advantages of modern equipment or location. This was his substitute for a capital (or rent) charge, intended to ensure that high profits due to the possession of lavish and modern capital equipment do not render a disproportionate reward. Another proposal, that of Vaag and Zakharov,[2] sought to achieve the same result by the revaluation of capital assets and making a capital charge of 20 per cent of their value annually, which would have the effect of increasing the relative costs of the better equipped enterprises. A capital charge also figured in the proposals put forward by Academician Trapeznikov[3] who in principle argued on 'Libermanist' lines, and has long been advocated by Nemchinov. Retained profits would be used for two principal purposes: bonuses to managerial and other staffs, who would thus acquire a direct interest in maximizing profits, and also for financing of decentralized investments. Liberman remained vague not only about the retention or abolition of materials allocation but also about prices. He naturally pointed to the fact that a price reform was highly desirable, but was anxious to have his system introduced even with imperfect prices. In his scheme, prices would be 'fixed and flexible'. This was no doubt deliberate vagueness. Presumably he had in mind fixed prices for basic materials, while many other items would be subject to negotiations between producer and customer.

The publication of his proposals in *Pravda* led to widespread argument. Outright opponents included Zverev, the former Minister of Finance who declared with colourful overstatement: 'Planning is one of the principal achievements of the October revolution; why abandon it?'[4] There were other more moderate critics. Thus, Gatovski was reluctant to accept profits as the *sole* criteria of enterprise efficiency. Others argued against the details of the scheme and in particular against the computation of bonuses recommended by Liberman. The whole question served the valuable purpose of

[1] E. Liberman, *Pravda*, September 20, 1964.
[2] *Vop. ekon.*, No. 4/1963, p. 88 ff.
[3] *Pravda*, August 17, 1964.
[4] *Ekon. gaz.*, October 13, 1962, p. 6.

bringing into the open the discussion of the role of market forces and profits in an economy of the Soviet type. Liberman was in fact open to quite serious criticism in principle. It was indeed clear that there had to be more decentralization to enterprise management, that profits had to play a substantially enhanced role. ('What is profitable for society should be profitable for the enterprise.') However, these considerations do not apply equally to all sectors of the economy. A Soviet enterprise is the equivalent of a single plant or factory in the west. Experience shows that there are a number of industries in which substantial economies of managerial scale exist, and in which it would be wrong to permit the management of a single plant to take decisions on production and especially on investment based on the profits of this plant taken in isolation. Electricity, steel, cement, many chemicals, are produced in the west either by nationalized industries or by large corporations which contain within themselves many production units, each of which would be enterprises in the Soviet definition of that word. The freedom of plant management within a western corporation is severely limited in most instances, and this is not necessarily a source of inefficiency. This suggests that the enterprise is not always the most suitable unit for decision-making, and so the Liberman proposals would need to be modified to fit the special circumstances of various sectors of industry.

This line of thinking has led the authorities into encouraging *obyedineniya*, possible Soviet corporations or trusts of the future. But, as shown in earlier chapters, the power and functions of these corporations are still vague. They *could* become commercially-orientated, profit-seeking, flexible equivalents in Russia of Du Pont, General Electric and I.C.I. Or they could in practice behave like the ministerial *glavki* whose powers they may well inherit. The 'traditionalist' opposition to reform may well adopt this second kind of *obyedineniye* as an apparently radical but actually conservative solution. It also looks like a way of avoiding competition, a concept which the 'conservatives' dislike.

It would be wrong to discount altogether the worries of the more conservative planners about the possible threat which the adoption of the Liberman proposals might cause to economic and financial balances. What if wage inflation were to take place in the absence of planned wages funds? What about the stability of budget revenues if enterprises can devise their own profits plans? In this and other respects, there is an evident danger that macro-economic magnitudes, which remain the responsibility of the centre, could not be effectively controlled. After all, the sum of micro-economic decisions make up those macro-economic magnitudes.

The reforms actually adopted in 1965 owe something to Liberman, as can be seen by referring back to chapter 1. But profits have not been accepted as the sole criterion. Furthermore, Liberman himself has been overtaken by many other, more radical, more consistent and more eloquent would-be reformers. Nothing so annoys them as when western critics bracket them with Liberman, or take his name as a symbol of reforming radicalism. A full account of all the 'reform schools' would occupy a book.[1] So what follows is a very brief survey of a vast subject.

There are, at one extreme, the advocates of a socialist market economy. These include, for instance, G. Lisichkin, who in a well-argued booklet sought to enlist Lenin in his support, using quotations from Lenin's declarations during the early days of NEP, when he did indeed urge state trusts to trade and to study and react to market conditions. Clearly, claimed Lisichkin, plan and market should be intimately interlinked, and without a market *valuation* the planners cannot really test whether their plans are correct.[2] The market situation then is seen as a regulator (if not *the* regulator) of produc-tion and of resource allocation. As another 'marketeer' put it, centrally-fixed prices are harmful, the market situation (*konyunktura*) should determine prices through competition, and 'socialist eco-nomics uses such things as profits, prices, credits, markets and supply-and-demand, which ideological enemies regarded as purely preroga-tives of the capitalists'.[3]

This emphasis on the market was too much for the 'conservatives'. Bachurin, deputy-chairman of Gosplan, attacked these ideas. He was against free choice of customers and suppliers, price-flexibility, com-petition.[4] But some of the radical reformers also demurred at what one of them called 'free market dogmatism'.[5] After all, the free market has not solved all problems anywhere, and in the absence of a free capital market it may fail to function as an effective regulator. Such 'moderate radicals' do, however, desire a much greater freedom of commercial or trade relations than the 'conservatives' could tolerate. Thus Birman takes it for granted that 'distribution by application and allocation' (*po zayavkam i fondam*) must be aban-

[1] It has. See E. Zaleski: *Planning reforms in the Soviet Union, 1962–1966*, University of North Carolina, 1967.
[2] *Plan i rynok* (M., 1966).
[3] B. Rakitski, *Komsomol'skaya Pravda*, October 19, 1966.
[4] *Ekon. gaz.*, No. 45/1966, pp. 7-8.
[5] A. Birman, in *Novyi mir* No. 1, 1967, p. 174.

doned as soon as possible. True, the market situation as seen at the enterprise level is not enough. He appreciates the existence of a national-economic profitability, but fears the departmental approach, and points out that 'the "possibility of voluntarism" (i.e. arbitrary political decisions) is inherent in the system, in the very process of planning'. Too often, for instance, output or investment decisions 'depend among other things on the relative pulling power of particular departments of Gosplan'. Then there was that case of super-voluntarism, when 8,000 out of the 12,000 brickworks in the USSR were closed by order, causing grave dislocation (this was the work of Khrushchev in his last years). Birman also appreciated the need for enterprise, for penalizing those who lack it, and therefore for some sort of bankruptcy procedure.[1]

The same Birman boldly bearded the dragon in his den, by having published in the house-organ of the Supply committee an article entitled '*Trade* in means of production!'[2] He dealt there with objections of the 'traditionalists'. Are there not scarcities? Are there not 'pushers (*tolkachi*) besieging many factories throughout the land?' Birman argues that these shortages are due to planning errors, to poor supply plans and inadequate or misplaced stocks and to a misapplication of a historically explicable scheme of priorities by the planners. Planners produce over-taut plans, and even 'include in the material balances goods which it is known will not be produced in the plan period'. He draws attention, too, to the practice of achieving or aiming at *aggregate* balance, which conceals shortages of sub-items. All these practices create a potential flood of un-satisfied demand which is at present held back 'by the lock gates of the supply system'. But a dynamic and growing economy such as the USSR cannot any longer tolerate the clumsy system of supply planning, with its *zayavki* six months ahead. So, in his view, 'the turn towards wholesale trade should be seen not as a regrettable necessity, but as the bringing of administrative practice into line with the requirements of the economic laws of socialism'.

The essential question is: How far can such reforms go without endangering the central plan? As already pointed out, the conventional definition between macro- and micro-economics provides no clear distinction in practice between those items which may be left free to respond to market pressures and those which the planners must control if they are to retain an effective grip on the basic

[1] Ibid, pp. 181, 184-87.
[2] *Materialno-tekhnicheskoe snabzhenie*, No. 11/1967, pp. 21 ff. (Grateful thanks to M. Feshbach for the reference.)

proportions of the economy and the pattern of its growth. If the clothing industry were planned solely on the basis of consumer demand, this would worry no one. This would be wholly in line with present policy. This means that cloth factories should provide the cloth needed for the fulfilment of the plans of the clothing factories. Logically it also follows that dyestuffs plans should be made on the basis of orders placed by the users. Then where does one stop? What about machinery for the textile and clothing industries? How far should investments be decided by the producers, so that they can adjust their output to changes in demand? If there is a large increase in this kind of decentralized investment, whose job will it be to ensure that the necessary capital equipment is produced? It should not be forgotten that the clumsy device of the centralized calculation and aggregation of *zayavki*, and indeed the entire system of planning by material balances, is designed to ensure that requirements for inputs and for investment goods are met. In a perfect market system the information is transmitted through market channels, and the pattern of investment responds to changes in demand for investment goods through the operation of the profit motive. But the Soviet Union has no capitalist class. Would it in fact be practicable to replace the administrative method of transmitting requirements for capital goods by a modified market mechanism? The answer to such questions is at least not obvious. The key problem is therefore one of linking effectively the centrally planned and the decentralized portions of a highly complex economic structure. The search for the appropriate balance between these various considerations will doubtless continue for some time.

Nemchinov, in his last year of life, presented the case for reform in a rather original way. He imagined the planning organs placing orders among various enterprises in accordance with plan requirements. The orders would relate primarily to final goods, not to intermediate products. 'Each enterprise will submit in advance to the planning organs its proposals as to the conditions upon which it is prepared to carry out this or that planned order for deliveries, with particulars of assortment, quality, delivery date and price. The economic and planning organs will then place their orders only with those enterprises whose proposals . . . are most advantageous for the national plan.'[1] In this conception enterprises would compete for orders, thus enabling the state to obtain its needs at lowest cost. Presumably enterprises would sub-contract to other enter-

[1] Nemchinov, *Kommunist*, No. 5/1964, p. 77.

prises, and the materials allocation system would largely disappear. Only some basic materials and fuels would be price-controlled, together with a few essential consumers' goods.

There are thus many schools contending. The level of discussion is now encouragingly high. There are many shades of opinion, covering those who believe in assigning a major and decisive role to the market all the way to those who would confine any reform to the utilization by planners of 'commodity-money relations' as one of several means to attain the objectives decided upon by the planners. The most extreme 'marketeers' do not deny that a plan is necessary, that the strategic development decisions belong to the state, that the state itself has objectives (e.g. national defence, education) which any plan must reflect. Even the more conservative and timid officials would agree that the product mix should accord more closely to user demand and that institutional changes (including the use of the profit motive) are needed to bring this about. But, as Birman (critically) formulates their arguments, 'the collection of *zayavki* from below and the sending down of allocation quotas (fondy) from above represents a logical scheme for the utilization of the national product, which can be cross-checked at each stage. The substitution of a market (for inputs) for allocations looks like a turn towards anarchy, a denial of planning.'[1] Birman himself, oddly enough, has little to say about prices in his 'market'. He argues rather that industrial materials should be planned 'like consumers' goods', which, after all, are not rationed. Yet logic surely demands that prices play an active role in any reform conducted in the Birman spirit, and one reason at least for the continuance of centralized allocation of supplies is that the price system is unresponsive to demand and so fails to convey information from user to producer.

The question has also been raised: at what level should decisions be taken, by reference to such economic criteria as profitability? As already suggested, this need not be the enterprise, in the sense of a plant or factory. There was a lecture during 1967 at the Academy of Sciences by Menshikov, at which he described the running of large American corporations. One of his audience, Aganbegyan, drew the conclusion: 'it is unscientific to regard the enterprise as the basic organizational unit' of the economy.[2]

Finally, among the sources of new reform ideas it is necessary to mention the Institute of Mathematical Economics, founded in Moscow in 1963, and also the activities of Kantorovich in Novo-

[1] Birman, op. cit., p. 28.
[2] *Vop. ekon.*, No. 8/1967, pp. 150-1.

sibirsk and of Novozhilov in Leningrad. Some of their theoretical notions will be gone into in chapter 11. Here it will be sufficient to give their views on reform. This is no easy task, since the 'mathematicians' are by no means united. Needless to say, mathematics as such is only a method, a technique, which could be used for very different purposes. None the less, the leading mathematical economists do have in some degree a common outlook.

They are not centralizers, in that they do not claim that ultra-centralized micro-economic planning could be made to function by means of computers. They are aware of the daunting complexity of such a task. There are something between six and seven million prices fixed at various levels of the Soviet economic administration. Each price represents an identifiably different good. It is quite evident that neither information flows, nor data processing, nor yet the decision-making procedures, could possibly cope with such a flood. Yet at the fully disaggregated micro-economic operational level, this is the kind of detail which must be the subject of administrative instructions, in respect of production, inputs, delivery dates, and so on, unless a criterion for devolving decision-making onto the lower echelons can be devised. This criterion, for reasons amply examined already, cannot be 'the plan', for this throws responsibility back to the centre. Therefore the 'mathematicians' generally advocate the use of market forces at the levels at which consumer (and generally user) demand impinges upon the process of planning. Decentralized demand, facing supply-and-demand balancing prices, albeit perhaps fixed by the planners,[1] must and should affect what is produced. Novozhilov, for instance, stresses the importance of the information-carrying function of prices at this micro-economic level.[2]

This information is seen as part of a two-way process of iteration. The planners would alter prices continuously while trying to achieve an optimal plan. The demand of the users (including the state itself as a consumer) is met by appropriate production and investment decisions, and their requirements affect the prices at which balance is achieved. At higher levels of aggregation, and in respect of key industrial goods and materials, all this can be the subject of a computerized programming process, aiming at the achievement of (or the closest approximation to) an optimum. The optimum must be related to the satisfaction of the needs of the people, since any

---

[1] Pugachev, a leading 'mathematician', drew attention in a paper to the Econometrics conference in Warsaw in 1966 to the danger of monopolist distortion if there is profit maximization under socialism.

[2] See, for instance, his article in *Ekonomika i matematicheskie metody*, No. 3/1966. See also chapter 11.

other criterion of optimality opens the door too wide to arbitrariness. The valuations attaching to the various commodities in the course of the programming exercise were called, by Kantorovich, 'objectively determined valuations', and we will have more to say of them in chapter 11. The mathematicians, logically enough, urge the use of prices, appropriate to decisions at lower echelons of the system, for finding the best use of new (and therefore scarce) machinery: naturally, if it is scarce it should, in their view, be priced at so high a level that only in its most productive uses will it be profitable.[1] By 'lower echelons' is meant here not necessarily the enterprise. The 'mathematicians' proved, in discussion, very conscious of the need for empirical research on the optimal location of decision-making in efficient hierarchical multi-stage structures. Both information and motivation are relevant factors here. But whether in Moscow or in the depth of the provinces, decisions need to be taken by reference to generalized criteria by perhaps junior officials. It is important to devise criteria so that 'every unit of the economy must have the possibility to take decisions, according to the principle that anything that is profitable for the economy as a whole must be profitable for each unit of socialist production.'[2]

These ideas have been challenged.[3] In any event, the mathematicians do not suggest that the exceedingly complex methodology and information-flows required for the implementation of their theories of optimal planning are available for use today. So it is certainly not the case that the political leadership are rejecting the clear and unambiguous advice of this (or any other) school of thought.

It is evident that progress is still slow, and there are many obstacles to rapid change. The old system has its inner logic. There is, too, what Birman has several times called the 'psychological barrier': old habits die hard, and everyone has been accustomed ever since anyone can remember to the system inherited from Stalin. Yet surely change will continue, and the trend is clear, even if the speed and extent of the advance are not. So far, the Soviet changes have not been nearly as far-going as those being implemented in Czechoslovakia and especially Hungary. More of these in a moment. However, it is premature to assume that the Soviet reforms will indefinitely hang fire, just as it is foolish to deny that there are some great difficulties in the way of a workable and viable combination of plan and market.

[1] K. Gofman, N. Petrakov, in *Vop. ekon.*, No. 5/1967, p. 32 ff.
[2] N. Fedorenko's paper on optimal planning and pricing, summarized in *Vop. ekon.* No. 5/1967, pp. 148-50.
[3] For instance see powerful attack by a mathematician on 'mathematical-abstractionists' by A. Skryabin, *Vop. ekon.* No. 11/1967, pp. 62 ff.

In agriculture, the granting of greater powers to reformed *kolkhozy* and *sovkhozy*, a reduction in the still very prevalent arbitrary interferences from *oblast'* party and other officials, is much overdue. Gradually, party control over everyday farming activities should come to be no more severe than is the case in industry. Indeed, it is already so in *sovkhozy*. The long standing tradition of treating *kolkhozy* so very differently in this respect will surely wither away, as the management of the enlarged *kolkhozy* becomes both politically reliable and well qualified, and as the internal organization of the *kolkhozy* comes to resemble *sovkhozy* more closely. The fall of Khrushchev, who was 'interferer-in-chief', was followed by promises of greater autonomy for farms. A revision of prices, accompanied by some form of more or less disguised payment of land rent, should increase the role of economic forces as determinants of farming decisions, though state procurements for essential purposes will doubtless continue to be compulsory. Any move towards a more flexible structure must depend, however, on improvements in production, since otherwise the party and state organs are all too likely to continue their present practice of interfering, to ensure that their needs are met.

In chapter 1 we have already seen that *sovkhozy* may be placed in so-called 'full *khozraschyot*', and that such a *sovkhoz* has a close resemblance to a *kolkhoz* which pays guaranteed 'wages' to its members at *sovkhoz* rates. The difference between the two types would then consist very largely of the principle of state as against co-operative property, with the corollary of an appointed director as against an elected chairman and management committee. Elections, we know, are often a legal cover for party nomination.[1] So one line of policy would be to have in the end only one type of agricultural enterprise, with some new name But on this question there is a long-standing disagreement: some prefer to strengthen the co-operative principle, and to unite *kolkhozy* into district, regional, republican, even national 'kolkhoz unions' (*kolkhozsoyuzy*). These would be representative bodies, which could also carry out local planning functions and administer inter-*kolkhoz* activities, including small-scale industrial production and building. Such an idea as this was advocated by Matskevich before Khrushchev dismissed him as Minister of agriculture. It figures among the resolutions of the twenty-third party congress. It is eloquently advocated in an article

---

[1] Or party dismissal. Thus the refusal of the peasants to dismiss a chairman at the *raikom's* behest was followed by the arrival of the *prokuror* and chief of militia, and by an apparently illegal arrest. (*Izvestiya*, August 16, 1967).

in a leading legal periodical. It is opposed by those who prefer to administer the two types of farm through the same hierarchy.[1]

The *kolkhoz* congress, which was to draw up a new statute, is, at that moment of writing, still to be held at some unspecified date in the future. No doubt the lack of agreement on such issues as the above explains its repeated postponement.

THE PARTY'S ATTITUDES

It is necessary to mention one significant obstacle to major reforms which enlarge the area of economic 'automatism' and restrict the range of decisions of administrative and party organs. This is the self interest of the many party officials and administrators whose present functions consist precisely in replacing the automatic functioning of economic forces. It is true that any conceivable reform of the Soviet economy would leave much to be settled by the central political authorities. For example, general questions of investment policy, the setting up of new enterprises, the provision of investment funds for new or rapidly growing industries, long term development plans, the drafting and amendment of the legal framework within which economic bodies operate, would certainly belong to the centre, and would keep the political leadership fully employed. But the party and state machines at lower levels, especially in the localities, would lose many of their present functions. They are not likely to approve of such reforms, and ideologists reflecting their viewpoints will surely argue that economic forces must be subordinated to deliberate political decision, and that such subordination is an integral part of the transition 'from the realm of necessity to the realm of freedom'. Party tradition would be on their side. Some would hold that this would decide the issue, that party self-interest must overwhelm all other considerations, including those of economic rationality. This, however, is not necessarily the case, because the party has other objectives than control. It is seeking to transform the USSR into the world's leading economic power. To achieve this aim it requires a more rational use of scarce resources, greater efficiency in planning and in production. It will doubtless seek to reconcile the achievement of greater efficiency with the pursuit of its narrow self-interest as a ruling group in society. But even this last phrase requires qualification, because 'the party' is not in fact the monolithic body which it claims to be. Within it, precisely because of its mono-

---

[1] Z. Belyaeva and M. Kozyr', *Sovetskoe gosudarstvo i pravo* No. 12/1967, pp. 83 ff. and I. Yudin and M. Lapidus, *Ekon. gaz.*, No. 30/1966.

poly of political power, there are divergent interests, and this applies even to the narrow group of professional party functionaries: we have already seen that the enlargement of economic 'automatism' does not unduly threaten the power position of the central leadership, while adversely affecting *obkom* secretaries.

For all these reasons, the attitude of the party towards ideas of reform is ambivalent; certain proposals may be rejected on ideological-political grounds, but others may have (albeit reluctantly) to be accepted if such acceptance is seen as the necessary price to be paid for a more efficacious pursuit of the aim of 'overtaking America'. The evident *impossibility* of carrying on in the old way makes acceptance of reform virtually irresistible.

THE CZECH AND HUNGARIAN MODELS

Until after the death of Stalin, most countries in the Soviet bloc copied the Soviet organizational scheme down to the smallest detail. Since the special reasons which, for better or for worse, gave rise to the Soviet system of planning were unlikely to apply in all other countries, this gave rise to grievous and probably quite unnecessary errors and irrationalities. So it was hardly surprising to find that several of these countries began to experiment with new ideas once they were free to do so. It is worth studying these experiments not only because of their intrinsic interest, but because they may well serve as a guide to possible future changes in the USSR.

Since the events of 1956, and increasingly in recent years, the countries which were once correctly described as Soviet satellites have acquired the power to conduct their own economic policies and adapt their planning system to their own requirements. Thus, when the Roumanians rejected plans proposed by the Soviet Union within COMECON, the fact that the Roumanian policy was not to the liking of the Soviet Government made no difference, and despite the incidence of a common frontier between the two countries there seemed to have been nothing that could have been done to ensure obedience. The Roumanian example related to a question which affected international economic policy. As for the solution of internal economic problems, there seems no evidence that the USSR even attempts to exert pressure in favour of this sort of solution. Consequently, various experiments and reforms have been tried in various countries. Some of the latter, like Poland and Hungary, possess a first rate tradition in academic economics and some very able economists. In Czechoslovakia too it was realized that major changes were essential, since the special problems of a small and highly industrialized country were unlikely to be solved by using methods copied from the experience of the Soviet Union.

By 1964 virtually all of the East European countries had embarked on major reforms. Space does not permit a detailed account of each of these. Two countries will be selected for a brief analysis, because they represent rather different approaches to reform: Czechoslovakia and Hungary.

In 1958 the Czechs[1] launched what was for its time the most radical attempt to transform the system, outside of Yugoslavia. (It is true that theoretical discussions in Poland had been much more far-reaching than this, but actual changes in that country were slow and cautious.) In Czechoslovakia smaller enterprises were amalgamated into larger units or trusts. Enterprises and trusts were to submit plans for approval to higher authority, i.e. the appropriate ministry, and these plans were to be based on customers' orders. The task of the industrial ministries was to be limited to ensuring that these plans were consistent with available resources. Most of the material allocations system was to be eliminated. The task of Gosplan was to be essentially one of drafting the long term plan, the taking of the necessary investment decisions and so effecting the shape and basis of expansion. To encourage enterprises and trusts to use their initiative to expand production of the right commodities, they were given a substantial incentive in the form of a share in profits. To encourage them to be honest about their production possibilities, the amount of profit retained was to be proportionately greater if the enterprises' achievements were part of the plan which it put forward for ministerial approval. Overfulfilment was thus relatively penalized. This borrowing from the rules of contract bridge may well have influenced one of the features of the Liberman proposals which have already been analysed. The actual rules for the amount of profit to be retained were complicated, being based in the main on planned increases over the previous period, modified by changes in labour productivity (used to discourage the unnecessary taking on of labour). The total amount of profits retained was greatly increased over the economy as a whole. They could be used partly for payment of bonuses and partly to finance decentralized investments. The latter could also be financed by bank credits, and in these ways as much as half of the total volume of investment was decentralized.

Three years later this entire reform was abandoned, and it is of

[1] For Czech read Czechoslovak throughout.

some interest to dwell briefly on the reasons for the failure of the reform, as similar difficulties could arise in other countries.

In the first place, there were errors in that part of the investment plan which was the responsibility of the central planners. This created disequilibria, tensions and shortages. Secondly, there was a lack of balance between the pattern of decentralized investment and the availability of investment goods. In other words, the machinery and engineering industry was not in a position to respond to the decentralized demand for their products. One is here reminded of the fact that the traditional planning system does provide a means of conveying information about requirements to those branches of industry whose task it is to meet them. The Czech 1958 reform failed to provide an alternative method of effectively conveying such information. Thirdly, there was no systematic amendment of the price system, without which the greater reliance on market forces could not be effective. The management thus faced irrational or inconsistent incentives and was unable to influence the behaviour of its suppliers by appropriate inducements. Finally, or so I was told in Prague, although the 'gross value of output' indicator was supposed to be banished from the scene, it none the less became the principal success indicator in practice. Apparently this was because increases in labour productivity were regarded as a vital criterion, and labour productivity was calculated by dividing the number of workers into the gross output.

After the abandonment of the reform, the Czech economy faced a period of serious difficulty, accentuated by a chronic balance of payments crisis. Major efforts were made to find a way out. In 1964 the economist O. Šik published a new reform plan, which was the basis of far-reaching changes gradually introduced after 1965. The essence of his scheme is as follows:

(a) Administrative allocation of resources is confined to a very short list of basic or temporarily very scarce commodities, such as energy, steel, heavy machinery. The rest is a matter for trade between enterprises, trusts, wholesalers, etc. and based on negotiated contracts.

(b) Save for the items on the administratively allocated list, enterprises are not 'sent down' any output plans. They make their own plans, based on their contracts with others. In principle, the planners' direction over the economy operates by control over investment.

(c) It is, of course, understood that prices must play an active role under the new system. It is also understood (quite correctly) that no one single principle of price determination will do. There are to be four price categories (I am referring here to wholesale or factory prices):—

(i) Centrally fixed prices. These will relate to a short list of basic items (energy, steel, etc.), the principal agricultural products and a few goods in very short supply.

(ii) 'Range' prices. Within maxima and minima, they will be subject to negotiation between enterprises.

(iii) In some cases, there will be average prices fixed, which will enable enterprises to negotiate more freely about assortment (e.g. clothing) or seasonal prices can be determined locally (e.g. vegetables).

(iv) Free prices, these applying to items 'in ample supply', fashion goods, local industry, miscellaneous services.

It was proposed that some 15-20 per cent of all sales of goods and services be free. The majority of commodities would fall in group (ii) above.

As a first stage, prices were recalculated by computers, based on enterprises' costs plus a profit margin (this being a percentage of capital assets). Prices were thus calculated for 27,000 product groups,[1] and were then further disaggregated, there being roughly 1,500,000 items with separate prices. The new prices were introduced on January 1, 1967. Two snags were encountered. One was that enterprises had succeeded in inflating cost estimates, and so the new prices were rather too high in some cases, while in other instances some of the highest cost enterprises have had to be subsidized. The second difficulty concerned excess demand, so that under conditions of a sellers' market it was not found possible to free more than about 5-6 per cent of prices, while two thirds remained fixed, and the 'range' prices all rose to the permitted maxima. The resultant price-inflexibilities have been one of the difficulties in implementing the reform. However, the materials allocation system has almost vanished, and production plans are based on free contract in most instances, unlike the present situation of the USSR.

Enterprises aim to maximize their contribution to the national income, or $v + m$ in Marxian terms. Their finances and incentives depend on the magnitude of $v + m$, or of net revenue (after paying for goods and services bought from outside). This net revenue is subject to tax, which is 18 per cent in industry and construction, and 30 per cent in retail trade. There is also a capital charge of 6 per

[1] M. Sokol, *Czechoslovak economic papers* No. 8/1967, p. 10.

cent, and a 2 per cent tax on stocks.[1] A tax on the wages fund is intended to discourage overmanning, it increases steeply if the wages bill is higher than in the previous year. What remains of v + m after tax is to be paid out in wages and salaries plus bonuses, or put aside as profit to devote to reserves or to decentralized investments. Wage minima are fixed, close to the *tariff* rates (which, in Czechoslovakia as elsewhere, are usually well below the actual earnings). If the minima cannot be met, a subsidy will be paid. Workers and managerial personnel alike would be interested in maximizing the net product, as any increase would have an immediate and predictable effect on incomes.

The budgetary revenues raised by way of turnover tax have been largely replaced by the 'net income tax' and capital charge.

All working capital is on credit, thus eliminating the practice of making free advances of working capital from the budget.

Investment is financed in three ways:—

(a) From the budget (but subject to capital charge, as above). This is for centralized, big investment projects.

(b) By bank credit, as part of the centrally approved plan, with appropriate calculation of rates of return, etc.

(c) Decentralized investments, partly financed by credits too, (with the banks deciding between competing requests for credit, perhaps by auction), partly out of enterprise profits.

Uncertainty, due to the partial failure of the price reform, is said to have affected the willingness of enterprises to invest, but this may prove temporary. A further uncertainty is the extent to which the so-called branch directorates (the Czech equivalent of *obyedineniya* or *glavki*) will run their respective branches of industry, and there have been fears that they may behave like ministries and interfere in excessive detail with enterprise autonomy. It is true that they do have an essential function in identifying market requirements at home and abroad, as well as putting forward proposals for sector investments. Time will show how they will use their powers.

The Czech reform has so far had little effect on the conduct of foreign trade, which remains in the hands of the specialized corporations. However, the replacement of Novotny by Dubček as party leader is likely to be followed by radical changes in this and also in many other aspects of Czech life, both economic and social-political.

Hungary's path to reform was different. Despite the events of 1956, and some ingenious improvements in the centralized planning

---

[1] *Nova soustova řizeni* (Prague, 1967), pp. 30-2.

system, changes of principle had to await 1966/67, and the reform is being implemented by stages as from January 1, 1968. The Hungarian model looks like the most radical of any, apart from Yugoslavia, and embraces some principles and doctrines not yet accepted even in Czechoslovakia, let alone the USSR.

Space forbids a detailed examination of the Hungarian reform. The following are those of its key features, which distinguish it, in content or emphasis, from the Soviet reform.

(a) As the Hungarian decree puts it, 'there will be continued justification for the private sector to maintain its complementary role, including small-scale industry and retail trade', and especially in the service sectors.

(b) 'A greater scope . . . for competition between enterprises' will be provided, to stimulate 'efficiency and satisfy the demands of the consumer more fully . . . Especially in the field of consumers' goods state enterprises (will) compete with each other or with co-operatives; furthermore in the field of the service trades compete with the private sector'. Where economies of scale are such as to favour the establishment of large enterprises which will have a semi-monopoly position, every effort would be made to ensure competition from substitutes or by imports, and control would be exercized to prevent exploitation of a monopoly situation.

(c) The role of the market in shaping national-economic plans is given prominence, and 'market processes may in fact cause departures from the plan', and the plan not then be insisted upon, unless this affects 'the realization of the basic proportion' of the economy.

(d) Enterprises are to have freedom to decide 'what and how much they want to produce and market', and 'from what enterprises and in what quantities they want to purchase for their own money' the inputs and capital equipment and transport and other services they require. Enterprises may buy directly from each other, or through wholesalers, as they please.

(e) Foreign trade plays a major part in the reform, as it does in Hungary's economy. Here the reform proposals go much further than any other communist-ruled country has yet gone, always excepting Yugoslavia. The aim is to grant the purchaser of inputs the right 'to choose between domestic and imported goods', while Hungarian sellers 'will have freedom to decide whether they want to sell their goods on the domestic market or foreign markets'. This will mean, for the first time, 'economic' control over foreign trade, primarily by exchange rates and tariffs, instead of its administration by specialized corporations. The latter will be retained as a species of commission agents, but large enterprises will be able to deal directly with foreign countries. Far from desiring to shield Hungary's economy from the outside world, 'the new economic mechanism will have to establish an organic connection between the domestic market and foreign markets. It will have to heighten the impact of external market impulses on domestic production, marketing and consumption'. While import and export licensing will exist, the primary form of control will be through what are called 'foreign exchange indices' (which are clearly intended to encourage trade to conform to the bilateral clearing situation, or to the relative advantage of earning convertible currencies). Not only productive enterprises but also retail trade will exercise choice in what to import.

(f) While large investments will be within the competence of government planners, decentralized investments out of retained profits and on bank credit will greatly increase. (The Hungarians were the first, after Yugoslavia, to introduce capital charges; they included them in costs.)

(g) Last but far from least, the role of prices is seen very differently from Sitnin's 'conservative' Soviet model. They are viewed as a key element in the system: they must provide the appropriate incentive and (of course) achieve 'a balance of supply and demand'. Three elements should enter price formation: costs, 'value judgments emerging from the market' and planners' preferences (i.e. considerations of economic policy). There must, furthermore, be 'an organic relationship between internal prices and foreign trade prices', achieved not by official exchange rates but 'with consideration of the average costs involved' in obtaining given foreign currencies (and doubtless also in the light of what can be done with them once obtained; these are the 'foreign exchange indices' referred to above). The freeing of prices from central control 'can be envisaged only by stages'. Like the Czechs, the Hungarians at present will have three categories: fixed, 'limit' (up and down) and free. But it is roundly asserted that 'the value judgments of the markets have to express themselves in prices', so that 'differentiation of profits should influence the shaping of the pattern of production and supply . . . and help in bringing about the equilibrium of the market'. Enterprises, subject to various safeguards and taxes, are to be made interested in profits through the creation of a profit-sharing fund and a 'development' (investment) fund.[1]

[1] All quotations are from the Resolution of the Hungarian socialist workers' party, circulated in English by the Information Service of the Hungarian Chamber of Commerce (undated).

It is, naturally, too soon to tell how much of this far-reaching programme will actually be fully implemented during 1968-69, the period of implementation specified in the decree. But it is obvious that in their much more vigorously logical approach to prices, their view of the role of foreign trade in internal economic activities, in the approach to competition and to the private sector, the Hungarians do differ radically from the Soviet moderate reformers.

Hungary has a powerful school of mathematically-minded economists, who have been seeking means of devising a planning-and-programming system in which optimization is reached by the centre and by autonomous sub-units in their interrelationship. The work particularly of Dr J. Kornai is becoming internationally known. Research on related lines is proceeding also in Czechoslovakia and elsewhere.

Space forbids further exploration of the reform in other countries. But a few lines should be devoted to Poland, if only to explain her omission. At one time Polish economists were in the van of 'reformist' thinking. Eminent men such as Lange, Kalecki, Lipinski, and distinguished younger economists such as Brus and Zielinski, have made important contributions to the economics of socialism. But there have been few big changes in practice, and Poland is at present in a somewhat depressed state. It seems proper, therefore, to concentrate on other countries.[1]

YUGOSLAVIA

The fascinating experiments in a 'socialist market economy' which have been conducted in Yugoslavia, especially after 1951, require a prolonged specialized study. Here it will only be possible briefly to indicate the respects in which this method of running the economy differs from the Soviet models.

Firstly, Yugoslav state enterprises are much more independent. With few exceptions, they have no output plan, other than the one they themselves adopt. This is based on commercial considerations, i.e. the demands of the customers. The enterprises compete with one another. This applies to wholesaling and retailing, as well as manufacturing enterprises. The overriding economic motive is profit.

[1] My colleague, Dr Zauberman, holds that there is a law ('Zauberman's Law') that 'the state of the economy varies in inverse proportion to the eminence of the economists'. This law would seem to have its application to Poland and Great Britain. For a valuable account of Polish developments, see J. M. Montias in *Value and Plan* (Grossman, ed.) (Berkeley, 1960), and especially his *Central Planning in Poland* (Yale, 1962).

Secondly, prices are much freer. In theory, they ought to be wholly free, so that a real market should operate. In practice, fears of inflation and a desire to peg the cost of living leads to the imposition of price maxima for many products. But this still leaves room for a good deal of price competition.

Thirdly, the bulk of the investment funds of enterprises are borrowed from the bank, which judges the various projects partly by reference to their profitability and partly in relation to state economic policies and long-term plans. At one period, it was thought possible to 'auction' investment capital to the highest bidder (among enterprises), but this is no longer done. The state influences the pace of development by directing a large part of its revenues to accumulation, and the direction of development by issuing instructions to the bank about whom to give preference among the claimants for investment funds. A capital charge is made, and investment credits bear interest.

Fourthly, enterprises have financial and organizational links with the local authorities ('communes'), and also, though to a lesser extent, with the republic (Serbia, Croatia, etc.) in which they are situated.

Fifthly, the directors' powers are exercised with elected workers' councils, which, at least formally, are much more powerful within an enterprise than are similar bodies in Poland or the USSR. The state enterprise is supposed to be administered by its workers, and wage levels depend, within limits, on the profitability of the given enterprise. However, to avoid various distortions (e.g. the exploitation by the enterprises of a monopoly position, or excessive inequalities between workers in different factories) the state closely controls the ways in which enterprise revenues can be disposed of, itself taking the largest share of the net product, discouraging 'overpayment' of wages by various fiscal measures. This has had the unfortunate effect of greatly diminishing the interest of the workers in the financial success of 'their' enterprise.

Finally, the bulk of Yugoslav peasants are owners of their land. Collectives, tried out in the 'Stalinist' period, have been almost wholly disbanded. The peasants are free to decide what to grow, there are no compulsory delivery quotas of any kind. They may sell what they wish in the free market. However, all state enterprises (including shops) must buy through peasant co-operatives, at prices which are decided by the state, and this means that any peasants who cannot take their produce to a large city, or whose produce is of a kind of which state enterprises are the only major buyers (e.g.

grapes, wheat), are virtually compelled to sell through co-operatives. However, since the peasants are free to decide what they grow, the state's powers in fixing prices are necessarily limited.

The role of the market mechanism, and the idea that enterprises are run by the workers who work in them, are contrary to current Soviet doctrine, but one suspects that neither the market nor the workers' councils are as free in the real Yugoslavia as they are in the 'Yugoslav model'. But then, as we have had many occasions to note, in few countries does the actual economy correspond to the imagination of the model-builders.

An economic crisis in 1965 caused drastic devaluation and a number of changes in the status of the enterprises, with the accent on stricter financial discipline and a yet freer market. There is a positively ruthless insistence on sound finance. Resultant unemployment has partially been relieved by migration to West Germany. Much has been done to liberalize foreign trade, and the convertibility of the new dinar is close to becoming a reality.

PART III: CONCEPTS AND IDEAS

CHAPTER 10

Some Basic Concepts of Soviet Economics

It is now time to discuss concepts, theories. The fact that this is being done last is not intended to imply any opinion concerning the primacy of matter over mind, of material as against spiritual. It is simply that the concepts and ideas which Soviet economists use are hardly comprehensible unless the institutional framework and practical problems are discussed first. It is true, of course, that basic ideology of Marxism-Leninism exerts a powerful influence on structure and on policy decisions. However, a discussion on the philosophical basis of Soviet communism falls well outside the scope of the present work.

NATIONAL INCOME

The Soviet concept of national income is in line with the classical tradition, in distinguishing between 'productive' and 'unproductive' activities, only the former being considered as generating a real product. As in Adam Smith, civil servants, soldiers, teachers, doctors, 'opera singers and opera dancers', etc., are deemed to be unproductive. The national income therefore consists of the total value of the material product. In the USSR, this value is deemed to equal the sum of the final selling prices of material goods, net of all double counting and of amortization (depreciation) of fixed assets. Since final selling prices of many goods contain turnover tax, this means that such taxes are included in the national income, which becomes the equivalent of a species of 'net national material product at market prices'. (This definition is inexact, because there is only a very restricted sense in which prices reflect market relations, but the essential point is that factor costs are not used as a basis.)

284

The adoption of a dividing line between 'productive' and 'unproductive' involves some awkward demarcational problems. In the Soviet Union, though not in all other eastern countries, passenger transport and personal postal services are excluded from the national income, though several economists have protested that this is an illogical procedure, and some have urged that not only passenger transport but also 'commercial services' (e.g. baths, laundries) should be included in the national income, but so far in vain.[1] The present concept involves, among other things, the idea that a railway signalman is productive when he lets a freight train past his signalbox, but unproductive when he performs an identical action on the approach of a passenger train. Similarly, a typist at a factory is productive, but the girl in Gosplan who may type the letter in reply is unproductive, because a line has to be drawn between 'administration' and productive enterprises, and the two typists find themselves on opposite sides of the line. However, before adopting a supercilious attitude, Western economists would do well to recall some of their own difficulties. Thus there is the old but true story that, in the Western concept, a man diminishes the national income by marrying his cook. Our definitions have also been challenged, by Western economists among them by Simon Kuznets and J. L. Nicholson.[2] If anyone considers that our own concept is simple to apply in practice, let him study the ways by which British statisticians estimate the net product of banking and insurance. The Soviet definition has, in fact, one quite impressive argument in its favour: that international (and to some extent also inter-temporal) comparisons of aggregates of material goods, however imperfect they may be, have a sounder basis than any aggregates of services. The latter are generally deemed in the West to equal the reward of the service provider—e.g. the value of a teacher or a soldier is equal to his pay. But suppose, as is the case, a US soldier's or teacher's pay is many times higher than that of a Russian soldier or teacher? One might well ask: what conceivable bearing have such figures as these on the comparative 'volume' of educational or military services? Whereas, at least notionally, steel can be compared with steel, and tractors with tractors, with no more than the usual index

---

[1] For a more detailed analysis of this controversy, see A. Nove in *Soviet Studies*, January, 1955, pp. 247-80. For the practice in other eastern countries, see E. F. Jackson, 'Social Accounting in Eastern Europe', *Studies in Income and Wealth*, Series IV (London, 1955). Also V. Sobol' and S. Strumilin in *Vest. stat.*, No. 4/1957, pp. 79, 85.

[2] See, respectively, *Economic Change* (New York, 1953), pp. 192 ff., and *Studies in Income and Wealth*, Series IV, pp. 145 ff.

number and physical comparability problems (though, alas, these are bad enough). It is important to note that the difference in incomes derived from services are in fact a measure not of the quantity or quality of the services, but of the productivity of the productive sectors. A little thought will show that this is so. Suppose that the material product—or more strictly the consumable material product—per head of population is four times greater in the United States than in Italy. Then, other things being equal, it is quite probable that an Italian hairdresser or civil servant will earn about a quarter of an American hairdresser or civil servant. In this respect, and perhaps others too, the use of the Soviet concept is more practicable and even possibly more logical than the West's. (However, for certain purposes, such as measuring resource allocation within a country, or the standard of living, the inclusion of services is often desirable.)[1]

In the application of the Soviet concept to the national accounts of the USSR, there are several points which could cause confusion in the minds of the unwary. The first is that some services, in themselves unproductive, do in fact form part of the national income, by being rendered to a productive enterprise. The latter's net product is calculated by subtracting from the total value of its output the 'material' expenditure, and also depreciation. But this means that certain services are not subtracted and so remain in the net product. This would apply, for example, to the services of lawyers and engineering consultants, or to journeys by passenger train of employees on behalf of the enterprise, and also to interest payments on credits. Consequently, these and similar services find their way into the national income—but not, as in the West, under heading of legal, technical, banking or transport services, but as part of the net product of the 'productive' branch of the economy to which they have been rendered. This affects the comparability of, for instance, the net product of industry under the Western and Eastern definitions, though, in the West too, the handling of such services by statisticians often lacks logic. The same services rendered to individuals, or to 'unproductive' sectors (for instance, education) would not appear in the national income in the USSR.

A somewhat odd situation arises with trade. It was common for Soviet economists to stress, in respect of the capitalists, the wasteful and unproductive expenditures involved (e.g. advertising, 'specu-

[1] Western national accounts have been attracting the attention of Soviet scholars. Thus see A. Vainshtein (ed.): *Statistika narodnova bogatstva narodnova dokhoda i natsional'nye scheta* (M., 1967).

lation', etc.). However, the use of retail prices for national income purposes necessarily involves including the contribution of trade in the Soviet total. Some theorists consider that this is justified because the bulk of expenditures consist of genuine handling costs (e.g. packing, unpacking, sorting). Others are not too happy about this, and consider that not all of Soviet trade should be treated as 'productive'.[1] However, in practice it is so treated.

It may seem unclear to those accustomed to Western concepts how national accounts can be made up on the Soviet basis. Essentially, there is a two-fold process. The first step is to build up the total net product of the 'productive' sectors, being the value of goods produced during the year (plus or minus change in unfinished production). This material net product is divided between sectors of origin as follows, using the actual figures for 1965:

	Milliards of (new) roubles
Industry	101·0
Agriculture	42·4
Construction	17·3
Transport and Communications	10·8
Others (Trade, procurements, material supplies, etc.)	21·1
Total	190·4

Source: N.Kh., 1965, p. 592.

In the same year, 1965, the total was divided as follows between consumption and accumulation (in milliards of roubles):

CONSUMPTION	140·7
of which: Personal consumption	123·9
Material expenses in institutions serving the public	12·4
Material expenses in science and administration	4·4
ACCUMULATION and other expenditure	49·7
of which: Increase in basic capital	28·9
Increase in stocks and reserves	20·8

Source: N.Kh., 1965, p. 592. (See also page 299 below)

[1] 'Buying' and 'selling' are in themselves regarded as unproductive. It is not clear whether free-market trade, which must be deemed to include a large element of 'speculation', is included as such in the national income.

The meaningfulness of all these figures is inevitably affected by the inclusion of most of turnover tax in consumption, and all of it in Industry. The share of agriculture, for instance, would be higher if it were 'credited' with a share in turnover tax revenue arising from agricultural produce.

In Soviet practice, the national income—or net national product —is built up from the production side, by means of data concerning the activity of productive enterprises in the sectors listed above. It is, of course, equal to the sum of incomes generated in the process of production, i.e. to personal incomes of those engaged in the 'productive' sectors, plus profits and other portions of the net product (notably, under the Soviet definition, turnover tax) which form part of the final selling prices of material goods.

Then comes the second stage; the material product is redistributed. It is transferred, through the budget and by other means, to maintain the 'unproductive' sphere. For example, part of the values created in the footwear industry, which are absorbed by the budget through turnover tax and/or profits levy, is used to finance education, defence or administration, and so, *inter alia*, to pay those engaged in these 'unproductive' pursuits. Education 'generates' no national income (though, of course, part of the education budget is spent on material products, such as desks and books, which figure in the net output of industry). But at the second stage, after redistribution, it becomes possible to say meaningfully that education expenditures constitute x per cent of the Soviet national income by use.[1] Western statisticians too use the term 'redistribution', to cover, for instance, social service payments by the state. However, the scale of redistribution is much smaller on the Western definition.

It is noteworthy that the total magnitude arrived at by applying the Soviet definition is not necessarily much smaller than the national income *at factor cost* in its Western concept, provided that the bulk of the 'unproductive' services are financed out of revenues derived from the productive sector. This is far from self-evident, and will be clarified by a simplified example. Supose that the only appreciable 'services' were defence, education and health, and that these were wholly paid for out of turnover tax levied wholly on industry. Using imaginary figures, one could envisage the following:

[1] For a useful detailed account of procedures, including their application to Western G.N.P. statistics, see M. Kolganov, *Natsional'nyi' dokhod* (Moscow, 1959). The G.N.P. of the United Kingdom was recalculated in detail into Soviet concepts by V. Kudrov, *Mirovaya ekonomika i mezhdunarodnye otnosheniya*, No. 6/1958, pp. 63 ff. See also A. Nove, 'U.S. national income à la russe' *Economica*, August, 1956, pp. 244 ff.

Soviet definition		Western definition	
Industry	500	Industry (factor cost)	250
(of which, turnover		Other productive	
tax)	(250)	sectors	300
Other productive		State services*	250
sectors	300		
TOTAL	800	TOTAL	800

*Defence, Education, Health, etc.

That this is not a wholly fantastic picture was shown in a calculation presented to a seminar at the London School of Economics by Professor Grdjić, of Belgrade; he showed that the national income of Yugoslavia comes to almost the same total by the two methods. Of course, if the 'western' calculation were in market prices, the total would be much higher. But it is wrong, in comparing a calculation in terms of factor cost with one in a Soviet definition, simply to add the value of services to the 'Soviet' total.

An interesting point to note is that, by long tradition, the Soviet statisticians include turnover tax in the net product of industry, even if the turnover tax burden falls primarily on the peasant producers of food or materials, or if the actual payment is made by wholesalers within the system of the ministry of trade. This undoubtedly leads to an overstatement, in terms of any economic reality, of the contribution of Soviet industry to the national income, and therefore to a relative understatement of that of other branches of the economy.

In comparing the structure of the national income expressed in the two definitions, we should be aware that the relative magnitudes of personal consumption, investment and state-provided services will look very different, as may be illustrated with imaginary figures based on the above table, still assuming that state expenditure is wholly on defence, education and health. One might then have the following (figures imaginary):

Soviet definition		Western definition	
Consumption (at	600	Consumption (net of	
market prices)		indirect taxes)	350
Investment	200	State services*	250
		Investment	200
TOTAL	800	TOTAL	800

*I am neglecting here the fact that part of the service expenditures takes material forms, and is either consumed or invested as such.

K

Of course, the two totals are in fact usually unequal,[1] in the two concepts, but this does not affect the fact that the separate appearance of (in this instance) state services in the breakdown sharply diminishes the share of consumption in the total. This is one of the reasons for the sharp contrast in the breakdown by use of the Soviet national income as given in Soviet and in Western publications.[2] Soviet statisticians commonly accuse their Western *confrères* of 'double counting', since they claim that the consumption of teachers and soldiers is already included (as indeed it is) under the heading of consumption, and that it is misleading for these sums to appear again as representing the 'service' rendered by teaching or soldiering. To the Western statistician, there is no double counting, since he includes the value of the services of the teacher or soldier on both sides of the account—as a product on one side and as an income on the other. This is no place to argue again the pros and cons of the two approaches; the reader must merely be warned of some of the many differences which follow from their use. The question of the availability and reliability of Soviet national income indices is discussed in the Appendix.

A curious change in the Soviet words for 'national income' occurred around 1950. Before that date, the term used was *narodnyi dokhod*, the literal equivalent of the German *Volkseinkommen*. Then, as by a signal, everyone used the words *natsional'nyi dokhod*. Certain quite senior Soviet academics, including Strumilin, have been urging a return to *narodnyi dokhod*. No change of real meaning is involved, and the philosophical significance of the change, though it presumably exists, is certainly not obvious.

Another change, of more recent vintage has been the publication of two national income indices for certain dates, one representing the 'production of the national income', the other 'the utilization of the national income for consumption and accumulation'. The difference between the two figures is usually attributed to 'losses', and to the foreign trade balance.[3] The latter would enter the picture in two ways; firstly, there is the export or import surplus, but secondly there is also the effect of revaluation of foreign trade statistics in

---

[1] Particularly when direct taxes play an appreciable role, for then the expenditures of the state on services would not be financed through the prices of goods. The same would be true if a high proportion of services were not paid for by the state but, as in the United States, by individuals and corporations. The figures in the Western 'factor cost' definition would be affected by a change in the relative importance of direct and indirect taxation.

[2] Another is the relative 'inflation' of Soviet consumption by the inclusion of turnover tax falling almost wholly on consumers' goods.

[3] *N.Kh.*, 1965, p. 814.

domestic prices. In these prices, the surplus shown in the trade statistics (in 'foreign-trade roubles') might be a deficit, or vice versa, for all we know. But the Soviet source draws attention to another source of difference. The 'utilized' index is calculated in current or 'actual' prices, and when it is converted into 'constant' prices the difference between it and 'produced' national income arises primarily because of differences in commodity composition. (But why *should* there be a difference in commodity composition, other than that due to losses on foreign trade? This is not explained unless the point is that they are calculated in different constant prices.) In 1965, 'produced' national income was 192·6 milliard roubles, of which 190·4 was 'utilized'. But the index for produced national income (1958 = 100) was 159, for utilized national income only 153.[1] Since there were losses also in 1958, and there was little change in trade balance, the reason remains obscure.

GROSS INDUSTRIAL OUTPUT

'Industry' (*promyshlennost'*) in the USSR includes all mining and manufactures, and excludes construction, which is regarded as a separate branch of the economy. It includes also the entire timber industry (except planting and looking after the trees), fisheries and all processing of agricultural products. The slaughter of livestock is regarded as an industrial, not an agricultural pursuit.

Figures on gross industrial output are the sum of the gross outputs of all industrial enterprises, whereas in the West the same designation relates to the output of industry with value-added weights. This affects not only the comparison of aggregate values—the use of the Soviet concept, which includes much double counting, will obviously give a much larger total—but, more important, it affects the index of industrial output.

There are two reasons for this. One is simply that the 'gross' weights used in the Soviet calculation give a disproportionate emphasis to highly fabricated products; in other words, relatively to a net weight calculation, a machine or a pair of shoes are relatively more 'important' in the index than the metal and the leather of which they are made, because the output values of machinery and footwear include the metal and the leather (and much else besides) entering into their manufacture. Clearly, this must have an influence on the index of growth. The second relevant factor is that the 'gross' total so calculated, and the index derived from it, is affected by the

[1] Ibid., pp. 814, 59 and 592.

degree of vertical integration or disintegration. This follows from the practice of adding together the output of enterprises. If, for instance, the same enterprise makes both the tractor and all its components, then, in this respect, there is no double counting; only the values of the tractors appear in the gross output totals. But if it were decided to make these same components in a specialized enterprise which has a juridically separate existence, then they *and* the completed tractors would be counted, at their gross values, and consequently the total and the index would be increased, without there being any additional output in reality. Of course, the opposite could also happen, with opposite results (but, precisely because of these results, which would affect fulfilment of gross output plans, integration might be deliberately avoided). The prices used for the purpose of gross industrial output indices are described as 'wholesale prices of the enterprise (i.e. excluding turnover tax).'[1] However, this does not mean that turnover tax is excluded altogether, since only the taxes levied on the products of the enterprise in question are omitted, whereas taxes already paid on materials used by that enterprise are 'in'. The vexed question of price comparison over time is closely related to that of the reliability and credibility of the official growth indices, and will be considered in the Appendix.

In calculating *net* industrial output, e.g. for national income purposes, double counting is eliminated, and with it the influence of turnover tax on weights *within* industry (turnover tax is added to the *total* net product of industry and thereby increases the weight of industry as a whole). No industrial index with net product weights is available for the USSR. However, some other countries have published calculations which enable comparisons to be made. Thus the volume of industrial output in Hungary is available as follows:

(1949 = 100)

	1955	1956	1957
Gross	271	247	276
Net	226	206	232

Source: Hungarian statistical handbook for 1958, (Vol. II, pp. 63-64).
For a critique of Soviet official figures, see Appendix.

GROSS AGRICULTURAL PRODUCTION

Agricultural statistics have a number of peculiarities and com-

[1] *N.Kh. 1959*, p. 831.

plications. Gross output data represent not the total value of output of enterprises, as is the case for industry, but the total value of farm products. There is double counting; fodder grain, for instance, is included as such even though it is consumed by livestock, and this double counting occurs even if the fodder grain in question is consumed by animals on the same *kolkhoz* or *sovkhoz* on which it has been grown. Thus each and every agricultural product is measured in physical terms, valued at the appropriate price and added together. The result is in no sense a measure of the end product of agriculture. The products of livestock slaughter are, as has been explained, deemed to be industrial. Agriculture produces not meat, therefore, but live-weight animals. However, other livestock products which do not involve slaughter, such as raw wool, milk and so on, are agricultural so long as they remain unprocessed. Gross agricultural output is also deemed to include any increase in the value of work done in connection with the following year's harvest (the equivalent of unfinished production) and work in connection with orchards or tea plantations which take many years to mature.

An important problem in valuing agricultural output concerns the large volume of unsold products, used on the farm or by peasants. Until 1960 the practice was to value the unsold portion of *kolkhoz* and private agriculture at 'average price of realization', i.e. at the average prices which *kolkhozy* and private individuals respectively obtained for their sales to the state and in the market.[1] *Sovkhozy* valued their unsold products at cost. In 1960 new rules were adopted, involving the valuation of *kolkhoz* produce at cost also.[2] The portion that is sold is (and was) valued at the price at which it is sold. Much of the information on details of product use, and also (notably in the private sector) on production, is obtained by sample survey.

An odd feature of agricultural output data down to 1958 was the inclusion in the statistics of the value of work done by the MTS as an additional, independent 'product' of agriculture. This quite gratuitous inflation of the total was attacked by several Soviet statisticians,[3] and disappeared with the disappearance of the MTS.

[1] This means that, since private persons sold a larger proportion of their products at the high free-market prices, that their 'average prices' were higher than those of other categories. In fact, they included some elements of Trade.
[2] See useful detailed article by A. Vikhlyaev in *Vest. Stat.*, No. 10/1960, pp. 54 ff. Also on all these questions see A. Nove, 'Some Problems of Soviet Agricultural Statistics', in *Soviet Studies*, January, 1956, pp. 248 ff.
[3] For instance, S. Strumilin, *Na putyakh postroeniya kommunizma* (Moscow, 1959), p. 53.

OTHER SECTORS

These present no especial conceptual problems, though, as in all countries, there are some difficulties in defining boundary lines. The gross 'output' of construction is the total value of building and installation work. It includes the value of building materials, excludes that of the actual installations. Material, fuel, etc., used up are excluded from any 'net' calculation. Similarly, the contribution of trade is the total trade margin (gross); these margins less the materials, fuel, etc., used by the trade network (packing costs, lighting, etc.) equal the net product. Transport and postal services are complicated by the somewhat artificial division between 'productive' and 'unproductive', mentioned above; some rough estimates are necessary in allocating common expenditures between these two categories; but otherwise the same principles hold.

'GROSS SOCIAL PRODUCT'

This concept represents the sum of the *gross* outputs of all the sectors, double counting and all. It is not to be confused with the national income. The purpose of such a total as this may appear far from obvious, but it exists, and a percentage breakdown by sectors has appeared in statistical compendia, alongside that of the national income.[1]

PRODUCERS' GOODS AND CONSUMERS' GOODS

An essential feature of Marx's pattern of analysis is the division of material production into two main 'departments', or 'sub-divisions' (*podrazdeleniya*), known as I and II. Department I is responsible for the production of all goods which are to be used in the process of production. Department II covers goods for consumption. Both include industrial and agricultural products. These categories are used in analyses concerning the basic 'proportions' of the economy, and as a means of relating these with growth.

More familiar, and much argued about, is the division of *industrial* production into group A (producers' goods) and group B (consumers' goods). Group A in its turn is sub-divided into A1 (producers' goods intended for making producers' goods, e.g. steel used in making machinery or machine tools), and A2 (producers' goods used for making consumers' goods, e.g. industrial sewing machines,

[1] For instance, *N.Kh. 1959*, p. 78. (Such a total is implied by the value figures of an input-output table à la Leontief.)

leather for shoes). Many careless commentators suppose A and B to be identical respectively with 'heavy industry' and 'light industry', but this is not the case. Thus the entire machine building (engineering) industry is classed as 'heavy', but passenger cars and domestic refrigerators made by this industry are classed as B, along with such products of 'light' industry as clothing and shoes, while that part of the textile industry's output which consists of cloth for the clothing industry is included with A. In principle, it is the *use* of any unit of the given product which determines its category, which means that many products are to be found in both groups. For example, cloth sold direct to consumers, rather than to the clothing industry, is in B. Electrical power is A, except when used for domestic purposes, when it is B. In a number of instances, however, when the end use is not precisely known, or one category of use is obviously very much the largest, the product is included in A or B in accordance to its 'predominant end use'.[1]

The share of A in total industrial output has increased steadily. It was 39·5 per cent in 1928, and 71·8 per cent in 1959.[2] It was an essential feature of Soviet economic theory that this has to be so, that producers' goods output (A) must increase faster than consumers' goods output (B), and that, within A, A1 should increase faster than A2. This is said to be a necessary precondition to what is called 'extended reproduction' (*rasshirennoe vosproizvodstvo*). This last term means growth, in the sense of more than reproducing the assets used up in the process of production.

There is much misunderstanding in the West—and in the East— about this allegedly necessary priority (which is strictly concerned with the superior growth of department I as against department II, though the discussion generally seems to concentrate on A and B), and the question deserves closer examination.

The priority of A could be 'justified' in various ways. One of these is not strictly a theoretical argument at all. To a régime whose overriding aim is growth, an emphasis on producers' goods is an aspect of the vital importance of investment, of the future as against present consumption. This is more than a matter of a propaganda theory; it is simultaneously an instruction to the planners about priorities, so that, in the event of a bottleneck, a shortage of goods wagons on the railways for instance, goods which are A (especially A1) are given preference over B. But there is also a serious econ-

[1] For a useful and simple account of the A-B distinction, see Rumyantsev, op. cit., pp. 12-17.
[2] *N.Kh. 1959*, p. 149.

omic case to be made, in three parts. One consists of the assertion that, if growth is to occur, A must, as a matter of economic and arithmetical fact, increase faster than B. The second emphasizes not just growth but also technical progress, the growing importance of machines and intermediate goods of all kinds; this argument is reminiscent of Western controversies about increases in the 'period of production', but it must also not be overlooked that A and B, like other Soviet industrial output aggregates, are 'gross' and therefore A grows relatively with any increase in production of intermediate goods in specialized enterprises, even if the goods concerned are ultimately used in the production of consumers' goods. Finally, it could be argued that, as the economy grows more mature, a larger relative amount of capital investment is used for replacement, and that for this reason an increasing share of investment goods (and therefore A) is needed to maintain a constant growth rate.

The A-B (or I-II) relationship is sometimes the subject of propagandist attack by the less well-informed Western critics, who overlook that the immediate result even of decisions to alleviate the lot of the citizen often takes the form of enlarging the output of 'A' goods, such as building materials for houses, water pipes for drainage, equipment for new shops and so on. Nor do such critics spend much effort on analysing the not unimportant question of whether *in fact* (especially given the Soviet method of computation of industrial output), growth necessarily involves the superior growth of A. On their part, Soviet economists generally adopt very crude lines of argument, using quotations from Marx and Lenin as 'proof'. This happened when, at the time of Malenkov's fall in 1955, it was considered politically necessary to denounce all theories which did not give due priority to A.[1] The economist A. Katz had put forward the view that a comparatively new trend towards economy of capital (i.e. 'a fall in the expenditure of basic capital per unit of production'), alters the picture; that, as a consequence, consumers' goods output could increase as fast as or even faster than that of producers' goods without stopping growth; he was attacked in consequence.[2] The same general line of thought was developed by the otherwise orthodox Polish economist Bronislaw Minc, who also—understandably in the context of Poland—brought in international trade as a modify-

[1] See particularly the unsigned editorial in *Vop. ekon.*, No. 1/1955, pp. 15 ff. and also A. Pashkov, *Ekonomicheskii zakon preimushchestvennovo rosta proizvodstva sredstv proizvodstva* (Moscow, 1958).
[2] Katz's ideas were deemed 'anti-Marxist' and were not published. They were summarized in a hostile spirit in *Vop. ekon.*, No. 1/1955, p. 18.

ing factor. However, Soviet economists had attacked his ideas also.[1]

The crudity of the official doctrine earned harsh comments from a number of western scholars.[2] In 1964 influential Soviet economists joined the ranks of the critics. Thus Arzumanyan, writing in consecutive issues of *Pravda* (February 24th and 25th, 1964) repeated the essence of Katz's arguments, and made the rather obvious point that, if the technical means exist of saving on the use of capital and intermediate goods, and so of increasing the share of final consumable output in the gross product, it will be absurd to forego this possibility in the name of the doctrine of the inevitable superiority of A over B. The fact that this argument was put in the context of Khrushchev's efforts to expand the chemical industry, which promised to be capital saving, did not diminish its validity. Indeed it is plainly the case that errors of planning, such as a mistaken decision about industrial location, would often tend to increase the relative rate of increase of producers goods. Thus the resultant unnecessary transportation would give rise to equally unnecessary production of railway equipment, which of course counts as 'A', but this would hardly be an achievement of which anyone should be proud. It follows that, other things being equal, the smaller the gap between A and B at a given rate of growth, the more likely it is that resources are being used without waste. A more recent criticism points to the 'excessive production for industry's own needs', as against final output in all its forms, as a species of waste stimulated by the measurement of industrial output.[3] The point, as Efimov put it, is to 'obtain the maximum final social product with the most progressive (productive) structure, from the standpoint of satisfying the overall economic needs of society.'[4] This whole question is closely connected with the problem of defining and identifying the optimum proportions in the economy, which is taken up in the next chapter.

It is noteworthy that Strumilin in a contribution to a high level symposium, queried the convention of including military hardware in the category of means of production on the grounds, to put it crudely, that they are not means of production. Nor are they con-

---

[1] See B. Minc in *Ekonomista* (Warsaw), No. 5/1956, and in Russian, *Vop. ekon.*, No. 12/1957, p. 63. The most detailed attempt at refutation is in Pashkov, op. cit., pp. 175-200.

[2] See in particular Alexander Gerschenkron's review of Pashkov's book in *American Economic Review*, September, 1959, p. 734. See also A. Nove, 'Towards a Theory of Soviet Planning' in *Soviet Planning*, Blackwell, 1964.

[3] L. Kochetkov et al., *Vop. ekon.*, No. 11/1967, p. 58. (We will say more about this in the Appendix.)

[4] *Plan. khoz.*, No. 5/1964, p. 14.

sumers goods, as had been claimed by Kronrod. Strumilin makes fun of such an interpretation: are they necessities consumed by workers or luxuries for the capitalists? His own belief is that they should belong to neither category and be treated as a separate item, perhaps as 'means of annihilation' or inevitable social losses.[1]

ACCUMULATION FUND AND CONSUMPTION FUND

Another means of dividing the national product is by reference to its use for consumption and for accumulation (investment). Clearly, this is an altogether different line of division to the one discussed above: for instance, an increase in stocks of shirts, which are consumers' goods, is accumulation.

The accumulation fund covers, in practice, very much the same area as a Western capital account: investment in fixed capital, plus increase (minus decrease) in reserves, stocks, etc. The rest of the national income is deemed to consist of the consumption fund, part of which is distributed in the form of personal incomes of 'productively' and 'unproductively' engaged citizens, and part is consumed in institutions of various kinds (e.g. feeding citizens in hospital, or in the army, and also the consumption within institutions of materials—for example, petrol in army vehicles, paper in government departments). It is customary in the USSR to make general statements to the effect that the accumulation fund is about quarter of the national income (in its Soviet definition) and the consumption fund correspondingly three-quarters. The relatively constant relationship of the two funds over a long period of time, during which investment (and the output of producers' goods) has tended to grow faster than consumption, is explicable in terms of changing price relationships: prices of producers' goods have tended to fall relatively to those of consumers' goods.

All this should be simple, but has been needlessly complicated by the assertions of some Soviet economists that the consumption fund is devoted wholly to the 'satisfaction of the personal and cultural requirements of the toilers', and that the remaining quarter of the national income covers not only accumulation but also 'other government and social requirements.'[2] If this were so, then the *material*

[1] *Planirovanie i ekonomiko-matematicheskie metody* (ed. Fedorenko), (Moscow, 1964), pp. 50-52.
[2] For a full discussion of the many formulations and reformulations of this thought, see A. Nove in *Soviet Studies*, January, 1955, pp. 274-6. See also the wording used, deliberately ambiguous, in *Politicheskaya Ekonomiya*, 3rd revised edition (Moscow, 1959), p. 644, and also useful article by Y. Shnyrlin in *Vest. Stat.*, No. 12/1960, pp. 59-65.

expenditures on defence and administration would be in the accumulation fund, which is clearly nonsense—unless, of course, the consumption of petrol in army lorries and paper in government offices could be deemed to give personal or cultural satisfaction to the toilers. There is one precedent for treating defence expenditure in a category of its own: thus Voznesenski did so in his book on the war economy,[1] and Strumilin more recently advocated the use of a separate category for military goods, as we have seen.

Statistics published in recent years have provided some further enlightenment on the composition of these 'funds'. Thus in 1962 the figures were as follows in milliards of new roubles:

Consumption	117·0	Accumulation 'and other expenditure'	45·9
of which: personal consumption	104·5	of which: Increase in basic funds (capital)	29·4
Materials consumed in institutions serving the population	9·5	(Productive funds) (Unproductive funds)	(20·1) (9·3)
Materials consumed in scientific and administrative institutions	3·0	Increase in material circulating capital and reserves	16·5

Source: *N.Kh. 1962*, pp. 483-4.

It may well be that military hardware, in so far as it is produced for stock, as is normal in peacetime, is to be found in the item 'circulating capital and reserves'.

[1] *Voyennaya ekonomika SSSR v period otechestvennoi voiny* (Moscow, 1948), p. 67. He gave, for 1940, the following: accumulation, 19 per cent, consumption, 74 per cent, defence, 7 per cent. Presumably the defence item refers to material expenditure only; soldiers' food, surely, is consumption.

CHAPTER 11

Soviet Economics and Economic Laws

Economics has been concerned with exchange relationships, with markets, with the unregulated activities of many men. What, then, is the economics of socialism? One possible answer, for which there is quite considerable warrant in the socialist tradition, is that the 'economics of socialism' is a contradiction in terms, and that the necessary administrative planning functions do not fall under the definition of economics at all. Engels showed himself affected by this kind of reasoning. For him, 'the only value known in economics is the value of commodities. What are commodities? Products made in a society of private producers' ... which 'enter into social use through exchange'. But from the moment when society enters into possession of the means of production, all these relationships change fundamentally. Social labour is no longer measured in money or value, but 'in its natural, adequate and absolute measure, *time* ... People will be able to manage things very simply, without the intervention of the famous "value" '.[1] It is clear from the context that Engels was not denying the existence of economic problems under socialism. However, he certainly thought that people would manage without 'commodities', i.e. without goods which acquire exchange values in relationship to one another, to which the analytical apparatus which Marx and he erected would have any significant application. Quantitative decisions by planners, which relate the desires of the citizens to the labour time necessary for satisfying these desires, would be sufficient, and this would be a 'simple' process, once private ownership of the means of production was eliminated. If Engels envisaged a transition period in the course of which value categories remained in being, he managed to conceal the fact.

Following him, Plekhanov made many observations in a similar spirit. One finds the most completely 'liquidationist' attitude to economics in Bukharin's famous *Economics of the transition period*, which appeared as early as 1920. Its title alone showed that he was

[1] *Anti-Dühring* (Marxist-Leninist Library edition, London, 1936), pp. 339, 340.

not contemplating some far-off state of pure communism when he wrote the following:

'Political economy is a science . . . of the unorganized national economy. Only in a society where production has an anarchistic character, do laws of social life appear as "natural", "spontaneous" laws, independent of the will of individuals and groups, laws acting with the blind necessity of the law of gravity. Indeed, as soon as we deal with an organized national economy, all the basic "problems" of political economy, such as price, value, profit, etc., simply disappear. Here the relations between men are no longer expressed as "relations between things", for here the economy is regulated not by the blind forces of the market and competition, but by the consciously carried out *plan* . . . The end of capitalist and commodity society signifies the end of political economy.'[1]

This view presented not only Bukharin's own ideas. As late as 1943, the famous article in *Pod znamenem marksizma*, of which more in a moment, criticized those who, in their lecture courses, alleged that 'since with the liquidation of capitalism the laws peculiar to it have been abolished, then economic laws in the socialist economic system do not and cannot exist'.[2] Incidentally, the Russian language distinguishes more sharply than does English between 'economics' or 'economic' in their strict sense (*ekonomika, ekonomicheski*) and the same words in the more general sense of dealing with material resources, which in Russian can be rendered by *khozyaistvo*.[3] The phrase 'socialist economic system' in the above quotation makes use of this second word, thus avoiding any apparent contradiction.

Illusions about the imminent end of economics were largely shattered by the introduction of NEP in 1921. However, there was now no need even to discuss the awkward problem of the role of economic laws within the state sector, since the survival of money and value relationships could be all too easily attributed to the existence of a large private sector. The outstanding contribution to the economic thought of the period came from E. Preobrazhenski, but he concentrated most of all on the relationship between the private and state sectors, the pace at which the latter could grow at the expense of the former ('primitive socialist accumulation').

For Preobrazhenski too, economic theory as such is related to

[1] *Ekonomika perekhodnovo perioda* (Moscow, 1920). Translation cited from an excellent essay in 'The Origin of the Political Economy of Socialism', by Adam Kaufman, *Soviet Studies*, January, 1953, pp. 273 ff.
[2] *Pod znamenen marksizma*, Nos. 7-8, 1943, p. 65.
[3] Also in German there is *Ökonomie* and *Wirtschaft*.

commodity production, i.e. is conditional upon the existence of private ownership. The 'science of collectively organized production' would replace 'the theory of political economy'.[1]

Such discussions were interrupted by the launching, in 1928, of the first of the five-year plans, which seemed in themselves to be proof of the primacy of governmental decision over real or alleged economic laws. The slogan 'there is no fortress the Bolsheviks cannot take' was widely used, the advice of cautious economists being widely disregarded. While planners and political leaders struggled with the crises and bottlenecks associated with the 'crash programmes' of the period, economics had little to say. No general textbook of economics appeared between 1928 and 1954, and indeed for several years it was found necessary to stop teaching 'political economy' in higher educational institutions.[2] This was a period of Soviet intellectual history when, to put it mildly, it was unhealthy for men to express critical ideas, and economic policy was so intensely 'political' that it was perhaps not surprising that men hesitated before developing theories which could be regarded as, by implication, providing objective criteria against which to judge official policy. Symbolic of the 'liquidationist' trend, coming logically enough during the first five-year plan, which most drastically disregarded 'normal' economic criteria, was the elimination of the word 'statistics' from the name of the Central Statistical Office. In 1931 it was renamed Central Office of National Economic (*narodno-khozyaistvennovo*) Accounting, known by its initial Russian letters as TSUNKhU, because 'statistics' was regarded as a word suggestive of the measurement of random, haphazard events, and therefore unsuitable for a planned economy.

In 1941, the name was changed back to Central Statistical Office, and this was a sign of a return to a more realistic approach. There is some evidence to show that the need for a new 'socialist economics' was felt by the authorities, since they too needed objective criteria if expensive errors were to be avoided. The period of 'hurrah planning'[3] was coming to an end. A new textbook was known to

[1] *Novaya ekonomika* (Moscow, 1926), p. 19.
[2] The cessation of teaching is referred to in *Pod znamenem marksizma*, Nos. 7-8 (1943, p. 56). The last textbook before 1954 was by I. Lapidus and K. Ostrovityanov, published in 1928. Then came *Politicheskaya ekonomiya, uchebnik* (1st edition, Moscow, 1954). I do not mention books devoted to tearing apart Western 'bourgeois' economics, which were fairly numerous, but irrelevant to the 'economics of socialism', or the very large number of books and articles on this or that actual problem of economic structure or policy.
[3] The term is borrowed from Dr Jasny, who used it to describe the early five-year plans.

have been in draft in 1941. The war interrupted the process, but in the very middle of the war there appeared an unsigned article in a very influential party journal, thought to have been inspired, or even written by Stalin, which was directly concerned with 'the law of value' in the Soviet system.[1] Here, as in other discussions, the law of value must be seen not as a term of abstract analysis, but as expressing the role of exchange relationships and of the entire body of associated economic phenomena (prices, profits, etc.) in society. Or, to put things another way, discussion of the role of the 'law of value' invariably involves the importance of economic laws in general vis-à-vis administrative decision based on political considerations.

The author of the article began by referring to a central committee directive to create a textbook ('short course') of political economy. He vigorously criticized the liquidationists. 'To deny the existence of economic laws under socialism means sliding down to vulgar voluntarism, which consists in the substitution of arbitrariness, accident, chaos, for the orderly (objectively determined, zakonomernyi) process of development of production' (p. 65). The author sought economic laws, and found them, or rather their expression, in industrialization, collectivization, planning, distribution of income according to work performed. This was dangerously near to equating economic laws and what the Soviet régime actually does, or has done, of which other instances will be cited. But Stalin, if Stalin this was, was looking for a 'criterion for the correctness of this or that line, this or that policy' (p. 65). Therefore, he was driven to restore the 'law of value' to Soviet economics. By carefully selected quotations from the Marxian classics, he endeavoured to make this appear orthodox. He deduced the survival of the law of value from the fact that labour is not paid an equal sum for each hour of work, that it is paid in money, that purchase and sale occur, that money is used. He treated goods, apparently all goods, produced under these conditions as 'commodities' (tovary), which enter into exchange. Therefore, the law of value applies—but, because its operation is restricted, because it cannot affect the distribution of resources within the state sector or the production programme of state enterprises, it applies only to a limited extent, 'in a transformed form' (p. 75). This was not very clear, or satisfactory, but became the basis of subsequent formulations until shortly before Stalin's death.

There the matter rested until 1951. In the interim, Voznesenski had expressed some harmless-sounding theoretical views in his book on the war economy, and was shortly afterwards shot. While he was

[1] Pod znamenem marksizma, already cited.

not—as far as is known—shot for his economic theories, a number of economists who had praised him had hastily to apologize, and the entire episode scarcely encouraged the profession to use its intellectual initiative.

In 1951, Stalin himself took a hand in a discussion around a new economics textbook. His contributions to the discussion were published in 1952, under the title of *Economic Problems of Socialism*. It proved to be his last work.

Although, as we shall see, he had much to say about the law of value, in two respects Stalin reflected the 'liquidationist' tradition. Firstly, he confined the said law virtually to the uncontrolled portions of the economy, and, secondly, he drew a sharp distinction between economic theory and the actual problems of planning. In a violent attack on a certain Yaroshenko, whom, paradoxically enough, he accused of a Bukharinist liquidation of the political economy of socialism, Stalin wrote: 'the problems of rational organization of productive forces, the planning of the national economy, etc., are not the subject of political economy, but the subject of economic policy of the directing (i.e. political) organs'.[1]

Stalin's most interesting contribution was an attack on the formulation concerning the functioning of the 'law of value in transformed form', of which he himself was thought to have been the inspirer and which had been obligatory for all economists. The law of value, and economic laws in general, cannot be 'transformed', he asserted. They exist, independently of the minds of men. The law of value applies to all transactions within the Soviet system in which purchase and sale takes place, i.e. in sales by co-operatives (especially *kolkhozy*) and peasants to the state, by them and by state retailing enterprises to the citizen, and also in foreign trade. In these cases, change of ownership occurs and such goods are 'commodities' in the Marxist sense. If their relative prices are fixed wrong, it affects production; thus (to cite the example he gave) an excessively high price for bread grains in relation to cotton would have discouraged the output of cotton by *kolkhozy*. However, goods circulating within the state sector, i.e. the bulk of producers' goods, are produced and transferred according to plan, without changes of ownership. Such goods are not 'commodities', are not as such subject to the law of value. Of course, they are transferred at a price, money does change hands, and such prices do indeed serve the valuable function of accountancy, efficiency check and so on. In that sense, value categories are relevant to the producers' goods sector. However, the influence of

[1] Stalin, op. cit., p. 72.

the law of value is substantially restricted under the Soviet system.

Stalin explained the need for a reassertion of the validity of economic laws by the danger of overconfidence of young cadres, who, 'overwhelmed by the colossal achievement of the Soviet régime . . . come to imagine that the Soviet régime can "do anything" '.[1] He sought, as in 1943, to provide criteria, to emphasize the objective limitations of policy. He gave special emphasis to the relationship of state economic policy to those uncontrolled or semi-controlled sectors where plans did not determine the behaviour of men, i.e. to the relationships between state organs and, essentially, peasants as producers, and the citizenry as a whole as buyers of consumers' goods. There, evidently, a wrong handling of exchange relationships was liable to lead to positive harm, and here arbitrariness was to be avoided by emphasizing the objective essence of the law of value and the 'commodity' nature of the goods concerned. But he failed to find an objective definition by which actual exchange relationships could be judged, and in his anxiety to assert that state planning decisions (especially about investment), are not guided by considerations of profitability, he had to take the producers' goods sector out of the class of 'commodities', and therefore legitimized a high degree of arbitrariness in price fixing and in investment decisions within the state sector.

THE POST-STALIN REVIVAL OF ECONOMICS

The economics textbook finally appeared after Stalin's death, but with his ideas incorporated in it. Its inadequacy was all too apparent. Even more apparent was the failure of the economics profession to advance new theoretical ideas. In 1955, a clarion call was sounded by the then director of the Institute of Economics, V. Dyachenko. 'Until recently, dogmatism and scholasticism (*nachyotnichestvo*) showed itself quite openly in quotationism. Instead of independent and deep economic research, the authors of many works busied themselves with a selection of, and commentary on, quotations. Facts were selected and presented merely to illustrate and to confirm the assertions contained in the quotations. Matters went so far that the number of quotations was regarded as an indication of the author's erudition. An economist who found a quotation which had not been used many times in the works of other economists considered himself a creative researcher. After serious criticism of dogmatism and scholasticism in the party press, quotationism dim-

[1] Stalin, op. cit., p. 10.

inished, but only on the surface. In many instances matters went no
further than the omission of quotation marks, editorial redrafting
of the quotations, but in essence things remained unchanged.'[1] He
went on: 'The elaboration of key problems of political economy is
most backward. For many years not a single solid theoretical work
in this field has been published.' And, even more significantly: 'Since
the economic discussions of 1951, it has become customary in every
work to refer to the objective character of economic laws of socialism, yet not a single work thoroughly examines in what the objective character of this or that law finds expression, how its requirement shows itself, in what respect and how breaches of these
requirements can be identified.'[2]

Thereafter a wide ranging discussion developed concerning the
nature of economic laws in the USSR, concentrating above all on law
of value and 'commodity' production. This discussion is still going
on, and in the interests of clarity and brevity only the main propositions of the various protagonists will be set out here.

THE LAW OF VALUE: DOES IT APPLY, AND, IF SO, WHY?

After a growing volume of discussion during 1956, a conference
on the law of value was held, and reported early in 1957.[3] This
opened the flood gates wide. At this conference, the majority held
that Stalin had been wrong in confining the law of value and the
designation 'commodity' to consumers' goods and the products of
co-operatives, that goods circulating within the state sector were also
commodities, and that the law of value had general application
throughout the economy. This remains the dominant view. True,
minority voices emerged, which repeated Stalin's argument, and, it
must be admitted, not without some logic on their side. Those who
denied that such goods were 'commodities' generally took for
granted the need for objectively determined prices, but held that this
need should not rest upon a false identification of these goods with
'commodities' in the Marxian sense. Indeed, one of those who hold
this view, Malyshev, has gone further and denied that *any* goods in
the USSR are 'commodities', and that the only sense in which the
theory of value applies is that there is need to measure and economize social labour, i.e. a sense in which it would continue to apply

---

[1] *Vop. ekon.*, No. 10/1955, pp. 3-4. Quotations, of course, were from the
holy writ of Marx-Engels-Lenin-Stalin.
[2] Ibid., pp. 6, 8.   [3] *Vop. ekon.*, No. 2/1957, pp. 71 ff.

even in the fullest and most perfect form of communist society. Yet this same Malyshev is an ardent supporter of pricing based on rational criteria.[1] One scholar even advanced the view that under socialism products have 'value' but yet are not 'commodities'.[2]

However, these were minority views. The majority accepted the arguments of Ostrovityanov, Gatovski and Kronrod to the effect that 'commodity' relations do exist in the USSR, that they extend into the state sector, that these relations, and therefore the 'law of value', relate to producers' goods made and used by state enterprises. The main case in favour of this proposition is essentially empirical: that the rational utilization of resources in general, and investment choices in particular, require that all goods be treated as commodities, and that therefore the law of value be deemed to apply to them. While agreeing thus far, some leading economists came to blows over the 'scholastic' question of why, in theoretical terms, this should be so, and indeed their arguments do seem more convincing on the purely practical than on the Marxist theoretical plane. Ostrovityanov accounted for the survival of value relations primarily by the continued existence of two species of property, i.e. of the non-state sector, which, so to speak, permeates the rest of the economy with the value and commodity categories which it renders necessary. Kronrod, on the other hand, asserted that 'commodity production is inherent in socialist productive relations. It is not brought into them from outside'. In other words, the existence of *kolkhozy* and so on is not the determining factor, but inside the state sector the movement of goods between enterprises is a process of commodity exchange, intimately connected with the necessity to pay the workers unequal sums of money wages.[3]

THE REAL CONTENT OF THE LAW OF VALUE

While the question discussed above could be regarded as an exercise in arid scholasticism, the problem of giving practical content in the Soviet setting to value and value relationships is clearly a matter involving fundamental economic policy. In particular, as we have seen in chapter 8 above, the correctness or otherwise of value

---

[1] Examples of such views may be found in the contribution of N. Khessin, in *Zakon Stoimosti* (Tsagolov), pp. 50 ff., and I. Malyshev, *Obshchestvennyi uchet truda i tsena pri sotsializme* (Moscow, 1960).
[2] I. Kozodoev, *Zakon Stoimosti* (Tsagolov), pp. 15 ff.
[3] Both these views are fully argued in *Zakon Stoimosti* (Kronrod), pp. 7-30, pp. 133-67. On the same subject, see K. Ostrovityanov, A. Pashkov, V. Cherkovets, I. Kozodoev, A. Tsagolov, all in *Zakon Stoimosti* (Tsagolov).

concepts is intimately connected with the discovery of objective criteria for prices. Many Soviet economists, aware of and hostile to the arbitrariness of 'Stalinist' prices, decided to use Marxian economics (as they understood it) as a criterion. If the term 'value' is to have any meaning at all, then the value of commodities in relation to one another must represent some real measure of relative cost. The latter must, in turn, find some expression in terms of socially necessary labour power, so as to fit into the framework of Marxian orthodoxy. The Marxian labour theory of value presupposes that labour alone is the source of value, and that value is equal to $c + v + m$ (or s) which stand respectively for constant capital (i.e. goods used up in the process of production), variable capital (reward of labour) and *mehrwert* (surplus value). The term 'surplus value' is usually rendered by Soviet economists as 'surplus product' when it is applied to the USSR, to avoid the implication of exploitation. Stalin urged that 'surplus product' be replaced by some more suitable term,[1] and some economists took to referring to v and m as respectively 'product for self' and 'product for society'. However, the designation used does not alter the problem, which is to identify some objective measurement of real values, real costs, so that these can be used as a guide in price setting and in choosing between alternatives. In applying the Marxian $c+v+m$ formula, most Soviet economists consider it possible to identify $c+v$ as equal to what could (not quite accurately) be called prime costs, (*sebestoimost'*), which include materials used up, depreciation of basic capital and rewards of labour. On the scale of the economy as a whole, m can be defined and calculated as that portion of the total value of the material product, i.e. the national income in its Soviet sense (defined in chapter 10), which is not paid out as rewards for labour. However, for each product separately m is not known, because its 'value' is not identifiable as such. As one economist put it, 'so long as we do not know the magnitude of the value of a commodity—and we do not know it—all our discussions about the divergence between prices and values have the character of guesswork'.[2] What, then, can be done to replace guesswork by an objective guide, in the absence of a market mechanism? The practical problem is to find a theory which helps the carrying out of economic policies and serves as a guide to the rational disposal of resources—for purposes determined by the political leadership.

Faced with this challenge, Soviet economists in recent years have

[1] Stalin, op. cit., pp. 18-19.
[2] A. Pashkov, *Zakon Stoimosti* (Tsagolov), p. 242.

proceeded on a number of different lines, but which can be divided into two main categories: theories based on 'cost plus', and those which would derive values from the tasks to be performed, from 'the requirements of society' or of the plan, or, finally, the market.

The first category of theories has the task of defining m, i.e. the amount to be added to $c+v$ to arrive at an objective basis. Some economists, notably Strumilin, take the labour theory literally. Since labour is the source of all value, then the total surplus product in the economy should be distributed proportionately to labour cost, in other words to v. Thus suppose c and v were, for a given commodity, each 100 roubles, and that the total value of the surplus product were 80 per cent of the total wages bill in the economy as a whole. Then the value of the product would be $100 + 100 + 80 = 280$.[1] However, another vocal school of thought advocates the share-out of the total surplus product proportionately to fixed and working capital, not to the wages bill. This school, typified by Vaag and Malyshev, find support in Marx's concept of 'price of production' (*Produktionspreis*) which, in volume 3 of *Das Kapital*, modified the pure labour theory by introducing the idea of a constant return to unequal quantities of capital.[2] The 1967 price reform, by providing for a capital charge and by accepting at least the principle of profitability percentage related to the capital assets of the enterprise, went some way towards accepting the arguments of the *Produktionspreis* school. Still another group advocate the shareout of m proportionately to cost, i.e. to $c + v$. The latter view could be consistent with a defence of the present practice of confining turnover tax almost wholly to consumers' goods, for, so long as wholesale prices are proportionate to $c + v$, wholesale prices would be proportionate to 'values' and would therefore fulfil an appropriate objective role.[3] On the other hand, the Strumilin and Vaag approaches, much though they differ in other respects, reject the present practice of separate systems and principles of pricing consumers' goods and producers' goods. They argue that 'real' costs, objective values, can and should be derived by relating m to one or more elements within costs and/or to the book valuation of capital assets. This is why they can bear the

[1] S. Strumilin, *Vop. ekon.*, No. 12/1956. The numerical example is mine.
[2] For such views see I. Malyshev, *Vop. ekon.*, No. 3/1957, L. Vaag in *Zakon Stoimosti* (Tsagolov), pp. 314-16, M. Kolganov in ibid., pp. 201-209. Strictly speaking, Marx's *Produktionspreis* presupposes that all of c, including the capital assets, are used up within the specified period of production, but this is so artificial an assumption that it is rightly ignored by the protagonists.
[3] For this argument, see P. Mstislavski, ibid., pp. 250-4. See also A. Bachurin, *Vop. ekon.*, No. 2/1957, p. 94, and D. Kondrashev in *Zakon Stoimosti* (Tsagolov), pp. 210 ff., for another variant.

label 'cost plus', even though they dispute among themselves about just what it is that should be added to cost. The weakness of such theories as a basis for pricing, or indeed for planners' decisions, has already been made clear earlier. These defects have led to consideration being given to the second principal category of ideas.

Or rather 'categories'. They include the many talented mathematically-orientated economists, and also those reformers who are above all conscious that prices must serve the practical purposes of allocating resources, and are thus impatient of any kind of cost-plus approach. In the minds of the economists concerned the ideas are not new. Thus Novozhilov and Kantorovich were expressing similar views when Stalin was still very firmly on his throne.[1] However, it was only in 1959 that they came fully into the area of public discussion, and Nemchinov did much to further such discussion.

Novozhilov's ideas depart very far indeed from $c + v + m$. He considers the application of such a formula to value relations in the Soviet setting to be quite misleading. In practice, he argued, Soviet planners have been making some allowance for scarcity as an element which increases real cost, but inconsistently and without any theoretical basis. In their work, the planners are constantly at grips with opportunity cost considerations, and—at least by implication —they value scarce goods by reference to alternatives foregone. The notional allowance for scarcity of capital, now widely accepted as part of the elaboration of investment criteria, should be regarded as a special instance of the general principle of opportunity cost. Theory lags badly behind practice. The effect on value of alternative uses is called by Novozhilov 'feedback costs' (*zatraty obratnoi svyazi*). Planners are handicapped by a theory of value which ignores these realities. 'The problem of measuring inputs (costs) and their results under socialism is not reconcilable with the measurement of inputs (costs) for each separate product by the labour required to produce it.' Indeed, it is only in the pre-capitalist period that, according to Marx, values fluctuate around labour cost. Under capitalism they fluctuate around *Produktionspreis*. Yet, argued Novozhilov, it would be wrong, contrary to the basic laws of dialectics, to assert that capitalism measures real costs less accurately than feudalism. There is no reason why socialism should return to a pre-capitalist form of value calculation, and a mechanical application of *Produktionspreis* formulae will not do either. It would also represent a

---

[1] Kantorovich's first work on a species of linear programming was published in 1939, while Novozhilov proclaimed his present theories in the *Trudy* of the Leningrad Polytechnic Institute, No. 1/1946. However, they were ignored or suppressed for many years.

misunderstanding of what Marx meant in volume 3 of *Capital*. It is wrong to regard the costs incurred in producing any one commodity in isolation as a basis for its value, since production processes of all goods, and the needs they fulfil, are inextricably intermingled. The real measure of the costs of producing any one commodity is 'that increment of social expenditures associated with its production'. This must include not only the prime costs of making the means of production, but also opportunity ('feedback') costs, a variable charge reflecting the use of scarce capital, natural and other resources.[1]

Novozhilov would relate pricing and valuation to the job in hand. If 'prices do not inform producers of *what* needs to be produced, nor of what *quality*, nor the socially-necessary limits on costs of production', then 'the missing information will have to be provided by plan-instructions . . . If the information contained in prices often contradicts the plan instructions, then the instructions must be strengthened by threats (*sanktsii*). But as the experience of centuries shows, fear is a less effective stimulus than economic or moral interest.' Socially-necessary labour, as a concept, 'expresses that expenditure of labour rendered necessary by the conditions of *production*, and on the other hand the expenditure of labour which is considered necessary by Society for its *consumption*'. If the decisions influenced by prices are marginal, then the prices should be marginal too. But Novozhilov is well aware that not all information can be carried by prices, and there are many decisions to which marginal cost pricing is inappropriate: thus large investment decisions affect future costs and scarcities, and technical progress affects costs. So the mathematically-devised long-term development plans would require planning or shadow prices very different from those which could be used to elicit some marginal production or marginal economies in the short-run with given resources.[2]

So for Novozhilov prices and values are a matter of efficiency in use, rather than of dogmatic speculation. It should be added that he

---

[1] See Novozhilov, op. cit., especially pp. 210-12. For a most useful summary, see A. Zauberman, *Soviet Studies*, July, 1960. It is interesting to note that G. D. H. Cole, in his introduction to Marx's *Capital* (Everyman's edition, Vol. I, pp. xxviii), made much the same point about the concept of value in the last volume of *Capital* as does Novozhilov. For the continuation of the arguments of Kantorovich and Novozhilov, and discussions on progress achieved, see reports on conferences on mathematics in economics, *Vop. ekon.*, No. 3/1963 and especially No. 9/1964, pp. 63-110 and also V. Glushkov and N. Fedorenko in *Vop. ekon.*, No. 7/1964, pp. 87-92. Also see symposium. *Ekonomisty i matematiki za kruglym stolom* (M. 1965).

[2] All this is in his article in *Ekonomika i matematicheskie metody*, No. 3/1966.

THE SOVIET ECONOMY

is sceptical about the attainment of the optimum which is sought by some of the mathematicians, and which he regards as impracticable.[1] The price-and-value logic of the mathematical optimisers leads them to seek what a Polish critic of this approach (Zielinski) has called 'parametric prices', i.e. a disaggregated and computer-determined set of prices (valuations) all integrally linked with the optimum plan. This is indeed the logic of Fedorenko,[2] though this is in his view associated with detailed disaggregation of his 'computed' and parametric prices by free negotiation between supplier and customer. Therefore, Novozhilov's ideas should be distinguished from those of some other 'mathematical' reformers. His argument is that, optimal or no, 'all planned tasks should be covered by means of production', that the plan will contain only those variants of output which cost less than rejected variants, and finally that prices, plans and *khozraschyot* are consistent with one another. Of course, these desiderata are very far from being achieved.

In many respects Kantorovich is in line with Novozhilov, as far as valuations are concerned. The former is much more concerned with programming techniques than with constructing an acceptable economic theory, but Kantorovich's 'objectively determined valuations' are for all practical purposes the same concept as Novozhilov's valuations derived from 'feedback costs'. Both are concerned to derive prices of factors of production and of commodities from the programme, from the electronic computer, essentially from and through an optimization calculation in relation to the general requirements of the plan. Both are, in essence, marginal in character, being concerned with the comparative valuation of increments at all stages.

Such a theory would go far towards freeing the Soviet economist from the stultifying effect of a theory which directs his gaze at direct costs, especially labour costs, as the objective basis of values and prices. Novozhilov claimed that his theory would make possible much greater devolution of decision making, since prices would be a more adequate guide to choice between alternatives. Therefore, he pointed to the 'democratic centralist' implications of his ideas. Kantorovich declared repeatedly that very wasteful misallocation of resources would be avoided if his ideas were accepted.

One of Fedorenko's ablest subordinates, the young economist Petrakov, had no difficulty in reconciling the attempt to find a

---

[1] In conversation with the author, he used the term 'super-cosmic mathematics'.
[2] See his speech to an important and fascinating session of the Academy, reported in *Vestnik Akademii Nauk SSSR*, No. 2/1966.

planners' optimum with a system of prices which reflect a market valuation. If there is a shortage there should be a rise in price. The higher coefficient of effectiveness which will then show itself 'will stimulate a redistribution of resources and in this way the basis will be found for a liquidation of shortages and the restoration of proportionality'. He then asserted: 'To recognize the existence of value under socialism . . . while denying the law of supply and demand is the equivalent of denying the unity between value and use-value. *Marx never called for the fixing of 'current' prices, i.e. prices corresponding to values.*' An equilibrium price, such as a value or *Produktionspreis* valuation would be, is evidently inapplicable to a situation of imbalance, of disequilibrium.[1] Is such an approach un-Marxist? Some, east and west, would assert that it is.[2]

UTILITY, SCARCITY, MARGINALISM AND LINEAR PROGRAMMING

Soviet economists have long shown a dislike for the concept of scarcity.[3] Of course, they are well aware that scarcity is a fact. In their capacity as planners, they are struggling with scarcities and bottlenecks virtually every day. They would argue as follows: yes, we are short of many things, and it is the task of planners to provide what is lacking by expanding production, as and when the priorities of the plan permit. It is true that land, and sometimes certain mineral deposits, are limited and can be treated as scarce in the sense that no decision by planners can overcome the shortage. There could be a case for expressing this sort of scarcity by attaching the appropriate price tags. But other scarcities are correctable by investment decisions, and these decisions should be taken by reference to a material balance analysis. It is wrong to attach scarcity prices to reproducible goods, because, so it is argued, this merely confuses calculations of real cost, which, in the long run, will be determined not by relative scarcities but by the costs at which, when the planners so decide, the scarce commodity could be produced.[4]

[1] N. Petrakov: *Nekotorye aspekty diskusii ob ekonomicheskom metode khozyaistvovaniya* (M., 1966), pp. 48, 51, 52. (Emphasis mine).
[2] For a western view, see R. Campbell: 'Marx, Kantorovich and Novozhilov: *stoimost'* versus reality', in *Slavic Review*, October, 1961.
[3] See Peter Wiles' stimulating paper, 'Scarcity, Marxism and Gosplan', in *Oxford Economic Papers*, September, 1953, pp. 288 ff.
[4] This would be consistent with G. Myrdal's views (*Economic Theory and Underdeveloped Regions*, Duckworth, London, 1957, p. 89): 'In fact a large part of the economic process . . . has to be directed by changing costs, prices and profit rates through modifying the conditions under which the price system functions.'

Since the decision will not be based on the profit motive, there is no point in 'rewarding' anyone with extra income merely by reason of a temporary scarcity. It is true that this involves rationing of scarce materials. (It is also true that, in the case of retail prices for consumers' goods, it is desirable not to ration, to avoid queues, and to fix a price by reference to supply and demand, thereby explaining the variable gap between wholesale and retail prices, i.e. big variations in turnover tax rates.)

This argument is intimately linked with the approach to subjective valuations in general, and also to marginalism. The opposition to a subjective theory of value is deeply embedded in Marxist theory. The source of value must be material, not spiritual, must be based on the conditions of production, not on people's thoughts. It is true that Marxists hold that, to have any value at all, a commodity must have some use, must receive 'social recognition'. But there is no room for greater or lesser degrees of utility in this theory, let alone marginal utility. The orthodox theoreticians do not deny that supply and demand play a role in price formation in a market, and that demand is affected by subjective considerations (though even here they are apt to stress the social nature of individual requirements). However, the conditions of production are regarded as determinants, while supply and demand explain fluctuations, or are the mechanism through which market prices adjust to a situation in which the conditions of production play the decisive role.[1] The key point made by the critics, when they are not merely aiming verbal missiles at 'bourgeois vulgar economics', is, to quote Gatovski again, that any proposed valuation based on marginalism and scarcity 'would make of scarcity of resources the economic criterion and guide, which means following a line involving a reduction in growth tempos of our economy, a change in the pattern necessary for such growth, and in particular the superior growth of production of means of production. The superiority in growth tempos engendered by the socialist planned economy would be unrealized. Instead of efforts being made to reduce costs and to adopt the most advanced productive techniques, more backward methods with higher costs would be prescribed, and the losses involved would be disguised by higher prices. All this would adversely affect the sources for increased accumulation. Marginalist schemes are deeply static.'[2]

[1] See, for instance, the attack on Novozhilov by A. Katz, *Vop. ekon.*, No. 11/1960, p. 95. It is also to be recalled that Marshall tended to give primacy to the conditions of production as price determinants in the long run.

[2] Ibid. See also P. J. D. Wiles' essay on 'Growth versus Choice', *Economic Journal* June, 1956.

Kronrod, himself a prominent critic of the existing price system, admitted the limited use of notional 'programming' valuations for specific tasks, but argued: 'To claim to plan the national economy on the basis of such valuations, and therefore to put them in the place of prices, costs, value, etc., this is merely the resurrection in mathematical dress of the old concepts of the subjectivist school, of the old marginalist pretentions. Their utter uselessness has long ago been proved by Marxist-Leninist political economy ... It is necessary to warn mathematicians and economists of the real danger of becoming too involved in formal patterns, empty abstractions, particularly abstractions of a marginalist kind, even if clad in a complicated system of equations. We need mathematical models which reflect real economic processes, based on strictly scientific Marxist economic teaching.'[1] As against this, Academician Kolmogorov argued that 'one should not be afraid that the mathematical apparatus of Marxist theory of the socialist economy will have some formal features in common with, for example, the theory of marginal utility of bourgeois economics. This is explained by the common nature of the mathematical apparatus for solving any variation problems, and ... in no way affects the specific nature of the questions before us, or the purity of the Marxian approach'.[2]

Yet what *is* 'the purity of the Marxian approach'? It is true that in Marxian theory there is the notion that economics, that 'commodity-money relations', will wither away. So, of course, should the state, the army, the police ... In the real world these things are not happening. In his challenging book, Ota Šik has argued that experience has proved that the expectations and ideas concerning the disappearance of commodity-money relations under conditions of social ownership were erroneous.[3] No Soviet economist would now deny the need for 'commodity-money relations'. But in that case one must accept their logic. A moment's thought would surely show that Marx derived his theory of value from studying a market economy, but he obviously did not and could not assert that the price of any commodity at a given moment of time either did or should conform to 'value' (or its modification, *Produktionspreis*). *Of course* he knew that the prices of candles or cabbages fluctuate with supply and demand changes, and it is obvious that variations from equilibrium prices are part of the dynamic mechanism of any

[1] *Vop. ekon.*, No. 8/1960, p. 106. This issue contains a fascinating discussion on 'mathematical methods in economics', of which this is a part.
[2] Ibid., p. 114.
[3] O. Šik: *Plan and Market under Socialism* (P.A.S.P., New York, and Prague, 1967), chapter I.

economy in which price and exchange relations play an active role. In this respect Petrakov was most certainly right. Marx asserted that labour is the source of all value, and abstracted from (rather than denied) consideration of increasing (or decreasing) marginal costs. It is true that he considered income from property to be in an important sense improper, illegitimate. But this did not prevent him from having a theory about differential rent, which is inherently a marginal theory, by the way. If efficiency considerations require payments *to the state* of a capital charge or rent by its own enterprises, an ideology designed to identify *private* exploitation is hardly likely to stand in the way of reform.[1] While some did argue that acceptance of such proposals would somehow involve the acceptance of a 'three factors of production' theory, resistance did not last long. One would have thought, in other words, that the principal obstacles to change are practical rather than theoretical.

It must be stressed at once that the problems facing anyone who wishes to devise a theory of value and price for Soviet conditions is an extremely difficult one, and mathematics does not provide any easy solution. It is true that in a sense linear programming techniques can be dynamic, in that the valuations which emerge from the mathematical model can be those which, in theory, should achieve the desired optimum over the time scale required by the planners. Thus these techniques would appear to be free from the reproach of being 'deeply static'. Yet the applicability of linear programming to the economy as a whole is in serious doubt on several grounds. Firstly, there is the question of the imprecision of and unpredictable changes in the parameters. It is hardly possible to define with the necessary clarity the aims of the programme, what it is that should be optimized. Many of the essential elements of the plan are in fact dependent on the calculations for which they are to serve as a base. The actual choice made by the planners, especially in the field of investment, alters scarcity relationships in all kinds of unpredictable ways. Then, perhaps even more important, programming techniques cannot take into account external economies, the consequences of indivisibilities. These severely limit the generalized use of 'objectively determined valuations', into which it is hardly possible to bring these considerations. The assumption of fixed technical coefficients also limits the 'dynamic' potential of programming, even within one sector, let alone on the scale of the entire economy, since investment decisions and technical progress change the coefficients.

[1] See A. Nove: 'Marxist Economic Theory Today', in *The World Today*, December, 1967.

In other words, linear programming is linear, life is not. To cite another critic: 'The universal utilization of solving multipliers [Kantorovich's methods] and the calculation on this basis of marginal valuations do not ensure a real dynamic optimum. Instead of making the scarcity of material resources dependent on technical progress and labour productivity, labour productivity is made dependent upon scarcity of material resources'[1] Admittedly, work is going on to develop non-linear, dynamic programming. However, as Kantorovich would readily admit, such computations are fraught with serious difficulties. (Input-output techniques, of course, are even more backward-looking, being based on relationships of some past years). For all these reasons, there is indeed a case for asserting that scarcity prices derived from the programme may mislead planners looking five or ten years ahead. A further difficulty is the immense complexity of the task of applying these techniques in a context wider than a specific industry or a specific problem. No doubt there is much to be said to refute the above objections, but the object of this paragraph is merely to demonstrate that this is not just a question of foolish or ideologically blinded economists refusing to adopt a self-evident solution to their problems.

Programming techniques are as yet incapable of coping with all this. They can be used at two stages. They can help in the process of making rough and rapid estimates of the implications of alternative plans in the very early stages of the long term planning process. This would have to be accompanied by a more traditional—albeit more sophisticated—kind of material balance calculation. Then, after these basic data become available, programming techniques can be used as consistency checks as part of an effort to approach optimization. This is not an all-inclusive use of optimization techniques, but on this less ambitious scale the experiments do show that the techniques can play a valuable part in planning. Great efforts are being made to reorganize information flows and to establish computer centres. The vast Institute of Mathematical Economics is launching its talented, youthful, enthusiastic staff into trying to solve these and other problems. Theoretical work of high quality is proceeding, and the voices of orthodox ideologists are heard less and less. It is therefore possible that major advances will shortly prove that the above judgements have been too cautiously pessimistic.

Nemchinov, who did much to 'legitimize' new ideas before his death in 1965, tried with some success to spread these ideas while minimizing the theoretical-ideological shock. He rightly stressed the

[1] Skryabin, op. cit., p. 68.

vital and necessary connection, lost sight of by the scholastic protagonists of labour value theory, between value and the satisfaction of wants. He did this, understandably enough, in Marxian language. 'The socially necessary expenditures of labour must be determined by reference not only to the expenditure of labour but also to its results. Only those expenditures are socially necessary which correspond to the requirement of society in given objective conditions of production.' The mere quantity of labour is not enough, one must determine 'how far (this) corresponds to socially necessary labour expenditure . . . Every enterprise must know the social valuation of all the objects of labour and tools of labour (materials and equipment) in units of socially necessary labour time.' But these valuations must be made on the scale of the national economy. These valuations must reflect the 'optimal plan balance, corresponding to the [political] directives and within the available resources (the amount available for capital investment, productive capacity, scarce resources)'. Nemchinov advocates the concept of a 'transformed form of value',[1] corresponding to real costs from the standpoint of the national economy (*narodnokhozyaistvennye izderzhki*), arrived at by adding to the prime cost ($c + v$) an amount composed of a standard capital charge plus a differential rent. The latter is to be derived from mathematical (for instance, vector matrix) analysis, i.e. from the programme. This would take into account the relative availability and relative advantages of land, minerals, factories, by reference to the intended results, to the basic lines of the plan. The plan, or programme, would be based on an elaboration of material balances. The implications of this differential rent, especially for factories (entitled 'buildings rent', but including, of course, the equipment), may not be visible at first sight, but reflection will show that they involve something close to marginalism in disguise—a better disguise, let it be said, than Novozhilov's. There is no suggestion that particular commodities' value has any relationship to marginal cost. Yet his model would in fact relate his 'values in transformed form' to average cost plus a variable margin which looks very much like Marshallian quasi rent, and the values resemble Kantorovich's. By relating values to the plan programme, i.e. to need, he tied them to the satisfaction of requirements, detaching them from a proportionate relationship to actual production cost, a relationship which was a major weakness both of the Strumilin and the *Produktionspreis* approaches. 'The essential feature of prices is

[1] Note the resurrection of the formula used in 1943 and attacked by Stalin in 1951.

precisely the fact that they depart from value and fluctuate around
it . . .'[1] Already in 1960, he was advocating some degree of price
flexibility. In his last year of life, as already noted, he moved to a
position of arguing that a wide range of prices be fixed by negotiation.

Nemchinov's theories, if accepted, would do much to correct some
major weaknesses in the hitherto orthodox theory, which virtually
ignored the connection between values and degrees of satisfaction
of needs. If two goods, both of some use, are unequally valued by
the user, then, although they may cost the same to produce, their
value is surely unequal. The user may prefer one good to another
for 'objective' reasons, as when it is better for some definable physical reason (as, for instance, if a lathe or drill is more effective in
operation), or the preference may be subjective, as when most
women prefer one dress material to another. In either case, it could
be argued in terms consistent with Marxism that the more desired
product receives a higher degree of social recognition, in which case
it could surely be held that a given amount of labour devoted to the
production of a more needed product is 'socially more necessary'
than the same amount used to produce something less useful. While
such formulations as these are not in the Marxian economic tradition, they will surely have to be adopted, explicitly or implicitly,
and we have seen that Nemchinov, as well as Novozhilov and Kantorovich, have moved in this direction, though by devious paths.[2]

The question of use-value has been receiving a good deal of
belated attention from Soviet economists. Thus Strumilin in the
work already cited wrote: 'Any new production (of goods) is valued
not in accordance with its absolute significance, but relatively to
those resources or goods which the given individual or collective
already possesses.' It follows from such an approach that Strumilin
is concerned with maximizing satisfaction, taking into account 'the
degree of saturation' of demand and something very close to the
concept of diminishing marginal utility.[3] He and others have shown
increasing interest in such concepts as demand elasticity, and have
no difficulty in reconciling these intellectual activities with Marxism.
Petrakov mocked those who under Stalin, considered compound

[1] *Vop. ekon.*, No. 12/1960, pp. 87, 89, 96, 100.
[2] Nemchinov (ibid., p. 90) praised V. Dmitriev, a pre-revolutionary Russian
mathematical economist, as a pioneer in the calculation of total real cost.
Dmitriev's book is not available here, but it is interesting to find a reference
to it in *Archiv für Sozialwissenschaft*, 1907, p. 34, where L. von Bortkiewicz
Its sub-title: 'An attempt at a synthesis between the labour theory of value
and the marginal utility theory.' Nemchinov, of course, did not refer to the
sub-title. (I owe thanks to Dr A. Zauberman for discovering the reference.)
[3] Strumilin, in Fedorenko (ed.), op. cit., pp. 53-55.

interest and demand or supply elasticities as in some indefinable sense 'illegitimate'.[1] All this is, of course, a reflection of the growing concern for quality, efficiency, and for the need to adjust output to user requirements.

Nor can one be satisfied with the still orthodox treatment of the problem of scarcity. While it is true that, viewed dynamically, the scarcity of today may be a misleading guide, none the less the concept needs to be taken more seriously by Soviet economists. Whatever the basis of long-term investment planning may be, many of the existing scarcities tend to be durable, and to some extent forecastable precisely because the long-term investment programme is known. If 'values', and therefore prices, express relative scarcities, then there could be less rationing (i.e. administrative material allocation), fewer *tolkachi*, much more 'self policing'; these points are rightly stressed by Joan Robinson. But many Soviet theorists are curiously reluctant to see scarcities as relative scarcities.

Progress in economic thought is exceedingly rapid in the USSR, and many ideas now expressed and even accepted would have seemed outrageously unorthodox a very few years ago. The 'mathematicians' are particularly challenging, and they are not in the least fearful of using western terminology, including (to the irritation of their critics) indifference curves and preference functions. The large majority found this shocking. L. Al'ter argued that such concepts told us nothing of degrees of preference, only that X was preferred to Y. V. Dyachenko contrasted his belief in the labour theory with Fedorenko's alleged belief in 'the theory of marginal utility'. This argument will obviously continue for years yet. It is intimately connected with the issue of the role of the market and of the plan, of consumer demand and planners, in deciding what is to be done.

SOME OTHER ECONOMIC 'LAWS'

From time to time, one encounters assertions that certain propositions constitute economic laws, though the word 'law' would appear to require inverted commas if the propositions in question are to have logical meaning. For example, there is said to be a basic *law of socialism*, defined by Stalin and frequently repeated since: 'the provision of maximum satisfaction of the constantly growing material and cultural needs of all society by means of a constant increase and perfection of socialist production on the basis of the highest

[1] Petrakov, op. cit., pp. 11-15, makes mincemeat of Stalin-period dogmatic economics.

technique'. Stalin also defined capitalism, though in somewhat less flattering terms (maximum profits, pauperization, exploitation, robbery, war, etc.).[1] This is partly just propagandist generalization, but also, so far as socialism in concerned, involves a politically convenient but analytically disastrous assumption that whatever decisions are taken by the Soviet government at any given time (for instance, about the satisfaction of the people's wants) necessarily conform to the above-named law, represent the objectively determined maximum at that stage of development.

The same is true of the often reasserted '*law of planned (proportionate) development of the economy*', which always appears in just this form, with the word 'proportionate' in brackets. As far as can be judged, this is little more than a statement to the effect that the economy is planned and that the planners, by reason of the social ownership of the means of production, can determine the correct 'proportions', e.g. between investment and consumption, industry and agriculture, and so forth. Occasionally, it is pointed out that it does not follow that the correct proportions are in fact observed, only that it is possible, and indeed necessary, for the proper functioning of the economy, that they should be. Stalin himself made this point.[2] In this case, it is a 'law' in a quite special sense, and a different word should be used. From time to time one comes across this 'law' in the course of arguments against excessive reliance on 'automatic' economic forces; in this guise, it amounts to emphasizing the primacy of conscious political control of the 'proportions' (i.e. primarily over investment). Unfortunately, it is seldom made clear by what objective criteria one is to judge whether the planners at any given moment are in breach of the 'law', save in those instances in which there are plain errors; for example, if the investment plan fails to provide the metal and energy required for the growth targets of the plan itself, clearly the 'proportions' are wrong. Similarly, the neglect of agriculture over many years could be regarded as leading to a breach of this 'law'. However, until the alleged disproportion is identified as such by the political leadership, it has hardly been possible to invoke the 'law' as a criterion.

Also involved is the doctrine concerning the priority of department I (or A goods) over department II (or B goods), discussed in chapter 10. This raises another species of question: how much priority is correct? What is *in fact* the limit on investment, on the rate of growth to be planned for? If accumulation is around 25 per

[1] Op. cit., pp. 38, 40.
[2] Ibid., p. 8.

L

cent of the national income, why not 40 per cent, or 15 per cent? Which is the 'legal' proportion? To this there is, as far as can be judged, one more or less orthodox answer, though it is seldom given in this form. Briefly, it is 'the principle of ensuring the *maximum possible* rate of technical progress, which determines the most rapid growth of social labour productivity, of the volume of social production'.[1] The object is the maximum possible growth rate. But what is at any given moment possible depends on a number of factors, some 'physical' (thus the labour force must be fed and clothed, which provides an essential floor to the consumption fund), some of a more intangible kind (thus, in normal times, incentives involve some more or less steady improvement in living standards). This may not sound like an economic law, but it may in fact be a fair definition of economic policy underlying the so-called planned (proportionate) development of the USSR. Unless it has meaning in this sense, the 'law' in question is merely an assertion that Soviet planners take the right decisions most of the time, and that they are not (or should not be) guilty of major inconsistencies. In this as in other branches of economic thought, Soviet theoreticians have opened up new areas of discussion in recent years about 'correct' proportions and objective criteria for discovering these. Thus, for instance, Notkin has been exploring this theory in several articles.[2] The question has in fact been partially 'dedogmatized' and is becoming linked to the discussions on optimization, economic effectiveness, programming and other such highly practical matters.

There is also a *law of the necessary conformity of productive forces and productive relations*. This may seem scholastic jargon, but in fact, when originally formulated by Stalin in 1938, it fulfilled an important political economic purpose. According to Marx, history progresses through contradictions, and one of the principal motive forces in historical change is precisely the fact that productive forces get out of line with productive relations; as, for example, when the potentialities of the machine age were held back by a feudal organization of society. In such cases, there was liable to be a strong tendency towards a revolutionary situation, in which the disequilibrium was corrected by violence. Stalin was concerned to exempt the USSR from this awkward species of contradiction. Hence the law of 'necessary conformity'. True, things do go wrong, there

---

[1] Katz, op. cit., p. 103. Emphasis mine. For a mathematical exploration of this problem of a maximum, see B. Ward in *Value and Plan* (ed. Grossman, University of California, 1960).

[2] See *Vop. ekon.*, No. 8/1964, p. 92, and *Plan. khoz.*, No. 6/1965, p. 1.

are difficulties, but, if these take the form of contradictions at all, these are 'non-antagonistic', do not lead to conflict, can be put right by appropriate party and government decision. Indeed, this 'law' in fact asserts that they *must* always be put right, since any suggestion that in any given instance it has not been done would be to allege that the law which cannot be broken has been broken. Therefore, this is yet another example of identifying state action (any state action) with objective necessity, politically very convenient but analytically useless, or meaningless. Some Soviet economists have been criticizing the theory, by emphasizing the role which 'contradictions' do in fact play in Soviet economic life.[1]

SOVIET ECONOMICS—AND OUR OWN

After a prolonged period of intellectual stagnation, Soviet economics has come to life, and, especially since 1956, has been the scene of genuine argument. This has also been the case in several other Communist countries. These arguments are an integral part of the search for a new balance between central orders and local initiative, between political 'campaigning' and an orderly utilization of economic forces; they are stimulated by the conscious search for a more effective utilization of scarce resources in a more mature and complex economy. In other words, the economists' debates are part of the general trend towards necessary reform in the economic field, and, because the party leadership's own economic aims render reforms and new thinking necessary, it is very improbable that the process will be stopped. Interesting though the debates have been, many of the ideas expressed have been rather obviously wide of the mark, and it is possible that some western economists would regard the confusions of their Soviet *confrères* with superior amusement. Yet such amusement should be tempered with a greater consciousness of the inadequacies of much western economic analysis of the dynamics of change, and with the thought that the problems of underdeveloped countries raise many of the questions with which Soviet economists have been wrestling.[2] If development is undertaken by deliberate government action, in a way which either modifies or ignores the pressures of the market, the guide lines provided by market relations are disrupted. They need to be

[1] For instance, see Y. Kronrod, in *Voprosy stroitel'stva kommunizma v SSSR* (Moscow, 1959). This 'law' is very well explained in the invaluable article by Kaufman, op. cit. Stalin's 1938 formulation appears in *Problems of Leninism* (1945 English edition), p. 586.

[2] More of this in the next chapter.

replaced—by what? If valuations are not provided by a market, can they be usefully derived from a pseudo market within an electronic computer? Are marginalism and the concept of factor cost only meaningful where there is a continuous process of adjustment to market pressures, where, so to speak, water can find its own level? Is a price theory derived from equilibrium analysis relevant to a state of affairs in which the scales are deliberately weighted?[1] Have western economists in fact any sort of agreed approach to the economic problems of development? Can we really be satisfied with the (usually unconscious) philosophical assumptions underlying welfare economics? Nor should we overlook the abstract nature of many of the more fashionable western models, growth models especially. While the oversimplifications and abstractions are doubtless justified for purposes of exposition and theoretical clarity, can we seriously suppose that in their present form they can serve as a basis for economic organization, reorganization, pricing, investment decisions, in the actually existing circumstances of any real country? (This, after all, is the challenge that faces the reforming economists in the USSR.) In the face of all these question marks, it is as well to approach the errors and omissions of Soviet economists without any undue superiority complex.

[1] This point arises in connection with the very interesting works of A. Bergson, listed in the bibliography.

CHAPTER 12

Assessment

THE SOVIET ECONOMY AND THE ECONOMICS
OF DEVELOPMENT

The Soviet economic system was developed in order to serve certain
purposes, notably the rapid industrialization of the Soviet Union.
Despite a justifiable degree of scepticism concerning exaggerated
official claims—of which more will be said in the Appendix—the
achievements of the system are indeed impressive. Despite great difficulties, big errors, much suffering and cruelty, and a destructive war,
the USSR today is second only to the United States. Once again, a
certain scepticism about the actual figures should not detract from
our appreciation of the magnitude of the achievement. Yet the economy seems to be suffering from a number of major inefficiencies, it
has been allocating resources irrationally; or such, at least, would
be the conclusions legitimately drawn from the data presented in
many of the preceding chapters. It may be asked: is there not an
inconsistency here? If the USSR has indeed succeeded in overcoming many serious obstacles to growth, has built up its economic
might so rapidly, then perhaps its policies and its economic structure were not, after all, so very irrational? Surely the system did
possess features which contributed to rapid growth in the Soviet setting? Perhaps the weaknesses and distortions analysed in earlier
chapters are the obverse side of methods of industrialization which
have, or had, a rationality of their own? Did we not, perhaps, adopt
implicitly standards of judgment too 'western', too narrowly economic, to form a sound basis for assessing the performance of the
Soviet system? These are serious questions, and the criticism which
they contain does have a certain validity. Unless we appreciate this,
we shall be in imminent danger of falling into the error of regard-
ing essential features of the Soviet economic system merely as aberrations, or as the projection into the economic field of power-seeking
megalomania of particular leaders. A particularly useful corrective
is to examine those features of the system which arose as a response
to problems of development as such. This task is facilitated by the

growing literature on development, produced by western economists who have studied how to overcome obstacles to industrialization in underdeveloped countries outside the Soviet bloc.

As a lead in to this analysis, let us take the Soviet habit of 'campaignology' in the economic field, with which so much waste and so many excesses are associated. The repeated appearance of campaigns are, to use the legal phrase, evidence of system. The Soviet method of industrialization was a series of leaps forward, of which successive five-year plans were a formal expression, and within them there was a concentration of publicity and resources on some particular sectors, with a neglect of other important matters, which led to bottlenecks which led to new campaigns, each of which tended to be 'overdone' in its practical application. There was wasteful discontinuity, the methods were highly political, economic calculation in its usual sense took a back seat. Why?

One reason, certainly, related to the political structure. Below the topmost leadership of the Communist party, the activities of officials and directors are more or less circumscribed within basic policy directives from the top of the pyramid. Any major change in investment policy, or even in technical method, generally requires a decision of the top leadership. But the men concerned are very busy, and often fail to take the necessary decision unless the need is extremely pressing, or fail to halt a campaign already current unless and until its harmfulness is abundantly obvious. By then another campaign may be necessary to set things right. This is in part due to the weakness of 'countervailing forces' in the USSR: in the West such forces would prevent excesses, and, by taking gradual initiatives in a decentralized way, render the campaign approach unnecessary in normal times. It should be added that the Communist party in the Soviet Union, in so far as it replaces spontaneously operating economic forces, organizes its own activities around campaigns, a point to which we shall return in a moment. Students of Soviet economic history know of a great many examples of belated decisions which, once finally taken at the centre, become campaigns; two recent examples are the drastic shift towards non-solid fuels and the decison to treble in seven years the size of the chemical industry. Soviet agricultural history is full of party-imposed 'panaceas', always taken too far and replaced by other campaigns.

But it is certainly not enough to seek explanations of 'campaignology' solely in the logic of political centralization. There are other reasons, which may indeed help to explain the high degree of centralization. One such reason has already been referred to in chapter 5, when a long quotation from Oscar Lange included the reference to a war economy as a parallel to the Soviet method of industrialization. Since Oscar Lange was a high official of a Communist state, some readers may well regard this as apologetics rather than evidence, and so it is worth citing an American scholar, who does not appear to have studied the Soviet Union or, in all probability, to have seen Lange's formulations. He wrote: 'One field of experience may provide some guidance: the planning of "total war". For a short time the present writer was engaged in wartime planning, and he has been struck since by the similarity between the *nature* of the problem confronting economic planners during the war and in underdeveloped countries ... The process required the breaking of a succession of critical bottlenecks ... In short, "total war", like planning development of poor and stagnant economies, involves marked and discontinuous structural changes, and resource allocation without reference to the market.'[1]

Myrdal, in his already cited book, emphasized the complexity of the task of development, the importance of politico-social factors, the frequent need to mobilize people around slogans devised by politicians if the forces of inertia and traditionalism are to be overcome. Equally relevant to our theme is the so-called 'unbalanced growth' school, of which Hirschman and Perroux may be cited as two outstanding representatives.[2] All the above-named economists are essentially concerned with development *strategy*. Given a decision to develop, the correct strategy is not to seek 'optimization' in its narrowly economic sense, or to attempt the impossible task of a balanced advance on all fronts; rather is it necessary to choose methods which will facilitate the breaking out of the 'interlocking vicious circles' which obstruct the movement forward. One should seek to set up creative tensions, seek out the kind of disequilibria which will act as stimuli for further change. The traditional economic criteria must be replaced by new ones, related to this concept of strategy. Some sectors should be given priority because, in Perroux's phrase, they 'exercent un exceptionnel pouvoir déstabilisant'.[3] Hirschman argues that 'in these basic types of investment decisions, it is, therefore, not sufficient to supplement, qualify and otherwise refine the usual investment criteria. We must evolve entirely new

[1] B. Higgins, *Economic Development* (New York, Norton and Co., 1959), p. 453.
[2] *The Strategy of Economic Development* (Yale, 1958), and *La Coexistence Pacifique* (Paris, 1958),
[3] Op. cit., p. 478.

aids to thought and action in the largely uncharted territory of efficient sequences and optimal development strategies'.[1]

It is instructive to note that the approach and priorities of the 'unbalanced growth' school have a number of things in common with
those actually adopted by Soviet planners. Thus they tend to emphasize not only the need for the conscious organization of development, but also for five or ten-year plans, and being ambitious: 'a
gradualist approach is almost certain to be self defeating'.[2] Hirschman and Perroux stress the need for capital-intensive, modern
methods in key sectors, despite the relatively great scarcity of capital
and the fact that other sectors or auxiliary processes within the
modernized sector remain 'hand operated', a situation typical of
much of the Soviet economy to this day, and treated by some critics
as self-evident proof of irrationality. The shortage of decision makers
is, for Hirschman, an argument for choosing those variants which
'set up incentives and pressures that make for ... induced investment decisions',[3] i.e. which compel other decisions to be made. By
these strategic criteria, heavy industry should be given priority: 'this
means intermediate or "basic" industries whose products are distributed as inputs through many industrial sectors besides going directly to final demand. It is clear that such industries should be given
preference over "last" [i.e. consumers'] industries, if they are at all
economically feasible'.[4] If such policies were to be applied, certain
traditional concepts of western economics must undergo modification. As Higgins puts it: '... Nor are the required adjustments
strictly marginal. In such countries growth itself must be managed,
and "sectoral planning" is necessary. The various rates at which
heavy industry, light industry, agricultural improvement, transport
and communications, housing and the like are to be pushed becomes
a matter of conscious policy. Planning of this kind involves a calculus, involving a cost benefit comparison, but it is no longer a
purely marginal calculus'.[5]

It is no part of the present book to argue whether the above-
expressed views are sound. The point is that they are not derived
from Soviet experience, yet—surely not a coincidence—they advocate an approach which does have some features familiar to the
student of the Soviet economy. Efficiency and rationality, it appears,
take on a new dimension in the context of development strategy, even
in non-Marxist and non-communist eyes.

There is a fairly obvious objection to the application of this ana-

[1] Op. cit., p. 79.   [2] Higgins, op. cit., p. 454.   [3] Op. cit., p. 151.
[4] Ibid., p. 118.   [5] Op. cit., p. 451.

lysis to the Soviet Union. It may be argued that the 'unbalanced growth' economists are concerned with stimulating spontaneous acts, whereas in a totally planned society such as the USSR it can all be done by deliberate action of the party and government. From this it might be thought to follow that balanced growth is possible—perhaps even only possible—in a Soviet type economy. Indeed, one of the protagonists of 'unbalanced growth', P. Streeten, has gone so far as to equate the 'law of planned (proportionate) development of the economy', so dear to Soviet theoreticians, with balanced growth.[1]

This last view, surely, is based upon a misunderstanding of this so-called 'law', or else upon an identification of the plan with intersector balance, even when the plan provides for extremely unbalanced growth between sectors. But, quite apart from this, the entire *rationale* of the Soviet 'campaign' approach to economic planning rests upon the inherent limitations of central control, or, more precisely, upon the need to stimulate not only the executants but also the controllers. Again, it is necessary to challenge the 'totalitarian myth' of the monolithic perfectly obedient society, in which everyone can be told precisely what to do, as if in the Soviet Union too there is no problem of overcoming inertia, even among the party officials themselves. Campaigns are, among other things, a means of goading the goaders, of mobilizing the controllers, of providing success indicators for officials at all levels. The deviations engendered by campaigns are the analogue to the distortions caused by success indicators at the 'micro' level and analysed in chapter 6 above. Of course, the importance of the controlling mechanism as a growth stimulator is all the greater where, as in the Soviet system, there is no built-in growth-inducing force, where the intervention of authority, and the targets set by authority, must act as a substitute for the automatic functioning of the profit motive.[2] Hence the vital role of campaigns as controller mobilizers. Hence the value of bottlenecks as stimulators to effort. Of course, it would be misleading to assert that Soviet planners deliberately create bottlenecks. But they adopt growth tempos which cause acute shortages and strains, while denouncing those who wish to adapt the growth tempos to the bottlenecks (as they say, *ravnyatsa na uzkie mesta*). Strain and campaigns go together.

Therefore, the campaign method seems to have a logic. It also

---

[1] 'Unbalanced growth', *Oxford Economic Papers*, June, 1959, p. 169.
[2] On all this, see a stimulating discussion by G. Grossman, 'Soviet growth: routine, inertia and pressure', *American Economic Review* May, 1960.

carries with it a big risk of waste, of gigantomania, of all kinds of bureaucratic deformations. Obviously, the logic of 'campaigns' as a method in no way argues in favour of any particular campaign, which may indeed be utterly wrong-headed, explicable by crude miscalculation, Stalin's megalomania and other irrational factors. It is also true that this whole approach must involve certain inherent weaknesses and gives rise to the many problems discussed in Part II of the present book. None the less, we must see that the adoption of such planning techniques were not due to the mere whim of an all-powerful dictator or to the self interest of the *apparatchiki*, though such things did play their role, and indeed still play a role, in Soviet economic development.

This line of thought should lead the critical reader to look again at the concept of rationality. Already in chapter 5 we noted at least two meanings: optimum resource allocation as such (i.e. without assuming any goals other than the efficient functioning of the economy), and the economically most rational means of achieving given ends. It is clear enough that these two concepts can contradict one another: arrangements which facilitate optimum allocation may be inconsistent with the pursuit of postulated ends. To take a non-Soviet example, the Irish government subsidises economic activities in Gaelic-speaking areas, to preserve a way of life which it regards as good. Given the purpose, this is not an uneconomic use of resources. However, as one thinks over the logic of 'development strategy', it becomes clear that there are other and more sophisticated 'levels' of rationality in the context of growth. For development involves actions which are political and social and have a logic of their own. In so far as such actions serve the cause of development, they must be held to fulfil economic purposes, yet these same actions *as such* may well inflict economic loss, and if one were merely seeking the *economically* most rational means of achieving given ends, they could well be utterly illogical and pointless. To take another non-Soviet example, borrowed from Myrdal, it could well be that the spirit of nationalism was an essential unifying factor, an essential motive force for development, in some countries; this may give rise in certain circumstances to the political necessity of taking measures against foreign firms, measures which, in themselves, actually harm development.[1] Irrationalities at one level may appear logical on another. In examining some rather obvious inefficiencies of the Soviet system, we should never completely lose sight of the aims pursued,

[1] Op. cit., p. 73.

and of the obstacles which had to be overcome. There are social-political 'external economies'.[1]

However, the claim that one is pursuing certain aims does not exempt the 'pursuers' from criticism at any level of their activities. The fact that obstacles had to be overcome does not mean that they were in fact overcome intelligently. In any case, one's realization that certain aims were pursued in no way implies that the aims were 'good', or worth the sacrifices which were imposed on a people which was given little choice about either ends or means. Value judgments about aims and means would take us far outside the scope of the present work, and the point is only made lest it be thought that the line of argument adopted in this chapter is an essay in apologetics. A more immediately relevant line of criticism concerns the fact that, in the Soviet Union, some obstacles were tackled with such crude brutality that the damage so done itself came to constitute an obstacle; the forced collectivization of the peasantry is an obvious example. Then the fantastically over-ambitious nature of the first five-year plan, and of some sector plans at more recent dates, led to waste on such a scale that a similar rate of growth could well have been achieved at far less economic and human cost if they hastened more slowly. Vast miscalculations occurred, resources were wasted on a prodigious scale on enormous 'prestige' projects (canals, 'transformation of nature', etc.) using much forced labour.[2] In no sense whatever should one argue that the errors and coercion which actually occurred were somehow 'necessary', let alone justified *ex post* by growth rate statistics or victory in war. Nor is it legitimate to claim that no other way existed for Russia to industrialize. Yet, without subscribing to the misleading doctrine that whatever is real is rational, that whatever happened had to happen, it remains true that what did happen had a certain logic, that it was connected with the problems of rapid development in post revolutionary Russia, that many of the problems encountered are common to underdeveloped countries in general, and that our picture of the relative efficacy of the Soviet economic system must take these things into account. This requires a view of rationality rather wider than that adopted by many western economists who examine the Soviet scene. It may be added that this broader view could with advantage be adopted by some western political scientists, who see the Soviet political struc-

[1] All this is further explored in A. Nove, 'Thoughts on Irrationality and Waste', *Survey*, July, 1967.
[2] On all this, see N. Jasny in *Soviet Studies*, April and July, 1961, and his *Soviet Industrialization, 1928-52* (Chicago, 1961).

ture (including its economic aspects) almost solely as the manifesta-
tion of power hunger on the part of totalitarian oligarchs. There
is surely much more to it than that.

But it is time to return to the questions posed in chapter 5, when
we spoke of the changing nature of problems. Even if it were accepted that the Soviet system did cope with some success—and at
heavy cost—with the task of building a great modern industrial
state, it may be legitimately argued that it is incapable of coping
effectively with running a modern industrial state once it has been
built. The evidence in Part II of this book points that way. So, indeed, does the nature and direction of the economists' arguments
with which we were concerned in chapter 11. Perhaps the (genuinely)
totalitarian elements of the Stalin system did, on balance, facilitate
the rapid building up of basic industries; by imposing priorities, enforcing a high rate of accumulation, destroying the power of social
groups to press for the satisfaction of their requirements (which
would have modified the priorities), the régime facilitated growth.
The institutional, political, psychological arrangements were geared
to these purposes, and sacrificed 'efficiency' to them, or rather, measured efficiency in terms of growth. But Stalin is dead, his system is
being modified. Do arguments derived from 'development strategy',
any longer apply?

CAN THE SYSTEM COPE WITH A MATURE ECONOMY?

The Soviet Union is at present in a stage at which it could be described as the least developed industrial country, or the most developed underdeveloped country. If such an assertion seems paradoxical in the light of the statistics of her industrial output, there is
none the less an important sense in which it is true. Soviet development has been extremely uneven, large sectors of the economy are
primitive, living conditions (housing especially) poor. Living standards have increased comparatively modestly from their 1928 levels, a
fact which contrasts strikingly with the very great rise in industrial production. Part of the explanation, in all probability, lies in the large
volume of misdirected industrial production, associated with the
major irrationalities in resource allocation which were typical of the
Stalin period; these raised the capital output ratio well above the
possible, and greatly increased the output of 'unnecessary' intermediate products, which go to swell the industrial output index without
providing a commensurate increase in the output of final products.

This was argued by a group of economists in the USSR, when they wrote, criticizing low levels of technique, quality and organization: 'All this led to excess expenditures of materials and equipment. But since at the same time the volume of gross output increased, the effect . . . on the economy did not receive its due reflection in economic calculations.'[1] In any event, growth was exceedingly unbalanced. Khrushchev endeavoured to advance on a broad front. He devoted resources and administrative effort to agriculture, he launched a housing drive, tried to provide more consumers' goods, better shops, amenities, schools, pensions. He laid stress on the need to win the economic race with America. He understood that the new circumstances called for new methods and he permitted widespread discussion and some economic experiments. Yet in the end he retained his preference for arbitrary political intervention and party-run campaigns. When growth rates declined after 1958 and economic difficulties accumulated, his solution to the various problems that arose took the form of repeated administrative reorganizations. When he was ousted, his successors stressed the necessity for more rational forms of management, an end to campaigning methods, a more intensive search for optimal planning.

Here we encounter a major 'contradiction'. The entire system of economic administration and party control is closely geared in with the old methods, was designed for development campaigns, leaps forward, is associated with straining after targets, success indicators and the like. It is altogether too easy to attribute the continuation of these methods, and of the centralization which goes with them, solely to the vested interest of the party machine. No doubt this vested interest is an important factor. However, it is also true that piecemeal reforms often prove self defeating. As we have had repeated occasion to observe in chapter 7, partial measures to give greater powers of decision to men on the spot frequently lead to even greater irrationalities and compel a return to centralization, because, in the absence of genuine market relations, only the centre is in a position to determine what is needed.

Yet the centre also lacks the necessary information about what is needed, or is unable to translate its requirements into precise and enforceable orders. We have seen how the planning organs are tending to be overwhelmed by the growing complexities of the task of linking a multitude of interconnected production and supply decisions. With the transition to a more mature economy, the nature of rationality has, so to speak, changed its meaning. The economic

[1] L. Kochetkov et. al., op. cit., p. 57.

discussions, the ideas of men like Nemchinov, Novozhilov, Kantoro-vich, the fact that their views are published and discussed, shows the existence of an influential school of thought which regards major structural changes as necessary. Their opponents use against them arguments which, in essence, are based on the view that the 'develop-ment strategy' is far from over, and that the old methods can be reformed without being discarded. The habits and self interest of the party machine may well incline them to support the 'conservatives' on this question, and they may respond with new slogans about new campaigns, which would simultaneously justify their leadership and the retention of the campaign techniques which go with it. Yet, as has surely been amply demonstrated in earlier pages, the old methods are both ineffective and discredited. Inefficiency in the use of re-sources, and particularly investment resources, has contributed to a decline in growth rates. Economic growth is an essential aim for the party leadership. To achieve the economic progress which it desires, it must revise its methods, whatever the contrary pressures of vested interested and habit. Radical changes are therefore due and are in-deed already in train.

THE EFFICACY OF THE SYSTEM IN COMPETITION WITH THE WEST

Until recently, comparisons between the western and the Soviet economies were, as a rule, thoroughly misleading. This was not due principally to statistical problems; these were and are, admittedly, very awkward, but the real point is a different one. Efficacy, if the word is to have any meaning at all, must relate to the ability of the given system or measures to cope with the situation which is ac-tually confronted at the given time and place. How, therefore, can one compare the functioning of an already developed economy, like that of the United States or Great Britain, with the methods used to industrialize, with a development strategy? It is like comparing chalk and cheese. However, with the emergence of the Soviet Union as an industrial power, and bearing in mind the insistence of its leaders that they intend to overtake the west in economic might, the possibility of meaningful comparison of systems increases. At least, it is possible to say something on the subject which is not meaningless.

None the less, before doing so it is necessary to utter a word of warning. The relative performance of the two systems in this or that sector must be judged by reference not to some abstract optimum, but to what is or would have been possible. This point can be

illustrated by taking as an example the very great superiority of the
United States in labour productivity in agriculture. Let us suppose,
for the sake of argument, that this is five times greater than in the
Soviet Union.[1] What conclusions can we draw from this? Surely, before saying anything worth while, we must take into account at least
the following. Soviet soil is, on average, less naturally fertile; the
climate is very much less favourable, the risk of drought and frost
damage much greater; there is a much greater density of rural population in relation to the area of cultivatable land, and it was
scarcely possible to shift peasants into non-agricultural employment
faster than was in fact done. One might also take the human situation into account: the Russian peasant is not an American farmer,
and a large proportion of the Soviet farm labour force consists of
women. All this in no way affects the many criticisms we can and
should make of the conduct of Soviet agriculture: we are indeed also
entitled to note that productivity of both labour and land has risen
more slowly than in many western countries during the past thirty
years, and might, therefore, conclude that there is nothing about
kolkhozy and *sovkhozy* especially conducive to the growth of agricultural output; many would, with some reason, regard this last sen-
tence as altogether too polite. Yet the fact remains that, even if
Soviet farm policies were ideal, productivity would certainly be considerably lower in the Soviet Union than in the United States. Relative efficiency is a tricky concept.[2] Its measurement by an analysis
of factor productivity, which has been attempted by several writers
in a highly sophisticated way,[3] is open to just these objections. It is
tempting to treat the resultant American superiority as evidence of
system, yet the relative productivity, in such terms, of (say) Turkey,
India, Italy and West Germany could lead to no conclusions of this
kind, since it is obvious that not only resource endowment but also
the whole historical-cultural experience of these countries have
helped to shape their economic performance. Efficiency, surely, should
be related to the possible, in the given place and at the given time.

No one, least of all Soviet economists, doubt that by any reasonable measure Soviet productivity is far below American standards,
and below what it could or should be. This, after all, is what the

[1] Soviet sources claim a 3:1 ratio (for instance, Y. Yoffe, *Plan. khoz.*, No.
3/1960, pp. 50 ff.), but they seem to add rather too generously to the published American labour force. Western estimates, on the other hand, have
tended greatly to overstate the Soviet farm labour force.

[2] For an excellent survey of factors affecting industrial productivity comparisons, see W. Galenson, *Labour Productivity in Soviet and American Industry*
(Columbia University Press, 1955).

[3] Especially A. Bergson: *The economics of Soviet planning* (Yale, 1964).

reform movement has been all about. It is true that on various occasions the Soviet leadership, in the person of Khrushchev, permitted itself the hope of overtaking the United States by 1970. However, not only was the relative volume of Soviet industrial output somewhat overstated, but the slower rate of Soviet growth since 1958 coincided with a speedup in American growth, so that the process of catching up has become decidedly slow. Khrushchev's successors have stopped arguing that it will be possible to overtake America at any date in the foreseeable future, but they still have confidence in the superior growth-potential of their system.

Is this so? Granted that the Stalin system was a means of rapid industrialization, is the Soviet system at its present stage able to keep up the pace? What are its elements of relative strength?

It can maintain a high rate of investment, a rate which will remain independent of business fluctuations and the uncertain preferences of individuals. While a larger proportion of these investments are apparently being devoted to the formerly neglected sectors (agriculture, housing, textiles, retail trade, etc.), a high degree of priority is still, and will continue to be, attached to the growth-inducing sectors of heavy industry. The movement forward is hardly likely to be interrupted by the crises or recessions which adversely affect the growth of western economies from time to time.[1]

The Soviet effort can glean advantage from the immense educational 'investments' of the past years. Much greater attention is paid to science, indeed to knowledge as such, not only by the authorities but also among the people, since the USSR has largely escaped the large scale 'commercialization of the moron' with its encouragement of mental laziness and ignorance. Although the Soviet educational system has its serious shortcomings too, they are least apparent in the scientific and technical field. The concentration of so many of the best brains in pure science must bring nearer the day when Russians will emerge as important innovators. Though hitherto they have tended to copy western methods, outside of a narrow and predominantly military field, there is no reason why, in the future, they should astonish us only with Sputniks.

The development of new ideas on industrial technique is extending the possibilities of automation in industry, and the Soviet econ-

---

[1] However, see J. Olivera's theory of cyclical growth under collectivism, *Kyklos*, 1960, pp. 229 ff. Also see the remarkable analysis of a species of growth cycle in socialist countries by J. Goldmann, of Prague, which appeared in English in *Economics of Planning* (Oslo), No. 2/1964, and in Italian in *Rinascità* January 16, 1965. Also his and A. Nove: contributions to *Is the Business Cycle Obsolete?* (M. Bronfenbrenner, ed.).

omic system may be especially well adapted to automation. This is because it can assure long runs of standardized products, planned well in advance, with few risks of unexpected changes, of uncontrollable competition or opposition from trade unions. Soviet scientists should be able to produce the necessary equipment, in view of their achievements in the related and more complex field of astronautics.

It must also be stressed that the system is in general well adapted to a rapid growth in the output of basic products—minerals, steel, cement, fuel and so on. As was already mentioned in chapter 6, the defects associated with the success indicator system affect such products very little, since they are more or less homogenous and so relatively easy to plan. Large scale investment in expansion of these basic industries is facilitated by the existence of a long term plan which makes possible a reasonable forecast of need for many years ahead, and by centralization of investment finance. The weaknesses which relate to adaptation to consumer demand and the finer adjustments of diversification hardly matter in these sectors.

A further very important 'advantage' in the growth race is backwardness itself, and this in two ways. In the first place, the existence of inefficiencies in resource utilization, of misemployed or underemployed labour in agriculture and so on, provides reserves in the move forward, which are not available in countries in which these reserves have already been drawn upon. In this sense, evidence of past or present inefficiencies is evidence of additional growth potential, unless it can be shown that the system is inherently incapable of curing the inefficiencies. A second 'advantage' of backwardness is the stimulus to growth which it provides, by the high degree of unsatisfied and urgent demands for more material goods. The Soviet Union is short of so very many things. The United States, by contrast, has reached saturation point in many sectors of its economy. Any major increase in its output of agricultural products, motor cars, washing machines, would be more likely to give rise to embarrassment rather than satisfaction; it is hard enough to sell what is produced already. Whereas in the Soviet Union there is need for expansion, and plenty of room for cost reductions through the introduction of modern techniques, especially in the consumers' goods field.

To this list of factors which, on balance, favour the Soviet Union some would add an alleged superiority in foreign trade. Dr Balogh, for instance, was apt to warn us of the likelihood of very intense Soviet competition on world markets, while less serious writers make our flesh creep with stories of massive trade offensives. It is impossible to discuss in detail here the reasons for viewing such alarms with scepticism, but there are certainly grounds for such scepticism. Despite a sizeable increase from the very low levels of the Korean War period, Soviet trade with the entire non-communist world in 1959 was still quite small, half or less of that of a country such as the Netherlands.[1] Except where the partner's trade with the west was disrupted by political quarrels (such as Cuba in 1960, for instance, or Egypt in 1956), Soviet share in trade has generally been very modest. The somewhat clumsy and bureaucratized system of foreign trade corporations is not conducive to efficient trading practices. While it is true that the monopoly of foreign trade has been used, and will doubtless continue to be used, to secure certain political advantages to the Soviet Union, the idea that the USSR is or shortly will be in a position to 'flood the world's markets' seems quite baseless; this presupposes very large exportable surpluses, over and above the internal needs of the Soviet Union itself and of its allies. There is no sign of a plan for such vast surpluses. Oil is, for the time being, a significant exception, but even oil is only embarrassing to the west because, thanks largely to the west's own import restrictions, it is sent to only a few countries, instead of being 'diluted' within the vastly larger world market. It is quite unrealistic to deduce the emergence of large exportable surpluses from statistics of projected increases in output. Obviously, it all depends on domestic utilization. For example, Soviet steel production has indeed risen spectacularly, but very little is exported, and indeed there are continued restrictions on its use in Russia, for instance, in construction.

Other analysts, for instance Isaac Deutscher, imagined that there is strength in the economic unity of the Soviet bloc, and in the specialization and joint planning which it makes possible.[2] The reader of the present book, who must have noted the grave difficulties in the way of proper co-ordination even within the USSR itself will surely approach such ideas with due caution. Undeniably, some form of planning and trade co-ordination exists, through COMECON. However, its limitations are all too easy to document. It has yet to be demonstrated that it is any easier for two Soviet countries than for two 'capitalist' countries to co-ordinate their economies through trade. The quarrel with China caused a great reduction in trade between that country and the Soviet Union, while Roumania has

---

[1] Soviet trade volume is generally compared with 1950 or 1937, when it was much below normal. Its growth looks far less impressive if based on comparisons with 1913, or even 1930.

[2] *The Great Contest* (Oxford, 1960).

disregarded the views of COMECON about her own pattern of development and trade. While it is true that long term trade agreements are made and are geared in with long term plans, it would be going too far on the evidence to ascribe any trade superiority to the Soviet system. COMECON is still struggling with bilateralism and non-convertibility.

It is unnecessary to analyse here the internal weak spots of the Soviet system, which must be set against the elements of strength listed above, since they have been dealt with at considerable length in Part II of this book. It is enough to recall some of the more important ones. There is, firstly, the tendency of planning organs to be overwhelmed by the complexity of their tasks, especially in the linking of production and supply decisions, while unable, in the absence of market and price criteria, to devolve decision making powers to local and enterprise levels. Secondly, agriculture is still inefficiently planned and wastefully administered. Thirdly, there is a marked failure to link demand and production; the position of the consumer and the citizen *vis-à-vis* those who minister (or should minister) to his wants is still unsatisfactory, and far below normal western standards. There are the complex and interrelated question of price reform, investment criteria, innovation, success indicators, discussed in chapters 6 and 7. One of the unknowns in assessing the prospects of the Soviet Union 'overtaking' the United States is precisely that we cannot tell whether, and how, the necessary adjustments will be made. These are the difficulties of adjusting the system to deal with problems of a developed, as distinct from an underdeveloped, economy, and they raise most serious questions of economic, doctrinal and political kinds. It is by no means clear whether these adjustments can be made without thereby slowing down growth rates, and indeed generating political and social changes which could have vast consequences.

A factor which may have an unpredictable effect is labour. On the one hand, large-scale movement of workers out of the villages is bound to slow down, since there are already severe shortages in many areas of skilled male workers who can operate and maintain the modern equipment which agriculture needs, and which will in the main replace unskilled women whose contribution to productivity elsewhere in the economy will not be very significant. On the other hand one factor which tended to slow down growth in the period 1958-64 has been reversed: this was the delayed effect of extremely low wartime birth and survival rates on the intake of young workers. In the most recent years the postwar birth 'bulge' has been reaching working age. We certainly cannot now assert that labour in general is a bottleneck. Yet labour is never 'in general', outside of the minds of model-builders (for whom, alas, labour is all too often seen as homogeneous). There is, as we have noted, geographical and occupational maldistribution. Population growth is far more rapid in the national republics of the south and south-east than in Russia proper or the Baltic republic, creating social problems. A very substantial improvement in housing, consumer services, amenities of all kinds, is needed and forms part of the government's plans. These are labour-using activities, necessary and urgent, but the effect on growth is not so easy to predict. Nor, indeed, is the effect of the reform on employment, unemployment, productivity.

There are a number of other factors which may tend to slow down growth. There is the difficulty encountered in expanding agricultural production, a difficulty only partially explicable by institutional weaknesses. With almost all potentially arable land in use, further advance requires very considerable intensification, much more fertilizer, irrigation, new roads, and many other things which cost much effort but which are now likely to yield diminishing returns. The location of certain important mineral and fuel reserves is causing a shift of industry towards the east, yet there are few towns there, few people, very few railways or roads. There must be heavy expenditures on social overhead capital. Yet part of the explanation for the very rapid expansion of earlier years lies in the fact that it was possible to utilize very much more intensively already existing railways and urbanized areas, and readily accessible natural resources. This led, of course, to great strain on railways and to acute overcrowding in the cities, but it did make possible the concentration of resources on industrial growth. The capital output ratio will probably increase. Finally, we earlier mentioned that backwardness itself acts as a growth stimulus. This stimulus must grow weaker as growth proceeds, not only in some vague psychological sense but in reality. Gradually the spectre of overproduction will raise its head—for a few products, as we have seen earlier, it has already raised it. But this will mean the end of a period in which what is produced can be lightheartedly 'adjusted' to the task of quantitative growth. The 'right goods' are needed, consumer requirements and quality cannot be ignored. There must be greater diversification. Yet it is far simpler to increase output if one is producing a few standardized articles at full capacity.[1] While not a major problem yet, because

[1] This point is vigorously stressed by P. J. D. Wiles, in his 'Growth versus Choice', already cited.

the economy does still suffer from so many scarcities, all this can surely lead to increasing difficulties as the Soviet Union gets nearer to American levels. (It may be worth remarking in passing that, while Soviet consumers' goods production must move towards greater diversity, there is a tendency towards standardization, or concentration on a very few models, in western countries. Perhaps in this respect at least there is convergence.)

The USSR, as it is compelled to adopt some elements of a market economy, and as profitability criteria become more important, is bound to run into some of our own familiar troubles. External economies and diseconomies are even now not perceived below the governmental level, because the problem of externalities has nothing to do with property relations, but arises out of the division of responsibility. If A, be he manager, minister or capitalist, is in charge of factory or activity X, the consequences of his actions to anyone else concern him little, are external to him. We saw this clearly when we considered regionalism and ministerial empire-building in the USSR. The same points apply, of course, to Soviet enterprises. It used to be argued that socialism would enable the all-seeing planners to overcome the sectional blinkered view, in the general social interest. Maybe they could, but they usually do not. Even Gosplan's own divisions give their own divisional interests priority, and this is one of the many problems of co-ordination. The problem arises from size, from the necessity of dividing the otherwise unmanageable into bits. Similarly, such troubles as river pollution, factory smoke, excessive tree-cutting in the most accessible areas, have been just as common in the Soviet Union under the stress of achieving production targets quickly, as they were in the United States in the days of the industrial robber barons. Once again, property ownership is not the point. Similarly, the concern for the future *vis-à-vis* the present is at least partially expressed in the west either through inheritance or by ownership of shares, since the latter do reflect in some degree an estimate of *future* earning-power. We know that this has not been sufficient in many cases, but even these considerations are missing in the Soviet system. The government, it is true, is the guardian of the future, and in its vast investment programmes expresses its own time-preference strongly, some say too strongly. But the same is not true of the executants of the government's plans, be they in ministries, regions or enterprises. And one sees nothing in the reform pattern which will make it any easier to take into account social cost. On the contrary, the whole logic of the reform is to strengthen the autonomy of the parts and the separate assessment of the profitability of separate activities. When opponents of change argue about the importance of not losing sight of 'national-economic profitability', they do have a point.

Nor should one fail to note that the 'new model', in so far as it can be discerned, does have some weak points. There are no clear provisions either for bankruptcy or for the autonomous setting up of new enterprises. A profit-orientated oligopoly with no (or a very limited) capital market may prove to be a source of confusion and disequilibria. Since Keynes we in the West have surely learnt that free markets do not automatically solve all problems. More than one Eastern theorist has been heard to say that some free-market enthusiasts in Prague, Budapest and Moscow have yet to learn this. Indeed some of the agricultural 'radicals' appear not to have heard of the cobweb. There may well be some hard lessons, and not a few shocks and setbacks, before a soundly-based alternative finally replaces the 'traditional' Soviet model. The effect of all this on growth is problematical.

Of course, in any full assessment of the relative pace of development of the Soviet and western worlds, it would be essential to take into account the economic policies and possible difficulties of western countries. While it is right to recall that, in recent years, such 'capitalist' countries as West Germany, Japan, Italy, have matched Soviet industrial growth rates, and that the western system has shown a marked superiority in resource allocation as distinct from aggregate growth, there are plainly no grounds for complacency about the west's relative position. On the other hand there is certainly no ground for pessimism. The very considerable slowdown in Soviet economic growth in the most recent years has underlined the fact that the Soviet planners face formidable problems as they search for a way of adapting their system to the requirements of the mid-twentieth century.

A MODEL FOR UNDERDEVELOPED COUNTRIES?

One of the more important ways in which Soviet ideas exercise an influence on people in the uncommitted world is through the quite widespread belief that the USSR—and perhaps China also[1]— demonstrates how it is possible rapidly to transform a peasant country into a great industrial power. In the earlier part of this chapter, we have seen that certain western economists who study

[1] A study of the Chinese economy, while certainly desirable, is well outside the scope of the present book and of its author's knowledge.

problems of development outside the Soviet bloc recommend policies which are in some respects similar to those pursued in the USSR. It is also to some extent true that the obstacles which were so ruthlessly tackled under Stalin's rule exist in many underdeveloped countries. The Soviet Communist party smashed through the 'interlocking vicious circles', to use Hirschman's phrase again. They forced the peasants and other private interests to conform to the priorities and financial requirements of the plans for rapid industrialization. They imposed an industrializing ideology. Through a one-party state, through party organization, through the suppression of any person or groups holding contrary opinions, they were able to mobilize the people to carry the process through despite heavy cost and much suffering. All this is another way of saying that the totalitarian aspects of Soviet rule, which we in the west find most distasteful, may actually be a source of attraction to some statesmen and intellectuals in underdeveloped countries, who find, for reasons analysed as some length elsewhere,[1] that they are unable to break out of the vicious circles, unable to mobilize their apathetic and sometimes obstructionist peasants, unable to overcome a variety of vested interests, unable to cope with the inflationary and balance-of-payments crisis which seems inevitably to accompany attempts at development. The practical consequences of the path advocated by Myrdal, Hirschman and others of their way of thinking may, whether they wish it or not, lead far along the road of political despotism and ideological enthusiasm, because this path can be effectively followed only by a government which can take charge of much of the economy and pursues the aim of development with a fervour not usually associated with democracy or tolerance. It is interesting to note that Bauer, who opposes this whole approach, is aware of this and uses it as an argument against state-sponsored industrialization.[2]

Yet there are a number of features of the Soviet model which should serve as a warning rather than as an example. It must be recalled that, when the first five-year plan was launched in 1928, the Soviet Union already possessed some industry, considerable technical, scientific and statistical cadres, a fairly extensive railway system, and, perhaps most important, food surplus. This provided a basis and a margin which most overpopulated Asian countries do

---

[1] See Myrdal and Hirschman, works cited. See also A. Nove, 'The Soviet model and underdeveloped Countries,' in *International Affairs*, January, 1961.
[2] See especially P. Bauer, *United States Aid and Indian Economic Development* (Washington, 1959).

not possess. The disasters of compulsory collectivization led to a sharp drop in farm output in the USSR; there was in fact widespread famine in 1933. To follow the Soviet model of collectivization, to launch a struggle with the property-owning peasantry, might have fatal results in Asia, for people and régime alike. True, the Chinese experience seems to have been rather different, and it is also true that some government-induced change in archaic systems of farming may well be indispensable. But it is surely right to say that, while the peasant problem is indeed a major factor in the interlocking vicious circles,[1] the Soviet way of solving it should not be a model for anyone. The Soviet-style industrializing ideology in fact tends to strengthen those elements which have contempt for peasants and are all too ready to neglect agriculture. Then the Soviet authorities largely destroyed handicrafts, the private small-workshop industry. This greatly contributed to the drastic fall in living standards in the first years of the 'thirties, and represents a loss in material and human terms which should surely be avoided. The same is true of the liquidation of the private trader, as part of the war on the 'speculator', when the state was incapable (indeed is still in certain respects incapable in the USSR) of effectively replacing him. Last but not least, the too complete rejection of conventional economic rationality criteria, the reliance on the campaign approach, untrammelled by free expression of opinion by those adversely affected, led to waste on a scale which underdeveloped countries should surely do all in their power to avoid. Such slogans as 'there is no fortress the Bolsheviks cannot take', and the many similar slogans directed in China against the so-called 'rightists', open the door far too wide to policies which are irrational in terms of any criterion.

Part of the 'magic' of the Soviet example also lies in the acceptance of official Soviet growth-rate statistics, which, were they really correct, would indeed be evidence of magic. It is the reluctance of western economists to believe that miracles happen in economics, even under a Stalin, which have led them rightly to question these indices.

At this point the author might be reproached for not citing actual growth rates. He will obstinately continue to refrain from doing so, for the following reasons. While Soviet indices undoubtedly suffer from 'inflation', Western recomputations, while most thorough and in their way admirable, cannot be accurate, primarily because of inadequate coverage. By 'coverage' is meant not only the omission

---

[1] On this whole question, see in particular A. Erlich, op. cit.

of items on which no usable figures exist, but also the inevitable imprecision of a complex and changing product mix (e.g. 'wool cloth', 'steel', 'locomotives') for which there are only global figures. Add to this the everchanging commodity composition of the machinery and metal-working sector, the problem of pricing new products, the doubts concerning the statistics of, and weights attributable to, agriculture, and the margin of error looks uncomfortably high. Recomputations through GNP do, of course, achieve full coverage in roubles, but the process of finding an index by which to deflate these figures once again involves comparability and coverage.[1] Frankly, all one feels really confident of is the assertion that, whatever the 'right' figure is, it is surely well below the official claims (and interested readers are earnestly enjoined to read the many books and articles on this theme listed in the bibliography). Of course, rapid industrialization of the USSR is a fact. But, properly deflated, the figures compare reasonably with those of Japan, and reminds us that there was also a Japanese road, neither western nor communist. But we cannot do more here than to mention it, in a book devoted to the Soviet Union.

Finally, it seems important to realize that, although the Soviet methods were crude and in important respects irrational, few will hearken to such warnings if those who utter them do not show awareness of the very serious problems which underdeveloped countries face on their road to modernization. The western path, a reliance on the free market, is often irrelevant, often leads nowhere. As one American economist put it, 'laissez-faire will not do the job, and totalitarian physical planning is unlikely to do the job well'.[2] Even if it were certain to do the job badly, men would still turn to it if other methods are ineffective. Hence the serious need for imaginative study both of problems of development in various countries and of the positive and negative features of the Soviet system at various stages of the industrializing process.

[1] Suppose investment totalled 1,000 in 1930 and 5,000 in 1940, in current roubles. To calculate the volume increase one would have, inter alia, to devise an index of machinery prices. To do so one must compare the cost of machines at the two dates, assign weights, take into account changes of model and the appearance of new models. Anyone who supposes this to be simple must read R. Moorsteen's study, referred to in the bibliography, or A. Gerschenkron: *A dollar index of Soviet machine output* (Rand Corp., 1951).

[2] B. Higgins, op. cit., p. 456

M

APPENDIX

A Note on the Availability and Reliability
of Soviet Statistics

Availability

A few years ago, it would have been easiest to make a quite short list of the few figures which were available. The fact that the contrary procedure is now the most convenient one is a measure of the 'liberalization' achieved since the death of Stalin, or rather since 1956, when the systematic publication of economic statistics gradually began again after a long interval. However, there are still some conspicuous gaps, of which the following are the most important.

(*a*) Output figures for some *industrial products* are missing, among them non-ferrous metals, ships, aircraft, many chemicals, some machines, as well as military weapons.

(*b*) While more is now appearing about the breakdown of the *labour force*, including agriculture and the military services,[1] numbers in particular industries are not given in any detail.

(*c*) While since 1964 we have had some average wage statistics, there is nothing about average pay in different industries, or as between different categories of workers, and hardly anything at all about actual earnings of peasants.

(*d*) There is no information given on the composition of turnover tax revenue, and only a few actual rates of tax are published.

However, let us give credit where credit is due. Gone indeed is the day when one had to search for statistics in leaders' speeches and make do with percentages of an unknown base. The statistical compendia on the economy as a whole, on agriculture, on various republics and localities, on transport, and so forth, together with the reports on the 1959 census, do give us a sizeable stock of statistics to work on, despite the remaining gaps. One difficulty is that many of the figures given are ill-defined; there is an unfortunate lack of explanatory notes; though minor attempts are being made to remedy

[1] Until it was decided to publish the numbers in the armed forces (1960), the number of peasants and the age and sex distribution of the population were unpublished, no doubt to prevent calculation by residual.

346

this, we badly need longer explanations, and a new edition of a handbook on economic statistics is much overdue.[1] The lack of clarity about definitions, and especially changes in definitions, is a constant danger; it affects budget data, and also a number of the output figures and indices.

Credibility: physical output figures

(a) *Industry*. Whatever the vagueness of definitions, the first question to ask is: are the figures true, or are they invented? Very few persons now believe that they are invented. The evidence against such a view is very strong. Despite captured documents,[2] despite the presence in the West of various Soviet officials who had defected, no evidence exists that the central Soviet statisticians invent figures to order, to produce propaganda effect. By this is meant that no one issues orders to print a figure of 400 knowing that the correct one is 350. Further support for this view comes from the fact that, when certain figures were discreditable, they were on occasion simply suppressed; many years later, they were published and showed that there was a fall in production in the 'suppressed' year. If it were possible simply to invent, then such behaviour would be pointless. Of course, we must note that selective suppression is a means of distorting a statistical table, but it is not invention. Not to tell the whole truth is not the same as telling a lie. Therefore we can legitimately conclude that when, for example, the Soviet authorities announce that 60 million tons of steel or 300 million pairs of shoes have been produced in a given year, this accords with the records of the Central statistical office in Moscow.[3] However, there are several qualifications to be made. One of these relates, not for the last time, to ambiguities of definition. Footwear sometimes includes only leather footwear, sometimes all footwear, the definition of leather footwear can and does alter, handicraft production can be omitted from the base-year without this being stated. Furthermore, most commodities for which statistics are published are not homogeneous, are in reality many different kinds of goods aggregated under a single head for statistical convenience. The methodology of aggregation is often unspecified. Of course, this is often true

[1] There used to be such an explanatory handbook, entitled *Slovar-spravochnik po sotsia'lno-ekonomicheskoi statistike*, but this was last published in 1948. Some notes do now appear at the back of the annual statistical volume.

[2] Especially the *1941 Plan*, published in America by the American Council of Learned Societies, after it had been taken from the Germans.

[3] This is also the broad conclusion of G. Grossman in his searching examination of *Soviet Statistics of Physical Output of Industrial Commodities* (Princeton, 1960).

of similar statistics in all countries. But the point is that rewards for growth are so important in Soviet industry that the definitional changes, and the adjustment to definitions at local level, can aim deliberately at whatever result looks best from the standpoint of statistical publicity. This point is also relevant to the reliability of aggregate indices, and we shall return to it.

The figures may correctly reflect the data available in Moscow, yet this data could be wrong by reason of statistical 'padding' by the reporting agencies, especially the enterprises. They are interested in claiming plan fulfilment, and this could lead them to exaggerate. Scattered reports of measures against directors who indulge in such practices confirm that such dangers exist, but measures are taken to minimize them. The close link between production and disposals (*sbyt*) puts a limit on the amount of likely cheating: to report non-existent production which one would be called upon to deliver is asking for trouble. There are also some temptations to conceal output, in order to keep extra stocks in hand or to cover up pilfering or some semi-legal deal. Defective goods, on the other hand, seem frequently to be foisted on customers in the guise of standard products, the quality inspectors being overruled. On balance, one should expect some exaggeration in reporting, and no doubt the possibilities of getting away with it vary in different sectors and at different periods. Unless it can be shown that the *extent* of exaggeration changes, the rate of growth remains unaffected, for obvious reasons; this is the 'law of equal cheating', which the author of these lines 'invented' in 1956.[1] There seems no evidence one way or the other, in industry at least, to suggest that the rate of growth since (say) 1937 or 1950 has been affected by falsification from below.[2] However, it is manoeuvring within the system of success indicators —without actually cheating—which seems much the most serious source of distortion. Reference back to the large number of plan-fulfilment 'dodges' listed in chapter 6 will provide a host of examples of how the wily director can distort the truth without actually breaking the regulations.

Clearly then, care is needed in interpreting the various figures, exaggeration is possible. But an excess of scepticism can lead to unfortunate results. Thus a certain American commentator noticed that cotton and wool cloth output figures were below the previous year in physical terms while the official statistical report claimed an increase, and jumped to the conclusion that this was evidence of

---

[1] In *Lloyd's Bank Review*, April, 1956, p. 3.
[2] This is also the conclusion of Grossman, op. cit., p. 133.

cheating. It was not; there had been a shift of statistical reporting from linear metres to square metres, the object of which was in fact to stop cheating by those who sought to fulfil plans by making cloth narrower. This illustrates the danger of using the 'cheating' hypothesis. Far better is it to assume that the figures represent some aspect of reality, and proceed, on that assumption, to examine with care the coverage and definition of the figures cited.

(b) *Agriculture.* For many years, until 1953, crop data were published in terms of 'biological yield', for reasons which cannot be gone into here.[1] It is very much to the credit of N. Jasny to have been the first to have documented and calculated with great ingenuity and surprising accuracy the extent of the consequent exaggeration.[2] This was due partly to the nature of the 'biological' statistics, which purported to represent the on-the-root crop, and were therefore gross of the considerable harvest losses, and partly to the tendency of the inspectors to exaggerate the on-the-root crop estimates, since certain delivery obligations of *kolkhozy* (payments to the MTS) were dependent upon them. In 1952, the grain harvest was said to have been 130 million tons. This has officially been revised downwards to 92 million tons, an exaggeration greater than many of the fiercest western critics thought possible.

Biological yield figures were dropped in 1953, and for several years no physical output data were published at all. Then they reappeared, and are now available in abundance, for every major farm product, down even to non-cow milk and non-sheep wool. However, there are several reasons for supposing that the 'law of equal cheating' may fail to operate in agriculture. Firstly, the large volume of unsold products makes it harder to keep track of reality. Secondly, a series of agricultural campaigns (grain, maize, meat, milk, and so on) have placed great pressures upon local officialdom, and we have Khrushchev's own word for it, at the January, 1961, plenum of the central committee, that it drove them into various kinds of simulation and exaggerated reporting (including the purchase of butter in the shops and its re-delivery to the state as new produce). Thirdly, the much better prices now paid for produce probably led to a discouragement of various forms of evasion by which production remained unreported.[3] Finally, the very large

---

[1] See A. Nove, 'Some Problems in Agricultural Statistics', *Soviet Studies*, January, 1956.

[2] See his *Socialized Agriculture in the USSR*, and other works.

[3] An interesting parallel may be found in Great Britain, where an increase in the official buying price for eggs shortly after the war led to a spectacular rise in the *reported* number of eggs laid.

proportion of meat and milk originating in the private sector is very inadequately counted, through a sample survey, and seems to be unreliable and possibly overstated. For all these reasons, there are grounds for supposing that both the absolute level of and the rate of increase in the output of some farm products are overstated, though we cannot tell by how much.

It is also noteworthy that the definition of meat includes offal, lard, rabbits, poultry, and so is wider than that usually adopted in the West. Maize figures included the grain equivalent of ensilaged cobs in the period 1955-64, but this has been abandoned. American analysts have claimed that milk sucked by calves is included in the Soviet milk statistics, but this has been denied.[1]

(c) *Foreign trade.* Very full data are published, but with some irritating omissions and one yawning gap in the figures. Two items which did appear before the war are not there. These are, using the trade classification numbers which were entered in the prewar figures[2] and which do not now appear at all:

> 28   'Objects of gold and precious stones'
> 31   'Pyrotechnical materials'

Does this mean that these items are no longer traded in, or rather that exports of arms and of some gold are kept out of statistical sight?

The gap mentioned above has become apparent since the USSR has divided its current trade statistics into three country categories: Socialist, capitalist-developed, and capitalist-underdeveloped. The first two present no problems at all: the figures for the obvious countries add up exactly to the import and export totals. The figures for the 'underdeveloped' do not, as the following figures show:

	1962		1966	
	Import	Export	Import	Export
TOTAL, 'underdeveloped capitalist countries'	525·9	889·5	783·5	1090·6
Total of all countries given	522·8	484·4	779·7	758·3
Difference	3·1	405·1	3·8	332·3

(*Sources: Vneshnaya torgovlya SSSR za* 1963 and 1966).

The difference for imports is consistent with the fact that some minor trading partners are omitted from the returns. The export figures are clearly incredible. Obviously, some sales of something to

[1] See *Comparisons of the United States and Soviet Economies* (Washington, 1959), p. 236, and V. Starovski, *Vop. Ekon.*, No. 4/1960, p. 105.
[2] *Vneshnaya torgovlya, 1918–40*, pp. 28-9.

someone have been statistically 'dumped' into this category. No explanation has been forthcoming. But logically this entitles one to query the other figures too, in which these not inconsiderable sums ought (somewhere) to belong.

Indices: are they credible?

According to the official statistics, gross industrial output rose almost twenty-one times between 1928 and 1955. The highest western estimate, by F. Seton, allows for a twelve-fold rise. The lowest, by W. Nutter, supports a much lower figure, a five-and-a-half-fold increase. There are some others in between.[1] There is not the space here to comment in detail on the many western attempts to reconstruct an index of industrial production, based on Soviet physical output series. The point is that all are unanimous in completely rejecting the official index, even while at odds with each other about the 'correct' figure. My own view tends to favour the Seton index, because the much lower figures of Nutter and some other analysts seem to me inconsistent with what is known and accepted about Soviet fuel utilization and freight transportation. However, this still leaves the official index way up above the realms of possibility.

It is not that this index is deliberately 'cooked'. But all indices are conventional aggregations, necessarily lacking in accuracy. So much depends on price weights and on the treatment of new products, especially where, as in the machinery sector, these are extremely numerous. Anyone who wishes to make any such calculations should take an awful warning from A. Gerschenkron's calculations, in which he showed that, from 1899 to 1939, American production of machinery increased more than fifteen-fold with 1899 price weights, but less than doubled with 1939 price weights, and he emphasized the enormous difficulties due to changes in type and design. What is 'truth' when such divergences are possible?[2] This is why the care and refinements of some attempts to aggregate all available physical output data for the USSR seem to me to lead to such uncertain results, which would remain uncertain even if there were none of the sizeable statistical gaps in the output series.

The official series suffers from the following defects:

(a) Until 1950, the weights used were those of 1926-27. Apart from giving 'preindustrialization' weights to the fastest growing sectors of industry, the introduction of new products gave an oppor-

---

[1] See bibliography for references.
[2] *A Dollar index of Soviet machinery output* (Rand Corporation, Santa Monica, 1951).

tunity (for directors) to manoeuvre so as to adopt for them high
'1926-27' prices. Despite occasional efforts to check this practice, the
big rise in costs in the 'thirties meant that the prices at which new
products were introduced into the index were higher than they would
have cost in 1926-27. There was then a tendency to concentrate on
the production of items bearing high '1926-27' prices, even at the
cost of underfulfilling plans for the less highly valued items, because
plan fulfilment was measured in 1926-27 prices. All this led to a
creeping inflation of the index, made easier by the fact that it was
genuinely difficult to determine what is a new product and what it
would have cost to produce in 1926-27.[1]

(b) It is a 'gross' index, in the sense described in chapter 10.
Therefore, it is affected by vertical disintegration.

Several Soviet writers have claimed that the behaviour of the
authorities is affected by the knowledge that by dividing up production processes between enterprises they can artificially increase
the growth rate, and thereby inflate the output of intermediate goods
in relation to the final product.[2]

(c) While since 1950 the index is no longer based on 1926-27
prices (it was calculated first in 1952 and then in 1955 prices), the
growth rates prior to 1950 were simply chained on to the new index,
and were not recalculated; or, if they were, the results have not been
published. Much remains unclear about how the index is compiled.
For instance, suppose that machinery output is expressed in 1955
prices, the problem of valuing new models remains, and, since in all
countries such valuations are somewhat artificial, this makes possible the systematic selection of the highest of a range of possible
figures, which can lead to distortion. It is only right to add that all
analysts agree that the post 1950 indices are markedly less unreliable than those for earlier years. However, whatever the price base
and whatever the regulations, the directors and local officials tend
so to choose between possible alternatives as to be able to report a
large increase in output. Because of the unavoidable imprecision of
the regulations and of the definitions, the index can be affected by
such choices in ways which are unlikely to arise in the West (where
there is also a degree of imprecision and of arbitrary comparison),
because increases in production as such are not vital 'success indicators' in a western firm.

---

[1] See A. Nove, '1926/7 and all that', *Soviet Studies*, October, 1957, pp. 117-
30. Soviet journals have denied these exaggerations, but contemporary evidence, cited in the above-named article, is against them.

[2] L. Kochetkov *et al.*, op. cit., pp. 57-8.

With so much room for more or less legitimate manoeuvre, Soviet statisticians can select the base and the weights which help them to show very large increases, and omit to publish calculations which reflect less credit on the system. For instance, base-year weights give a larger increase in output than end-year weights, so, in discussing industrial production indices, one Soviet statistician went so far as to proclaim that end-year weights were contrary to science, a remarkable doctrine indeed.[1] Yet, when Soviet statisticians calculate a cost of living index, they are careful to use end year weights,[2] which minimize the increase in prices and so represent real wages in a more favourable light.

National income

The official index is at all times to be treated with a degree of suspicion. The official claim to a seventeen-fold increase in the period 1913-55, for instance, is utterly incredible. Thus it seems very widely agreed, by Soviet economists among others,[3] that the national income of the Russian empire in 1913 was approximately a fifth of that of the United States. If the official claim were even remotely correct, the Soviet national income would now be well ahead of that of the United States, which, even allowing for the familiar vagaries of index numbers, just is not acceptable. Then it is decidedly odd that the national income can increase by seventeen-fold when one of its principal components, agriculture, showed a rise (in gross output) of only 70 per cent. The computational methods are not properly explained. There seems to have been a substantial overstatement of the growth of the net product of trade and construction, at least during the period of '1926-27' prices.[4] But even in more recent years strange things happen to national income data. Thus an increase of 5 per cent in 1964, given by several reliable Soviet sources, including Kosygin, was suddenly transformed into an increase of 7 per cent in the statistical report published in *Pravda* on the 30th January 1965, and then converted into an increase of well over 9 per cent in the statistical handbook for 1964, without (so far) a word of explanation. One can but show reserve in using official claims, and seek explanations where possible to clear up doubtful points.

---

[1] D. Savinski, *Vest. Stat.*, No. 10/1958, p. 39.
[2] A. Gozulov, *Ekonomicheskaya statistika* (Moscow, 1953), p. 359.
[3] Y. Kronrod in *Sovetskaya sotsialisticheskaya ekonomika, 1917-57* (Moscow, 1957), p. 168.
[4] See A. Nove, '1926/7 and all that', already cited.

Some other items

Housing data (in square metres) may be given in *living* space (excluding kitchens, corridors, etc,) or in *total* space (*obshchaya ploshchyad'*). The former is roughly two-thirds of the latter, and the unwary are sometimes confused between them.

Real wage and other such figures are sometimes given by reference to the year 1940, or to some early post-war year. It should be noted that these were not good years for the consumer, and that a fairer picture of progress achieved requires a calculation based on some better year, say 1937 or 1928. This is never done by the official statisticians. It is important to distinguish data on real wages, which, allowing for the chosen base year, check well against other figures, from vague and barely credible claims about 'real income per head'; these include estimates of the value of social services and such indirect 'income' as the length of vacations with pay, and the methods used are never explained.

Conclusion

Despite some justifiable scepticism about certain Soviet data, it should be clearly stated that the published physical output series and many other figures must be taken seriously, that they generally represent an expression (though sometimes an ambiguous or distorted expression) of reality. Much greater doubt attaches to some of the index number series, which are in some instances just not credible. Yet these comments are by no means intended to deny that the Soviet system has achieved rapid growth. Undoubtedly it has, though not at the tremendous pace which the official indices allege. Its achievements have, indeed, been such that it is surely about time that some of the wilder claims were quietly buried.

BIBLIOGRAPHY

A SHORT BIBLIOGRAPHY

NOTE.—Copious references to Soviet books and periodicals have been made in the text and will not be repeated here, save for those cases where titles of books and periodicals have been given in footnotes in abbreviated form.

Space is not available for a full bibliography and the very large number of relevant books and articles in Western languages. The list given below represents a selection of books, together with a few references to particularly useful articles. Many other articles are referred to in footnotes in the text.

(A) *Books and periodicals abbreviated in text:*

Direktivy KPSS: Direktivy KPSS i sovetskovo pravitel'stva po khozyaistvennym voprosam, 4 vols., Moscow, 1958.

Zakon Stoimosti (Tsagolov): *Zakon stoimosti i evo rol' v narodnom khozyaistve SSSR* (ed. Tsagolov), Moscow, 1959.

Zakon Stoimosti (Kronrod): *Zakon stoimosti i evo ispol' zovanie v narodnom khozyaistve SSSR* (ed. Kronrod), Moscow, 1959.

N.Kh. Narodnoe khozyaistvo SSSR (statistical compendium), published in various years from 1956.

Sel. khoz 1960: Sel'skoe khozyaistvo SSSR (statistical compendium), Moscow, 1960.

Ekon. gaz. Ekonomicheskaya gazeta, organ of the Central Committee.

Plan khoz.: Planovoe khozyaistvo. Organ of Gosplan.

Vop. ekon.: Voprosy ekonomiki. Organ of Institute of Economics.

Vest. stat.: Vestnik statistiki. Organ of Central Statistical Office.

Sots. sel. khoz.: Sotsialisticheskoe sel'skoe khozyaistvo.

(B) *Some works in Western languages:*

ECONOMIC HISTORY OF THE PERIOD

A. Baykov: *The Development of the Soviet Economic System* (Cambridge and New York, 1947).

E. H. Carr: *A History of Soviet Russia: Socialism in One Country*, vol. 1 (London and New York, 1958).

M. Dobb: *Soviet Economic Development Since 1917* (London, 3rd edition, 1966).

A. Erlich: *The Soviet Industrialization Debate* (Cambridge, Mass., 1960).

N. Jasny: *Soviet Industrialization 1928-1952* (Chicago, 1961).

A. Nove: *Was Stalin really necessary?* (London and New York, 1964).

A. Nove: *Economic History of the USSR* (Lane and Penguin, London, 1968).

H. Schwartz: *Russia's Soviet Economy* (London, 1966).

N. Spulber: *Soviet Strategy of Economic Growth* (Bloomington, 1964).

E. Zaleski: *La planification de la croissance economique* (Paris, 1962).

GENERAL DESCRIPTION OF THE ECONOMY

E. Ames: *Soviet Economic Processes* (London, 1967).

B. Balassa: *The Hungarian Experience in Economic Planning* (New Haven, 1959).

A. Bergson: *The Economics of Soviet Planning* (Yale, 1964).

E. Boettcher: *Die Sowjetische Wirtschaftpolitik am Scheidewege* (Tübingen, 1959).

R. Campbell: *Soviet Economic Power* (Cambridge, Mass., and Boston, 1960), (Second edition 1966).

J. M. Montias: *Central Planning in Poland* (Yale, 1962).

B. Ward: *The Socialist Economy: a Study of Organizational Alternatives* (Berkeley, 1967).

P. Wiles: *The Political Economy of Communism* (Blackwell, Oxford, 1963).

PROBLEMS OF GROWTH AND ITS MEASUREMENT

A. Becker: 'Comparisons of US and USSR National Output: Some Rules of the Game,' *World Politics*, October, 1960.

A. Bergson (ed.): *Soviet Economic Growth* (Evanston, 1953).

A. Bergson and S. Kuznets, *Economic Trends in the Soviet Union* (Harvard, 1963).

M. Bornstein 'Comparisons of Soviet and US National Products', Reprinted in F. Holzman (ed.): *Readings in the Soviet Economy* (Rand, McNally & Co., Chicago, 1962).

R. W. Campbell, 'Problems of US/Soviet Economic Comparisons' (also reprinted in the above).

G. Grossman: 'Soviet Growth—Routine, Inertia and Pressure,' *American Economic Review*, May, 1960.

D. Hodgman: *Soviet Industrial Production, 1928-51* (Harvard, 1954).

N. Jasny: *The Soviet Economy during the Plan Era* (Stanford, 1951).

Joint Economic Committee of the us Congress: *Comparisons of the U.S. and Soviet Economies* (3 vols., Washington, 1959).

N. Kaplan and R. Moorsteen: 'An Index of Soviet Industrial Output,' *American Economic Review*, June, 1960.

R. Moorsteen: *Prices and Production of Machinery in the Soviet Union, 1928-1958* (Harvard, 1962).

A. Nove: *Soviet Economic Strategy* (N.P.A., Washington, 1959).

W. Nutter: 'Some Observations on Soviet Industrial Growth,' *American Economic Review*, May, 1957.

F. Seton: *Soviet Industrial Expansion*, Manchester Statistical Society paper, 1957.

F. Seton: 'Soviet Progress in Western Perspective,' *Soviet Studies*, October, 1960.

D. Shimkin and F. Leedy: 'Soviet Industrial Growth,' *Automobile Industries*, January 1, 1958.

P. Wiles: 'The theory of International Comparison of Economic Volume,' in *Soviet Planning* (ed.) Degras & Nove (Blackwell, Oxford, 1963).

THE STATE ENTERPRISE AND MANAGEMENT

J. Berliner: *Factory and Manager in the USSR* (Cambridge, Mass., 1957).

D. Granick: *Management of the Industrial Firm in the USSR* (New York, 1954).

D. Granick: *The Red Executive* (Garden City, New York, 1960).

J. Kornai: *Overcentralization in Economic Administration* (London and New York, 1959).

NATURAL RESOURCES

D. Shimkin: *Minerals, a Key to Soviet Power* (Cambridge, Mass. 1953).

AGRICULTURE AND COLLECTIVE FARMING

K. Bush: 'Agricultural Reforms since Khrushchev', in *New directions in the Soviet Economy* (U.S. Congress, 1967).

N. Jasny: *The Socialized Agriculture of the USSR* (Stanford, 1949).

R. Dumont: *Sovkhoz, Kolkhoz ou le Problématique Communisme*, (Paris, 1964).

J. Chombart de Lauwe: *Les Paysans Sovietiques* (Paris, 1962).

J. Karcz: 'The New Soviet Agricultural Programme', *Soviet Studies*, October, 1965.
J. Karcz (ed.): *Soviet and East European agriculture* (Univ. of California, 1967).
R. D. Laird (ed.): *Soviet Agricultural and Peasant Affairs* (Lawrence, Kansas, 1964).
A. Nove: 'Soviet Agriculture Marks Time.' *Foreign Affairs*, July, 1962.
O. Schiller: *Das Agrarsystem der Sowjetunion* (Tübingen, 1960).
H. Wronski: *Le Troudoden* (Paris, 1957).

THE COMMUNIST PARTY ORGANIZATION

M. Fainsod: *Smolensk under Soviet Rule* (Cambridge, Mass., 1958).
L. B. Schapiro: *The Communist Party of the Soviet Union* (New York and London, 1960).

NATIONAL INCOME

A. Bergson: *The Real National Income of Soviet Russia* (Harvard, 1961).
J. Y. Calvez: *Revenu National en URSS* (Paris, 1956).
'An Estimate of the National Accounts of the Soviet Union,' *Economic Bulletin for Europe*, vol. 9, no. 1 (May, 1957).
M. C. Kaser: 'Estimating the Soviet National Income,' *Economic Journal*, March, 1957.

LABOUR AND WAGES

Emily C. Brown: *Soviet Trade Unions and Labour Relations* (Harvard, 1966).
Janet Chapman: *Real Wages in Soviet Russia Since 1928* (Harvard, 1963).
W. Galenson: *Labour Productivity in Soviet and American Industry* (New York, 1955).
W. Hoffmann: *Der Arbeitsverfassung der Sowjetunion* (Berlin, 1956).
S. Schwarz: *Labour in the Soviet Union* (New York and London, 1953).

BUDGET AND PUBLIC FINANCE

R. W. Davies: *The Development of the Soviet Budgetary System* (Cambridge, 1958).

G. Garvy: *Money, Banking and Credit in Eastern Europe* (New York, 1967).

F. D. Holzman: *Soviet Taxation* (Cambridge, Mass., 1955).

ECONOMIC THEORY AND MARXISM

R. Campbell: 'Marx, Kantorovich and Novozhilov, *Stoimost*' versus Reality', in *Slavic Review*, October, 1961.

H. Chambre: *Le Marxisme en Union Soviétique* (Paris, 1955).

G. Grossman: 'Notes for a Theory of a Command Economy,' *Soviet Studies*, October, 1963.

T. J. Hoff: *Economic Calculation in the Socialist Society* (London, 1949).

O. Lange: *On the Economic Theory of Socialism* (The Hague, 1938).

O. Lange: *Political Economy* (Warsaw, 1963).

W. Leontief: 'The Fall and Rise of Soviet Economics', *Foreign Affairs*, January, 1960. (Republished in *Essays in Economics*, Oxford, 1966.)

Joan Robinson: *An Essay on Marxist Economics* (London, 1942).

J. Schumpeter: *Capitalism, Socialism and Democracy* (London, 1943).

VALUE, PRICE, ECONOMIC RATIONALITY

A. Balinky, J. Hazard, A. Bergson, P. Wiles: *Planning and the Market in the USSR in the 1960's* (Rutgers, 1967).

M. Bornstein: 'The Soviet Price System', *American Economic Review*, March 1967.

M. Bornstein: 'The Soviet Price Reform Discussion', *Quarterly Journal of Economics*, February 1964.

M. Dobb: 'Soviet Price Policy,' *Soviet Studies*, July, 1960.

D. Granick: 'An Organizational Model of Soviet Industrial Planning,' *Journal of Political Economy*, April, 1959.

G. Grossman: 'Industrial Prices in the USSR,' *American Economic Review*, May, 1959.

G. Grossman (ed.): *Value and Plan* (Berkeley, 1960).

N. Jasny: *The Soviet Price System* (Stanford, 1951).

A. Nove: 'The Politics of Economic Rationality,' *Social Research*, summer, 1958.

A. Nove: 'The Changing Role of Soviet Prices,' in *Economics of Planning* (Oslo) No. 3, 1963.

Myron E. Sharpe (ed.): *Planning, Profits and Incentives in the USSR* (Rutgers, 1967).

P. J. D. Wiles: 'Scarcity, Marxism and Gosplan,' *Oxford Economic Papers*, September, 1953.
A. Zauberman: 'Economic Thought in the Soviet Union,' *Review of Economic Studies*, vol. xvi, no. 39, 1948/49.
A. Zauberman: 'New Winds in Soviet Planning,' *Soviet Studies*, July, 1960.

INVESTMENT CRITERIA

H. Chambre (ed.): 'Le Developpement du Bassin du Kouznetsk,' *Cahiers de l' ISEA*, Paris, no. 100 (April, 1960).
H. Chambre: 'A propos des Critères du Choix des Investissements,' *Cahiers de l' ISEA*, Paris, no. 104 (August, 1960).
J. M. Collette: *Politique d'Investissement et Calcul Économique* (Paris 1965).
M. Dobb: 'The Problems of Choice between Alternative Investment Projects,' *Soviet Studies*, January, 1951.
G. Grossman: 'Scarce Capital and Soviet Doctrine,' *Quarterly Journal of Economics*.
F. Holzman: 'The Soviet Ural-Kuznetsk Combine,' *Quarterly Journal of Economics*, August, 1957.
N. Kaplan: 'Investment Alternatives in Soviet Economic Theory,' *Journal of Political Economy*, April, 1952.
A. Zauberman: 'A Note on the Soviet Capital Controversy,' *Quarterly Journal of Economics*, August, 1955.

PLANNING METHODS

H. Chambre: *L'Aménagement du Territoire en URSS* (Paris, The Hague, 1959).
M. C. Kaser: 'The Reorganization of Soviet Industry, in *Value and Plan*, cited above.
M. C. Kaser: 'Welfare Criteria in Soviet Planning,' in *Soviet Planning*, ed. Degras and Nove.
H. Levine: 'The Centralized Planning of Supply . . .,' in *Comparisons of the U.S. and Soviet Economies*, cited above.
J. M. Montias: 'Planning with Material Balances in Soviet-type Economies,' *American Economic Review*, December, 1959.
E. Zaleski: *Planning Reforms in the Soviet Union, 1926-66* (Chape Hill, 1967).

MATHEMATICAL ECONOMICS

J. Hardt and others: *Mathematics and Computers in Soviet Economic Planning* (Yale, 1967).

L. Kantorovich: *The Best Use of Economic Resources* (London, 1965).
V. Nemchinov (ed.): *Mathematics in Economics* (London, 1964).
A. Zauberman: *Aspects of Planometrics* (London, 1967).

TRANSPORT AND OTHER SECTOR STUDIES

G. Gardner Clark: *The Economics of Soviet Steel* (Cambridge, Mass., 1956).
A. Gerschenkron (with A. Erlich): *A Dollar Index of Soviet Machinery Output, 1927/8-37* (Santa Monica, 1951).
M. Goldman: *Soviet Marketing* (London, 1963).
P. Hanson: 'Structure and Efficiency of Soviet retailing and wholesaling', *Soviet Studies*, October 1964.
H. Hunter: *Soviet Transportation Policy* (Cambridge, Mass., 1957).
M. Kaser: *Comecon* (second edition, London, 1967).
F. Pryor: *The Communist Foreign Trade System* (London, 1963).
E. Williams, Jr.: *Freight Transportation in the Soviet Union*, (Princeton, 1962).
A. Zauberman: 'The Criterion of Efficiency of Foreign Trade in Soviet-Type Economies, *Economica*, February, 1964, pp. 5-12.

EDUCATION AND SOCIAL SERVICES

A. G. Korol: *Soviet Education for Science and Technology* (New York, 1957).
N. de Witt: *Soviet Professional Manpower* (Washington, 1955).
Discussion articles, 'Towards a Communist Welfare State?' *Problems of Communism*, nos. 1 and 3, 1960.

STATISTICS

C. Clark: *A Critique of Russian Statistics* (London, 1939).
A. Ezhov, *Industrial Statistics* (Translated from Russian, Calcutta, 1960).
G. Grossman: *Soviet Statistics of Physical Output of Industrial Commodities* (Princeton, 1960).
N. Jasny: *The Soviet 1956 Statistical Handbook: a Commentary* (East Lansing, 1957).
N. Jasny: 'Some Thoughts on Soviet Statistics,' *International Affairs*, January, 1959.
Symposium on 'Reliability and Usability of Soviet Statistics,' *The American Statistician*, 1953.
(see also under 'Problems of growth . . .,' above).

Index of Subjects

'Accounting prices', 147
Accumulation fund, 298–9
  policy, 332
Administration, expenditure on, 54, 56, 122
'Advances' to peasants, 140
Agricultural tax, 62, 116, 123
Agriculture, labour force, 335, 337
  machinery, supply of, 100, 188–9
  planning, 51, 72, 99–103, 205–13, 332, 338
  prices: see Prices, agricultural
  procurements: see Procurements
  production, definition and valuation of, 292
    (See also Gross Agricultural production)
  statistics, reliability of, 349–50
  ministry of, 100, 101, 205
  relative priority of, 166
Allocation, certificates, 41, 92
  of materials: see Material supplies
Allocations to national economy (budget), 119–21, 123
Amortization, 38, 123, 126, 237
'Anti-Party group', 73
Arbitrariness, in economic life, 17
Arbitration, 107
Artisans, co-operative: see Co-operatives, producers'
  individual, 65, 116, 344
Assortment of products, problems of, 20, 171
ASSR (Autonomous Socialist Soviet Republics), 25
Audit, 106–7
Autarky, in international trade, 217–8

regional: see 'Regionalism'
Average cost principle, 146

Bachelor tax, 116
Balances: see Material balances
Banks: see Gosbank, Savings Banks
  Investment Banks, Stroibank
Bankruptcy, 107, 128
'Big regions' 86–87
Bilateralism, 214
Biological yield, 349
Bolshevichka and Mayak: see Planning, new experiments
Bonuses, for directors, 33, 177, 179
  in collective farms, 138, 140
  staff, 134
Bottlenecks, 88, 89, 163, 164, 329
Bread, tax on, 113, 154
Brigade, in a collective farm, 50
Budget, expenditures, 119–22
  republican rights, 87, 125
  revenues, 58, 112–18
    (See also under headings of various taxes)
  state, 97, 111–23
Building: see construction
Buildings tax, 117
Bureaucracy, 73, 104, 159
By-products, utilization of, 74

'Calendar' planning, 177
'Campaigns' in economy, 162, 166, 326
Capital assets of enterprises, 31, 40
Capital charges, 39, 147, 231, 237–8, 308, 318
Capital fund, collective-farms, 55–6, 126, 140
Capital repairs, 127

363

Index of Names

370

GEORGE ALLEN & UNWIN LTD

Head Office:
40 Museum Street, London, W.C.1
Telephone: 01-405 8577

Sales, Distribution and Accounts Departments:
Park Lane, Hemel Hempstead, Herts.
Telephone: 0442 3244

Athens: 7 Stadiou Street, Athens 125
Auckland: P.O. Box 36013, Northcote Auckland 9
Barbados: P.O. Box 222, Bridgetown
Beirut: Deeb Building, Jeanne d'Arc Street
Bombay: 103/5 Fort Street, Bombay 1
Calcutta: 285J Bepin Behari Ganguli Street, Calcutta 12
P.O Box 23134, Joubert Park, Johannesburg, South Africa
Dacca: Alico Building, 18 Motijheel, Dacca 2
Delhi: 1/18B Asaf Ali Road, New Delhi 1
Hong Kong: 105 Wing on Mansion, 26 Hankow Road, Kowloon
Ibadan: P.O. Box 62
Karachi: Karachi Chambers, McLeod Road
Lahore: 22 Falettis' Hotel, Egerton Road
Madras: 2/18 Mount Road, Madras 2
Manila: P.O. Box 157, Quezon City D-502
Mexico: Liberia Britanica, S.A., Separio Rendon 125, Mexico 4, D.F.
Nairobi: P.O. Box 30583
Rio de Janeiro: Caixa Postal 3537-Zc-00
Singapore: 36c Prinsep Street, Singapore 7
Sydney, N.S.W.: Bradbury House, 55 York Street
Tokyo: C.P.O. Box 1728, Tokyo 100-91
Toronto: 145 Adelaide Street West, Toronto 1

ALEC NOVE

WAS STALIN REALLY NECESSARY?

In this book Professor Nove deals with many aspects of Soviet political economy, planning problems, and statistics. Starting with an attempt to evaluate the rationality of Stalinism, he discusses the possible political consequences of the search for greater economic efficiency, and this is followed by a controversial discussion of Kremlinology. The next two groups of chapters are respectively concerned with industrial and agricultural problems, and they include an analysis of the situation of the peasants as this is reflected in literary journals. The essay on social welfare (unlike some of the author's other work) has been used in the Soviet press as evidence against over-enthusiastic cold-warriors, among whom the author is not always popular. There are also elaborate statistical surveys of occupational patterns and the purchasing power of wages, and a chapter which seeks to examine the irrational statistical reflection of irrational economic decisions. The final chapter seeks to generalize about the evolution of world communism. All those interested in Soviet affairs will find a great deal to interest them in this thought-provoking volume.

WITH J. A. NEWTH

THE SOVIET MIDDLE EAST

The Soviet Middle East covers the national republics of Central Asia and Transcaucasia, which were absorbed into the Russian Empire and are now part of the Soviet Union. They have considerable economic achievements to their credit, and have also shown rapid progress in health and education. How does their present situation compare with the rest of the USSR, with their non-Soviet neighbours, with their own past? How were these developments financed? How far was progress due to, or made possible by, the immigration of large numbers of Russians? Is the economic and political relationship of these republics to Moscow a form of colonialism or neo-colonialism? Is there evidence of economic exploitation of these areas by Moscow, or, on the contrary, has there been a net flow of resources into these republics from the rest of the USSR? How far has their development in fact been conditional upon subordinate status, upon the republics being sub-units of a much larger political and economic organism? What was the relevance of the Soviet planning system and Soviet ideology?

A discussion of such questions as these is of interest not only for its own sake, but also for the bearing which it may have upon the problems of developing countries. There are also questions involving the political stability of the Soviet Union as a multi-national state. Will the economic and social evolution lead to a dangerous growth of so-called "bourgeois nationalism"? Or have the Soviet authorities, by providing good opportunities of promotion for the ambitious, succeeded in taking the sting out of such discontent?

GEORGE ALLEN & UNWIN LTD